W9-BWD-112

DESERT SAINTS

DESERT SAINTS

The Mormon Frontier in Utah

By

NELS ANDERSON

Phoenix Books

THE UNIVERSITY OF CHICAGO PRESS

CHICAGO AND LONDON

This book is also available in a clothbound edition from
THE UNIVERSITY OF CHICAGO PRESS

Standard Book Number: 226-01782-6

THE UNIVERSITY OF CHICAGO PRESS, CHICAGO 60637
The University of Chicago Press, Ltd., London W.C. 1

 Published 1942. Fourth Impression 1969. First Phoenix Edition 1966. Printed in the United States of America

DEDICATED TO

The Mormon Pioneers, especially
Lyman L. Woods, of Clover Valley,
Nevada, and his family

Thomas S. Terry, of Hebron, Utah,
His three wives and
Their many children

With these families I had a home
And we have remained friends

ACKNOWLEDGMENT

FOR a considerable part of such merit as this book may have the author is indebted to many people. The list is not complete. None of the persons named here share the responsibility for the shortcomings of the book. Without their help the imperfections would have been more numerous.

For financial aid during the summer of 1933: the Social Science Research Council and the Social Science Council of Columbia University.

For statistical and documentary materials made available: the United States Bureau of the Census, the National Archives, the Writers' Project and the Historical Records Survey of the Work Projects Administration in Utah, and the Historian's Office of the Church of Jesus Christ of Latter-Day Saints.

For voluntary service, advice, and encouragement: W. O. Bentley, president of the St. George Stake; George F. Whitehead, president of the St. George Temple; also Juanita Brooks and Judge LeRoy Cox, of St. George; Professor William J. Snow, of the Brigham Young University; Maurice Howe, Nathaniel Rogg, Frances A. Moore, Ray Millard, Bertha Schwartz Eisen, Mildred Stock, and Bess Feltman.

For reading the manuscript at various stages of its development: Joseph A. Brandt, president of the University of Oklahoma; Floyd Dell, of the Work Projects Administration; Bernard De Voto, of *Harper's Magazine;* and Professor Louis Wirth, of the University of Chicago.

For valuable documentary contributions, pertinent page-by-page suggestions, and the careful checking of factual data the author is especially indebted to Dale L. Morgan, director of the Writers' Project of the Work Projects Administration in Utah. M. Hamlin Cannon, who is preparing a history of the Mormon War, permitted me access to many of his notes.

FOREWORD

THE study of Mormonism has a strategic significance for the understanding of America. The Mormon Church is a religious body of American origin. It embodies typical American values in its own peculiar forms of expression, and it has recapitulated in its own history important long-term trends to be observed in the history of the nation as a whole. From the time of its foundation in upstate New York in 1850 to the present, the Mormon Church has presented the spectacle of a separate and different religious community which managed at the same time to be an integral part of America. The irony of this situation is made manifest by the fact that its integration into the larger national society involved a considerable measure of coercion by the federal government.

From 1831 to 1846 the Latter-Day Saints attempted four times to build a city of their own in the Middle West. The first of these efforts, in Kirtland, Ohio, ended in financial disaster, internal dissent, and external antagonism. The other three attempts—two in Missouri and one in Illinois—found initial success quickly followed by hostility which culminated in the Mormons' expulsion from the area. The migration to Utah came after these attempts, and there the group, recovering its poise after defeat and at the cost of great suffering, built its own community based upon irrigation farming in the valleys of the intermountain West. In April of 1847, 148 Mormon pioneers, led by Brigham Young, who succeeded the murdered prophet Joseph Smith, left Nebraska for the West. In 1877 when Brigham Young died, there were some 357 Mormon settlements in the West with a total population of around 140,000. Moreover, in this settlement effort, which was continued after the death of Brigham Young, conflict with non-Mormons—with "Gentiles" as the Mormons called them—remained an important element of the Mormon situation. Utah, whose settlement began before the California gold rush, was one of the first areas in the western region to support a sizeable population and was among the last territories to be given statehood. This delay was the direct result of the conflict between the Latter-Day Saints and the United States government.

Here is a history that is significant for the serious scholar and fascinating to the general reader. The reissue of Nels Anderson's book in a paperback edition by The University of Chicago Press will gratify both. Anderson's book, originally published in 1942, was a pioneer effort in the study of Mormonism. It was also an important beginning in the application of social science and historical method to the study of a subject. The achievement of the Latter-Day Saints in the West and the heroism that characterized their efforts have long been attractive to writers of various kinds. In the serious study and analysis of these subjects, however, much is to be learned about the significance of the experiences of men in the settlement of this continent and about the character of social life and its general development. Anderson's work ranks today among the best of social science scholarship. Its reappearance is to be welcomed.

Maitland once declared that anthropology must become history or become nothing. The judgment may be exaggerated and harsh, but its warning is not to be ignored. Sociology, whether the work of anthropologists or of sociologists, needs the complement of history, just as history profits from the explicit conceptualizations of sociologists. Sociology has increasingly developed theoretical sophistication, but the true worth and utility of its conceptual tools of analysis can never be fully realized if cut off from a sense of history and an appreciation of the perspective and skills of the historian's craft. In this book, Nels Anderson gives us both an early and a successful product of such a combination. He sees his subject whole and in detail and in the context of temporal setting.

Mormon history is, as we have noted, one that fascinates both specialized scholar and general reader, and for similar reasons. Freedom has been an important element and a significant value in our national history. The record of religion in this country reveals what freedom means in providing an environment in which aspirations of common men can find expression. Potentials long dormant or hemmed in and limited by inhibiting institutions in older societies achieved fruition in the American setting. In Europe, religious revolt tended to settle into a new religious conservatism, but in America the implications of protest and its anti-authoritarian impulses found easier outlet and more varied expression.

Mormonism was the product of the "burned-over district" of northern New York State, where the fires of evangelical fervor and the spirit of religious innovation reached a kind of apotheosis. The Mormons turned away from religious orthodoxy, even the orthodoxy of the quite unorthodox. They combined within their new system of beliefs Christian elements from tradition and the Bible and ideas drawn from the popularization of science and philosophical speculation. Of this admixture they made a dynamic ideology capable of inspiring men to effort and courage. To the question posed by social philosophers of what happens when established restraints are removed or weakened, Mormonism gives one historically specific answer. It may be objected by theologians that such freedom and opportunity for expression as America gave the common man resulted in the vulgarization of the Christian content of the Protestant tradition and of the non-Christian notions which Mormonism wove into its fabric as well. Yet the vigor of the movement testifies to the fact that democratization of theological conceptions did not deprive Mormonism of the capacity to arouse the enthusiasm of the native Americans and European immigrants who joined the new church and came to Utah in the nineteenth century.

The Mormon record shows a sectarian group which grew under conditions of opposition and hostility into a large body whose members conquered a wilderness and left their mark upon a sizeable community of Americans. The Mormons acted on the basis of two dominant ideas—one consciously in their minds, the other built into their thinking and feeling by the previous two centuries of the American experience. They consciously imitated the model of biblical Israel as it was re-presented to them in the revelations and exhortations of their prophet-founder. The Bible is above all the story of a people who shared convictions about their status as elected by God. It depicts the development of institutions, secular and religious at once, which embody the collective existence of this people. And finally, the Bible proposes for this people a common homeland—set apart and appointed by the Lord—a promised land to be occupied, possessed, and rendered their own. In nineteenth-century America the Mormons chose this model for emulation.

Heeding their founder Joseph Smith and his successor Brigham Young they withdrew from the secular Babylon and attempted to build the New Jerusalem as they conceived it. In such efforts they were, of course, neither original nor unique among Christian sectaries; but their circumstances proved both more arduous and more propitious than those that faced many other groups with similar aspirations. The result was the projection and eventual construction of a Zion in the wilderness where the desert was indeed made to blossom as the rose. After four attempts to build a holy city in the Middle West, during which decade and a half they suffered defeat but developed their own particular folk tradition and sacred history, they moved West, conceiving themselves to be the "Camp of Israel." And there, in the open territory afforded them between the mountain chains, they built their sacred community on a grander scale. They were not to leave Gentile opposition behind, however; it followed them to their new home, this time assuming the form of a hostile federal government and an indignant national opinion. There were times in this Mormon-Gentile conflict, in this often bitter contention between Mormon Utah and the forces of American order and respectability, when a desire for separation from the United States showed itself among the Saints: there were times when Mormons began to think that it might become necessary—to use Brigham Young's words—to cut the ties that linked their kingdom with the kingdoms of this world. Various factors, not the least of which was the Saints' strong patriotic attachment to America, inhibited the realization of any such separatist potentiality.

Here again the Mormons were not unique, for separatism was in the thinking of other westward-moving Americans as well. With Mormonism, however, such notions were, like everything else they said and did, given a peculiar religious cast. Instead of independence, the Mormons sought a form of corporate autonomy as a state in the Federal Union. Theirs was a pre-Civil War notion of pluralism, in which state autonomy seemed a realistic possibility. That they did not finally abandon such aspirations until almost two generations after the final defeat of such ideas at Appomattox testifies to the reality of their partial secession from the national community. Congress turned down the Mormon proposal for a State of Deseret (from a word in the *Book of Mormon*) and established in its stead a much reduced and federally supervised Utah Territory. The long struggle against Mormon autonomy and the peculiar Mormon institution of plural marriage delayed Utah's admission to the Union until 1896.

The sect that began amid the religious enthusiasms of upstate New York became not only a church embracing large numbers of people but coterminal with a vast expanse of territory upon which the Mormons imprinted their peculiar stamp. It became in that process an indigenous community, developed under American conditions, with its own experience enshrined in the memory of its saints and heroes, who were united by common beliefs and values, common and particular institutions, and a common homeland identified with their own sacred history of suffering and achievement. Biblical Israel had found an American fulfilment. Beneath this conscious model and impenetrating it was the idea—the call—that had moved so many others in the new land—the idea that opportunity for a better life, fulfilment, freedom, and something new and beckoning, lay to the west. The Mormons had reinterpreted old Christian ideas and blended them with those of a popular and democratic secularism. Mormanism had followed a biblical model which was at the same time a theologized projection of an American dream. Peculiar, but thoroughly American, religious and secular at once, the Mormons became Americans of a special type. They represent the clearest example to be found in our national history of the evolution of a native and indigenously developed ethnic minority.

Despite its undeniable singularity, Mormonism has rightly been called an America in miniature. For within Mormon history have occurred the same processes to be seen in the history of America as a whole. The Mormons were American in origin; they experienced in their own history the same encounters and challenges faced by other Americans outside the faith. In their own theologized way they shared important American values, particularly those emphasizing the significance of worldly activity and the importance of work, health, education, and recreation. Thus they represented one of many strands in the humanizing and secularizing of an original Puritanism. Their sacral utopianism was secular American utopianism in religious guise. They experienced conflicts with the parent American society resembling those of the original colonists with the mother country. They carried on city building and attempted to achieve a better life in the present world. A signfiicant factor in the general westward movement of Americans from the Appalachians to the Pacific, they settled on free land and poured their ample energies into its improvement and development. They attracted immigrants from Europe with their secular-religious, American-biblical projection of a land of promise, thereby reenacting much of the entire immigrant experience. And they were finally reintegrated into the national world from which they had seceded, much as the nation was reintegrated into the larger European world on which it had originally turned its back. As the nation found that world transformed, the Mormons found the nation far larger and very different from that from which they had originally fled. And today the problems of an affluent society, the communications revolution (which has everywhere sounded the knell of provincialism), urbanization, and the social problems of advanced societies are to be found in Utah in the very heart of Mormondom. A decade has passed since the majority of Utah's citizens derived their livelihood from agriculture; here again Mormon history parallels that of the country at large.

Mormonism is also of interest from the perspective of the social sciences. It offers an important example of institutional experimentation in a situation of relative freedom. Inspired by novel religious tenets, the Mormons developed economic organizations to provide a context for their efforts to master a difficult terrain. The Mormon religion was born in a region and at a time which experienced the founding and operation of various utopian socialist colonies. Moreover, the first large group of converts to the church were members of Sidney Rigdon's socialist community in Kirtland, Ohio. Joseph Smith was not favorably disposed toward such utopian economic doctrines, despite the undoubted importance of this group of converts and of Rigdon himself; however, this encounter with a religious variety of socialism resulted in his attempt to reconcile economic co-operation under church hegemony with individual management and responsibility. Smith announced a "revelation" embodying the "Law of Consecration," in which properties were consecrated to the church but were distributed to be developed by private initiative. In spite of the fact that it did not work successfully and had to be abandoned in 1838 in favor of tithing, this compromise was a great creative conception of the Mormon prophet. The synthesis of private control and community-minded co-operation which it set forth remained the central Mormon ideal and influenced Mormon enterprise for many decades. In the 1870's a more extreme communistic form evolved in the second United Order and was propagated and approved by Brigham Young himself. At his death this effort was given up and replaced by a form of co-operation among businessmen in Zion's Board of Trade. Here too the emphasis was upon community co-operation and welfare. When the depression came to Utah in the 1930's, the Mormons initiated the Church Welfare Plan, a program of religious socialism practiced within the Church itself which still exists in an expanded form. It is not true, as some have claimed, that the Mormon Church completely took care of its own and that its people neither needed nor utilized federal relief measures. But the co-operative Welfare Plan was, ironically, the proposal of those church leaders who were most opposed to the New Deal and the welfare efforts of Washington.

The second important area of institutional experimentation in Mormon history was plural marriage. This deviation from the marriage mores of the general American community was in practice before it was recorded as a revelation given by the Lord to the prophet and was practiced secretly until its public announcement in Utah in 1852. As an institutional experiment it was abortive. There was neither time nor sufficient calm for it to work itself out in terms of institutional patterns accepted by the general Mormon group. It met with tremendous resistance from outsiders and the government, and it was less than wholeheartedly accepted by numbers of Mormons themselves. As in all polygynous societies, plural marriage, although the ideal form, was practiced by only a minority. Psychological resistance seems never to have been completely overcome, although the identification of the institution with essentials of the faith increased the feeling of duty concerning its practice. In the long contention between Mormon and Gentile, this singular marriage institution was a central issue. The Supreme Court of the United States found in 1878 that a group could not in the name of religion violate the general marriage practices of the country and legitimate itself in terms of the First Amendment. Seeking free expression of their aspirations and ideals within the context of American constitutionalism, the Mormons here tested and indeed found the limits. At the Constitutional Convention of 1887, when some 200 Saints were in jail for "cohabitation," the Mormons took the initiative and made polygamy a crime. In 1890 the church president, Wilford Woodruff, renounced the doctrine as effective church teaching, although it remained a remote and unrealistic ideal long afterward. It was not, however, given up without a covert struggle in intra-church councils, and there exists in Utah and the West today a group of excommunicated Mormon "Fundamentalists," sporadically prosecuted by the authorities of the state and numbering several thousand, who continue to practice plural marriage and who have organized a schismatic church of their own.

Mormon efforts at institution building are also interesting in terms of regional development and intelligent planning. Nowhere has the Mormon co-operative economic ideal had such effect as in the development of irrigation. In Utah the Saints found themselves for the first time in a land of low rainfall. They built their settlements on the basis of co-operative irrigation and developed the Mutual Irrigation Company in which co-operative control of water supported and made possible individual family farming. This sharing of the access to water, which replaced riparian rights in territorial and state law, was a development of the church—in early Utah the primary and parent institution of settlement. Also within the church, Bishop's Courts to adjudicate and adjust disputes developed. The Mormon settlements were fertile ground for innovations and for their translation into institutional forms, many of which proved their functional utility under the harsh tests of western existence.

It is this story that Nels Anderson tells in his account of the desert Saints. He tells it as a social scientist, as a historian, and as a man having empathy with the problems, the thinking, and the feeling of the Mormons. His book, unlike many other works on Mormonism, starts in southwestern Utah, in Utah's "Dixie," where a somewhat different Mormonism prevailed. It was in southern Utah that the more utopian United Order flourished, and here too that Mormons related themselves to the Indians in a manner unique in the experience of American pioneers. In their conflict with the government the Mormons at times found themselves allied with the Indians, whom they believed to be the descendents of apostate Hebrews. In the infamous Mountain Meadows massacre Mormons and Indians united in an attack upon an emigrant train from Missouri. But this book is not just about a part of Mormondom or a section of Utah; it is a book about the Saints and their struggle to build a new Zion in the West.

Since the first appearance of Nels Anderson's *Desert Saints*, a number of impressive works on Mormonism have appeared—history, sociology, biography, and plain story. Much original research and a good deal of analytical thinking have been applied to the subjects of Mormon history, institutions, and religion. Consequently, the significance of the Mormon experience—in itself and as part of a larger setting—has received increasing consideration. Yet this early book continues to hold its place among the significant works on Mormonism.

Anderson's work, and its subject, are of interest because the Mormon story is a continuing one—the Mormon way of life exists today in the midst of a rapidly changing American society. Mormonism is itself undergoing a great transformation—one that may be said to have begun with the church's accommodation to American society as symbolized in the abandoning of some of its peculiar institutions and the admission of Utah to the Union. The urbanization of the Wasatch Front area of Ogden, Salt Lake City, and Provo, the development of modern business and the creation of modern tastes for consumer goods and an affluent life, the rigidification of church organization into older patterns not necessarily appropriate to new conditions, and the inevitable secularization of Mormon life are all in advanced stages of development. All the problems of modern society—from juvenile delinquency to a mounting toll of highway deaths—are now to be found in the kingdom of the Saints. Moreover, Utah has three universities which confront young Mormon minds with modern thought. Impersonalization of life, religious crisis and doubt, and a search for new values and new identities can also be found.

In other respects as well one may observe Mormonism's special combination of peculiarity and typicality. Like many Western States, Utah each year receives more back from the federal government than it pays in taxes; and like many of those states, Utah also contains a sizeable body of opinion which opposes a strong federal government taking an active role in internal affairs. Here the Mormon Church is usually regarded, not without reason, as a strong conservative influence. Like other states of the mountain area, Utah has shown its vulnerability to nostalgic right-wing ideologies which would resist modernity. Yet Utah has generally followed the national trends in voting, whether one considers the Roosevelt landslide of 1936 or the Johnson landslide of 1964.

During the last half-decade the frustrations and confusions involved in the current social changes in Utah have found amorphous and unclear expression in popular political thinking; but here too Utah is hardly unique. In Utah, as in much of the country, there has been a confused groping for ideological and symbolic expression of the emerging responses to the strains of transition. Such groping has found a distinctly Mormon symbol in Utah. It is a strange symbol, considering the historical facts and the current situation. Mormonism has long denied membership in its elaborate lay priesthood structure to Negroes. This is itself an irony since as northerners the Mormons in Missouri were suspected of abolitionism—a suspicion that contributed to the difficulties of their situation there. There is only a small Negro community in Salt Lake City, and it has never been an important factor in local life. Nor can it seriously be suggested that Negroes today, concerned as they are with issues crucial to their lives and welfare, are clamoring for membership in the Mormon priesthood. (One might interpret the case of the Nigerians who have organized an independent Mormon Church on the basis of Mormon literature which came into their possession as an exceptional case.) Yet the issue of Negro admission to the priesthood has become a major controversy in Utah's public and political life. The liberal elements, and many of the young, use it as the reference point for protest against the "standpatism" of the local "establishment." Conservatives in the church, on the other hand, see it as a symbolic issue in holding the line. Mormons in Utah are acting out their own inner conflict with modernity in terms of this issue. Consequently, its meaning as the master symbol for pro- and anti-modernity factions obscures its realistic significance for civil rights and local community relations. Picketing and protest, demands for positional statements and clarification, evasion, resistance, and recalcitrance have all made their appearance. For many on the local scene the issue has been realistically dramatized by the "social problem" created by the importing of Negro athletes into the nearly all-white student communities of two of the state's universities. While symbolic reactions of this kind enable people to give expression to deep anxieties and insecurities and thus provide relief for a deeper malaise, it is to be doubted that such expression and catharsis contribute much to the kind of clarification of issues that would prove helpful in a realistic confrontation with Utah's contemporary problems of growth and transition. Understanding what underlies such protest and resistance is important to Utah today, as it is important throughout the nation, for in periods of change like the present, symbolic expression may create false issues and deflect attention from those aspects of the situation which must be faced before solutions to the problems of a rapidly changing society can be found.

Here too Anderson's book is important, for the study of contemporary situations must be made against the background of their history. Scholarly and scientific contributions to the understanding of human behavior must be part of our analytic equipment. Nels Anderson's *Desert Saints* continues to be significant among such contributions.

THOMAS F. O'DEA

COLUMBIA UNIVERSITY

PREFACE TO THE 1966 PRINTING

IN THE summer of 1934 I went to southern Utah to spend four months gathering data on a grant from Columbia University. My purpose was to tell the story of Mormon settlement in that region—called "Dixie" by the Mormons—paying special attention to two communities. These communities, Enterprise and St. George, were well known to me from a previous stay, as were the people who lived there and much of their family history.

My earlier arrival in that region, in 1908, was unexpected. A teen-age hobo, I was bent on going places, working awhile, and then moving on. My goal was Panama, where I intended to help dig the canal. A freight-train crew stranded me in the most uninviting of places, and after one thing and another, I came to a ranch among the Mormons, was made genuinely welcome, and felt at home. Panama went out of my mind, and the lust for wandering lessened.

Several years later I was still there, living either in Enterprise or in St. George. If I left for work on the railroad or in the mines, these communities remained my home. In 1915 I finished at the Dixie Academy in St. George and went to Brigham Young University and then to the University of Chicago to study sociology. The Dixie story gained a new perspective, and my wish to make a study of it grew, although realizing the wish seemed hardly possible then.

Because of my background, I was drawn into studies of hobos, prisoners, and other fringe elements, until I felt myself a pariah among respectable sociologists, with little hope of finding a professorship. The chance that came in 1934 allowed me to demonstrate my research ability. Here was something I could do, something I was glad to do partly because the story would be a bit my story too.

The year 1934 was a depression one. I was lucky to have even a year-to-year instructorship at Columbia. Then—as much by chance as my first arrival in Dixie had been—four months after returning from Utah I was asked to take a job in Washington. This was mainly owing to the reputation I had been trying to live down. Once in the public service, I could hardly afford to take a teaching job, nor was I especially interested. I was deep in real sociological problems; teaching could come later.

So began twenty years of one kind of public service after another—never once a dull job, never once a job without challenge. Half of that time was spent with special agencies overseas. I reached retirement abroad and then became associated with a research institute there. A professorship came to me—unexpected and unsought—ten years after retirement, long after the idea had been put aside.

The writing of *Desert Saints* was slow work; it was done in Washington as my regular job allowed. As the fact-gathering continued, my "project" became my hobby, taking every hour I could spare over six years. As is usual with hobbies, it became a work of love. The book served as a link between my real occupation and the one I had dreamed of.

While the book was not condemned by the leaders of the Mormon Church, it did not draw much praise. One of the Twelve Apostles, who reviewed it for a Mormon periodical, said to me personally, "The book might have been great; if you had written more with the Spirit of the Lord, you would not have included some of the passages which to me seem negative."

A story circulated in Dixie that I had tricked my way into the St. George Temple and without authority had read sacred Mormon records. This criticism against me was probably aimed indirectly at George Whitehead, the uncommonly intelligent old gentleman who was President of the Temple and who was always present when I went there to work. He sat beside me much of the time, reading the same records, and he was fascinated by their contents. The records contain little that the Mormon Church needs to keep secret. President Whitehead knew that I never overstepped the line dividing the sacred from the profane. Both of us knew that there was then no rule to keep me from looking at the records under such supervision. Moreover, I was not an outsider. I had joined the Church in 1909, and I still regard myself as a Mormon.

NELS ANDERSON

MEMORIAL UNIVERSITY OF NEWFOUNDLAND
ST. JOHNS, CANADA

TABLE OF CONTENTS

INFORMATION FOR THE READER

IN MORMON folklore the name "Deseret" means a honeybee and stands for the simple virtues of industry. Before there was a Utah the Mormons, then newly settled in the Salt Lake Valley, tried to obtain from the government a charter for a state of their own; and the area of that proposed state of Deseret included all of the present states of Utah and Nevada, as well as parts of the present states of Idaho, Wyoming, Colorado, Arizona, and California.

But the Congress of the United States disregarded the pleas of the Mormons. In 1850 the proposed Deseret became the Territory of Utah. Utah's southern border was laid down at the thirty-seventh parallel of latitude, and the northern border at the forty-second parallel. Still later, all of the state of Nevada was carved away from Utah's western area. There were three slices in favor of Nevada. Later one helping from the eastern border was given to Colorado and another to Wyoming.

Although Brigham Young's dream of a great ideal commonwealth suffered by these territorial reductions, the dream of a perfect Mormon state was not surrendered. Deseret was the Mormon ideal of the democratic state, peopled by god-fearing people—a state without political corruption, without poverty or immorality. There would be in that ideal commonwealth no rich and no poor.

Deseret failed for statehood in 1850 and again in 1856 and 1862. For a period following 1862 it had a sort of ghost government. The officers of the ghost state of Deseret included many of the leaders of the church. Brigham Young was re-elected each year as "governor." Each year the ghost government met in legislative session and adopted the laws of the Territory of Utah. Deseret was held in readiness against the time when Congress might grant to her statehood status.

When Utah finally gained statehood, it was not the state of

BRIGHAM YOUNG

Born in Vermont, 1801; joined the Mormon church in 1832 in New York; ordained one of the first apostles in 1835. In 1844, on the death of Joseph Smith, he succeeded to the control of the church. Was made president of the church in 1847 and held this position until his death, in 1877.

Deseret. That vision belonged to the frontier period, and it passed with the frontier character of the Mormon community. The memory of a Deseret unrealized is probably all the brighter because the ideal was denied and the compromise state, "Utah," came in its stead.

Deseret would have been a state in which all interests—social, economic, and political—would have been subservient to the leadership of the Mormon church. It might have been a state of democratic profession but not a democracy in fact. There could not have been within its borders more than one political party, more than one social or economic philosophy; and religious minorities would have found Deseret intolerable. Deseret democracy would have been typical of democracy in any utopia. It could survive only by the miracle of all citizens having a single heart and mind.

Back in 1850, when the dream of Deseret was brightest, a request was submitted to the people of Utah for a stone to be contributed to the George Washington Monument. Those who visit the Washington Monument and walk down the five hundred feet or more of inner stairway will see placed in the walls many gift stones from states, cities, volunteer fire companies, military units, religious bodies, and others. There, too, is a stone from the state of Deseret. It was sent after the Utah territorial government had been established. The placing of that stone was as near as the Mormon dream of Deseret came to winning a standing in the sisterhood of states.

Deseret, the perfect state, was none other than Zion, God's kingdom on earth, as revealed to Joseph Smith, prophet, seer and revelator, and founder of the Church of Jesus Christ of Latter-Day Saints. It is believed by the Mormons that Joseph Smith received by divine revelation the intelligence and guidance by which their church was established; that he walked and talked with gods and angels; and that personages from heaven delivered to him the golden plates on which were inscribed in ancient hieroglyphics the record of an extinct people that once inhabited this continent and developed here a mighty civilization.

JOSEPH SMITH

Prophet, seer, and revelator; founder of the Church of Jesus Christ of Latter-Day Saints. Born in Vermont, 1805; martyred in Illinois in 1844.

Whether Joseph Smith was a prophet or merely a paranoiac would be a matter of great importance to his followers, but it is not an issue here. Too much has already been written on that subject. Scholars and skeptics have debated it with believers, and all have returned from their debates with minds unchanged. Joseph Smith's status as prophet is not provable except to those who accept him in faith.

Other prophets stood before the world during the first half of the last century bearing the same message. They, too, called on the pure in heart to gather round them; but their kingdoms did not increase, and few endured. Some of the other prophets and their people were persecuted and driven, but none were persecuted as were the Mormons.

Zion first gathered at Kirtland, Ohio, near the shore of Lake Erie to the east of Cleveland. Here the Saints built their first temple. Here they attempted that communal type of living, known as the "United Order." Other religious groups attempted to live under some form of Christian communism. Some of those groups failed when their plans of communal living failed. Not so the Mormons. They suffered failures but did not fail.

While Kirtland was utilized as a place of first gathering, Smith promoted a plan for building Zion in western Missouri. Between 1832 and 1839 Smith and his Latter-Day Saints tried twice, without success, to establish Zion in Missouri. Next they went to Illinois. Again they met with the same economic, political, and religious opposition. This time the prophet lost his life, but the elements of his plan did not perish with him. The church then migrated to western Iowa and later to Utah, seeking a place to build the Zion of which Deseret would have been the civil counterpart.

Mark Twain once remarked that the Mormons were a curious people: "Their religion is singular but their wives are plural." Those who are acquainted with the history of the Saints are impressed with the relatively minor place of polygamy in that history. It was not an issue in their Ohio and Missouri difficulties. In fact, although "celestial marriage" was introduced by Joseph Smith about 1842, it was scarcely associated with Mormonism prior to their Utah settlement. It was a serious issue after 1852, but already the church had passed through twenty years of persecution, internal change, and sacrifice.

Although polygamy gave the Mormons front-page notoriety, it was but one of their unique characteristics. They were a temple-building people, and in their temples their work for the dead introduced a new element in religion. In their temples the living and the dead are united in family groups, which link an everlasting past with an eternal future. In this distinction is seen one of the doctrinal differences between Mormons and other sects.

Other doctrinal differences need to be mentioned for the part they played in arousing the opposition of ministers of other sects. Mormons believe in continuous revelation, which is rank heresy to other creeds. Mormons believe they have the original Old Testament priesthood, restored through Joseph Smith. That claim is offensive to other creeds. Mormons set up other books—the Doctrine and Covenants, the Book of Mormon, and the Pearl of Great Price—as companion works with the Bible. To other creeds this is sheer blasphemy.

Major emphasis in this book will be placed on the struggle of the Rocky Mountain Saints to establish for themselves an insular economy. They tried to protect their ideal of economic and social isolation by their own self-sufficient political organization. Actually, the long struggle between the Mormons and their opponents, the Gentiles, was not primarily concerned with the polygamy issue. That was a good and high moral issue, but behind it were more potent economic and political differences.

Polygamy was really an incident in Mormon frontier history. The basic story concerns the struggle of a persecuted people to find a haven of refuge and to establish homes and communities in a forbidding, ungrateful desert environment. Continued persecution caused them to bless their insular habitat for the security it afforded. Recognizing the importance of this home-making mission, Bernard De Voto has criticized gentile literature for the exaggerated importance it has given to the polygamy issue. Had there been no persecution, polygamy in Deseret would have perished of its own disabilities.

It is pertinent, at this point, for the writer to indicate his own interest in the subject of this volume. He went to Utah in 1908, and for ten years he lived in various Mormon communities and with Mormon families in eastern Nevada and southern Utah. He attended high school at the Dixie Academy at St. George and in 1920 graduated from the Brigham Young University at Provo. He joined the Mormon church in 1909 and has retained a nominal affiliation with the Latter-Day Saints.

In 1933 he secured from the Social Science Research Council a grant-in-aid. A grant was also received from the Social Science Council of Columbia University. These research moneys were made available for a study of the Mormon community and family. The author at that time proposed to confine his efforts to some small community in southern Utah, the area of his former acquaintance. St. George was selected because of the complete records in the public and church files. He found an abundance of written information, and the church officials were very co-operative in making this available.

For the pioneer period, church records were more abundant than public records, as would be expected for the decades when the priesthood was the primary government for the faithful. In a great vault room in the basement of the St. George Temple were stored hundreds of record books of more than twenty communities of southern Utah and some for communities now in Nevada. In these were reported the doings in the local church groups. Besides the local records, the author had access to the minutes of the High Council of the St. George Stake of Zion, the governing body of the church in southern Utah. These were great bulky volumes reporting on trials and actions of the Council from 1863 to the present.

Access was also gained to a considerable number of private journals and to a manuscript history of the Southern Mission—four large scrapbooks of day-to-day information about happenings in the region. Some of the personal journals were made available later through the co-operation of the Writers' Project and the Historical Records Survey of the Works Progress Administration, now the Work Projects Administration. Scores of private journals and brief biographies were collected and copied.

These are on file either at St. George or with the Historical Records Survey at Salt Lake City.

More than any other frontier people, the Mormons were keepers of records. Every company that crossed the plains named a person to keep the day-to-day record of the journey. Every group of families sent to form a settlement had its historian, and that functionary was as important a member of every settlement as was the fiddler who went along to supply music for the dances.

It was later realized by the author that a comprehensive account of Mormon family and community life could not be written in terms of a single community and selected typical families. This was attempted with commendable success by Maurine Whipple in *The Giant Joshua* and less sympathetically by Vardis Fisher in *Children of God*. There have been other novels in which the subjects were Mormon families and the settings Mormon communities, but in each case the writer was confronted with the problem of relationship networks by which the individual or family was linked to all others in his community, and his community was but a segment of a larger unity.

Since this is the first time such an abundance of local materials has been assembled, the author could not resist the temptation to use a great deal of it. Most books about the Mormons are centered in and around Salt Lake City. The hundreds of hinterland communities have been neglected, and unfortunately so, because in those places the Mormon way of life in its greatest purity prevailed. It remained unadulterated there much longer than in the more cosmopolitan areas around Salt Lake City and Ogden.

Dixie, the "Cotton Country," was the inland capital of the Mormon empire. It was there the first temple was completed. It was there that the United Order was established in 1874. It was there that Brigham Young went in winter to enjoy the milder climate, and often his presence in St. George served to transfer church headquarters to Dixie during winter months. Also, St. George, with the surrounding area, was the base of operations for extending the Mormon frontier into Nevada,

Arizona, New Mexico, Colorado, and across the border into Mexico.

A Mormon temple is a sacred place, and Saints are admitted there only on the recommendation of their bishops. Because of this fact, a word of explanation is due regarding the search by the writer of the records filed in the vault of the St. George Temple. The writer did not venture into the upper floors of the temple, where the sacred ordinances are performed. His work was confined to the basement only. Each day he passed the huge cast-iron baptismal font which rests on the backs of twelve cast-iron oxen, but he entered none of the ordinance or other rooms. He never asked questions about what was to be seen in other parts of the building. Moreover, he was scrupulously careful not to be in the temple unless an attendant was present. This explanation is made to protect the integrity of temple officials who might otherwise be subjected to the censure of their brethren.

It will be noted that the first twelve chapters of this book are historical and that the final four chapters deal with special subjects. Originally there were more subject chapters and fewer historical. The change was made to give greater continuity to materials relating to frontier development. This done, the writer still felt the need of the additional chapters dealing with phases of the Mormon culture. No defense is made for this mixed method of presenting the subject.

One reader of this manuscript raised a question about the different character of the concluding historical chapters. He thought they lacked the detail of earlier chapters. This raises the question about the date at which the frontier period ends. When the writer was confronted with the task of cutting the manuscript to its present length, he was forced to the conclusion that the detail of the final two chapters could be eliminated with the least damage to the completeness of the frontier picture.

The high point of Mormon frontier history was about 1859. From that point on, church power was curtailed little by little. When Brigham Young died in 1877, the church was entering its final battle; but the end of the polygamy struggle was not then in doubt. Only after the church yielded was statehood possible. Except for the settlement of this issue, the frontier period was over at Young's death. For this reason the writer "tapered off" the historical section in the twelfth chapter. Again, this is a matter of opinion, and the writer believes the frontier period ended in the late seventies.

The pioneers are presented herein as a hardy, although at times a fanatical, people with a mission. In some respects Mormon ardor was rendered the more zealous by the zeal of the opposition. Many of the Gentiles who opposed them were no less fanatical and were as determined to destroy the church as the Mormons were to build it. Brigham Young was no less intolerant than men like Judge Eckles, Judge McKean, or the Indian agent Dr. Hurt. Many crusading politicians and preachers who fought the Mormons and their system were well-intentioned persons, but they were so biased that they could not see any virtue in their opponents. The same must be said of some of the Mormons. These issues ran their course, reached a climax, and then faded out. And with them faded the vision of that perfect state, Deseret.

CHAPTER I

GOD'S CHOSEN PEOPLE

ENTERPRISE, UTAH, is a small farming town in the extreme southwestern corner of the state at the edge of the Escalante Desert, where in the Pleistocene period was the shore of a great lake, the northern limit of which was near the Idaho-Utah line. Great Salt Lake is the remnant of that extinct inland sea known to geologists as Lake Bonneville. Much of the old lake bottom is a desert, which embraces areas of western Utah and eastern Nevada. Around the edges of this desert, from northern Utah to Enterprise, is an array of small Mormon villages, located wherever the streams flow from the mountains.

In 1908 Enterprise was a new town of a hundred families. It was laid out along the lines of pioneer tradition. Each farmer had his land in the "field" and a plot of ground in town. In the "field," where the crops were grown, there were no dwellings, not even sheds or barns. All the farmers lived in the town. They were building their homes in 1908, planting shade trees, laying out gardens, and some families had small lawns.

Each morning the Enterprise farmer did his chores, milked his cows, took care of the chickens and pigs, ate his breakfast, then hitched up the team and started for the "field"—a distance of three, four, or five miles. At night he drove back, did his chores, worked a little in the garden, and perhaps after dinner (supper, to him) went to some social at the meeting house, the same meeting house where he danced on Friday night and worshiped on Sunday.

The year 1908 was one of thanksgiving for Enterprise. The founders of the community had been laboring co-operatively for years to build the dam and ditches to bring the irrigation water from the mountain, down Shoal Creek Canyon to the desert. The work had been finished, the water was running to the fields, the crops were growing; and so all Enterprise was gathered together on Pioneer Day, July 24, in double celebration.

It was on July 24, 1847, that the first pioneer Mormon company pitched camp on the gray parched flats where Salt Lake City now stands. On every anniversary of that occasion the Saints of the Rockies had thanked God for bringing them over the plains to the valleys of the mountains. But on July 24, 1908, the people of Enterprise were gathered also to thank God for the water in the irrigation ditches and for their first full crop.

Enterprise was honored on that occasion more than any Mormon village from the Salt River in Arizona to the Big Horn in Wyoming; two members of the Quorum of Twelve Apostles were present. For any Mormon community on July 24 to have one apostle present for a half-day was a signal honor. Enterprise had two apostles all day.

For Apostle Anthony W. Ivins the occasion was a homecoming. From boy to man, he had lived many years in that part of the state. He was a man past middle age, garbed in a gray business suit. He wore a sharply trimmed beard, which might have caused him to be mistaken for a doctor or a professor. He looked much less the apostle than his companion.

The other apostle was a George Albert Smith, distantly related to Joseph Smith, Jr., who founded the Mormon church in 1830. This Smith—tall, thin, of gentle voice and kind manner—was born, it seemed, to the clergy. He was of less worldly appearance than Ivins. He wore the same type of whiskers, but his chin was less firm; however, he was also more spiritual of countenance.

Pioneer Day celebrations in Mormon towns followed approximately the same pattern. In the forenoon there were races and games for the children, some pageantry reminiscent of pioneer times, and at the end gathering at the meeting house. In the afternoon there were horse races with betting on the sly, "busting" of broncos, and a baseball game between the married and single men. In the late afternoon came the children's dance, and in the evening the regular dance for grownups.

For Enterprise that day the high point of the outdoor features was the "handcart parade," prepared for the occasion because the people felt in a pioneer mood. The men who took part in the parade had permitted their beards to grow. Time and labor had been spent creating the costumes, fitting out the handcarts, and rehearsing so that the pageant would carry through without fault. Even the young men in the role of marauding Indians had rehearsed their attack on the handcart company.

The paraders assembled in a vacant tract a half-mile from the meeting house, from which point the villagers could view the procession. They could see the "Indians" lurking in the sagebrush. They could see the weary emigrants dragging their overloaded handcarts, the women carrying their babies, and the small children trailing behind. As the handcart pioneers neared the ambush, the suspense deepened, turning to anguish when the "Indians," with fierce whoops, pounced upon the unsuspecting travelers. The women and children scattered; the men heroically threw themselves into the battle. After five minutes of shouting, shooting, and pantomime the attackers were put to flight. The company reorganized and continued on its way toward the meeting house, singing: "We'll find the place God for us prepared, far away in the West."

The rest of the people followed, filling all the seats and standing around the back of the hall and down the sides. Still there was not room, and some of the young men found seats in the open windows.

Bishop George A. Holt escorted the apostles to the platform. Several of the leading elders followed and took their places on the stand. The meeting opened with the congregation singing "The Star Spangled Banner." A prayer was offered, and that was followed by a song to the Mormon homeland: "O Ye Mountains High." The bishop stood up and told of "this great day for our people"; how they escaped their enemies and found safety "in these mountain valleys."

Apostle Smith, the first speaker, said he came to mingle with the people as a neighbor. He hoped to meet many personally before the day was through. He talked of the home, the family, and the Mormon way of life. Apostle Ivins spoke of the pioneers who settled that part of Utah, who extended the Mormon frontier into Arizona and down into Mexico. He knew personally many of those pioneers; some of whom were in the audience. One, who would speak to them as orator of the day, had been known to him since childhood. This trusted frontiersman had served wherever sent, and he asked no reward save the joy of service.

Bishop Holt invited Grandfather Lyman L. Woods to the stand. "We are all happy that Brother Woods is so well after the long ride from Clover Valley. We want him to speak as the spirit directs. He is the only person among us whose memory reaches back to the days of Prophet Joseph." An aged man started for the platform. With some effort he straightened from his apparently usual stooping posture. His hair, white and almost bushy, was brushed straight back and smoothed down severely. He wore a beard covering his face entirely except for a clean-shaven half-circle between the corners of his mouth and the line of his chin, and his moustache was clipped close. Those who knew the venerable patriarch knew also why he cut his beard and mustache so. Since his youth he had been a chewer of tobacco, a habit not in keeping with the Mormon "Word of Wisdom," which forbids the use of alcoholics, tobacco, coffee, and tea.

By shaving his chin in that way Grandfather Woods avoided the telltale tobacco stains. His conscience, however, in the matter was clear, because Brigham Young, the master whose word was law, once said that the Lord would overlook minor aberrations on the part of loyal frontiersmen. With the same clear conscience the old veteran would drink his cup of strong coffee each morning, certain that the good marks on his record would insure his soul for the Judgment Day.

His teeth, upper and lower, were all gold-crowned and glistened as he spoke, but this display of gold did not seem conspicuous. His hands were impressively huge and big jointed, his arms long, his shoulders sharp and square. His physique was reminiscent of past strength of body, as his manner and speech confirmed his distinction as a frontiersman. He began:

> I cannot make a fine speech because I never had the book learning; but if the Lord will brighten my memory, I will tell of things I have seen with my own natural eyes and heard with my own natural ears.
>
> As a boy I saw and talked with the Prophet Joseph. Once he put his hand on my head and blessed me. I have seen him wrestle with the young men on the green. He was quick as a squirrel and strong as a mountain lion, but he was gentle as a lamb. I have seen him on a white horse wearing the uniform of a general.

Woods asked a boy sitting on the floor in front of the audience to stand. "That's how big I was when I saw the Prophet last. He was leading a parade of the Legion and looked like a god."

The narrative followed, step by step, those dramatic events after the martyrdom of Prophet Joseph and his brother, Patriarch Hyrum Smith: the false charges against them; the trial, when they went "like lambs to the slaughter"; the mob that slew them at the Carthage jail; and the failure of Illinois to apprehend the "mobocrats" who sought to destroy the church and scatter the Saints. But God raised up a new leader in Brigham Young, and the Saints followed him out of the land of persecution.

Grandfather Woods talked to the children, as if they alone were present. The parents listened with the same rapt attention to a recital they had heard hundreds of times before. And a few of the aged ones present had lived through some of those pioneer experiences. But the story about themselves and their origins took on new beauty as it unfolded from the lips of this pioneer, whose tongue had been blessed with the genius of narrative.[1]

What did it matter to that audience if the story did not follow the true sequence of events or if the memories of the storyteller became confused with the memories of others? This was their story, too—how God started the church and how the Devil tried his old tricks. When the Saints gathered in Ohio, the Devil was there to cause trouble. The church moved to Missouri. Again, the Devil showed up to enter the hearts of men. At every turn there were "mobbings and burnings and drivings," but the prophet led his people to safety.

Once the Devil sent his blackface mob, but the flood arose and stopped the mob. They put the prophet in jail, but he always got away. Evil spirits entered the bodies of the Saints, but the elders laid on their hands and the spirits were cast out.

Woods remembered that hour of trial in June, 1844, with Joseph and his brother martyred, and how the leaderless Saints were fearful. "I saw strong men weep like children. Every home in that beautiful city had lost a loved one. But the God of Israel watched over us, and Brigham Young was raised up to lead the people out of that unhappy place."

Different men claimed that the prophet's mantle had fallen on them. The people listened but were not convinced until Brother Brigham rose to speak. They saw his face light up like the noonday sun, and in the brightness of his countenance they saw the face of Joseph. "That," said Grandfather Woods, "was the testimony none could deny except those who wanted to follow the Devil."

The congregation listened and praised God that the days of persecution were over. They echoed "Amen" when Grandfather Woods concluded: "We had fifty years of persecution, but now we are safe. The church of God is planted on the mountain tops where all the world can see."

In all the Mormon Zion in 1908 not a hundred persons could boast a memory span equal almost to the life of the church. There is none today. They saw their church grow from its hazardous infancy through a turbulent adolescence to an adult institution.

To those pioneers who viewed their experiences through eyes of faith the story of Mormonism was ever told in simple numbers. It was merely a struggle between the hosts of heaven and the legions of hell. Every man of faith knew what the outcome would be. It was no less true of the Mormons of Enterprise who heard the Pioneer Day oration. Joseph Smith was no mystery. He was to them a plumed knight on a white charger, a battler for the right, a seer and revelator. He was leader because God willed it, than which there can be no better answer for the questioning mind.

Who was this man who had the genius to gather about him thousands of people; whose followers in spite of poverty, assault, and ridicule retained their loyalty, some even to the sacrifice of life; and whose martyrdom elevated him to a place in the hearts of his people which to this day remains only a little less than godhood?[2]

Joseph Smith was born December 23, 1805, on a backwoods farm near Sharon, Windsor County, Vermont, the fourth child of ten in the family of Joseph Smith, Sr., and Lucy Mack Smith. Of the Smiths much has been spoken, both good and evil. Of their poverty there is no question, but there is dispute about their character. In the chronicles of Mormonism they were simple, devout, hard-working farmers who moved from place to place, as did many families of the time, in search of a chance to work and live.

In 1815, when young Joseph was in his tenth year, the Smiths moved to Palmyra on the Erie Canal, then being constructed, and remained in that general vicinity the next several years.

Young Joseph was a boy of spiritual leanings and some intellectual curiosity, but he had little opportunity for formal education.[3] That was a period of intense religious controversy and of pentecostal cults. Throughout the northern frontier, from Vermont to Ohio, rival sects and religious isms competed for converts. Strange preachers wandered the highroads, claiming to be prophets and calling the people to repent. Some predicted judgment day soon at hand; all preached fear; and each claimed that all the rest were wrong.

Bewildered, young Joseph turned to the Bible, and there he read that he should ask God for guidance. So he went into the woods to pray. As he prayed, the heavens opened, and two personages appeared in a shaft of light. "This is my beloved Son, hear ye Him," spake the elder of the two. Then the other personage told Joseph that he should join none of the churches, for all were wrong. All drew near to God with their lips, but their hearts were elsewhere. That was the story the boy told his friends and family. Members of his family listened and believed. The neighbors scoffed and branded Joseph a falsifier, a visionary, even a victim of Satan. But he would not deny his story or change it. That was some time in 1820.

Three years passed. Joseph was reaching man's estate, and he grew in wisdom. On the night of September 21, 1823, while he was in bed, he received a second visitation. This time it was a personage who is now known in Mormon folklore as the "Angel Moroni" and whose image in gold stands on the topmost spire of the Salt Lake Temple.

Moroni led Joseph to a hillside and showed him where was buried a record on gold plates, the contents of which he would one day reveal to the world. Moroni gave instructions to Joseph. The next year at the same time he appeared again, and again he told the youth of the great work in store for him. Moroni made other visits, preparing Joseph for his great mission.

In September, 1827, Moroni permitted Joseph to take the records into his possession. It was, according to Joseph's own report, a sheaf of thinly hammered gold plates. Each page was about six by eight inches, and all the pages made up a volume of six inches thick, bound together by three rings. Buried in the stone box with the book was a breastplate and a device to be worn as spectacles. The spectacles, "Urim and Thummim," were to be used in translating the record.

During the period of preparation Joseph had proved he could keep his counsel, withstand the jibes of tormentors, and could not be distracted by the Devil. He was permitted to have possession of the golden plates and to begin the translation, as God would guide his mind, of the strange hieroglyphics inscribed thereon.

The forces of evil tried frantically to frustrate young Joseph. He was forced to flee from place to place lest the golden plates should fall into vulgar hands. A schoolteacher, Oliver Cowdery, of the same age as Joseph and also a Vermonter, served as amanuensis. They worked with a curtain between them, Joseph translating and Oliver writing as he dictated. This story of the birth of a new Holy Writ, which was called the Book of Mormon, has been told in so many places that for the present volume it is sufficient to mention the matter briefly.

The Book of Mormon was published in March, 1830. A month later, on April 6, the prophet, his brother Hyrum, his brother Samuel, Oliver Cowdery, and two Whitmers, at Fayette, New York, joined to form the organization which was later named the "Church of Jesus Christ of Latter-Day Saints."

From 1820, when the youthful Joseph had his first vision, until the founding of the church in 1830, Mormonism was little more than a promise. Smith walked with angels and talked with God, received revelations and dreamed dreams; but these experiences were confined to himself. He did make a few friends, and some friends were loyal to him. That decade may be called the "years of apprenticeship." The next decade belonged to Brother Joseph and the church. They were years of trial and error but also years of growth. During that period the church met with resistance and persecution experienced by no other group, political or religious, in American history.

The decade from 1820 to 1830 was one in which Joseph Smith was tested, and even his critics will concede he was not found wanting. He grew to an impressive physical manhood, and inwardly he grew to a spiritual and mental stature equally impressive. Each succeeding year, as he mingled more with men, he may have been spoiled by the forces of circumstance; but he also grew wise in the ways of the world. As the decade before 1830 was the testing period for the prophet, the following decade was the testing period for the church.

During that second decade Smith gradually found himself in a new role. The "peep-stone" associations connected with his translation of the golden plates were replaced by associations of a different character. He became in the public eye a leader and promoter. Perhaps to some he was merely another climber, a demagogue with a vision. In history he turns out to be, in his last years, a man on a white horse, just as he was remembered by Grandfather Woods.

The cornerstone of Smith's new plan of life and salvation was the Book of Mormon. Here was new light on the gospel of Christ. He would call his church the "Church of Christ."[4]

THE THREE WITNESSES TO THE BOOK OF MORMON

Above, Oliver Cowdery, who acted as scribe in the translation of the book as Joseph Smith dictated from behind a screen. *Below*, David Whitmer and Martin Harris. The latter helped finance the first publication of the book. All three left the church but later came back into the fold. At the bottom is shown the hill Cumorah, where Joseph Smith reported that he dug up the golden plates.

There would be two sacred books—one from the Old World, one from the New World.

Briefly, the Book of Mormon purported to be the record of a race of people who once inhabited this continent. They came from the Near East in a strangely constructed boat which drifted over the Pacific Ocean without benefit of sails or help of oars. These people came to shore on the western coast of Central or South America.

Lehi, the man who headed that strange expedition, had four sons, and each son came with his wife and family. The two older sons were Laman and Lemuel. They became the leaders of a hunting tribe and lived in the woods and the swamps. Because of their chronic badness, God cursed them with dark skins, and in the Book of Mormon they are called the "Lamanites."

Lehi's two younger sons were Nephi and Samuel. They were industrious men, faithful to the Lord and obedient to Father Lehi. They became farmers, herders, and builders. The Mormons claim that the remains of cities found in Central America are reminders of those "white and delightsome people," the Nephites, whose culture began about six centuries before Christ.

According to the record as translated by Brother Joseph, Christ also visited this continent and set up a church with apostles and principles not unlike those established in Palestine. With the Nephites the church continued three hundred years or more. Eventually, about four centuries after Christ, the Nephites and Lamanites engaged in a sort of last-man war. All the Nephites, except Mormon and his son, Moroni, were slain. Moroni hid the record and the translating spectacles in the hill Cumorah. Centuries later he returned to deliver these treasures to Joseph Smith.

It was on the story of the Book of Mormon and the doctrines contained therein that Smith took his stand. As converts were made, they were loaded down with copies of the much publicized "Golden Bible" and sent along the highways. They sold books, taking in return lodging, produce, or cash. They asked people to read the book and pray.[5]

Joseph Smith found himself confronted with many issues and problems. If his church was to fill the entire world, where would the place of beginning be? Where would the new Zion have its central point of control? There were questions of organization, regarding lines of authority, levels of administration, economic control, and discipline. Many of the new converts began, in their zeal, to receive revelations. Joseph, as he was confronted by one issue or another, went to the Lord. The Lord answered with revelations.[6]

Revelation No. 32, received in September, 1830, concerned the Indians of the western regions. In accordance with the mandate of the Book of Mormon, the new Gospel was to be taken to the Lamanites. Four men—Oliver Cowdery, Parley P. Pratt, Peter Whitmer, Jr., and Ziba Peterson—were sent from Fayette, New York, to preach to the Indians.

These missionaries, following the road westward, came to Kirtland, Ohio, where they met Sidney Rigdon, a former disciple of Alexander Campbell. He was a visionary and a promoter, an advocate of a form of Christian communism, and pastor of a congregation of believers. Rigdon and most of his followers accepted Smith's gospel and were baptized. Rigdon hurried to New York to meet the prophet and invite him to Kirtland.[7] About January, 1831, Smith and a following moved to Kirtland, accepting that location as the first gathering place.

Parley P. Pratt and his party reached Independence, Missouri, in the spring of 1831. They followed the usual route down the Ohio River Valley, over the Mississippi, and up the valley of the Missouri. They found the land there rich and abundant. They came to the western boundary of Missouri and entered the Indian territory beyond, but that land was not available for settlement. The elders returned to Independence in Jackson County, then a town of about three hundred persons. Kansas City, later the metropolis of the county, had not yet started.

During June and July, 1831, after the return of Pratt's party, Smith was actively encouraging elders to migrate to Jackson County. Smith, in company with his new associate, Sidney Rigdon, and several others, arrived at Independence late in

July. In the party was the recently converted W. W. Phelps, who entered Mormonism from the editorship of an anti-Masonic periodical in New York. Phelps was put to work publishing the first Mormon paper, the *Evening and Morning Star*, which began to issue from Independence in June, 1832. Also in the party was Martin Harris, Smith's friend, who two years earlier was supporting him financially in getting the Book of Mormon published.

On August 1, Smith received a revelation confirming Jackson County as the location of Zion. The next day the area was consecrated to the gathering of the Saints, and on the third day of August the brethren selected and dedicated a site for the temple.[8]

After some two weeks in Jackson County, Smith on August 9 set out on his return journey. In that short interval he received four revelations. En route to Kirtland, where he arrived on August 27, two revelations were received, and two more were received shortly after his arrival there. In the main, these revelations concerned the movement of the Saints to Jackson County.[9]

This absence of about two months was his first of such a length from his rapidly growing flock. On his return he found considerable confusion. Some of the new converts had been seeing visions. It was for him to let them all know that he alone was prophet. Smith alone talked with God.

More baffling were the economic problems of the Saints. Some of the converts arriving at Kirtland were in dire poverty. Smith felt impelled to persuade other converts to share their goods or to "consecrate" their surplus.[10] The idea of consecration assumed that a Saint recognized that all he possessed belonged to the Lord; that he should give his surplus to God's agency, the church.

In the early months of 1831, before leaving for Missouri, Smith received a number of revelations in which the communal doctrine of property was mentioned. In Missouri he saw families arrive in such naked poverty that he mentioned in his revelations the need there and then of "dividing the inheritances."[11]

There was a pooling of funds to buy public land which sold at $1.25 per acre. Clearly, it did not cost a great deal to get a foothold on Missouri soil, but some of the Saints did not, upon arrival, have enough even to buy an acre. They were encouraged to buy land collectively.

Besides expediting the movement of families from Kirtland to Zion, consecration provided the means to aid in the gathering of new converts. Some help was needed for the missionary service, although generally the missionaries traveled without purse or script. But occasionally they needed funds for travel.

Apparently, the handling of these matters of property caused friction among the brethren, which may explain why Joseph Smith, in September, moved his family from Kirtland to Hiram in Portage County, some thirty miles distant, where he remained the next several months. The reasons for the friction are not pertinent at this point except that on March 25, 1832, Smith and Rigdon were set upon at Hiram by a mob of disaffected Saints and severely beaten. In addition, Brother Joseph was given a coat of tar and feathers. A few days later he received a revelation, Section 78 of the Doctrine and Covenants, instructing him to hasten to Missouri. He reached Independence on April 24.

On that trip he was impressed with the magnitude of the Zion-building task. Most of the converts were poor, although pious, people. Few of them had the means to migrate from the Kirtland area to Zion. The scheme of voluntary consecration of surplus goods was not adequate. A more systematic co-operative economy was needed. It is not surprising that two days after arriving in Jackson County, Smith received his important revelation on the United Order of Enoch.[12]

Within two weeks Joseph Smith, Sidney Rigdon, and others again set out for Kirtland, where they arrived in June, after a journey of miraculous experiences. The next five years Smith was much occupied, going to Missouri, visiting neighboring states, settling disputes between his subordinates, promoting the United Order, teaching the principles of the Gospel, directing the missionary program.

Although a busy and harassed man, Smith was never a frustrated one. He moved in and out of difficulties with the skill of a contortionist, and he had the genius to capitalize to his advantage many a situation which might have proved embarrassing to a less gifted person.

Some difficulties were of his own making because he lacked the ability of Brigham Young, his successor, to pick the right men for the jobs to be done. He lacked Brigham Young's capacity to assign work and to delegate authority. However, his deficiency in administrative ability was compensated for by the loyalty he was able to command. Converts who were inspired to follow him blindly, and who remained in the faith for that reason, later, with the natural maturing of the church, found a place and a role in it.

Among his faithful followers were such practical men as Newell K. Whitney, who operated a store at Kirtland. This man, when he joined the church, was soon to become, with Martin Harris, Sidney Rigdon, and Oliver Cowdery, a central figure in the United Order. Another man of practical good sense was Edward Partridge, first bishop of the church. It was Whitney, in partnership with Sidney Gilbert, who opened a Mormon store at Independence in April, 1832. This store was part of the United Firm and was designed to be the trading center for the United Order.

The United Order of Enoch was to function under three agencies: (*a*) The Storehouse, in which the church would gather goods by gift or consecration and dispense charity. (*b*) The United Firm, designed as an outlet for the goods collected in the Storehouse. Like the co-operative stores started later in Utah, it was expected that the Firm would have a monopoly of Mormon trade. (*c*) The Printing Concern, which was managed by W. W. Phelps. Two papers were to be published for sale: the *Evening and Morning Star*, a monthly; and the *Upper Missouri Advertiser*, a weekly. This plant was also to publish books.[13]

While it is generally recognized that the Order failed to get beyond the organization stage, the Gilbert and Whitney store was established and did operate as a Mormon monopoly. The

Gentiles in Jackson County regarded the proposed venture as a threat to their security. In their zeal the Mormons perhaps said too much about taking over the country. The United Order was another evidence of their exclusiveness and aggressiveness; so concluded the Gentiles.

As a further irritant, the first issue of the *Evening and Morning Star* carried an editorial entitled "Free People of Color," which touched on the slavery issue. Phelps, who had formerly crusaded against the Masons, found in slavery another evil to battle.

Mob action against the Mormons did not begin until July 20, 1833, when the printing plant of the *Star* was destroyed. Until the end of that year there were frequent attacks by gangs of gentile rowdies. Houses were stoned at night; haystacks burned; the store was raided; and Mormons found alone were beaten.

When the news of mob action in Jackson County reached Smith at Kirtland, he learned that the Saints were discouraged and that some were asking: "Did not Brother Joseph say this land would be ours, and would not be taken from us?" Smith asked God why this "calamity" had come to Zion. On December 16, 1833, he received a revelation and was assured that "Zion shall not be moved out of her place, notwithstanding that her children are scattered."

While this promise may have been cheering to the faithful harassed Saints in Jackson County, the revelation also contained a sting. It mentioned "jarrings and contentions and envyings and strifes and lustful and covetous desires among them, therefore by these things they polluted their inheritance." Yet God assured Joseph: "My bowels are filled with compassion toward them."

The refugee Saints, deprived of their goods, were glad to escape over the Missouri River into Clay County, which is immediately north of Jackson County. They were made welcome by Clay County citizens but were given only a temporary haven. Again they appealed to Joseph Smith, who was much occupied at Kirtland. Smith appealed to the Lord and on February 24, 1834, he was assured that God in his wrath was ready for action. "Zion is to be established, no more to be thrown down."[14]

This revelation instructed Smith to organize an army of five hundred men called "Zion's Camp." If he could not find that number after diligent effort, "peradventure ye may obtain 100." Before the end of April at New Portage, fifty miles west of Kirtland, Zion's Camp was organized. Each man was required to furnish his own arms and equipment and no less than five dollars in cash. About two hundred men gathered at the recruiting-point.

The march of Zion's Camp, as secret as they could make it, began on May 1. Smith, as "General," with bodyguard and standard-bearer carrying a white banner on which was inscribed in red "Peace," led the way.

This amateur army aroused the curiosity of strangers, whose queries were met with vague answers. It was no less a mystery to its own members. These soldier-Saints were men of various backgrounds who stood now on a common ground, their faith in the prophet who called himself "General." They knew not the enemy they would battle, but they believed that the hosts of heaven would intercede and scatter the Gentiles before them.

Occasionally along the route they stopped to engage in sham battle or to perform other military exercises, about which Smith presumed to know much. They saw miracles in every strange manifestation of nature. One day they brought three snakes to Smith. Should they be killed? He ordered them not to hurt the snakes. "Men must become harmless, before the brute creation; and when men lose their vicious dispositions and cease to destroy the animal race, the lion and the lamb can dwell together, and the sucking child can play with the serpent in safety."[15]

As the brethren approached the Mississippi River to cross into Missouri some were fearful lest the Gentiles should gather in force against them. Others rebuked them for their lack of faith. They arrived in Missouri on June 5 but met no opposition. The Camp advanced across the state, knowing that news of their coming had gone ahead and that resistance might be expected, but nothing happened.

Nothing happened until June 19, when they reached Fishing River, a tributary of the Missouri. Smith wrote that during the day "the Jackson County mob to the number of about two hundred, made arrangements to cross the Missouri River, above the mouth of the Fishing River, at William's Ferry, into Clay County, and be ready to meet the Richmond mob near Fishing River ford, for our utter destruction."[16]

There came a storm of such magnitude that the shallow stream became a flood, and the Missourians were dispersed. Smith wrote that the "earth trembled and quaked . . . . it seemed that the mandate of vengeance had gone forth from the God of battles, to protect His servants." God was with them, surely.

Rumors spread that Zion's Camp was marching on a mission of revenge, and the Jackson County Gentiles organized for defense. Negotiations had been in process between a gentile committee and a committee of Mormons. Both groups had written to Governor Daniel Dunklin, who faced the threat of private war but was doing nothing positive to prevent it. Very properly he took the stand that the Mormons had the right to migrate into the state, but the Gentiles had rights too. He believed that the religious doctrines of the Mormons had caused the trouble. Mormons had a right, however, "to worship Joe Smith as a man, an angel, or even as the only true and living God, and to call their habitation Zion, the Holy Land, or even heaven itself."[17]

Apparently, neither Gentiles or Mormons were satisfied with the efforts of Governor Dunklin to keep the peace. Nor was he of any help in the negotiations for settling the question of the losses to both sides when the Saints were driven from Jackson County the previous year. The opposing committees were trying to decide whether the Mormons should buy the holdings of all Gentiles in Jackson County or whether the Gentiles purchase the properties from whence they had driven the Mormons. No agreement was ever reached.

Critics of Joseph Smith have made the most of his Zion's Camp venture, claiming it as evidence of his eccentric character and his itch for military fame. But the sword that he waved with such a flourish when the march began in Ohio was quietly replaced in its scabbard when Zion's Camp reached Missouri. He entered Clay County with the solemn declaration that his was a mission of peace.[18]

Smith's punitive expedition ended unhappily. Soon after the Fishing River episode several of the company fell ill with cholera. Some elders rebuked the disease as the work of the Devil. Elder John S. Carter, one of the rebukers, was the first victim of the plague, which in four days afflicted sixty-eight members of the company and took fourteen lives.[19] Smith received a revelation, which is Section 105 of the Doctrine and Covenants, rescinding previous plans about the redemption of Zion by the sword. God's people would have to wait for a while. Vindication would be delayed.

The reason for this change of plan was laid to the people. Some had transgressed; so the campaign of pulling down "the towers of mine enemies" was postponed. The Saints would "sue for peace, not only to the people that have smitten you, but also to all people."[20] Smith returned to Kirtland.

No doubt the change of plan relieved the stricken Saints of much trouble. They were not prepared for such armed conflict; so they turned to the job of finding new homes in Clay and Ray counties. Two new counties, Caldwell and Daviess, were formed farther to the north. This was open and inviting country in which few Gentiles had settled. During the following three years the Mormon emigrants poured into that area without much opposition.

Trouble did not break out again in Missouri until 1838. The causes were not unlike those in Jackson County in 1833. The Mormons still talked of building a Zion that would embrace all the region around. Gentiles were still regarded as enemies. To the Saints, Caldwell County was hallowed ground, for Prophet Joseph had told them that here was the place where the Lord appeared to Father Adam.[21]

On July 4, 1838, the Saints gathered at Far West to celebrate. They were again feeling secure and mighty. Gentiles were also present, and there must have been a spirit of good will prevailing. The occasion was used for laying the cornerstone of a new meeting house. Sidney Rigdon was orator of the day. His speech was unfortunately intemperate.

Rigdon declared that if the enemies of God's people again opened hostilities, "it shall be between us and them, a war of extermination." The Saints would be patient no more but would carry the seat of the war to the families and homes of the enemy. He likened the ungodly outsiders to the salt that must be thrown away when it has lost its savor and is of no use save "to be trodden under foot of men." That oration was later known as the "salt sermon."

Joseph Smith was present on the occasion of the Independence Day celebration, although he may have been innocent about the substance of Rigdon's oration. Apparently he did not disapprove, for he wrote in his journal for the day that "a shout of Hosanna" went up afterward. Smith had arrived at Far West on his final trip from Ohio on March 14, 1838. Since the Zion's Camp experience he had been in Missouri but once, and that for a month in the autumn of 1837. The winter of 1837–38 had been a difficult one for him at Kirtland. This was partly due to the failure of a banking venture, but there had also been some friction between him and certain persons who had left the church or were cut off.[22]

Perhaps the time was ripe, or it may have been only a coincidence that trouble with the Gentiles should arise so soon after his arrival in Missouri. Perhaps the new trouble in Missouri was aggravated by the influx, during 1837 and soon after, of a considerable number of the Kirtland families, thus suddenly increasing the size of the settlement. This growth of Zion, coupled with the attitude expressed in the salt sermon, served to arouse the Gentiles.

On Monday, August 6, Missouri had a state election. Gentiles in Daviess and Gallatin counties attempted to keep Mormons from voting, fearing that the Saints would capture the political machine. Fights ensued. Stories circulated that the Mormons, five hundred strong, were preparing to attack. Gentiles in all that section took down their rifles.

Governor Lilburn W. Boggs, the same who had, as lieutenant-governor in 1833, encouraged the mobbers of Jackson County, now ordered the militia to keep the peace. By the issue of this order certain of the Gentiles, enemies of the Saints, had been transformed into soldiers. The military identification did not alter their Mormon-baiting urge one whit.

Realizing that the power of the state might be against them, the Saints, nevertheless, organized for the battle that ended in their expulsion. Open hostilities began early in October, when crops were ready or stored, and possibly that was a factor in timing the raids of the Gentiles. Eighty families were driven out of Carroll County, where earlier the Gentiles had complained that the Mormons had "threatened to assassinate some of our most valuable citizens."[23]

In a few localities it was claimed the Mormons retaliated by burning gentile homes. Joseph Smith denied the charge. The governor did get such reports, and thereupon issued the following order, which earned for him the perpetual hatred of all Mormons: "The Mormons must be treated as enemies, and must be exterminated or driven from the State if necessary for the public peace—their outrages are beyond all description."

That order was sent to the militia, on October 27, less than four months after Rigdon's salt sermon. "A war of extermination" was what Rigdon said it would be. Here was the gentile answer.

Governor Boggs had been hasty and possibly moved by bias in issuing his extermination order, but he was doubtless under great pressure from the Gentiles. Three days before the order there had been a skirmish between armed Gentiles and Mormons at a ford on Crooked River. The Gentiles were put to flight, and the Mormons suffered the loss of two men killed and several wounded. One of the men slain was Apostle David W. Patten.

Three days after the Boggs's order, on October 30, a company of militia, led by one Colonel W. O. Jennings, attacked a community of Saints at Haun's Mill on Shoal Creek. The raiders killed seventeen men and boys and plundered homes.[24] On the same day, about two thousand men, under General Samuel D. Lucas, surrounded the city of Far West. Three Gentiles in the place were given an opportunity to leave town. There were conferences under a truce which delayed the attack. Perhaps the Gentiles, finding that the Mormons were dug in for battle, lost their daring. Instead, they submitted terms requiring that the Mormons:

1. Give up their leaders to be tried and punished.

2. Make an appropriation of the property of all who had taken up arms, to the payment of their debts, and indemnity of damage done by them.

3. Leave the State, and be protected out by the militia, but to be permitted to remain under protection until further orders were received from the Commander-in-Chief.

4. Give up the arms of every description, to be receipted for.

Elder George M. Hinkle, colonel in charge of the Mormon forces, accepted the terms. The Mormons were disarmed. They surrendered Joseph Smith, Sidney Rigdon, Lyman Wight, Parley P. Pratt, and George W. Robinson. But they were not given militia protection against the pillaging of their homes.[25]

Upon receiving Smith and the other leaders as hostages, General Lucas, with his subordinate officers and certain prominent gentile citizens and preachers, conducted a military trial, a sort of hound-and-rabbit, drumhead court. He sentenced all five to death and ordered General A. W. Doniphan to take the prisoners to the public square at Far West on the morning of November 2 and shoot them. Doniphan refused, and the executions did not take place.

During the next month the politician militia leaders found themselves increasingly embarrassed. The force of public opinion, slow to find expression in those days of tardy communication, finally began to assert itself. There was rivalry among the generals for the custody of the prisoners. General Lucas took them to Independence, where he paraded them through the streets; but before putting them through that ordeal, he paraded them before the Mormons at Far West. He permitted the men to visit their families. Hyrum Smith, who elected to accompany his brother, was permitted to see, but not comfort, his pregnant wife.[26]

From Jackson County the prisoners were taken to Richmond in Ray County. For several days, in the bitter cold, without bedding, the Mormons were detained in a vacant residence until charges could be formulated. According to the church records, the prisoners were subjected to much personal abuse and taunting. As reported by Parley P. Pratt in his *Autobiography*, they said to the prophet: "Come, Smith, show us an angel; give us one of your revelations, show us a miracle . . . . if you are apostles or men of God, deliver yourselves, and then we will be Mormons."

The lawyers and generals finally agreed to charge the prisoners with "treason, murder, arson, burglary, robbery, larceny and perjury." Before the trial started at Richmond, more than thirty Mormon leaders had been brought in on some or all of the above charges. A number of Mormons testified against the prisoners. They were all cut off the church.[27]

After seventeen days the trial adjourned without result. Some of the prisoners were released; but the Smiths, Rigdon, Pratt, and six others were held in jail several months longer, during which time various gentile lawyers managed to extract from the Saints considerable sums for defending their imprisoned leaders. On April 8, 1839, the trial began again, but it did not proceed well. A change of venue was obtained, and the prisoners were started under light guard for Boone County. En route the guard got drunk, and Prophet Joseph and his brethren escaped.

Joseph Smith had come to Missouri a fugitive from Ohio justice, and now he was again a fugitive fleeing from Missouri to Illinois. During the next three years several unsuccessful attempts were made by Missouri to extradite him. The burden of organizing and moving the Saints out of Missouri fell upon the shoulders of Apostle Brigham Young, who had not been rounded up with the hostages. Possibly it was due to the sound sense of this man that the Mormons were permitted to remain in Missouri until the break of spring, although they were not to put in another crop. While Smith, Rigdon, and the rest languished in prison, it was Brigham Young who salvaged the remnants of Zion.[28]

It was Brigham Young who guided the migration eastward over the Mississippi into Illinois, although none knew where they would settle in that state or if they would be permitted to stop at all.

It was Brigham Young who purged the church of all the apostates whose faith had been shaken because of the mobbings and of all who had turned against their prophet. In spite of the skepticism of a few, Zion did not fail but moved on and planted her foot in Illinois.

NOTES

1. Lyman Lafayette Woods was known to the writer from 1908 until his death in 1917. He was born in Fredonia, New York, July 23, 1832. The village of his origin later gave birth to the Women's Christian Temperance Union and the Grange, which evidences the spiritual character of the people in that locality from whence the Mormon church gained some of its first converts. When Woods was two years old, his mother joined the Mormons. This conversion resulted in her separation from her husband. In 1836 she moved to Kirtland, Ohio, and later to Nauvoo, where she died. The child was taken in by the Rockwood family and bore the Rockwood name. He drove an ox team across the plains from Iowa to Utah in 1849. In his late teens he left the Rockwoods and took his own name.

Between 1850 and 1860 Woods served as a scout for Brigham Young. He carried the mail between Utah and Missouri, engaged in expeditions against the Indians, served as guide to companies going to California, and later hauled freight from California. He settled at Provo but was called from that place in 1869 to take charge of the Clover Valley settlement. There he remained, living poor when he might have moved somewhere else and prospered. He had been called by Brigham Young to live in Clover Valley, to hold the land against the Gentiles, and to keep peace with the Indians. He would not ask to be released. When he died in St. George, his body was taken back, according to his wish, to Clover Valley.

2. Many books have been written about Joseph Smith and the church. Probably the first book on the subject was that written by E. D. Howe, *Mormonism Unveiled*, in 1834. E. D. Howe, who lived at Painesville, Ohio, near Kirtland, was already well known as publicist and writer for his *History of the War of 1812*. A more friendly non-Mormon book is *Joseph Smith and His Mormon Empire*, by Harry M. Beardsley, published in 1931.

3. Beardsley (*op. cit.*, p. 21) gives what is often noted as the "gentile opinion": "Joe Smith reached the adolescent age under unfavorable conditions that were to color his entire life. Undernourished, unschooled, he grew up in an atmosphere that tended to accentuate the natural vagaries of the period. His father, an irresponsible vagabond, joined the son on the open road when the wanderlust came. His mother, a religious fanatic, got a vicarious ecstasy out of the religious experience of her son, and encouraged his tendencies toward emotional excess."

The mother, Lucy Mack Smith, wrote *Biographical Sketches of Joseph Smith, the Prophet, and His Progenitors for Many Years*. The contents of this weird and visionary document are the basis of most of the opinions such as those expressed by Beardsley.

4. According to the *History of the Church, Period I*, by Joseph Smith (II, 62–63), a conference of elders held at Kirtland on May 3, 1834, decided that the official name of

the Mormon church should be changed from the "Church of Christ" to the "Church of the Latter-Day Saints." The Saints then objected to the name "Mormon," or "Mormonite." On April 26, 1838, Smith received a revelation (Doctrine and Covenants, Sec. 115) indicating that the name would be the "Church of Jesus Christ of Latter-Day Saints."

5. Mormon missionaries might have been content to rest their case on the Book of Mormon. Sectarian preachers constantly challenged them in this wise: "If this new book is in harmony with the teachings of the Bible, then prove to us from the Bible that your doctrines are true." Before many years the Mormon elder delighted in nothing more than a challenge from a minister for a public debate on the Bible.

6. Critics of Joseph Smith have endeavored to prove from the revelations and other expressions given in his capacity as prophet that he was either a fraud or a paranoiac. Beardsley (*op. cit.*, p. 79) indicates that the prophet had a diseased mind. The same view is offered by Woodbridge Riley in his *The Founder of Mormonism*.

7. Beardsley (*op. cit.*, pp. 24, 39–51, 57, 95) sets forth the claim, held by some, that Rigdon was the inspiration of Smith. In western Pennsylvania, Rigdon had been a Baptist preacher. For doctrinal differences he left the Baptist church and joined the Campbellites. For other differences on points of religion he left the Campbellites and started the organizaton over which he presided at Kirtland. It is alleged by Beardsley that Rigdon, years earlier, had obtained a document called "The Manuscript Found," written about 1812 by Solomon Spaulding. This manuscript, a work of fiction, concerned a civilization which supposedly existed on this continent centuries ago. Rigdon, according to this report, had taken the manuscript to Palmyra, where it fell into the hands of Joseph Smith. It has also been claimed that there had been a secret friendship between the youthful, impressive Joseph and the more mature, brainy Rigdon. These surmises lack connected proof, but there is enough evidence to keep them alive.

8. In the *Publications of the Missouri Valley Historical Society*, Vol. I, No. 2, is a quotation from an old resident of Independence who said that on August 3, 1831, Smith and his elders "boldly walked out on a part of the southeast quarter of Section 3, Township 49, Range 32, and at a point indicated by Joseph Smith, the Seer, they dedicated the Temple Lot and gave to God a tract of land that neither they nor the Church owned, but which belonged to Jones H. Flournoy." On December 19, 1831, they bought the 63 acres for $130. Before the end of 1831 they bought about 2,000 acres.

9. Of the revelations reported in the Doctrine and Covenants, which are probably the most important ones claimed by the prophet, 18 were received before 1830; 19 in 1830; 35 in 1831; 16 in 1832; 23 in 1833. Only 5 were reported for 1834 and 2 for 1835. There were 3 in 1836 and but 1 revelation for 1837. Apparently, as Smith became more sure of himself he called less on the Lord and was less in need of revelation.

10. Joshua V. Himes on August 14, 1832, published in Boston a leaflet warning citizens against "Mormonite" preachers trying to "propagate their strange and marvelous doctrines." He said that fifteen persons had been converted, including "two individuals who are defenceless females." One of these was alleged to have given $800 savings and the other $1,500 savings to the Mormon church.

11. The "inheritance" was the reverse of the "consecration." What was given to a member or what he was permitted to keep was his inheritance. It was the basic purpose in "dividing the inheritances" that no man would have more than he needed or could use. The surplus would be used to help the poor, but they were expected to work hard to increase their inheritances. This is discussed by Joseph A. Geddes in *The United Order among the Mormons*, pp. 48–57.

12. References to sharing the wealth, to consecration, and to mutual aid are found in Sections 38, 42, 45, 51, and 57–61 of the Doctrine and Covenants. Section 82, given on April 26, 1832, set forth the plan of the United Order of Enoch. It was apparently

not the purpose of the Order to abolish private property but to garner into the hands of the church all property not actually needed by private owners, that it might be distributed to others.

13. There was a fourth unit of the Order, called the "Literary Firm." This was the book-publishing phase of the Printing Concern. Joseph Smith and others on November 1, 1831, held a meeting at Hiram, Ohio. It was decided to collect Smith's revelations and publish them in a Book of Commandments. Later, when the Firm was organized, it took over this publishing responsibility. At the time the printing press was destroyed, only a few copies of the Book of Commandments had been completed (see Geddes, *op. cit.*, pp. 79–84). "Carefully selected" revelations were later compiled at Kirtland and were published in 1835 as the Doctrine and Covenants (Joseph Smith, *op. cit.*, II, 243–51).

14. This is Section 103 of the Doctrine and Covenants. Verse 15 reads: "Behold, I say unto you, the redemption of Zion must needs come by power." Verse 27: "Let no man be afraid to lay down his life, for whoso layeth down his life for my sake shall find it again."

15. Joseph Smith, *op. cit.*, II, 71. On p. 95 Smith reported that Martin Harris "boasted to the brethren that he could handle snakes with perfect safety. . . . . I told them it was presumption for anyone to provoke a serpent to bite him." Smith thought that this was tempting the Lord.

16. *Ibid.*, pp. 102–15, contains the report of the episode on Fishing River and the subsequent plague of punishment. This ending was in contrast with a note written by the prophet on May 27 (p. 73). "Notwithstanding our enemies were continually breathing threats of violence, we did not fear, neither did we hesitate to prosecute our journey, for God was with us, and His angels went before us, and the faith of our little band was unwavering. We knew the angels were our companions, for we saw them."

17. This letter was written by the governor to Colonel J. Thornton on June 6, 1834. Thornton was given authority in the letter to aid in maintaining peace. The governor was then under the impression that the Mormons were about to march under arms against Jackson County (*ibid.*, pp. 84–87).

18. On June 21 Smith signed a statement regarding his purposes in going to Missouri. "In the first place, it is not our intention to commit hostilities against any man, or set of men. . . . ." This statement was made the day before receiving his revelation (Sec. 105 of Doctrine and Covenants) telling him the redemption of Zion must wait (*ibid.*, pp. 106–8, 121–22).

19. A brief statement of the Mormon version of this episode is given by Joseph Fielding Smith, *Essentials in Church History*, pp. 170–78.

20. Upon his return from the march of Zion's Camp, Joseph Smith on August 11 was tried before the High Council at Kirtland on charges submitted by Sylvester Smith alleging undue rebukes and misuse of company funds. The charges, according to the record, were not sustained. Smith wrote of the trial: "Accordingly I was met in the face and eyes, as soon as I got home, with a catalogue of charges as black as the author of lies himself; and the cry of Tyrant—Pope—King—Usurper—Abuser of men—Angel—False Prophet—Prophesying lies in the name of the Lord—Taking consecrated monies—and every other lie. . . . ." Sylvester Smith "for fear of punishment," confessed his error in accusing the prophet. Later he relented and confessed his error without adding "for fear of punishment" (Joseph Smith, *op. cit.*, II, 142–46, 160).

21. According to Joseph Smith (Doctrine and Covenants, Sec. 107), Adam, three years before his death, gathered his posterity about him on the site of Adamondi-Ahman in Daviess County. As Adam was blessing his posterity, the Lord appeared and blessed

Adam, naming him the head of a multitude of nations. Hearing that this area was regarded as hallowed ground, as was Jackson County, further irritated the Gentiles.

22. Smith's time in Kirtland had been much occupied with missionary work; with building a temple, which was barely finished when the Saints moved away; with obtaining the means to send migrants to Zion; and with the organization of a bank, the Kirtland Safety Society. The Mormon version of the failure of this bank is reported by Joseph Fielding Smith, *op. cit.*, pp. 196–98.

23. From the *Missouri Republican* (St. Louis), August 18, 1838. During this period the *Republican*, being more removed from the scene of conflict, was inclined to be sympathetic toward the Mormons.

24. Joseph Young, who arrived in Caldwell County from Kirtland earlier in the month, had gone to Hauns Mill on October 28 and found the Saints there preparing to defend themselves. He was present when the attack came two days later. His statement is found in Joseph Smith, *op. cit.*, III, 183–86.

25. Mormon historians condemn Hinkle for this surrender. At the time, whatever the after claims on either side, the action appeared wise. The argument in favor of surrender is found in *A Brief History of the Church of Jesus Christ of Latter-Day Saints*, by John Corrill, formerly a faithful builder of Zion. To quote from p. 48, his word to the Saints: "Did not your prophet proclaim in your ears that the day was your own, and you would overcome; when in less than a week you were all made prisoners of war, and you would have been exterminated, had it not been for the exertions and influence of a few dissenters, and the humane and manly spirit of certain officers?" For a statement of the Mormon view see Joseph Fielding Smith, *op. cit.*, pp. 234–44.

26. The baby born a few days later on November 13 to Hyrum's wife was Joseph Fielding Smith, later an apostle, and president of the church from 1901 to 1918. He became a polygamist and the father of 21 sons and 21 daughters, 11 of them born between 1890 and 1904.

27. Joseph Smith wrote (*op. cit.*, III, 178–82) of the evil spirits "raging up and down the state to raise mobs" against the Mormons. Also Satan was busy among the Saints; "and among the most conspicuous of his willing devotees was one Dr. Sampson Avard." Whether with good intent or otherwise, Avard organized a band of secret avengers, first called the "Daughters of Zion," a name to fool people, but later called the "Brothers of Israel." Then they called themselves the "Sons of Dan," concerning whom it was written in Gen. 49:17: "Dan shall be a serpent by the way, an adder in the path that biteth the horse's heels so that his rider shall fall backward."

Did Smith, although he excommunicated Avard, then take to himself the leadership of the Danites? There have been many reports that some of these brothers who swore to "ever conceal and never reveal" their secret purposes remained loyal to Smith. It was often charged that Smith had his spies, informers, and strong-arm men. It would be strange if he did not have some such organization, in view of the opposition against him and in view of the secret character of that opposition.

28. Joseph Fielding Smith (*op. cit.*, p. 252) gives the estimate of losses to the church because of the final expulsion from Missouri. This move involved from 12,000 to 15,000 persons. Some of the Saints managed to sell their holdings, although at a loss. On December 10, 1838, a memorial of grievances was sent by Brigham Young, Heber C. Kimball, Edward Partridge, and others on the church committee asking the Missouri legislature to "do for us, after mature deliberation, that which your wisdom, patriotism and philanthropy may dictate." The matter was presented by John Corrill, representative from Caldwell County, on December 19. No action was taken (Joseph Smith, *op. cit.*, III, 217–39).

CHAPTER II

GOD'S PEOPLE IN BITTER RETREAT

MOST of the Missouri refugees crossed the Mississippi at Quincy, Illinois. The people of the Quincy area organized a relief fund to aid them. The influx of several thousand refugees, however, caused some concern lest the oversupply of new workers should lower prevailing wages, but this fear passed when they were assured that the Mormons wanted only a chance to settle on the land and be farmers. The governors, Carlin of Illinois and Lucas of Iowa, indicated an attitude of welcome. Both states needed settlers. The Mormons were known to be good farmers. They were land-breakers and town-builders. Such industrious people were scarce. There were also political reasons for this friendliness. A presidential election was one year away. By 1840 the Mormons would be voters.

Governor Thomas Carlin, Stephen A. Douglas, later a senator and a candidate for the presidency, and other Democrats of western Illinois saw in the Mormon vote the prospect of victory over the Whigs. Naturally, they had no objection to a mass Mormon vote in the hands of a single man if that man were friendly to them. Whig leaders countered with the argument that the Mormons should join with them, reminding the Saints that the Democrats had driven them from Missouri. Obviously, whichever faction they favored, the Mormons, voting as a group, would incite the enmity of the other.[1]

Remaining, for the time, noncommittal on the political issues, the Mormon leaders turned their attention to finding a home. In Hancock County, which lies north of Quincy on the banks of the Mississippi, opposite the southeastern corner of Iowa, was a large area quite uninhabited. Here extensive tracts of land were available for purchase. A Dr. Isaac Galland owned several hundred acres in the vicinity of a small village called "Commerce." Smith bought Galland's holdings, and on that location he laid out the city of Nauvoo, soon the first metropolis of Illinois.[2]

Within and near Nauvoo the Mormons made other purchases. In some cases they were able to exchange the titles they held for lands in Missouri. While the buying and moving was getting under way, Joseph Smith, with Sidney Rigdon and others, went to Washington armed with affidavits from Saints who had suffered violence in Missouri. He carried a bill of the losses, amounting to upward of a million dollars. He would "importune for redress."

The mission to Washington failed. Smith and his party returned in March, 1840. They got sympathy but were told frankly that the federal government could not enter on an issue involving the police power of a state. Among other national figures, Smith talked with Henry Clay; and Clay put this question: "Why don't you go to Oregon?" This suggestion did not please Prophet Joseph; but, although he rejected it, within two years he himself was prophesying that the Saints would yet find safety beyond the Rocky Mountains.

Smith faced the problem of determining upon the method of settlement in Illinois. As the refugee families crossed from Missouri, they scattered and found homes in several counties, where they could find labor or land. Some of the leaders favored that manner of settlement. They believed it would be more conducive to peace to mix among the Gentiles, claiming that the Missouri settlements failed because the Mormons had been too exclusive.

Smith did not accept this view. He was building Zion; and if Zion would grow, the Saints must be united. They would join farm to farm, house to house, into a compact community. Any argument to the contrary was of the Devil, and the Devil could take any who were of contrary mind. The question was settled when Brother Joseph on January 19, 1841, received a revelation calling all families remotely situated to gather in Nauvoo.[3]

Prior to the "gathering" order, Joseph Smith had been occupied with the task of obtaining from the Illinois legislature a charter for Nauvoo. In this effort he was greatly aided by Dr. John C. Bennett, an adventurer who came offering to help. Bennett possessed a genius for promotion, and he knew Illinois politics. He held the position of quartermaster general of the state militia. Bennett conveniently shared Smith's views on all issues, even his anger against President Van Buren.[4]

Through Bennett's aid the Mormons in December, 1840, obtained from the Illinois legislature a liberal charter, a document which received the approval of Abraham Lincoln, then a member of the legislature. The city was permitted to establish its own university, which would have been the first municipal university in this country. Authority was also given to

> organize the inhabitants of said city, subject to military duty, into a body of independent military men to be called the "Nauvoo Legion," the court martial of which shall be composed of the commissioned officers of said legion, and constitute the law-making department, with full power to make, ordain and execute all such laws and ordinances as may be considered necessary for the benefit, government and regulation of said legion. . . .

By this unusual charter, wangled by Bennett, Nauvoo had its own army. Not only was the prophet a man on a white horse, but he could and did make himself a general. He was not long in donning a fine uniform, and the Legion under him stood out as a church army, the only one of its kind in the United States.

Bennett joined the church and became the first mayor of Nauvoo, a city which began to attract notice. Within four years the number of Mormons in Nauvoo and near by approximated twenty thousand. They were industrious farmers and diligent craftsmen. Their homes were neat, and their yards orderly. They took pride in gardens and flowers. There were no rich among them, and every man made hard labor a sacrament.

Brother Joseph was busier than any of the rest. A man of boundless energy, compelling optimism, unrelenting determination, and plausible egoism, he often in a single day, from sun to sun, talked to hundreds of people. He gave advice here, rebuked there, comforted one, or consulted with another; there was

LIEUTENANT-GENERAL JOSEPH SMITH ADDRESSING HIS NAUVOO LEGION

His brother, Hyrum, stands behind him. This picture, from a painting by John Hafen in 1888, is often reproduced in publications of the church with the following quotation from Smith: "I call upon God and the angels to witness that I have unsheathed my sword with a firm and unalterable determination that this people shall have their legal rights and shall be protected from mob violence, or my blood shall be spilt upon the ground like water, and my body consigned to the silent tomb. While I live I shall never tamely submit to the domination of cursed mobocracy."

scarcely a person in that city not known to him personally. Nauvoo was his own city, a sort of proprietary domain where he was a law unto himself and the lawgiver for all who called him God's vicegerent on earth.

Nauvoo was a city ruled by a benevolent monarch—the fish market, so to speak, of the world, where catches from every nation, kindred, and people were gathered together, the good kept, and the bad cast off. It was a city of work and worship, but it was also a city of pious aloofness and self-isolation from the Gentiles.

Geographically concentrated and self-sufficient, the Mormons in and around Nauvoo so reinforced one another in the ardor of their faith that the Gentiles had no place among them, nor were they wanted. The same tensions that grew up in Jackson County and later in Daviess and Caldwell counties began to appear in Nauvoo. The situation here was more complicated because the Mormons were more numerous. They felt more secure because of numbers and wealth, because they had learned to use their political strength, although not wisely, and because they found behind the Nauvoo Legion the illusion of power.

In Illinois, Smith received respectful notice. Perhaps he lacked experience in the ways of public affairs, for in Ohio and Missouri he had received little attention, save from notoriety. However, his boundless self-confidence expanded until he was not uncomfortable in the role of a big man in the state. Some Gentiles thought he was a little overbearing and oversure; others found him quite the opposite.[5]

Politicians are adaptable people; and, whatever Smith's personal qualities, they tried to keep in his good graces, for he had in his vestpocket several thousand votes, which could swing a state election either to the Whigs or to the Democrats. Smith lacked the political genius to play with that kind of fire.

Following the order for the Saints to gather in Hancock County and to build there a great city, Prophet Joseph and his leaders carried out the organization of a Mormon militia. They had such a unit in Missouri; but here they would have a militia in uniform, of which Joseph Smith had command and Hyrum Smith was one of the brigadier generals. Other church leaders were generals, colonels, majors, captains—pretty much in direct relation to their rank in the priesthood. Every able-bodied man was a member of the Nauvoo Legion. Much time was spent in parading, drilling, and fighting sham battles.

Some Gentiles, uneasy about so much military show, wondered to what it was leading. Josiah Quincy in his *Figures of the Past*, published in 1883, recalled his interview with the prophet. He asked Smith if he had not assumed more power than was safe for one man to hold. Smith answered that in the hands of any other man so much power would be dangerous, but it was safe with him because he was a prophet of the Lord. His followers would have answered likewise.

If the concentration of the Saints and their military demonstrations served to cause gentile uneasiness, among the Mormons there was also unrest. While they all had a common interest in the future of Zion, they were of many backgrounds. There was considerable friction before these people could be brought to a unity of mind and feeling. Some who came to Nauvoo with a burning faith turned out to be converts of shallow conviction. There were disaffections. Also, there was rivalry between leaders.

There were many men who did not fit into that type of society; and the most conspicuous was John C. Bennett—doctor, preacher, soldier, politician, and promoter. Bennett wrote Smith twice in July, 1840, praising the Mormons and hoping to become one of them. He would keep his job as quartermaster general of the state of Illinois and would also like to practice as a physician. Smith was pleased and indicated his desire to make Bennett's acquaintance.[6] Smith made him the first mayor of Nauvoo, chancellor of the Nauvoo University, and a major general in the Nauvoo Legion.

With all these offices Bennett should not be blamed for feeling that he had achieved the headship of the community. He soon learned that Smith, as the head of the church, was also head of all else. Bennett chafed under his tutelage and before long found himself the center of a group of unhappy subordinates. They did not openly rebel against the prophet, but he soon learned of their opposition through his faithful informers. The break came in May, 1842, when Smith accused Bennett of plotting to take his life. Charges of adultery were also brought against Bennett. He resigned from the office of mayor. He was cashiered out of the Legion and excommunicated from the church.[7]

Dr. Bennett was never quite inside the prophet's closed circle of trusted associates, but he was near enough to know that polygamy was being practiced. When he entered into a plurality relationship on his own account, Smith and the inner circle brethren called it adultery. He was furious and set out to expose Mormonism with the same zeal he had previously exhibited in joining the church.

On May 14, 1842, when the Bennett case was disturbing the Mormons, word came that former Governor Lilburn W. Boggs, who issued the "extermination" order driving the Mormons from Missouri, had been shot. He survived the attack, but blame was placed on Joseph Smith and his "Danites." Another attempt was made to arrest Smith. There was great concern lest the exiled Bennett join the Missourians in their efforts to arrest and convict Smith; but Bennett had other interests, for that year he wrote and published his *History of the Saints*; *or an Exposé of Joe Smith and Mormonism.*

After the publication of his book, Bennett returned to the task of undermining Smith's Nauvoo empire. There was no lack of issues. He and a few others who left the church supplied the leadership.

Mormonism was also maturing. Many of the rough edges of Smith's plan of life and salvation had been rubbed away, and his system began to take on form and unity. With diligent and tenacious Bible-reading the elders of Israel were able to find substantiating evidence to support the new Gospel from the records of the old. They discovered in obscure passages, rarely noticed by sectarian preachers, hidden meanings; and they found also evidence of a hundred prophesies fulfilled in the restoration of the Gospel by their prophet.

In the course of this search the elders evolved the doctrine of salvation for the dead through ordinances performed in the temples by the living. It was this search of the Scriptures that raised the question of polygamy. Apparently the subject had received some attention several times before 1840, but it was not until after that date that the institution was given serious thought. For Joseph Smith to give any subject serious thought was the preface to action. He found ample biblical support for the principle. If polygamy was good for the ancient men of God, would it be less a blessing for men of God in these latter days?

When John C. Bennett turned on Joseph Smith, the charge of polygamy proved discomfiting, and there was no defense save denial. But there was no worry about issues that could be tried in local courts, where the faithful would not, and others dared not, speak out.[8]

When Bennett was removed from office, Smith became mayor, as he had been, in fact, all the while. Governor Ford, possibly in response to complaints about the excessive powers of Smith, recommended in December, 1842, that the Nauvoo charter be modified. William Smith, brother of the prophet, was a member of the legislature. He was not able to prevent the passage in the lower house of a bill to curtail the powers of the Nauvoo charter. The bill failed in the senate.[9]

Tensions multiplied in 1842 and 1843. Smith had clashes with a number of men who had long been faithful to him. There was a quarrel with his old friend, Orson Pratt; and another with Sidney Rigdon. It was reported in the first case that Smith had made advances to Pratt's wife and in the second that Rigdon would not give his daughter to Smith in marriage.

With numerous attempts to arrest Smith, with various charges leveled against him, with his conviction that there were plots to take his life, it is not surprising that during 1842 and 1843 he began to talk of the church moving to the Far West. The first recorded prediction of such a move was on August 6, 1842. He then said the Saints would endure persecution until they would "be driven to the Rocky Mountains."[10]

For Joseph Smith, 1843 had been a year of dodging and hiding, lest he be kidnapped and taken to Missouri for trial. The prophet entered 1844 in a political mood. He wrote letters to various candidates for the presidential election, asking their views on the Mormon question. Among the candidates that year were Henry Clay, Daniel Webster, John C. Calhoun, Lewis Cass, and Martin Van Buren.

Clay, Calhoun, and Cass answered the inquiry, but their responses were noncommittal. Smith was angry. Some of those close to the prophet urged that he might become the next president. On January 29 the twelve apostles and other friendly brethren met to discuss candidates. They concluded that all the men mentioned above were morally unfit to be elected president. They nominated Smith.[11]

Smith responded on February 7 with his *Views of the Powers and Policy of the Government of the United States*, a long statement on the decline of justice in government. He would open the West for settlement, buy the slaves into freedom, and abolish prisons. He poked fun at the other candidates, especially Martin Van Buren, whom he referred to as "poor little Mattie." Local Mormon papers, the *Times and Seasons* and the *Neighbor*, published editorials supporting Smith's candidacy.

The vice-presidency was offered first to General James Arlington Bennett, of New York, who had evidenced a friendly attitude toward the Mormons. When Bennett declined, the next choice was Colonel Solomon Copeland, of Paris, Tennessee. Copeland did not accept, and the honor was tendered to Sidney Rigdon, who had moved to Pennsylvania following his disagreement with Joseph Smith. This gesture healed the breach. Rigdon accepted.

A convention was held at Nauvoo on May 17. Smith, as a candidate, set forth his views on government. Resolutions were written, and a national convention was planned at Baltimore to convene the following July 13. Smith's party of "liberty and equal rights, Jeffersonian democracy, free trade and sailor's rights, and the protection of person and property," did not get much further. Elders went forth to stump for their prophet, but it all ended with his death on June 27.[12]

While Smith was fixing one eye on the presidency, his other

eye was concentrated on the matter of migration. If he became president, he would use his power to open the West for settlement. He wrote in his journal on February 23 that he had discussed with the apostles the desirability of an Oregon and California exploring expedition:

> Send twenty-five men; let them preach the Gospel wherever they go. Let that man go who can raise $500, a good horse and mule, a double-barrel gun, one-barrel rifle and the other smooth bore, a saddle and bridle, a pair of revolving pistols, bowie knife and a good sabre. Appoint a leader and let them beat up for volunteers. I want every man that goes to be a king and a priest. When he gets to the mountains he may want to talk with his God; when with the savage nations, have power to govern, etc. If we don't get volunteers, wait till after the election.[13]

During the previous year Apostles Amasa M. Lyman and Lyman Wight, with Bishop George Miller, had been occupied in the "pineries" of Wisconsin, getting out shingles and lumber for the Nauvoo temple, then nearing completion. They came to the conclusion that the Saints should consider migrating to Texas. This matter had been presented to the prophet. He was sufficiently impressed to send Lucian Woodworth to visit the republic of Texas. Woodworth returned with a favorable report; but other interests intervened, and after Smith's death Brigham Young rejected the scheme. Later Miller and Wight led a few Saints away to Texas, but they were cut off from the church.[14]

The fall of Smith came about through the machinations of a number of former Saints who had quarreled with him. Among these disfellowshiped men were the brothers William and Wilson Law, William Marks, Dr. Robert D. Foster, and Leonard Soby. They were joined by John C. Bennett and received financial assistance from various Gentiles in Hancock and neighboring counties.

The former Mormon group began to proclaim information, which history has confirmed, about the "spiritual wife system." Two of the outlawed faction, Joseph R. Jackson and Robert D. Foster, brought perjury charges against the prophet in the circuit court at Carthage, the county seat. At the same time an indictment charging polygamy was issued by the grand jury on the testimony of William Law. The prophet went to Carthage on May 27 to face trial; but the case was postponed, and he was released, to be called later.[15]

Then followed a month of intense action—the month that was to end with Brother Joseph gaining the martyr's halo. On June 7 was published the first and only issue of the *Nauvoo Expositor*, a daring and scorching sheet, put out by the gentlemen who had been consigned by Smith to the buffetings of Satan. It was the usual spread of charges against the prophet and his aides, but this time the charge of polygamy was added. It was claimed that "whoredoms and all manner of abominations are practiced under the cloak of religion. Lo, the wolf is in the fold, arrayed in sheep's clothing." Smith was pictured by the angry men responsible for the *Expositor* as, among other things, an egotist, a dictator, a cheat, and a perjurer.

Brother Joseph might have used the occasion as an example of tolerance to Missouri, where, eleven years before, the plant of the *Evening and Morning Star* had been raided and destroyed by Gentiles. Instead, he put the *Expositor* on trial as a nuisance. The Mormon historians claim he used a legal procedure, but it was the legal machinery over which he alone had control. The municipal authorities decided that action should be taken against the offending paper. On authority from the city council and the order of Mayor Smith the offending press was broken and all obtainable copies of the *Expositor* burned.[16]

On June 11, the day after the raid on the printing press, the owners of the plant had Smith and several others arrested for destruction of property and causing a riot. Smith, on his own demand and in accordance with the law, was tried before the nearest justice of the peace, a Mormon. The charge was dismissed. On June 13 there was held at Warsaw in Hancock County a mass meeting of Gentiles. The destruction of the *Expositor* was denounced. Every citizen was called upon to arm against attack from the Mormons. The Gentiles appealed to Governor Ford for action against Smith. Smith at the same time reported to the governor, giving his side of the case.

Then followed ten days of terrible tension. There were rumors in Nauvoo of an invasion from Missouri. Outside Nauvoo the Gentiles were arming. Local units of the militia came together. Threats were heard against the life of the prophet.

In his capacity as mayor and lieutenant general Smith illegally placed Nauvoo under martial law and called the Nauvoo Legion to arms. The governor took a hand and sent a posse to the "Holy City." The posse arrived on June 23 and demanded Joseph and Hyrum Smith. The prophet sent word to the governor that they would surrender, but they demanded protection. They were taken into custody on June 24.

The brothers Smith were lodged in the county jail under guard of a Mormon-hating local militia unit, the Carthage Grays. Technically, Governor Ford provided protection, but there was doubt about his sincerity. He might have removed the men to another county. Actually, he left them helpless in the hands of their foes. On the morning of June 27, with no resistance from the militia, a mob raided the jail and shot both Joseph Smith and his brother Hyrum.[17]

Brother Joseph had often said, and he said again before departing, that he would at last seal his testimony with his blood. He told close friends when he rode away: "I go like a lamb to the slaughter"; and while they were sorrowed by his words, there was none with the imagination to sense the profound void that the death of the prophet would leave in their midst. To quote again the words of Grandfather Lyman L. Woods, spoken to the Saints at Enterprise on Pioneer Day, 1908: "It was as if every home in that beautiful city had lost a loved one."

Other blows followed in rapid succession. By state authority the Nauvoo Legion, already disarmed, was disbanded. Perhaps the governor feared that the Legion might become an avenging mob or that there might be local civil war, as there had been in Missouri. Gentile militia units in the remainder of the area came together under the guise of emergency police.

Who would lead the church? There were so many candidates for Joseph's mantle that the people were confused. Most of the apostles were away preaching or campaigning, and for a few weeks the people were all but leaderless.[18]

Sidney Rigdon returned from his voluntary retirement at Pittsburgh and proposed a "guardian" for the church. Apparently Rigdon had always regarded himself as Joseph's natural successor. He did not propose that he should be named president of the church, "for none can take Joseph's place," only that he should be guardian, which would have been merely another name for the same role.

There were other aspirants, including John C. Bennett, who made it known that he would be willing to lead the church if asked. There was, too, one James J. Strang, recently converted, who had been on friendly terms with the prophet. There was also a group who argued that church leadership rested with the direct heirs of the prophet. Leaders of this movement were Joseph's widow, Emma Smith, and William Smith, brother of the prophet.

After all had pressed their claims, Brigham Young, as senior member of the apostolate and its president, announced to the people that, as far as he was concerned, he did not care who led the church. Of one thing he was sure, the "Keys to the Kingdom" and all the authority of the priesthood, to which every adult male belonged, resided in the apostolate. The people could follow any leader they wished, but none of these factions would be authentic, and none would survive. The people were convinced, and a shout of approval went up for Brother Brigham and the "Twelve."[19]

Rigdon, when his "guardian" plan was rejected, went away to Pittsburgh and established a small branch, which never grew. James J. Strang, temperance lecturer, lawyer, journalist, and prophet by his own claim, established a church in Wisconsin. This body was very active and included among its members various dissenters, not the least of them John C. Bennett, who was soon cast out. Later Strang took his church to Beaver Island in Lake Michigan. Here he established himself as "king." He introduced polygamy and the United Order. His venture proved a controversial one and incited the opposition of the outsiders. The Michigan people about 1856 raided the island, killed Strang, and scattered his kingdom.

Lyman Wight, obsessed with the "Kingdom of God" idea, attempted a colony in Texas. He claimed that this plan had been approved by Joseph Smith. After a few years Wight's venture failed.[20]

The one faction which has not failed is the Reorganized Church of Jesus Christ of Latter-Day Saints, established about 1860 around Emma Smith, William Smith, and other members of Prophet Joseph's immediate family. This "Josephite" group with headquarters in Iowa, has remained under the leadership of direct descendents of Joseph Smith. Its membership in 1940 was about ninety thousand.

The Mormon church began as a young man's movement. It is in the hands of old men today. Joseph Smith was in his twenty-fifth year, and the average age of his close associates was 28 years. In 1844 the average age of the church leaders was 39 years, that being Smith's age at his death. Brigham Young was 43 years of age when he took charge. Today the average age of the men who lead the church is over 65 years. President Heber J. Grant in this year (1942) is 86 years of age. The prospect is that he will be succeeded by one of the senior apostles, who will be 80 years of age or older.

This citation of ages at the top of the priesthood pyramid, if it has any value at all, brings out a vital comparison between 1844 and 1940. Brigham Young and his aides were coming into the prime of life. What a different story the record of Mormonism would have been had the median age-level of the church leaders in 1844 been between 60 and 70 years!

By virtue of his headship Young also was prophet, seer, and revelator; but he sought no revelations. Perhaps he concluded that, for the time being, there had been sufficient revelation. Or perhaps Brigham Young was a different kind of man. It was said of him that he did not listen to the spirits; he commanded them.

Brigham Young also had important problems; but, when he emerged from his chamber of prayer, it was to give instructions and not to read a new revelation. One suspects, after reviewing his record, that he acted first and prayed afterward. Although

Smith and Young approached problems differently, both exhibited the same positive self-confidence.

Joseph Smith was not an effective administrator. He planned and prophesied and pointed vaguely to far goals, but he was not skilful at delegating responsibility for immediate tasks. Brigham Young was a master of men. If he planned a job, he could pick the man to do it. He was also a visionary, but his visions did not skyrocket into space, for he staked them to the earth.

Young was a practical and puritanical Vermonter. He had been a mechanic, a carpenter, and builder. Smith had had no occupation. He was more of a reader than his successor, and he often displayed his knowledge of books. Brigham Young was too busy to be a reader, but he entertained no feelings of inferiority because of this lack. Toward the end of his days Joseph Smith developed a fastidiousness in dress and a liking for his general's uniform. Not so with Brigham Young; his tastes remained simple. The fact that he did not don the spangles and otherwise parade his person did not evidence any lack of ego on his part. Brother Brigham knew too well that wherever he sat, there was the head of the table. That he was the head was something he did not have to prove to himself or others with each rising of the sun.

The primary objective of Brigham Young's headship over the church can be stated in simple terms. He would gather the remnants of Israel together; he would move Zion to the Rocky Mountains; he would drill into the Saints the principles of the Gospel laid down by Brother Joseph; he would continue to send missionaries to gather in the chosen from all corners of the earth, and he would build the church so strong that all the legions of hell could not uproot it. Such were the objectives of Joseph Smith. It took a Brigham Young to attain them.

Probably never in his life was Brigham Young jealous of the place that Brother Joseph held in the hearts of the people. He kept the spirit of Brother Joseph in the saddle astride that white horse. He sold the prophet to the Saints so well that his own place in their hearts was neglected, and only now are the Mormons discovering the majesty of their Moses who led them out of bondage and possible extinction.

The idea of a westward migration had not been planted in the minds of the Saints, however much it had been discussed by the prophet and his aides. Most of the Saints had permanent interests in Nauvoo, which was the main reason for their support of the temple-building project.

As the conviction grew that Nauvoo was no longer a place for them, it became apparent to the leaders of the Brighamite faction that migration could not begin before there was unity of the church. It was estimated by some that there were twenty thousand Saints in the vicinity of Nauvoo. That probably included all brands, from the warm to the cool, and those who later pulled away with one or another of the factions.

The gentile committees were anxious for a Mormon exodus. Perhaps there were some men who hoped to profit financially if the Saints could be forced to move in a hurry—too quickly to sell their holdings except at a loss. It is not known how many moved in 1844, especially from the outlying places, where they feared to remain even to harvest their crops.

Brigham Young, as head of the apostolate, became head of the Nauvoo Legion; and, although Daniel Spencer was named mayor, Young took over Smith's role as head of the community. Under his guidance life in Nauvoo was less hectic; but however peaceful the intentions of the Mormons, the Gentiles carried on the drive for their expulsion. The opposition turned to the legislature, demanding that the Nauvoo charter be repealed and the Legion be abolished. This demand was granted by the legislature in January, 1845.

By this act of the legislature the Mormon population was transformed from citizens of a city to refugees in a county, the control of which was in gentile hands. Their city officers were stripped of authority, even to the keeping of the peace; but that was only a legal setback, because the same men who ordered the city's affairs continued to govern the people.

Work on the temple was stubbornly continued. To finish the job was more important than escape. In October, 1845, the church had the satisfaction of holding the last Nauvoo conference in the all but completed building. On May 1, 1846, fulfilling the prophesy of Joseph Smith, the splendid edifice was dedicated. The Saints submitted to sacrifice beyond measure to finish the job, knowing they would have to abandon the holy structure to gentile pollution.

Gentile committees in the surrounding counties in September and October, 1845, demanded the removal of the Mormons from Illinois by spring. The Mormons answered that they would move if they could get help in finding buyers for their property.[21] However, on February 4, 1846, the exodus began, the refugees crossing the Mississippi on the ice. A temporary camp was established in Iowa on Sugar Creek, nine miles from the river. It appears to have been the plan to remove as many women and children as possible from the trouble zone. Mormon records indicate that nine babies were born at Sugar Creek the first night of the encampment.

However, while most of the Saints had crossed the river before the summer, many remained behind to wind up affairs. From other places in Illinois there had been an influx of families called "new citizens," who purchased Mormon holdings. While not many such sales were made, the new citizens were interested in keeping the city intact; and when, in September, mob activities were again renewed, these people joined with the Mormons in demanding militia protection until the evacuation could be completed.[22]

During 1846 possibly as many as fifteen thousand persons crossed the river to Iowa. During most of that period the city was under the protection of a militia unit; and, although the soldiers may have disliked the Mormons, they were fairly orderly and they did keep back the mob-minded Gentiles who were itching to sack the city. Late in September there was a change in the command. Discipline of the militia broke down. Soldiers began to turn on the people; and before the Mormons could get out of the city, they were sacking and robbing. It was reported that some of these soldiers, to celebrate their victory, placed a cannon on the portico of the temple and fired at the Mormons on the opposite bank of the Mississippi.[23]

What became of all those people who crossed the river? They did not all remain together. There must have been a general dispersion on the Iowa side. During the next decade most of the families that remained in the faith gravitated to Utah.

For those who stayed with the main body of marchers a work plan and organization was devised. The route of the march was westward along southern Iowa just north of the Missouri border. It was a curious kind of march, and unique in the history of migration. Beginning in mid-winter, small groups of men were sent out. These were the industrial column. Most of the land over which they traveled was unsurveyed public domain not yet for sale. These labor battalions worked in relays. Some staked out the land to be cultivated and did other preliminary work. Others plowed, and still others followed and planted. All who moved over the route were part of a co-operating work crew. At the end of the season crops were ready for the harvest at several points along the route.

The plan of the exodus was to cover as much ground with as many families as possible before the farming season began. This was the great imperative, so that horses and oxen which were pulling wagons would be free for pulling plows and harrows and for other tasks essential to building temporary quarters for the winter. "Headquarters" of this moving procession was located anywhere at the front, center, or rear, wherever Brigham Young happened to be. Headquarters on March 7 was 55 miles west of Nauvoo and by April 25 he had reached Garden Grove 155 miles west of Nauvoo. On June 14 headquarters were established at Council Bluffs on the Missouri.

So organized, "15,000 Saints, 3,000 wagons, 30,000 head of cattle," not to mention other livestock and properties, with the minimum of loss and confusion, finally arrived in western Iowa.

Indirect benefits resulted from the march of the camps. Brigham Young and his leaders were learning how to organize people for labor and travel. Families were grouped in companies of one hundred. Each hundred was divided into fifties. Sometimes there were smaller groups of tens. Over each unit was placed a captain. Brigham Young was president over the entire camp of Israel. In the organization of the camps every man and boy each day had something to do, and none could dodge his share of duty.[24]

Discipline was swift and inclusive, but not unduly harsh for the faithful. For example, two of the brethren quarreled. One challenged the other to a duel. The camp clerk issued an order that the challenger be banished, and he could not return unless the congregation was willing to forgive him.

Some of the refugees crossed the Missouri into Nebraska. The rest remained on the Iowa side. In either case they were on Indian land, and it was necessary to get permission from the government to stop until they could prepare for the move westward. On either side of the river, even before getting permission from the government, they started to build communities of log huts. The Nebraska station, first called "Winter Quarters" and later "Florence," is now a suburb of Omaha. Kanesville is now Council Bluffs, Iowa.

There was no opposition to the Mormons from the scattered gentile settlers of western Iowa, but there was some concern in the Missouri settlements farther down the river.[25] For the first time in Mormon history the church enjoyed a friendly relationship with the federal government.

Joseph Smith's prophesy that the Saints would migrate to the West is pertinent at this point. His own struggle against personal enemies and his campaign for the presidency may have interfered somewhat with his plans. However, in March, 1844, he sent Orson Pratt and John E. Page to Washington with a plea for federal assistance in the proposed migration and bearing an "Ordinance for the Protection of Citizens of the United States Emigrating to the Territories and for the Extension of the Principles of Universal Liberty."[26]

The prophet proposed that Congress authorize him to raise an army of one hundred thousand volunteers; that the government protect him in this venture; that, as head of the venture, he should be made an officer of the United States Army; and that with this force he should march into Oregon or Texas and establish a commonwealth which would be loyal to the United States. Clearly, the plan was to organize a new Zion's camp for the purpose of settling the Saints in the West. Although some members of Congress and the Senate favored the scheme, nothing came of it.[27]

When, in the autumn of 1845, the various gentile committees were demanding the removal of the Mormons, Brigham Young wrote to Samuel Brannan, editor of a Mormon paper, the *Messenger*, in New York: "I wish you, together with your press, paper and ten thousand of the brethren, were now in California at the Bay of San Francisco, and if you can clear yourself and go there, do so." Three weeks later, on October 8, President Young addressed an epistle to all Saints in the United States reminding them that migration was imperative; "therefore dispose of your properties and inheritance, and interests for available means, such as money, wagons, oxen, mules and a few good horses adapted to journeying and scanty feed."[28]

On November 8 Orson Pratt, head of the Saints in the "Eastern and Middle States," wrote to all the branches under his direction that the great migration to the West would begin as soon in the spring as grass would grow and water run. He advised that it would be cheaper and more convenient for the Saints in the East to go by sea, that it would cost less to reach California or Oregon by boat than to reach Nauvoo by wagon.[29]

Samuel Brannan, at the head of a seagoing company, chartered an old sailing vessel of 450 tons capacity. For this ship, the "Brooklyn," a rental of $1,200 a month was paid. The company of 238 included 70 men, 68 women, and 100 children. They took aboard tools of all kinds for building, lumbering, farming. They took 2 cows and 40 pigs, food for several months, seeds of many kinds, a printing press, and a library of 179 books. Each adult person was required to pay $50 for fare and have an additional $25 for provisions. Children went for half-fare. The amount collected was sufficient to pay the hire of the boat for eight months.

Actually, the "Brooklyn" made the journey around the Horn to San Francisco Bay in five months and twenty-five days. The voyage began at New York on February 4, 1846, which, by a coincidence, was the same day that the westward exodus started from Nauvoo, and ended July 29, at the time the advance guard of the camp of Israel was locating itself for the winter on the Missouri. In the course of the voyage the war with Mexico had started. A few days before the arrival of the "Brooklyn" at San Francisco, then called Yerba Buena ("Good Herbs"), the American flag had been run up over the fort at that place.[30]

Yerba Buena in July, 1846, claimed fewer than two hundred inhabitants. The Brannan company just about converted the town into a Mormon community. They selected a tract of land for co-operative farming, with Brannan assuming the role of master and proprietor. This effect did not have an opportunity to materialize, because the discovery of gold in California six months later frustrated all plans. In the meanwhile Brannan started a newspaper, the first bona fide sheet on the West Coast, the *California Star*.

Although determined to migrate, whatever the outcome, Mormon leaders had not given up the hope of getting financial aid from the federal government. On January 20, 1846, Brigham Young wrote to Jesse C. Little, who had recently succeeded Apostle Orson Pratt as presiding officer over the eastern region. Little was advised that "if our Government shall offer any facilities for emigrating to the western coast, embrace those facilities, if possible. As a wise and faithful man, take every honorable advantage of the times you can."[31]

Little gained an audience with President Polk soon after news reached Washington of hostilities with Mexico. Polk wrote in his journal, June 3, concerning Elder Little and his request:

> I told Mr. Little that we were at war with Mexico and asked him if 500 or more of the Mormons now on the way to California would be willing on their arrival in that country to volunteer to enter the United States army in that war, under the command of a United States Officer. He said he had no doubt they would willingly do so.

On June 19 an order was written at Fort Leavenworth by Colonel S. W. Kearny of the First Regiment Dragoons to Captain James Allen of the same command, directing him to conduct recruiting among the refugee-Saints. Captain Allen with an escort of three dragoons appeared at Mount Pisgah on June

26. The Mormons, still tense from experiences with the militia of Illinois were unwilling to believe the captain. Finally it required the efforts of Brigham Young to convince them that soldiers could come among them with other than punishing purposes. Brigham Young called a public meeting of all the camps on July 13, by which time most of the people had concluded that the offer of enlistment was heavenly arranged. Allen got his recruits at once.[32]

Captain Allen named a number of Mormons to posts of command in the Battalion. Most of the recruits had been members or officers of the Nauvoo Legion. When the recruits marched away to Fort Leavenworth to be outfitted for the expedition, special messengers went after them. Each soldier was to receive an advance payment of $42 for his year's expenditure of clothing. Apostle Parley P. Pratt brought back $5,860 of this allowance, which, in all, was about $21,000. It was expected that the men would spend some on clothing and send what they could spare to their families.

Leaving Leavenworth on August 12, the Battalion reached Santa Fe, New Mexico, on October 12. Howard Egan and John D. Lee, special messengers from Brigham Young, met the soldiers at Santa Fe with mail from home. They brought back from the soldiers 282 letters and about $4,000.[33]

As soon as the recruiting of the Battalion was over, Young dispatched Apostles Orson Hyde, Parley P. Pratt, and John Taylor to England. They left at the end of July and arrived at Liverpool early in October. This mission was urgent for several reasons: (*a*) it would report the true status of things in the United States; (*b*) it would review the spiritual state of the Saints in England, where the membership had grown so fast without effective leadership; (*c*) it would prepare the Saints in England for the new gathering, keeping the poorest back until means could be provided for their travel; (*d*) it would collect funds for aiding the first migration westward from the Missouri.

Under inexperienced leadership the Saints in England had invested a considerable amount of money in a joint-stock company, a co-operative agency that had good objectives but poor management. The purpose of the stock company was to finance the migration of the Saints. The venture failed because of bad faith or ignorance, and its leaders were disciplined.

Although the apostles were sent to England on a mission of administrative character, they also had another mission: to secure help from the British government. Apostle Taylor during late October and early November, 1846, interviewed various prominent public officials of England with a view to interesting the government in appropriating funds to settle the British Saints in western Canada.

Some time in November a memorial was addressed to Queen Victoria, begging the "Queen's Most Excellent Majesty" to consider the plight of some of her poor but honest subjects and to extend her "Royal aid" that they might "find a field of labour and industry" somewhere in Canada. Some interest was stimulated, but Parliament was not willing to provide the necessary funds.[34]

It must be remembered that going to "Oregon" in 1846 had reference to an area which included also what is now Washington, Idaho, and parts of Wyoming and Montana. "California" included most of the Great Salt Lake Basin and practically all of the Colorado River Basin. The Salt Lake Valley and the Bear River Valley were generally regarded as part of "Upper California," also called "Alta California," the territory taken from Mexico.

In 1846, when Jesse C. Little obtained his audience with President Polk, the way had been effectively opened for him by Colonel Thomas L. Kane, a Philadelphian, who became interested in the Mormon cause. Kane went to Iowa and was present at the time the Mormon Battalion was recruited. This visit was the beginning of a lifelong friendship between Kane and Brigham Young. Kane was helpful in obtaining permission from the Mormons to occupy temporarily Indian lands along the Missouri, pending their preparations to move westward. Young wrote to President Polk on August 9, 1846, indicating his intention to seek a "location west of the Rocky Mountains and within the basin of the Great Salt Lake or Bear River Valley."

Why did Young, within the space of a few weeks, apparently change his mind about his destination? Mormons say that the Lord guided him. The other answer is that Colonel Kane helped him reach a conclusion.[35]

So the Saints began singing a song about their new destination in the intermountain region:

> In upper California, O! that's the land for me,
> It lies between the Mountains and the Great Pacific Sea;
> The Saints can be supported there;
> And taste the sweets of liberty,
> In Upper California, O! that's the land for me.
>
> We'll burst off all our fetters and break the Gentile yoke;
> For long it has beset us, but now it shall be broke;
> No more shall Jacob bow his neck;
> Henceforth he shall be great and free,
> In Upper California, O! that's the land for me.

NOTES

1. Thomas Ford, governor of Illinois from 1842 to 1846, wrote a *History of Illinois, 1818–1847*. Concerning Mormons in politics, he wrote (p. 329): "But the great cause of popular fury was that the Mormons at several preceding elections had cast their vote as a unit, thereby making the fact apparent that no one could aspire to the honors or offices of the country, within the sphere of their influence, without their approbation and votes. It appears to be one of the principles by which they insist upon being governed as a community, to act as a unit in all matters of government and religion." Elsewhere in the volume Ford described the bitterness of party politics in Illinois.

2. Smith said that Nauvoo was a Hebrew word meaning "the beautiful." The author has a letter from the postmistress of Nauvoo, Alabama, named by one Thomas Carrall, who had visited Nauvoo, Illinois, where he had been thrown into jail during the Civil War. He reported that Nauvoo was an Indian word for "beautiful place."

3. The Lord, in calling "all my Saints from afar," said further: "And send ye swift messengers, yea, chosen messengers, and say unto them: Come ye, with all your gold, and your silver, and your precious stones. . . . ." On January 8, 1841, the first presidency issued a proclamation calling all Saints to gather to Nauvoo and build in the county a great city (Joseph Smith, *History of the Church*, *Period I*, IV, 267–73).

4. Upon his return to Nauvoo, Smith wrote: "On my way home I did not fail to proclaim the iniquity and insolence of Martin Van Buren, toward myself and an injured people, which will have its effect upon the public mind; and may he never be elected again to any office of trust or power by which he may abuse the innocent and let the guilty go free." According to Smith, Van Buren listened to his plea for redress and then said: "Your cause is just, but I can do nothing for you" (*ibid.*, p. 89). Mormons proudly tell how Van Buren failed of election twice thereafter.

5. Governor Ford described Smith as "the most successful impostor in modern times; a man who though ignorant and coarse, had some great natural parts, which fitted him for temporary success. . . . . His lusts, his love of money and power, always set him to studying present gratification and convenience, rather than the remote consequences of his plans . . . . he was full of levity even to boyish romping; dressed like a

dandy and at times drank like a sailor and swore like a pirate. . . . . He could as occasion required, be exceedingly meek in his deportment. . . . . He always quailed before power and was arrogant to weakness . . . ." (*op. cit.*, pp. 354–55).

6. Joseph Smith, *op. cit.*, pp. 168–72. Bennett was born in Massachusetts in 1804 and was a year older than the prophet. He had been professor at Willoughby University in Ohio, apparently non-existent now.

7. *Ibid.*, Vol. V, frequent references in the first 130 pages of this volume.

8. An investigation by the state legislature of polygamy charges might have been very disturbing then because Smith in 1842 was keeping the matter a strict secret among a few friends, but it was not too secret. Church records show that Smith married the following women in the order named: 1841, Louisa Beeman, Prescindia Huntington, Zina Huntington Jacobs; 1842, Eliza R. Snow, Sarah Ann Whitney, Desdemona W. Fullmer; 1843, Helen Mar Kimball, Eliza Partridge, Emily Lawrence, and Sarah Lawrence. None are reported for 1844. These names and others are listed by Harry M. Beardsley in *Joseph Smith and His Mormon Empire*, pp. 388–89.

9. Joseph Fielding Smith, *Essentials in Church History*, p. 336. Other cities protested because of the powers given to Nauvoo but not included in other charters.

10. This prophecy was made two days before Smith was arrested for "being an accessory before the fact, to an assault with intent to kill by one Orrin P. Rockwell on Lilburn W. Boggs." Rockwell had already been arrested. Both were released by Nauvoo authorities. Different versions of this prophecy have been given (Joseph Smith, *op. cit.*, V, 85–86).

11. When offered the nomination on January 29, Smith said: "You must send every man in the city who is able to speak in public throughout the land to electioneer, advocate the Mormon religion, purity of elections, and call upon the people to stand by the law and put down mobocracy. . . . . There is oratory enough in the Church to carry me into the presidential chair the first slide" (*ibid.*, VI, 187–232).

12. *Ibid.*, pp. 386–97. In the convention there was outspoken bias against lawyers in government.

13. *Ibid.*, p. 224.

14. On February 15, 1844, Wight and Miller wrote from Black River Falls, Wisconsin, to the presidency of the church, reporting on their labor in the pineries. They described the region there as barren, dreary, and cold and suggested that a lumber company be sent to Texas, Mexico, or Brazil. Before the prophet's plan to go to California or Oregon took possession of his mind, he entertained the dream of a Texas location. Wight's colony of about two hundred and fifty persons was located in Bandera County. In the University of Texas Archives is a manuscript, dated 1920, by Herman Hale Smith, entitled "The Lyman Wight Colony in Texas, 1846–1858."

15. Smith wrote an item in his journal on June 6 that word reached him concerning the desire of Robert D. Foster to be taken back into the church. The report indicated that if he could be reinstated to various former positions he would deliver "all the affidavits of the anti-Mormons under his control." Smith did not respond. Next day Foster circulated a story that Smith had offered him a "hatful of dollars" (Joseph Smith, *op. cit.*, VI, 429–30).

16. *Ibid.*, 437–49, contains the minutes of the trial of the *Expositor* and the charges of Smith and his aides against the anti-Mormon group.

17. Enemies of Joseph Smith were wont to describe him as a coward, but his surrender to the civil authorities at Carthage was an act of unusual courage. He could have fled into Iowa, and his people would have gloried in his escape. Technically, the Smiths were charged with treason for having called out the Nauvoo Legion under their com-

mand to resist a *posse comitatus* sent to arrest them previously (Ford, *op. cit.*, pp. 337–39).

When Smith reached the jail, he was jeered by the militia there to guard him. He spoke to the militia, saying: "Nothing but my blood will satisfy you." He prophesied that most of those present would "witness scenes of blood and sorrow to your entire satisfaction." He said their souls would be saturated with blood and that many would face the mouths of cannon. B. H. Roberts in his *Comprehensive History of the Church*, II, 256–57, mentions that a regiment from this area faced slaughter at Buena Vista and that the losses in life sustained by these people in the Civil War were excessive.

18. On June 20 Smith wrote in his journal that he had sent word to the apostles to come home immediately. Eleven of them were in eastern cities (Joseph Smith, *op. cit.*, VI, 519).

19. W. W. Phelps, who might have dubbed himself the "Wizard of Words," in 1841 devised the following laudatory titles for the church leaders: Brigham Young, "Lion of the Lord"; Parley P. Pratt, "Archer of Paradise"; Orson Hyde, "Olive Branch of Israel"; Willard Richards, "Keeper of the Rolls"; John Taylor, "Champion of Right"; William Smith, "Patriarch of Jacob's Staff"; Wilford Woodruff, "Banner of the Gospel"; George A. Smith, "Entablature of Truth"; Orson Pratt, "Gauge of Philosophy"; John E. Page, "Sun Dial"; Lyman Wight, "Wild Ram of the Mountains"; John C. Bennett, "Joab, a General in Israel." William Smith, Page, Wight, and Bennett fell by the way.

20. The "Kingdom of God" would have included most of western Texas as it was in 1844, when that republic embraced parts of the present states of Oklahoma, Kansas, Colorado, Wyoming, and New Mexico. Dale L. Morgan, of Salt Lake City, has under preparation a manuscript of the "Kingdom of God" plan.

21. The Mormon response is found in Roberts, *op. cit.*, pp. 508–11. Much of the leadership in this demand for the Mormon removal was in Quincy, where the refugee-Saints in 1838 and 1839 found haven after the Missouri persecutions. Brigham Young put every mechanic to work preparing wood and gathering iron to make wagons. Concerning sales, Young wrote on November 30, a few weeks after they had promised to move: "Very few sales of property are being made, the citizens of the country around instead of aiding us to sell our property, are using their influence to discourage sales and the authorities constantly haunt us with vexatious writs, efforts are made to bring us into collision with the authorities of the United States by means of vexatious writs from the federal courts. The brethren are doing their utmost to prepare amidst all the discouragements that surround us for a general exodus in the spring . . . . " (Joseph Smith, *op. cit.*, VII, 536).

22. On January 13, 1845, a few days before the city's charter was repealed, the Nauvoo Council declared that, owing to the activities of the Gentiles, such a state of lawlessness prevailed in the county that evil men were being attracted to the area. Thieves, robbers, "bogus makers," and murderers were tempted to operate in Hancock County, knowing that whatever they did would be blamed on the Mormons by the Gentiles and on the Gentiles by the Mormons. On January 17, Joseph A. Kelting, a deputy sheriff of the county, and a Mormon, charged that these criminals from without were operating with persons in Nauvoo alleged to be Mormons (*ibid.*, pp. 252–61).

23. Joseph Fielding Smith, *op. cit.*, pp. 412–41. The temple was burned on November 10, 1848, the Mormons allege, by an incendiary who thought the unused building would tempt the Mormons to return.

24. Roberts (*op. cit.*, III, 54) cites as an example of organization, Garden Grove, April 25, when 259 men were on hand for work. One hundred were sent to split rails, 10 to build fences, 48 to build houses, 12 to dig wells, 10 to build bridges, and the rest were assigned to clearing the land to plow for planting.

25. Frank A. Golder in his *The March of the Mormon Battalion*, pp. 94–96, reports two anti-Mormon letters written by persons in the northwestern part of Missouri. One of these was written on June 23, 1846, to G. A. Parsons, adjutant general of the Missouri militia, by J. Brown Horey. Horey charged that the Mormons were "armed to the teeth, and supported by batteries of heavy ordinance." He feared they might invade Missouri. The second letter was written on July 4, 1856, to the president of the United States by L. Marshall, of Putnam County. Marshall demanded that the Mormons be disarmed and expelled "from our border."

26. This ordinance and memorial was written by Joseph Smith on March 26. He seemed to favor, at the moment, going to Oregon, a region "without any organized government" and exposed to foreign invasion (Joseph Smith, *op. cit.*, VI, 275–77).

27. Orson Hyde, who was later sent to join Orson Pratt and John E. Page in the effort at Washington, on April 25 and 26 wrote of his progress. The Smith plan found some friends. Some congressmen favored the Mormons going to Oregon and forming a state or even nation of their own (*ibid.*, pp. 269–377).

28. References to the Brannan venture are found in *ibid.*, VIII, 445–80, 515, 586. There had been some correspondence between Brannan and Young on a corporation proposed by some political promoters in Washington. These gentlemen offered to obtain from the government protection for the Mormons and would set up trading relations with them in their new location if the Mormons, in return, would agree to set aside for the company every other lot and tract of land. Brannan was favorable to the plan. Young vetoed it.

29. *Ibid.*, VII, 515–17. Pratt said the Saints had the "choice of death or banishment beyond the Rocky Mountains." In the expressions of leaders during 1845 and 1846 there is no indication of any locality being visualized, or in which region of the West it would be. Pratt advised taking ship because more goods could be taken than by wagon and it would be cheaper.

30. Brannan was born in Maine in 1819. He moved to Ohio in 1833 and learned the printing trade. He had been in the church several years when, at the age of 27, he was placed in charge of a shipload of emigrants. For committing some indiscretion, which also involved William Smith, younger brother of the prophet, he had been subjected to discipline. He made the journey to Nauvoo and gained forgiveness. Although a type of adventurer, Brannan did that one job well. No plague broke out on the "Brooklyn," although there were ten deaths. Two children were born on the voyage. They were named "Atlantic" and "Pacific." Brigham Young never had much confidence in Brannan. His judgment was later vindicated. Brannan apostatized, made two fortunes, and died a pauper. The story of his life was reported by Andrew Jensen, in the *Deseret News*, Church Section, March 26, 1938.

31. Little approached his friend, John H. Steel, governor of New Hampshire, and was given a letter of introduction to Colonel Thomas L. Kane, of Philadelphia. Kane, then a young man, was the son of a Judge Kane. He became interested in the Mormon case and went to Washington with Little. He was instrumental in getting President Polk interested in giving to the Mormons five hundred enlistments. Kane became a lifelong champion of the Mormons and a lasting confidant of Brigham Young.

32. In point of fact, the five hundred enlistments were so many jobs and were accepted as missions for the church. Most of the money paid the soldiers was sent back and was used in fitting out the pioneer company that went to Utah the next year. The Mormon Battalion was the goose that laid the golden egg. On September 13, 1857, when Brigham Young was angry because an army was being sent against Utah (*Journal of Discourses*, V, 231), he charged that the government in 1846 issued a "damnable dastardly order." It was not an order but an offer. Young charged that the government

was testing the patriotism of the Mormons when they were weak. A full report is found in Roberts, *op. cit.*, Vol. III, chaps. lxxiii–lxxv and lxxxvii.

33. *Journal of John D. Lee*, edited by Charles Kelly, entry for November 21, 1846, indicates that the money was turned over to Brigham Young. Later entries indicate that there was some complaint from a few families. Apparently Lee received some of it for compensation after that daring ride exposed to Indians and robbers.

34. The memorial was printed in the *Millenial Star*, November 28, 1846. Since "all of America was Zion," it may have been the plan to move the British Saints to Canada, whereas the main body of the church would locate somewhere in Oregon or California. J. B. Munro in *Washington Historical Quarterly* (Seattle), Vol. XXV (October, 1934), indicates that officials of the Hudson's Bay Company were opposed to Mormon settlers in Canada unless they would be friendly partisans in case of trouble with the United States. If the Mormons should not be friendly to the interests of Great Britain, "it would be quite impossible for us, even if assisted by the natives, to dislodge them."

35. The Mormon leaders had been reading the reports of John C. Fremont of his explorations of the Bear River Valley and a part of the Salt Lake area. See Thomas L. Kane, *Private Papers and Diary*, p. 51 (referring to the Mormons going to Salt Lake Valley): "I am free to say that I earnestly counselled it; because I was convinced that it was a measure greatly for the benefit of both the Mormons and the United States. This country, though not likely for many years to be desirable in the eyes of ordinary emigrants on account of its secluded interim situation, has many advantages." He then enumerated his reasons for this belief.

CHAPTER III

ZION IN THE MOUNTAINS

WINTERING on the Missouri was an occasion for discipline and preparation. Once again the Saints enjoyed a period of security from opposition, except for the buffetings of Satan. The organization of church government embraced in the province of its management every family and camp. Level by level, the whole community was linked through the priesthood to the one man at the top.

At Winter Quarters was laid out a town of 41 blocks with 820 family lots. Also, on the Iowa side of the river hundreds of little cabins were erected before winter set in. The men went to work making harness, repairing wagons, and fencing in the fields to be planted with the break of spring. Those with nothing else to do were assigned to making baskets and bushel measures to be sold to farmers in Iowa and Missouri, the proceeds to go into the "common fund."

W. W. Phelps and other men of learning were occupied with writing textbooks. When there was not work for the adults, there was study of the Gospel; and if there was leisure, the musical instruments were brought out for dancing. The dance was religiously introduced into the Mormon culture that winter.[1]

There were Indian troubles. The Omahas, a weak tribe, were attacked by neighboring tribes. They fled to the Saints for shelter. These poor redskins had to be fed by the Mormons most of the winter. Some joined the church, which made them the more unpopular with enemy tribes.

During the late summer there was much sickness in the camps of Israel. Various estimates of the ravages of the plague place the number of deaths at about six hundred. The ailment was called by some "black canker"; by others, the "blackleg." Colonel Kane, who was present at the time, believed the resistance of the people had been lowered because of exposure the previous winter.

B. H. Roberts submits the observation that the plague was heaviest near the Missouri River, "where the prevalent southwest winds wafted to them the miasmata" of the stagnant pools along the river bottoms, where the cattle were grazed. As soon as cold weather set in, the plague abated.[2]

In the autumn Brigham Young received a visit from the explorer-priest Father De Smet, who had spent several years wandering over the intermountain regions and who brought information concerning the country he had seen. Church leaders had a map of Captain John C. Fremont's route to California. From these and other sources, they were able to piece together sufficient information to guide their planning for the journey in the spring. This they did know, that there was a road to the West, that the main road passed north of the Salt Lake Basin and then branched, one fork extending northwest to Oregon and the other bearing south of west, over the Sierras into California's Sacramento Valley. They also knew that for at least two decades the entire mountain area had been the hunting and trading domain of a hardy set of trappers and explorers.

However general or inaccurate the information may have been, the Mormons had some knowledge about the country over which they would travel and in which they hoped to locate. It was substantially the same information that was available to other companies moving westward.[3]

The earliest record of any white man visiting the Utah area was the report of Father Silvestre Velez de Escalante, who in 1776 led an expedition from Santa Fe seeking an overland route to Monterey on the Pacific Coast. He reached Utah Valley in September and then turned southward. Following the contacts made by this hardy priest with the Indians of the area, the way was open for the traders from Santa Fe.[4]

Still later, a lively fur trade was carried on in the mountain region by British and American trappers. A group of men employed by the Ashley Company camped in northern Utah during the winter of 1824–25. This company, formed in St. Louis in 1822 by William H. Ashley, explored the region north of Great Salt Lake. Leader of one of the parties of the Ashley Company was Jedediah S. Smith, who in 1827 formed a partnership which bought out Ashley.[5] There was some rivalry between American traders and those of the Hudson's Bay Company, which resulted in the latter company's withdrawing northward to that part of Oregon definitely believed to be British territory.

In 1830 the Smith partnership sold out to a group headed by James Bridger, who formed the Rocky Mountain Fur Company, which entered into bitter competition with Astor's American Fur Company. The rivalry ended with the triumph of the latter but not until the supply of beaver in the mountains was about exhausted. Moreover, the beaver business had been injured by the trend of fashion from beaver to silk hats.

Foremost among the traders and explorers of the Utah area was Peter Skene Ogden, a representative of the Hudson's Bay Company, whose name is planted in the region on streams, canyons, mountains, and a city. He was the trader who discovered the Humboldt River area.[6]

From the trading and trapping enterprise there gathered in the mountain country a class of men who were later a problem to the Mormons. Many of these men married into the Indian tribes and became tribal leaders, known as the "mountain men." Unable to subsist longer on the trapping business, some of these veterans hired themselves as guides to exploring parties or to emigrant companies going to the West.

First to take wagons westward over the pack trails from the Missouri Valley was Captain Benjamin L. E. Bonneville, of the United States Army. In 1832 and 1833 Bonneville made wagon tracks over the South Pass as far as the Green River. This was an exploring expedition, and possibly Captain Bonneville was also interested in determining the extent of British occupation and control in the mountains of Oregon. Bonneville apparently did not visit the Salt Lake area, although the great extinct inland sea, of which Great Salt Lake is a remnant, bears his name. It was a detail of his company, under the command of

Joseph Walker, that visited the Salt Lake Valley; but Bonneville got the credit through a book by Washington Irving, *Adventures of Captain Bonneville.*

After Bonneville took the first wagons to the Green River, in 1833, the feat was not tried again until 1836, when a party of missionaries, under the leadership of Marcus Whitman, broke a wagon road to Fort Hall, near the present city of Pocatello, Idaho. A member of the Whitman party was a boy of 16 years, Miles Goodyear. He joined the company about forty miles west of Fort Leavenworth.[7] One of the first migrant youth to go west, Goodyear gained the distinction of being the only resident of Utah when the Mormons arrived. He left the Whitman company at Fort Hall and became a trader in his own right. He married an Indian and located on the Weber River.

In 1841 the John Bartleson company of 48 men and 15 women, with 5 carts and 13 wagons, went through to Oregon; and the next year the Caleb Greenwood company broke a wagon trail to California.[8] Each year thereafter the stream of emigrants to Oregon and California increased, so that the road as far as the Green River and points in Oregon was wide open at the time of the Mormon exodus.

Active preparations for the journey over this trail into the country of the "mountain men" began in the Mormon camp on January 14, 1847, when Brigham Young proclaimed his first and only revelation, the "Westward Ho!" order for Israel, which was recorded as Section 136 in the Doctrine and Covenants.

This revelation set up the plan for organizing companies and equipping them with teams, wagons, and provisions. So detailed were the preparations and so efficient the organization that all could have packed and moved at a few days' notice. However, it was not intended that all should go, only that all should be ready to do so. Place was made in the companies for every widow and orphan, for those who had no teams as well as for those with good equipment. According to the revelation, those companies that did not migrate during the coming summer would work, producing food.[9]

Brigham Young, with his advance company, began the westward trek on April 16. It was his plan to go himself with a well-equipped work group and for a larger company of families to follow. The advance company would reach the valley in time to prepare for the second company a place of security for the winter. His party included 73 wagons, 143 men, 3 women, and 2 children. The original plan was to have "twelve times twelve men," 144; but one of the men took sick and turned back. The three women included one of the wives of Brigham Young, one of the wives of his brother, Lorenzo D. Young, and one of the wives of Young's first counselor, Heber C. Kimball.[10]

Sometimes the wagons traveled two, three, or even five abreast, as was possible over the prairie country; this was safer than traveling in a single file stretched over a distance of two or three miles. The former manner, the usual practice of wagon emigrants, offered protection against surprise by the Indians who skulked out of sight but would be more than likely to attack persons caught singly or in pairs away from the rest of the party.

Mormon travel procedure was the customary routine. They usually got off with a daylight start and covered from eight to sixteen miles a day, depending on the streams to cross, hills to climb, bogs to pull through, or other obstacles. At night the wagons formed a circle with an opening at each side, making a corral into which the animals were driven when there was danger of Indian raids. When there was no danger, the oxen and horses were night herded. The company usually stopped early enough in the afternoon to make the necessary preparations before nightfall and to permit the animals to do as much daylight grazing as possible.

William Clayton's journal of the movement of the company shows that each day's journey was a repetition of the previous day. There was the usual recording of temperature at 4:00 or 5:00 A.M., a statement about the weather, health of the company, and the total distance traveled. Here they were delayed five hours crossing a stream. There the Indians had burned the grass. At another place the Indians came begging and were not satisfied with the amount of flour and tobacco given them.

Here was a notation and there another that Brother Brigham had reprimanded someone. Several guards went to sleep one night, and the brethren for a joke purloined their rifles and hats. There was a laugh all around and then a severe rebuke.

The Mormon party followed the north bank of the Platte River, whereas the well-traveled road followed the south bank. It seems that Brother Brigham selected the more difficult route because in a few weeks the other companies bringing the women and children would follow. They would be less molested on the north bank. The two parallel roads did not converge until near Fort Laramie, about five hundred miles from Winter Quarters.

Clayton's record reports of miracles and healings. For example, on April 18 a tree fell on an ox owned by Father James Case. A limb of the tree "drove one of its eyes into the socket out of sight. About ten minutes afterward the eye returned to its place, and the ox seems to have sustained little injury." On Sunday, April 25, Brother Elijah Newman was baptized for his health. He "had been afflicted with the black scurvy in his legs to such an extent that he could not walk except with sticks or crutches. But after the baptism and confirmation, he returned to camp without any help."

En route the men fared better than the animals. In places grass was short; and elsewhere the Indians had burned the prairie over, not to inconvenience the white travelers, but to bring the buffalo. They believed that by burning off the dead grass the new grass in the spring would grow faster. The Mormons had a good supply of buffalo meat and caught some fish from the streams. Special men were named to be hunters, and the camp journal recorded the big bags. For example, on May 1 the buffalo kill was one bull, three cows, and six calves, possibly about a ton of fresh meat.

The pioneer party did not travel without trouble. It was the case with emigrant groups that they had to become a sort of civil community to themselves, to make their own rules and administer discipline. The kangaroo court, or its counterpart, came into general use. It must have been resorted to by Brother Brigham's company; and there it had no place, in his way of thinking. The priesthood was with them, and that was sufficient government. He was also provoked at the horseplay and cutting-up of the younger men. Some of the older men were grumbling, wondering if this venture was really the Lord's plan. They lacked the faith needed to drive on, mile after mile, into the unknown.

Strong action was needed. The issue ripened and burst on May 29, a cold and wet day, when the company remained in camp. Brigham Young called all the men together. He preached to the text: "I am about to revolt from traveling with this camp any further with the spirit they now possess." He ended his admonitions by calling on the several apostles present to step forward and humble themselves before the Lord and to make their intentions manifest. Next he called on the high priests, then the elders and all the rest. The next day, Sunday, May 30, groups "went into the valley of the hills; and according to the order of the priesthood, prayed in a circle." The spirit of contention and muttering departed.[11]

This was the discipline of faith, invoked time and again in bringing companies over the same dreary stretch. If the spirits of weary and hungry people could not be sustained by the ordinary devices for morale, by singing and prayer, the leaders would employ the power of fearful admonition. The strong would be called on to stand up and declare their faith, and thereby the faith of the weak was fortified.

On approaching Fort Laramie the Saints learned that a company of Missourians had preceded them by a few days and that the head man of the company was former Governor Lilburn W. Boggs of "extermination-order" fame. It was recorded in the company journal that the Boggs party was in poor discipline and that there had been frequent desertions. The Mormons later met emigrant parties from Missouri from whom they expected the worst, but their relations turned out to be friendly.

At Fort Laramie the pioneers were met by a company of 17 Mississippi Saints. This little group, with 5 wagons and a cart, 11 horses, 24 oxen, and 32 other cattle, had wintered with the "sick detachment" at Pueblo on the Arkansas River. They brought news of the Mormon Battalion, the first for several months. Before the Battalion started on its march over the southern deserts to the Pacific Ocean the previous October, Colonel Philip St. George Cooke eliminated 141 men as unfit, because of physical or other reasons, to make the long, grueling infantry march.

The Battalion members and possibly fifty other Saints from Mississippi were still encamped at Pueblo waiting for instructions from Brother Brigham. Apostle Amasa M. Lyman was sent to bring them along to the Rocky Mountains. This company arrived in Salt Lake Valley five days after the pioneer party.

Leaving Fort Laramie, which was about the halfway point in their journey, the pioneer company followed the north fork of the Platte River. They were overtaken and passed by two companies of Gentiles going to Oregon, one company with 11 wagons and the other with 13. They were also passed by 3 men with 15 horses, most of them pack animals. These men were en route from Santa Fe to San Francisco by way of the Great Salt Lake. On June 12 the pioneers came to the point, 124 miles above Fort Laramie, where the road crossed the Platte. Normally the river could be forded, but the waters were high and swift. They found the two Oregon companies camped there and trying to make rafts. The Mormons had with them a large boat made of leather, called the "Revenue Cutter," which would carry about 1,500 pounds. This was pressed into service to help the Gentiles ferry their goods over the river, in payment for which the Mormons received flour, meal, and bacon. Some empty wagons of the Gentiles were then pulled across with ropes. That method of crossing proved unsatisfactory; so the Mormons took a little more time to make rafts.

While the pioneers were ferrying their wagons over the river, two companies of emigrants came along. They employed the Mormons and their rafts. The pioneers received provisions—flour, meal, beans, honey, and two cows—in payment. The crossing of the Platte occupied the whole of six days, during which time the livestock had an opportunity to rest and feed on good grass. When the march to the West was again started,

A DRAWING, BY WILLIAM H. JACKSON, OF INDEPENDENCE ROCK ON THE SWEETWATER RIVER ABOUT 1860

This location was then in Nebraska Territory but is now in east central Wyoming. When the emigrant trains went into camp for the night, the wagons were drawn up in circles for defense against Indians. In case of attack, all the animals were driven into the nine men were left behind to build a ferry for the convenience of the Mormon companies to follow. The ferry would be available for hire to other travelers and a source of revenue.

From the Platte the route followed the Sweetwater River by gradual ascent to the South Pass,[12] where the pioneers arrived on June 26. Finding the precise dividing-line between the westward and eastward flow of the water, Apostle Orson Pratt made his calculations and recorded the altitude, 7,085 feet above the sea. The actual altitude is 7,550 feet. The distance from Fort Laramie "as measured by our mile machine is 275½ miles."

The next day was Sunday. The company wished to spend the Sabbath in fasting and prayer, giving thought to the death of Prophet Joseph and his brother Hyrum, three years before; "but the Gentile companies being close in our rear and feed scarce, it was considered necessary to keep ahead for the benefit of our teams." They followed the Little Sandy, a tributary of the Green River; and, although the stream was small, the country barren, and the grass scarce, the pioneers were happy to be where the "current ran west instead of east."

On June 28 the pioneers met that wiry and wily trader of the mountains, James Bridger, on his way with two men from Fort Bridger to Fort Laramie. He stopped to camp and held council with the apostles. They talked about Salt Lake Valley and the Bear River country. Then he had supper with Brigham Young.[13] Two days after the meeting with Bridger the Mormons came to the Green River, where they met Samuel Brannan and two other men of the company that sailed from New York to the San Francisco Bay in the "Brooklyn," on February 4, 1846.

Brannan and his companions set out on April 4, going up to the Sacramento Valley past the establishment of John Sutter and over the Sierras even before the passes were free of snow. They managed to cross the hazardous Humboldt region without being waylaid by the Indians, and then on to Fort Hall. They passed over part of the trail where several months before the ill-fated Donner party had met with disaster. More than half the party had died of starvation and exposure. They saw the bones of the victims strewn along the way. It was a daring trip that Brannan made, considering his lack of frontier experience.[14]

Brannan brought news of the "Brooklyn" and of the landing of the ship at San Francisco; of the conquest of California and the safe arrival of the Mormon Battalion. However, he was not warmly received, apparently not even by Orson Pratt, who had shared in getting the voyage of the "Brooklyn" under way. His praise of California's climate and fertile soil fell on deaf ears. He brought with him several issues of his own newspaper, the *California Star*.[15]

Brannan's praise of California failed to move Brother Brigham. He had already weighed California and Oregon in the balance. His mind was made up. He would not deny that California was like Eden, but would California be secure? Everyone else was heading that way or to Oregon. He, too, would follow the sun, but not so far. He would take the desert; and there the Saints, by dint of hard labor, would build their own Eden. Woe to anyone who argued with Brother Brigham when his mind was made up!

On July 7 the pioneers reached Fort Bridger on Black's Fork of the Green River, and on the record was written: "397 miles from Fort Laramie or Fort John." Here they found about fifty lodges, most of them inhabited by white men married to squaws men with whom their relations a few years later were not very friendly.

At Fort Bridger the pioneers left the traveled road, following the Hastings route, leading directly to the Salt Lake Valley. It was over this route that the Donner party had gone the previous year. It was not a road, merely a wagon track, and the Mormons had to do a great deal of work to get their loads over the route at all. It required about two weeks to cover the 113 miles from Fort Bridger to their destination. A work party of 42 men with 23 wagons under the direction of Apostle Orson Pratt went ahead to make the route passable. Later Apostle Erastus Snow was sent to join the party, with instructions from Brigham Young regarding the general direction to be taken. Apparently, on information he had gained from James Bridger and others, Young did not want to locate too near Utah Lake, the habitat of a strong Indian population.

The work party under Pratt and Snow entered the Salt Lake Valley on July 23; and on July 24 the main body of the pioneer party, including the Mississippi Saints, arrived. Brigham Young had been sick with mountain fever for several days. He was riding on a bed in Apostle Woodruff's carriage. Concerning his first view of the valley, there is a legend that he raised himself up on his elbow and, after viewing the scene a moment, said: "*It is enough. This is the place. Drive on.*"

What precisely Brigham Young did say may not be important, even though the Mormons have made "This is the place" the subject of a Utah song. Wilford Woodruff wrote later his own impressions of the scene and his report on the reactions of Young, who "expressed his entire satisfaction at the appearance of the valley as a resting place for the Saints. While lying on his bed in my carriage, gazing upon the scene before us, many things of the future concerning the valley were shown to him in a vision."

There are legends that President Young had seen the valley in a vision and that his expression "This is the place" was a confirmation of his vision. Even the skeptics were convinced. There was none to listen to Samuel Brannan.

Whatever Brigham Young may have said about "the place," coming into the valley was an occasion for dreaming dreams and seeing visions. Here was a haven found after seventeen years of wandering in Babylon. After four times failing to establish Zion in the midst of the Gentiles, they were now in a place of safety. If they could not attain the perfect society in this isolated mountain haven, then perfection was not within mortal reach.

Here was "the place" where the city of Zion would be erected, where they would "dig in," as Prophet Joseph predicted, and the Devil would not again root them out. In this place they would build Zion by their own plan, live life by their own pattern, and no law of gentile design would be foisted on them.

In this mountain place at long last Zion would plant her feet to grow strong and mighty, never again to be driven by the black-face mob or thrown into the dust by the enemies of truth. This was "the place" where the weary trail emerged from the wilderness. Here were met in "the place" of God's selection, God's chosen people and his appointed time.

July 25, the second day in the Salt Lake Valley, was Sunday. All met to hear Orson Pratt, the pioneer of the pioneers, preach to the text: "How beautiful upon the mountains are the feet of him that bringeth good tidings," and so was portrayed a vision of hosts of angels rejoicing at the deliverance of Zion.

Then Brigham Young rose to speak. He was still weak from illness. He was never more eloquent or ever more brief. He described the blessed society that would inhabit this new home.

> No man can buy land here, for no one has any land to sell.
>
> But every man shall have his land measured out to him, which he must cultivate in order to keep it.
>
> Besides, there shall be no private ownership of the streams that come out of the canyons, nor the timber that grows on the hills.
>
> These belong to the people: all the people.

It was verily true that no one had any land to sell, for all the area was being lost to Mexico and did not pass over to the United States until the treaty of Guadalupe Hidalgo on February 2, 1848, several months later. When the Mormon Battalion veterans, working at Sutters Mill, discovered gold on January 24, 1848, all of California was still Mexican territory.

When the conquered territory became a part of the United States, it was still true that no one had any land to sell, for the new land became Indian territory, not open for settlement. These legal technicalities did not greatly bother Brigham Young.

The location was surveyed for a city, and the land was divided into town lots, small farms, and larger farms. Each family head was given land of a type and in amount to meet his needs and circumstances. For example, mechanics and shopkeepers, who would be part-time farmers, were given small one- to five-acre lots near the center of the community. Men who lived by farming alone were given the larger lots, the ten- to eighty-acre tracts farther out.

The size of a man's farm was determined by the size of his family. A man with one wife and a few children would receive a few acres, perhaps up to fifteen. A man with two or more wives and many children would receive proportionately larger farms, even up to eighty acres. Once it was determined what acreage was due to the head of a family, the location of his farm would be settled by drawing lots.

While these preliminaries were being arranged, Captain James Brown, on July 29, brought into the valley the second pioneer company, about two hundred persons, including about one hundred and forty Battalion members and the remainder of the party of Saints from Mississippi. With this addition there were in the valley at the beginning of August about three hundred and fifty persons.

On August 9 Samuel Brannan, James Brown, and several others left the valley for California. Brannan carried instructions to the Saints who had voyaged on the "Brooklyn" to California the previous summer. They were to settle down on the West Coast and hold their company together until further instructions could be sent the next year.

Captain James Brown was sent with instructions to the Battalion members, whose term of enlistment had already closed on July 16. This meant that the one hundred and forty Battalion members who had migrated to Salt Lake Valley with Captain Brown would also be mustered out, but they would have to go or send to California to get their pay. The instructions he carried were for the members of the Battalion to remain in the West, get such employment as they could, and, in the spring of 1848, gather in Salt Lake Valley, bringing such supplies of seed, cattle, horses, and food as their earnings would buy.

There was much to do before Brigham Young and the apostles departed for Winter Quarters. Initial steps were taken for irrigating and plowing. Some crops were planted but did not mature, because the season was too late. A site was located and a stake driven where the temple would be built. Then before Brother Brigham left the valley group, all the adults went into the water and were baptized to renew their covenants.

The first company for Winter Quarters left on August 17 with 71 men. Young left with the second company, 108 men, on August 29. Most of the pioneer party returned to Winter Quarters; also, a number of Battalion members went along to join their families. A few men went along to meet their families then on the way to the valley. It is not known how many of the 179 who went away with Young and the seven apostles later returned to winter in Salt Lake Valley.

The 1847 Mormon family migration from the Missouri included 566 wagons and 1,553 persons. These companies did not reach Salt Lake Valley until September. Their number swelled the new settlement to about eighteen hundred persons,[16] including the Saints from Mississippi, the discharged members of the Mormon Battalion from Pueblo, and a few Battalion members from California. Still in California were about two hundred members of the Battalion and all of the Saints who had made the voyage with Brannan from New York in the "Brooklyn."

Without doubt, the Mormons who constituted the first winter colony in Salt Lake Valley deserved Brigham Young's description of them, "the finest people on earth." Here were men, women, and children joined in faith to face a winter of hunger and cold. They brought wheat, barley, and other grains; but this was for seed and could not be used for food. They had a considerable herd of cattle; but these were needed for breeding, and the oxen for work.

These people faced the prospect of living off the environment, which was not an encouraging prospect. Roots were scarce, and wild game limited. Even the Indians in that habitat were living on the verge of starvation. They knew only that the winter would be severe and that they were confronted with the prospect that their livestock might be starved for the want of feed. Moreover, they had to be on guard lest the animals they would not kill for food might be driven off by the Indians.

There were other worries. If they could make their shoes and clothing last the winter, what of the summer? Could any crops be produced without irrigation? Some believed sincerely that irrigation would not be needed. The Lord would provide the rainfall required.[17]

When Orson Pratt's advance company were finding a way into Salt Lake Valley, they came upon the trader and trapper, Miles Goodyear, the only resident in the valley. His presence was a matter of concern. Even one Gentile, and that one fifty miles away, was too many for the brethren. They learned that Goodyear would sell but that he would have to be paid in gold. Captain Brown was making his rush trip to California with instructions for the Battalion members. He returned early in November, bringing the back pay of the veterans in the valley, about $3,000. With $1,950 of this money Captain Brown obtained from Goodyear a quitclaim deed, 75 cattle, 75 goats, 12 sheep, 6 horses, and a cat.[18]

It may be mentioned here that the Mormon Battalion, by its march from Santa Fe to San Diego, made a place in American military history. However important the Battalion's service to the nation, the more important service of those veterans on missions came from the use of their earnings to finance the pioneer expedition and this first land purchase in settling the valley.[19]

The Battalion reached San Diego on January 29, 1847, having marched 1,870 miles over trackless desert. Colonel Philip St. George Cooke by this time had come to admire his Mormon soldiers with a measure of respect that lasted through the years.[20] His order No. 1 contained this compliment: "History may be searched in vain for an equal march of infantry. Half of it has been through a wilderness where nothing but savages and wild beasts are found, or deserts where, for want of water, there is no living creature. There, with almost hopeless labor, we have dug deep wells, which the future traveler will enjoy."

The Mormon officers of the Battalion, who were also leaders of the men as church members, dutifully carried out the purposes of the church and looked over the country as they passed. Captain Jefferson Hunt, highest among his brethren in military rank, being head of Company A, took the lead in viewing the country for settlement locations.[21]

When the Battalion was mustered out on July 16, 1847, at the close of its enlistment, about eighty officers and men elected to reinlist for six months. Army officials wanted more to enlist for a longer period, but the men were willing to remain only until they could get news about the settlement plans of the church. Approximately two hundred and forty of the veterans, under the leadership of Captain Hunt, set out for the northern part of California, expecting to meet Brigham Young en route to that destination.

Hunt and his party came to Sutter's Fort on the Sacramento River, where some of the Mormons got employment with John Sutter, whose holdings were extensive and whose work crew numbered several hundred men. It was reported that he produced in his fields 40,000 bushels of grain and that his cattle herd numbered 12,000 head. He owned 2,000 horses and mules and more than 10,000 sheep and hogs. He had his own shops for making clothing, harness, saddles, and a good share of his farm equipment.[22]

Apparently still uncertain, the Battalion veterans decided to have Captain Hunt, with a few men and pack horses loaded with grain, go ahead and learn the whereabouts of the westward-moving pioneers. They had been told about Brannan departing on the same errand three months earlier.

After September 5, having crossed the Sierras, Hunt and the veterans met the Brown-Brannan party and learned of Brigham Young's plans, but they continued on to Salt Lake Valley. Brown and Brannan next came to Sutter's Fort, left their instructions, and went on to collect the pay for the Pueblo detachment.

Late in the autumn Sutter organized a crew of workers, including seventeen or eighteen of the Mormons, and sent them to a place called "Coloma" on the south fork of the American River to build a sawmill, under the supervision of James W. Marshall. In order to furnish power to operate the mill, several of the men were put to work digging a millrace. Henry W. Bigler kept a journal of his activities. He reported as follows for Monday, January 24, 1848: "This day some kind of mettle was found in the tail race that looks like gold, first discovered by James Martial, the boss of the mill."

That was the line that made history for California and the

Mormons. Bigler wrote in his journal again on Sunday, January 30: "Clear and has been all the last week our metal has been tride and prooves to be goald it is thought to be rich we have pict up more than a hundred dollars woth last week."

When the news got out, the face of all the United States turned to California. The discovery was made six months to the day after the arrival of the pioneer party in Salt Lake Valley and but a few days before California became territory of the United States by the Treaty of Guadalupe Hidalgo.

When Jefferson Hunt and his advance party arrived in Salt Lake Valley on October 16 with a pack train of grain and their pockets full of army gold, Brigham Young had just about reached Winter Quarters. Hunt's report about the attractions of southern California had to wait. There were more pressing problems.

Realizing they could not return to California so late in the year by the northern route over the Sierras, Hunt, in company with Porter Rockwell and eighteen other men, decided to follow the southern route, as described to them by Miles Goodyear. Over this unmarked course the traveler went great distances between watering places, encountering desert stretches that could not be traversed in the heat of summer. After two months of riding, Hunt reached the valleys of California through the Cajon Pass, from whence he found his way to those places in southern California already known to the Mormon Battalion. Early in the spring the Hunt-Rockwell party started back with a supply of seed grain and about two hundred head of cattle. They reached Salt Lake Valley in May, 1848.

In Winter Quarters on the Missouri the first pressing problem was the reorganization of the church. Control had been with the Quorum of the Twelve Apostles. In December, 1847, the leaders of the church elected Brigham Young to be their president. Heber C. Kimball and Willard Richards, until then members of the apostolate, were named, respectively, first and second counselors. This action gave the Saints a new sense of security. Apostle George A. Smith led the congregation in the shout of praise: "Hosanna, Hosanna, Hosanna to God and the Lamb.

Amen! Amen! and Amen!" That, according to B. H. Roberts, Mormon historian, is to be given by the Saints only when the acme of joy is experienced.

On December 23, 1847, shortly after the reorganization of the inner council, a "general epistle" was addressed to the latter-Day Saints "dispersed throughout the earth." Joy was expressed that Zion's resting place had been found in the bosom of the mountains, and "we anticipate, as soon as circumstances will permit, to petition for a territorial government in the Great Basin."

Saints migrating to the Missouri River, preparatory to making the long journey over the plains, were instructed to gather at Kanesville, Iowa. Such migrants coming to this gathering place would bring whatever of value they could afford to carry.[23] Since those who would cross the plains would pass through lands infested by savages, they should bring good firearms. The Saints in California were instructed to remain in that place "until further notice."

In all the world converts were instructed to migrate. The document ended on this note, "Come, then, ye saints of Latter-days, and all ye great and small and wise and foolish, rich and poor, noble and ignoble, exalted and persecuted, rulers and ruled of the earth . . . . your reward shall be an hundred fold, and your rest . . . . glorious."

Some fifteen hundred Saints in 1848 were "squatting" along a stretch of about thirty miles on the Iowa side of the Missouri. This land was not yet on the market but was soon ready for sale at a price of $1.25 per acre. The Iowa legislature in 1847 set apart most of the land occupied by the Mormons as Pottawattomie County—a Mormon county with Mormon officials.

With this turn in events the Saints decided to set up in western Iowa a halfway base from which, each spring, the emigrant parties would be outfitted for crossing the plains and mountains. This would be their food-producing base. Migrants bound for Utah, but not yet able to make the trip, would be encouraged to linger there until more favorable arrangements could be made.

Apostle Orson Hyde was placed in charge of Kanesville. Perhaps it was not a good choice, he being a polygamist, which stimulated gentile criticism. He established a newspaper, the *Frontier Guardian*, the only Mormon sheet in this part of the country except Samuel Brannan's *California Star*, which did not operate as an organ of the church.

At the break of spring, preparations were under way at Winter Quarters for the 1848 migration. The name "Winter Quarters" was used to describe the entire settlement of Saints on the Missouri, including Mormons on both sides of the river. Here is an inventory of the expedition:

Persons	1,891	Chickens	904
Wagons	623	Dogs	134
Oxen	2,012	Cats	54
Horses	131	Geese	10
Mules	44	Doves (pigeons)	11
Cows	983	Beehives	5
Loose stock	334	Ducks	5
Sheep	654	Goats	3
Pigs	237	Squirrels	1

To move so many people and animals over a thousand miles of the most difficult road imaginable was a feat beyond compare. Brigham Young was emulating the story of Noah and his ark. The record contains little information regarding the difficulties involved in moving—for example, more than two hundred pigs as much as fifteen miles per day, especially in hot weather.[24]

The 1848 migration was divided into three companies, and these companies were divided into smaller groups. This was necessary to avoid crowding at the water holes. To move with four thousand or more animals on a small stream might cause a stampede if all the animals were abnormally thirsty after hours in the dust and heat and if there proved to be not enough water. Moreover, it was easier to drive small herds of animals than larger ones. When the companies reached a river and faced the problem of crossing by ferry or ford, it was a saving of time to have the units small.

President Young's division, which started on May 26, reached the Salt Lake Valley on September 20. The second division, under command of Heber C. Kimball, arrived four days later. Willard Richards, brought in the third dividion of the 1848 migration on October 11.

On Brother Brigham's return to Salt Lake Valley he found that, while the pioneers had endured a hungry winter and spring, they had just finished producing their first crop. Between three and four thousand acres had been put under irrigation. Most of the land was fenced. Ditches and dams had been constructed for a larger acreage another season. Obviously, the crop would not be sufficient for a colony of about four thousand persons.

In the spring of 1848 the outlook for a bumper crop had been good. There was rejoicing in the colony during March and April. Although most of the pioneers were experienced farmers, they declared they never saw grain grow so strong and healthy. But in the month of May came the invasion of black crickets. Millions of these hungry creepers invaded the fields of grain and devoured every green stock down to the roots. The pioneers fought back with every device at hand. They filled the irrigation ditches with water. They tried plowing the pests under. Finally, their own resources exhausted, they fell on their knees and called on heaven for aid against the crickets.

Suddenly, and miraculously, there appeared in the skies a white cloud from the direction of Great Salt Lake. Thousands of seagulls swooped down on the fields, devouring the crickets. They ate to their fill and then disgorged their gullets to fill up again, and so repeated the process. The people left the fields and gathered to send up their prayers of gratitude. The seagulls had done their work well. The crop, or the half of it remaining, was saved.[25]

Reports on the harvest of 1848 vary greatly, as might be expected when the realities of a situation had to be squared against the proclaimed expectations. Reports varied, too, on the basis of the kind of farming that was done. Some Mormons were so convinced that the Lord would send ample rain that they neglected to irrigate. Others went to work with a will and made use of irrigation, so that their crops were damaged less by the drought. In some sections of the valley the crops were injured by early frosts.

However, in spite of the partial failure of some crops due to the crickets, the drought, and other reverses, the Saints in the valley called a day of thanksgiving on August 10. Some food had been produced, but there would be none to spare. It meant another winter of living on rations.

It was this second winter that took its place in Mormon history as the season of hunger, when the people went into the canyons to dig thistles and the roots of the sego lily, which in honor has become Utah's state flower. Again the temptation was strong to butcher their breeding and milch cattle and eat their seed wheat, but again they resisted it.[26]

Possibly there were some who were tempted to move with the spring to California, where the gold fever had taken possession of the entire population, but they remained to till the soil. They might have moved to the gold fields en masse, arriving there months ahead of the forty-niners.

Practically all of the Mormons of the 1847 and 1848 emigrations were located within a few miles of the "temple site" in Salt Lake City. The only other community then under way was Brownsville, which had been established by Captain James Brown on the Weber River. This settlement was on land purchased from Miles Goodyear with gold furnished by Battalion members. Other families joined the settlement in 1849. Lorin Farr was placed in charge; and Brownsville became Ogden, the second stake of Zion.

During 1848 some of the families and most of the Battalion members in California had moved to Salt Lake Valley. The California Saints were virtually stranded, having been on the West Coast about three years. These people, who came from the eastern missions by boat, never lived under the discipline of Joseph Smith or Brigham Young. They went from the mission fields to the frontier, and with no leadership save that of the unstable Samuel Brannan, who proved to be an irresponsible shepherd.

When Brannan heard about Sutter's gold, he shed his church

duties and joined the rush for the American River. He operated a store near the fort, and it was reported that this "shirt-tail" establishment did a good business. Brannan would sell anything on credit but whiskey. For that he asked gold on the spot. It was not long before he was on his way to wealth.

It is interesting that while the Saints under Brannan were being neglected by him, there is no record that they were in trouble. The driving authority of the church was absent. It was quite the reverse in Kanesville, Iowa, where the Saints were under pious discipline, their leader being Apostle Orson Hyde. They were having trouble with the Gentiles. Came the presidential election of 1848. Whigs and Democrats appealed for Mormon support. The question of political preference was settled by Brother Brigham before his departure in the spring of 1848.

For some reason not explained, Brigham Young decided that the Mormon vote would be given to the Whigs, perhaps because the Whig candidate, General Zachary Taylor, popular hero of the Mexican War, appeared a certain winner. For Young to commit the entire Mormon vote to the Whigs was asking some of the Saints, chronically Democratic, to make a considerable sacrifice. However, the Mormons voted as told. Taylor was elected, but the Whigs lost the election in Iowa. This meant that the Mormons could expect trouble from the Iowa Democrats.

Iowa Democrats proposed a bill to abolish Pottawattomie County, in which resided most of the Mormons. It was the intent of this proposal to divide Pottawattomie and transfer the area to the several surrounding counties. The division would have so gerrymandered the county that Mormons would have been the minority group in each of the counties. The bill was defeated, thanks to the energy of a small number of Whigs, who held the balance of power in the upper legislative chamber.[27]

Useful though Kanesville was to Zion's emigration program, the Mormons there found their welcome had worn thin after the political error of 1848. This halfway station was abandoned in 1853. Some of the gentile opposition was because of polygamy, which, unfortunately for the Saints, was openly practiced there.[28] Kanesville had a population which ranged from 2,000 to as many as 8,000, depending on the season. Its regular population was small. The rest were Saints waiting for the next wagon train for Utah. Most of them lingered but a few weeks or months.

NOTES

1. Joseph Smith frowned on dancing at first. When Brigham Young gave dancing his blessing, he is reputed to have said: "Many preachers say that fiddling and music come from hell; but I say there is no fiddling, there is no music, in hell. Music belongs to heaven, to cheer God, angels and men. If we could hear the music there is in heaven it would overwhelm us mortals."

2. Roberts, *A Comprehensive History of the Church*, III, 153.

3. Pioneer trading and exploring in the mountain regions has been reviewed briefly in *A History of Ogden* by the Utah Historical Records Survey. The writer is indebted to Dale L. Morgan and his researches in connection with a forthcoming book on the Humboldt River. See *Utah: A Guide to the State*, pp. 48–51.

4. Father Escalante's "Diary and Travels" may be found in W. H. Harris, *The Catholic History of Utah* (Salt Lake City, 1909).

5. The work of Ashley, Smith, and others of that period has been reported by Harrison C. Dale in his *The Ashley-Smith Explorations and the Discovery of a Central Route to the Pacific, 1822–1829*.

6. For the record of Ogden see Hiram M. Chittenden, *The American Fur Trade in the West* (New York, 1935).

7. *Miles Goodyear: First Citizen of Utah*, by Charles Kelly and Maurice L. Howe, contains an item quoted from the *History of Oregon* by William H. Gray, who was a member of the Whitman company. He described the boy as "having on an old torn straw hat, an old ragged fustian coat, scarcely half a shirt, with buckskin pants, badly worn, but one moccasin, a powder horn with no powder in it, and an old rifle." He had wandered west from Connecticut and was going to the Rocky Mountains.

8. In 1844 Caleb Greenwood published his *Emigrant's Guide to Oregon and California*, probably the first of a series of books sold to prospective travelers to the West. For a detailed mile-by-mile report of the history of the road over which the Mormons took, as well as other trails, see *The Oregon Trail* (New York, 1939). This is one of the "American Guide Series" compiled by the Writers' Project of the Work Projects Administration.

9. John D. Lee wrote in his journal for February 15, 1847, that the captains of the hundreds, fifties, and tens reported on preparations. Brigham Young gave instructions regarding the case of women whose husbands were in the army. It was the plan to have a place for every man, woman, and child that would go with the companies to follow later. Families of the Battalion members were given preference because Battalion money had been used in fitting out the expedition.

10. The information in this account of the march of the pioneer company was taken mainly from *The Historical Record*, Vol. IX (1890). This volume, edited and published by Andrew Jenson of Salt Lake City, contains the day-by-day report of the pioneers

going to Utah and later returning to Winter Quarters. The original material was written in the journal of William Clayton, Heber C. Kimball, and others.

11. On May 29 Wilford Woodruff wrote in his journal some of the words of Brother Brigham: "I had rather risk myself among the savages with ten men that are men of faith, men of mighty prayer, men of God, than be with this whole camp when they forget God and turn their hearts to folly and wickedness." He recounted their follies, card-playing, "hoeing down," or boisterous dancing, playing checkers, and holding mock trials, as did the gentile emigrants. "Now, it is quite time to quit it . . . . before you will be fighting, knocking each other down and taking life."

It is reported that on this trip, or the one of the following season, Brigham Young called on William Clayton to write a song that would strengthen the brethren in their faith. Clayton wrote before morning, "Come, Come; Ye Saints," a parody on an English song of the same title. This became a Mormon classic, and its spirit is felt in these typical verses:

> We'll find the place that God for us prepared,
> Far away in the West;
> Where none shall come to hurt or make afraid,
> There the Saints will find rest.
>
> And should we die before our journey's through,
> Happy day! All is well!
> We then are free from toil and sorrow, too;
> With the just we shall dwell.

12. On June 27 the pioneers met Moses Harris, a "mountain man," who offered to hire himself as a guide, claiming that he was familiar with the Bear River and Salt Lake country. He had with him for sale a stock of jackets, shirts, and pants made of buckskin, but his prices were thought to be high. He then left to meet other companies on the road, to hire as guide or to sell his wares.

13. Bridger reported favorably on Salt Lake Valley but seemed to favor the Utah Lake or Bear River area. His report of the Indians at those locations may have persuaded Brigham Young to locate not too near either Bear River or Utah Lake. Bridger reported that the Indians could be routed easily, but he did not advise it. He thought it would be better to enslave them. It was at this meeting that the legend began that Bridger said he would give $1,000 for an ear or a bushel of corn that could be grown in Salt Lake Valley. If he said it, he may have had reference to certain desert tracts.

14. The Donner party, sometimes called the Reed-Donner party, included 36 men, 21 women, and 30 children, led by George Donner. They were emigrants from Iowa, Illinois, and Tennessee going to California. They followed the Hastings Cutoff around the southern shore of Great Salt Lake and then over the desert. They were caught in the deep snows of the Sierras. From exposure and starvation 39 members of the party perished before they reached Sutter's Fort. The tragedy was the subject of much scandal, because it was alleged that some of the survivors had resorted to cannibalism. See Charles Kelly, *Salt Desert Trails*, pp. 81–95.

15. At Monterey on August 15, 1846, appeared the first issue of the *Californian*, a paper of one page containing but a few hundred words, edited by Walter Colton. Brannan's *California Star* appeared on November 1, 1846. Colton had a small bag of type with some of the letters missing. The papers later joined and became the *Alta Californian*. In 1849 Brannan sold his interest to Colton for $800.

16. These companies, in addition to the 566 wagons, had 2,213 oxen, 124 horses, 887 cows, 358 sheep, 716 chickens, and a number of dogs used for hunting and herding. Some of the cows were used to the yoke with the oxen.

17. The faith and optimism of some of the pioneers is indicated by a letter written on August 7, 1848, published in the *Millenial Star*, X, 370. In this letter Parley P. Pratt reported on Zion's fertility. He said a man planted 11 pounds of wheat the previous autumn and reaped 22 bushels. "Barley that was sowed, ripened and was reaped and

carried off, the ground irrigated, and produced from the roots a fresh crop four times the quantity of the first crop." One critic, commenting on Pratt's praise of Zion's crop, said he may have been thinking of the babies, of which 248 were born the first year.

18. Brigham Young learned about Miles Goodyear from James Bridger. Some days later Orson Pratt's advance company met Goodyear, and within a few weeks the Mormons were offering to buy him out. See Charles Kelly and Maurice L. Howe, *Miles Goodyear*.

According to Kelly and Howe, Goodyear set out at once for southern California, his pack train loaded with peltry. He left behind his Indian wife and two half-breed children. With his gold and the gains from his furs and skins Goodyear bought a drove of horses at prices from $2.00 to $4.00 each. These he took to Fort Leavenworth, hoping to sell them to the army. Finding no market, he wintered the horses on the bottoms along the Missouri River. In the early spring of 1849 he started for the West along the Oregon Trail, back over the mountains and past his old hunting ground, then over the desert and the Sierras to the gold diggings. After driving his horses more than four thousand miles, he found back in California a market and prices that paid for all his labor. While preparing to establish himself in California, he died in the autumn of 1849. His brother, Andrew, took over his property and later brought from Utah the two half-breed chiildren, but the squaw widow of Miles Goodyear remained in Utah.

19. Most of the money received by the Battalion members was sent home. These soldiers did not spend their earnings on pleasure, since they were on missions. Pay ranged from $7.00 per month for a private to $50 for a captain. Counting money allowed for clothing, Battalion members must have received for the year in excess of $50,000—possibly nearly $75,000, when travel and other allowances were included. We don't know how much of this ultimately went to the social use of Zion, but we do know that the Mormon Battalion Monument at Salt Lake City cost more than double all the money earned by the Battalion veterans.

20. See *The Conquest of New Mexico and California* by Colonel Cooke for his report of the march of the Battalion. Daniel Tyler, a member of the Battalion, later wrote a *Concise History of the Mormon Battalion in the Mexican War*. Colonel Cooke was an officer on General Johnston's staff when the United States forces occupied Utah in 1858. Some of the members of the Nauvoo Legion that opposed Johnston were former members of the Battalion. When Cooke marched with his troops through the streets of Salt Lake City, he saw some of these men standing at attention on the side lines. He removed his hat as he rode by them.

21. *The March of the Mormon Battalion*, by Frank A. Golder (pp. 251–52), contains a letter, dated May 14, 1847, signed by Jefferson Hunt and other members of the Battalion, addressed to Brigham Young from their camp "By the Town of the Angels." Since they did not know where Young was, it was probably intended as a report for later delivery: "We are in perfect suspense here. In two months we look for a discharge and know not whither to steer our course. We have a good offer to purchase a large valley, sufficient to support 50,000 families, connected with our excellent country, which might be obtained. The rancho connected with this valley is about thirty miles from this place, and about twenty miles from a good ship landing. We may have this land and stock consisting of eight thousand head of cattle, the increase of which was three thousand last year and an immense quantity of horses, by paying five hundred dollars down, and taking our own time to pay the remainder, if we had only the privilege to buy it. There are excellent water privileges on it."

22. John Sutter came to the United States from Switzerland in 1834 and opened a store in St. Louis. He later went to Oregon; then to Honolulu, where he bought a share in a tramp ship bound for Alaska. Later he arrived with the vessel in the Bay of San Francisco, where he sold his interest and obtained permission from the Spanish-Mexican governor to locate a tract of land suitable for farming. He selected a site which included

the area of the present city of Sacramento. After 1840 Sutter's Fort was the port of entry to California from the north. When California came under the United States and the gold rush began, the diggings were on his land; but he failed to prove title. He later left California and died in Pennsylvania in 1876, a relatively poor man. See Erwin G. Gudde (ed.), *Sutter's Own Story* (New York, 1936).

23. The epistle of December 23, 1847, advised the Saints to bring to Zion "Every book, map, chart, or diagram that may contain interesting, useful and attractive matter. . . . . " The Saints were told to bring every type of plant, beast, fowl, machinery, or designs for such equipment. The epistle bristled with flowery rhetoric and exuded optimism about the beauty, order, and efficiency that would be Zion. It was written by Apostle Willard Richards.

24. In 1865 (*Journal of Discourses*, XII, 287) Brigham Young said: "We had to bring our own seed grain, our own farming utensils, bureaus, secretaries, sideboards, sofas, pianos, large looking glasses, fine chairs, carpets, nice shovels and tongs, and other fine furniture, with all the parlour cook stoves, etc.; and we had to bring these things piled together with the women and children, helter skelter, topsy turvy, with broken-down horses, ring-boned, spavined, poll evil, fistula and hipped; oxen with three legs and cows with one tit. This was our only means of transportation, and if we had not brought our goods in this manner we should not have had them."

25. There is today a monument to the seagull on the Temple Block in Salt Lake City. The gull is now a sacred bird, protected by Utah law, although farmers sometimes find them as much of a pest when they come to eat the cherries as they were a blessing when they ate the crickets. Kimball Young, in "A Story of the Rise of a Social Taboo," *Scientific Monthly*, XXVI, 449–53, refers to the seagull monument as "a kind of attenuated amorphous totem pole."

26. Of 1848 Parley P. Pratt wrote in his *Autobiography*: "I had plowed and subdued the land to the amount of nearly forty acres, and had cultivated the same in grain and vegetables. In this labor every woman and child in my family, so far as they were of sufficient age and strength, had joined to help me, and had toiled incessantly in the field suffering every hardship which human nature could well endure. Myself and some of them were compelled to go with bare feet for several months, reserving our Indian moccasins for extra occasions. We toiled hard and lived on a few greens, and on thistles and other roots. We had sometimes a little flour and some cheese, and sometimes we were able to procure from our neighbors a little sour skimmed milk or buttermilk."

27. Hyde wrote in the *Frontier Guardian* of April 4, 1849, his report on the failure of the Pottawattomie bill saying: "Our readers may forget as soon as they can, the injustice which the Democrats sought to do us. Indeed, the sooner the better; but never forget that four Whig members of the Senate stood by our interests to the very last hour—manfully defending them, and defeated our oppressors." The bill had received the approval of the lower house.

28. See the recollections of Dexter C. Bloomer in *Annals of Iowa*, Ser. 3, II (December, 1896), 599. In his youth Bloomer had lived in Pottawattomie County. Concerning polygamy, he wrote: "In Kanesville, many of the well-to-do men—and no others were allowed to have them—had several wives. Elder Hyde set the example and his dwelling was well supplied. I have already referred to John D. Lee with his ten wives in 'Winter Quarters.' George A. Smith, who had his residence in the valley, just beyond the eastern limits of Fairmont Park, in Council Bluffs, had seven, while Mr. Miller, who opened several farms adjacent to Stringtown on the bottom, had four or five, whom he kept at work in his fields during the summer, and many others of the 'Saints' had a plurality of wives 'sealed' to them."

CHAPTER IV

DESERET: THE MORMON STATE

THE two thousand Mormons left in the desert in the autumn of 1847 were probably as well organized a group as could be found. They needed no vigilantes to keep order, for they had the priesthood, and the priesthood was so constituted that there was no problem of authority and control.

Brigham Young had no cause for worry about the discipline of the pioneers left behind in the valley of Great Salt Lake. He may have been concerned about their health, about their food supply, or about the Indians falling upon them, but he had no worries about their being able to maintain order. Before leaving, he called the brethren together. Arrangements were made to establish a governing body, the High Council. They agreed that if Father John Smith, uncle of Joseph Smith, was in the company soon to arrive, he would be acceptable to preside over them.[1]

Young and his pioneers, returning to Winter Quarters, met the emigrant party near South Pass on September 5. John Smith was with one of the companies. A High Council for Salt Lake City was named, with Smith as president. Charles C. Rich and John Young were named as his counselors. Twelve other men, including some in the party en route westward as well as some already in Salt Lake Valley, were named as members of the High Council. Smith carried a letter of instructions, signed by Young, addressed to the brethren in Salt Lake Valley.

On October 3, about a week after the arrival of the emigrant companies, a conference was held in Salt Lake Valley under the auspices of the High Council. Brigham Young's nominations and suggestions were approved. A military commander was named. Albert Carrington was named to be clerk, historian, meteorologist, and postmaster for the community. John Nebeker was appointed marshal and "public complainer."

As an example of deference to higher priesthood authority, although John Smith was president of the High Council, the real control was in the hands of the two apostles who were present, John Taylor and Parley P. Pratt. The apostolic authority was informal.[2]

One of the first acts of the High Council was to name a committee to draft a code of laws "for the government of the people in the valley." A committee was also named "to receive the claims on the plowed land and adjust them." In the same meeting of the Council the occupied area was divided into five wards with a bishop over each.

The High Council for Salt Lake Valley wrote its regulations one by one as it was confronted by special problems. There were family difficulties, quarrels between neighbors, and disputes about property. There were special problems, such as the establishment of a cemetery and the appointment of a sexton. A bell post had to be set up and a bell-ringer appointed.

The authority of the High Council rested with the priesthood, and that body did not need the report of the Committee on Laws. The purpose of the committee was to set up certain guiding ordinances which gave the work of the Council a more legal appearance. The report was received on December 27, 1847, and the several ordinances proposed were publicly accepted and went into effect on January 1, 1848.

Five provisional ordinances were included in this pioneer code. The acceptance of these indicated that the people would be governed thereby until it was determined at the peace conference between the two governments whether the valley would be placed under the rule of Mexico or the United States. Robert S. Bliss wrote in his journal that these provisional laws were less needed for the High Council than for the morale of the people, who were accustomed to living under law and were restless and insecure without it.[3]

The five ordinances passed by the High Council were of elementary character, as this summary will indicate:

1. Ordinance against any person "idling away his or her time." Any person who did not do his assigned labor would have his land taken away by the Council and managed so that his family would not suffer. The charge of managing his affairs was made against his property.
2. Ordinance for dealing with disorderly or dangerous persons. Such would receive not exceeding 39 lashes on the bare back or fined not less than $5.00 or more than $500.
3. Ordinance for cases of adultery or fornication. Such culprits were to be given up to 39 lashes on the bare back and (*not* or) fined not to exceed $1,000.
4. Ordinance for dealing with stealing. The offender to receive up to 39 lashes on the bare back and to restore the theft fourfold.[4]
5. Ordinance for dealing with "drunkenness, cursing, swearing, foul or indecent language, unnecessary firing of guns . . . . or in any other way disturbing the quiet or peace of the community." Such were to be fined not less than $25. No lashes were provided for these.

There were later ordinances regulating the use of timber products, lest some acquire more than they needed; ordinances regarding loose livestock, driving stock on the range, branding and marking livestock, and permitting studs or jacks to run loose; and ordinances regulating the use of irrigation water, the making of whiskey, and the sale of guns.

The High Council continued to be the government of Salt Lake Valley through 1848. It was during this year that the Brigham Young doctrine of the community ownership of land, water, and timber resources was supported by decisions. The control of these resources was placed in the hands of individuals, who charged the users to pay for their service. This social doctrine regarding the use of timber prevailed until gentile opposition broke it down. Gentile opposition was beneficial because the grants from the High Council, and later from the legislature, gave undue privileges to favored church leaders. The grantees did not always use their monopolies for the purpose of protecting the timber and assuring a fair distribution of it.

During 1849 the High Council approved a paper currency for the people, the money to be backed by gold coin or gold dust. In the name of the provisional government of Great Salt Lake City some gold coins were minted. The Kirtland notes were legalized. These were notes that had been circulating among the Saints since the failure of Joseph Smith's Kirtland bank, which he called the "Kirtland Safety Society." Although the bank failed in Ohio in 1837, Brigham Young arranged to have the Council in Salt Lake Valley in 1849 legalize the notes. Thus,

DESERET CURRENCY

Above, a $20.00 note of the Kirtland Safety Society, dated February 20, 1837, to the demand of O. P. Good, signed by Joseph Smith, Jr., cashier, and Sidney Rigdon, president. "Kirtland notes" were issued to circulate as money. When the bank failed, Smith told the people to keep the notes, because some day they would be redeemed. Some were redeemed in Salt Lake City in 1849.

Below, coins minted from California gold, some of it brought in by the Battalion veterans. At the left is a $20.00 coin, dated 1849, showing clasped hands. The initials G.S.L.C.P.G. stand for Great Salt Lake City Provisional Government. At the right is a $5.00 gold piece of the same minting. In the center is a $5.00 piece minted in 1860. The Deseret alphabet characters read: "Holiness to the Lord." The lion was Zion's symbol for Brigham Young, "The Lion of the Lord."

the prediction of Joseph Smith, that the notes would some day be as good as gold, had been fulfilled. It is not known how many were redeemed or who held these notes.[5]

This provisional ecclesiastical government, for all the fault the Gentiles found with it, did with dispatch and without discrimination whatever needed to be done, and it served until other government could be provided. It was not corrupted by money and could not be used for gain. It was a curious combination of the New England town hall mixed with priestly authoritarianism. No parallel is found in any other frontier state, except, perhaps, Texas, and the state of Franklin, out of which Tennessee emerged.

By the Treaty of Guadalupe Hidalgo, on February 2, 1848, all of Alta California, called the "Mexican Cession," was passed over to the United States. Not until May 30, when the respective congresses of the two countries had ratified the treaty and the agreements had been exchanged, was the treaty in effect. Possibly Brigham Young, already on his second and last trip to Utah, did not hear the report until August or later.

It is quite apparent that the church leaders had already considered a course of action if their valley became United States territory. This was indicated in a letter to Brigham Young by Apostles Ezra T. Benson and George A. Smith from Kanesville on October 10. They pointed out the difficulties involved in the territorial status and urged that the Mormons should try to become a full-fledged state. Otherwise the country would be overrun by a "set of starved office seekers, hungry for a loaf from some quarter to be governor, judges, and big men, irrespective of the feelings or rights of the hardy emigrants who had opened the country. . . . ." The letter ventured the opinion that if the Democrats won the 1848 election and if the Mormons acquired territorial status from them, there would descend upon Zion "a hoard of coching sycophants in the shape of big men to feed out of our crib."[6]

Congress was slow to take action about the newly acquired territory. A military government had been established in the western part of California, but the eastern part was left suspended. Beginning in December, 1848, through March, 1849, when a petition was complete, Brigham Young, Heber C. Kimball, Willard Richards, and others were giving thought to the language of a memorial to Congress. To this document was affixed 2,270 names, possibly all the adult members, including aliens in the valley. On May 3 Dr. John M. Bernhisel started for Washington with a memorial and petition from "residents of that portion of North America commonly called Western California" to obtain "a Territorial Government of the most liberal construction authorized by our excellent Federal constitution, with the least possible delay, to be known by the name of Deseret."[7]

Dr. Bernhisel also carried proposals regarding the geographical limits of the envisioned Deseret. It would include mainly all the land of the Great Salt Lake Basin and the Colorado River Valley. The area included present Utah, all of Nevada, sections of Idaho, Wyoming, and New Mexico, most of Arizona, and part of California. Within the proposed area were about 265,000 square miles of desert and mountain land. The present area of Utah is 84,476 square miles.

Before Dr. Bernhisel's departure steps had been taken to prepare a constitution for a state of Deseret. This was drawn up in a convention held early in March. Except in minor particulars the constitution was similar to that of other states. Suffrage was restricted to "white male residents"; the Bill of Rights was included as a guaranty of religious liberty; and a singular deviation from other constitutions was that no provision was made for the remuneration of officeholders, except the governor.

According to the constitution, there was to have been an election of officers for the proposed state on the coming May 7. Actually, the officers were elected at the general public meeting on March 12. All formalities were dispensed with, even the formality of waiting until the general assembly was elected. These were the officers named in the general meeting:

		Position in Church
Governor	Brigham Young	President of the church
Secretary of state	Willard Richards	Counselor to Brigham Young
Chief justice	Heber C. Kimball	Counselor to Brigham Young
Associate justice	Newell K. Whitney	Presiding bishop of the church
Associate justice	John Taylor	Apostle
Marshal	Horace S. Eldridge	One of the Seventies
Attorney-general	Daniel H. Wells	Only an elder then
Assessor	Albert Carrington	Only an elder then
Treasurer	Newell K. Whitney	Presiding bishop of the church

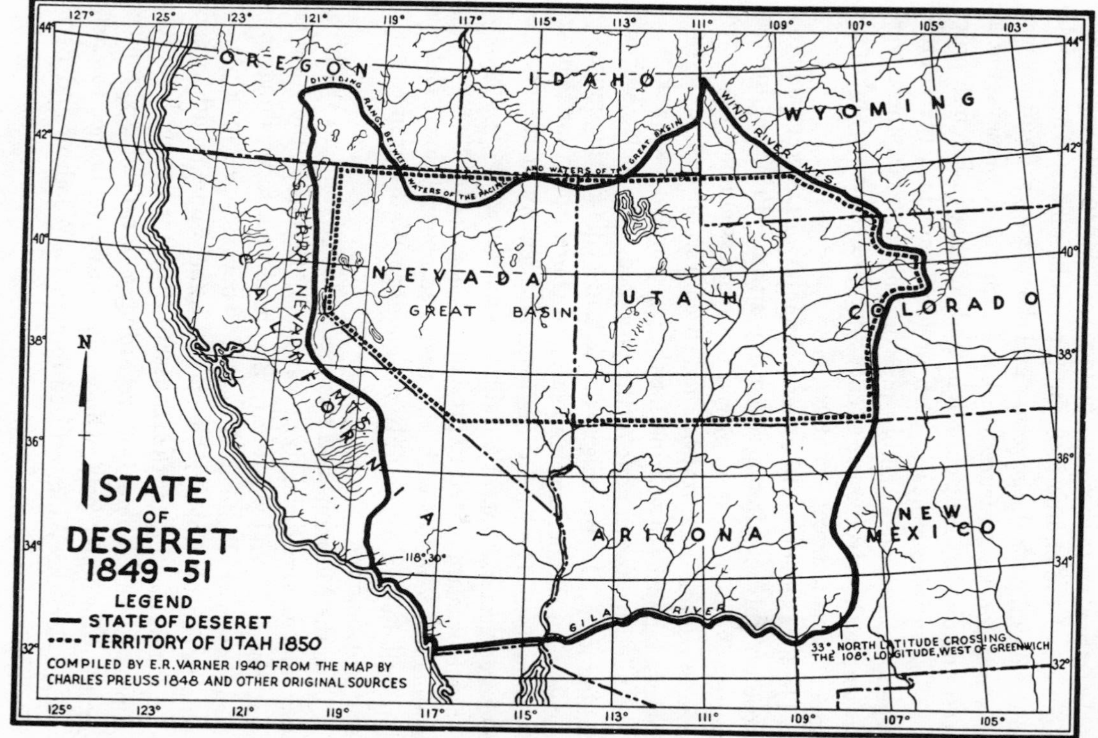

Source: "State of Deseret," *Utah Historical Quarterly*, Vol. VIII (Nos. 2, 3, 4 [April, July, October, 1940], in one volume)

There is little need for comment on the above line-up. In an ecclesiastical state there was no inconsistency in voting the leading men of the church into the top public offices. That would hold especially for the governor and the treasurer. Whitney was in a position, as treasurer, to handle all public moneys, but as presiding bishop of the church he had charge of all church property and all the tithes in cash or kind paid into the church. When the general assembly met on July 2, 1849, there were present in the lower house twenty-six representatives and in the upper house fourteen senators.

The first session of the general assembly of Deseret came to a close on July 9, after a seven-day sitting. Principal interest centered on writing a memorial to Congress announcing that a governmental organization had been established, and then followed months of waiting for the government's answer.

While the government of the proposed state of Deseret was taking form, Dr. Bernhisel was at Kanesville getting more signatures on the petition and later en route from that point to Washington. On July 5 the general assembly of the state of Deseret elected Almon W. Babbitt as its "delegate to Congress." Babbitt was appointed to present to Congress the memorial for statehood, together with the proposed constitution.[8] Babbitt left Salt Lake City on July 27, going to Washington to ask a seat in Congress.

Thus the Mormons had two memorials en route to Washington: one for territorial status carried by Bernhisel, the other for statehood carried by Babbitt. Bernhisel went to Washington in company with Wilford Woodruff. They stopped in Philadelphia to consult Colonel Thomas L. Kane. Some months previous to this meeting, at the request of Brigham Young, Kane had approached President Polk regarding a territorial government for the Mormons. Polk, who was about to yield office to Zachary Taylor, the Whig, refused to act. To Woodruff and Bernhisel, Kane said:

> You are better without any government from the hands of Congress than with a territorial government. The political intrigues of government officers will be against you. You can govern yourselves better than they can govern you. I would prefer to see you withdraw the bill, rather than have a territorial

government, for if you are defeated in the state government, you can fall back upon it again at another session, if you have not a territorial government, but if you have, you cannot apply for a state government for a number of years. I insist upon it, you do not want corrupt political men from Washington strutting around you.[9]

Kane spoke wisely; a territorial government would only bring the Mormons under political supervision. They would do better with their own priesthood government. If statehood were granted, to quote Kane, "Brigham Young should be your governor. His head is not filled with law books and lawyers' tactics, but he has power to see through men and things."

On August 30, about a month after Babbitt's departure for Washington, Salt Lake City received a visit from General John Wilson, newly appointed Indian agent for the Deseret area of Alta California. Wilson came on other business than Indian affairs. He brought a special message from President Zachary Taylor, proposing that all the western California area join with the people in Salt Lake Valley and petition for statehood. According to the plan, the two areas would enter beforehand into an agreement which would result in a later division to form two states. It was thought then that neither region had enough population at the beginning of 1849 to qualify for statehood but that later there would be enough people for either to qualify.

Although the Mormons had been favorable to Zachary Taylor, their friendliness for him had cooled. However, Brigham Young accepted the proposal made by Wilson. By any means possible he was determined that the Saints must have a state of their own. He therefore wrote a letter, probably sent with Wilson, addressed to Apostle Amasa M. Lyman, then in California. As governor of the provisional state, he authorized Lyman to enter into any practical arrangement thought best, but he said:

We are to have a general constitution for two states. The boundaries of the one mentioned by us, before referred to, is our State, the other boundaries to be defined by the people on the coast, to be agreed upon in a general convention; the two States to be consolidated in one and named as the convention shall think proper, but to be dissolved at the commencement of the year 1851, each having their own constitution, and each becoming a free, sovereign, independent State, without any further action of Congress.[10]

Young advised Lyman that the chief handicap of the Mormons was a lack of population, but that was a temporary inconvenience and should not be used by California as the excuse for assuming undue power in the arrangement. He would tolerate no yoke that would reach over the Sierras and fasten on them. He had no objection to an arrangement that would save the nation, but the Saints had also to think of saving themselves.

While the Mormons were occupied with organizing their provisional government, a similar movement was under way in California. Already a number of the essential steps had been taken when Brevet Brigadier General Bennett Riley arrived to take his post as military governor. Since most of his soldiers ran away to the gold fields, he was helpless to carry on a military government; so he joined hands with the citizens in forming a civil government. Californians, being less of one mind, could not settle everything in a single meeting, as did the Mormons. Their constitutional election was held on August 1, 1849, and the convention met on September 3. It required more than a month to draw up their constitution, a job which the Mormons did in four days.

General Wilson was delayed in getting over the mountains. He arrived in California when the constitutional convention was in the midst of its deliberations. There was no interest in the proposal of joining with Deseret; in fact, Californians were offended at the thought.

According to the constitution of Deseret, the general assembly would meet each year on the first Monday of December, unless a special session were called by the governor. Apparently the first session met a month earlier, since the first ordinance passed by that body was on November 12, 1849. This first ordinance was a law regulating elections. It was followed, on December 8, by an ordinance regulating the militia of the state of Deseret. This militia had been organized earlier in the year by the High Council of Salt Lake Valley. The Mormon militia was again called the "Nauvoo Legion," and it continued to have as officers the men who had been officers in Nauvoo, some of whom had also served with the Mormon Battalion.

The December sessions of the general assembly appear not to have been frequent. The members were probably occupied with preparing ordinances. The real work apparently began after the holiday recess, when the brethren lawmakers met on January 8, 1850. The next day a law was passed to provide for the organization of the judiciary according to the constitution. This law, in later years, aroused considerable opposition from the Gentiles because of the provision which left with the general assembly the authority to name, in addition to the justices of the supreme court, the state marshal, the attorney-general, and the judges of the county courts.

Before the legislature adjourned on March 2, several ordinances were voted which need only passing reference: the incorporation of the University of the State of Deseret, with an appropriation of $5,000; an ordinance relating to the work of the county recorder; a law creating the office of surveyor-general; ordinances relating to firearms and the sale of liquor; and a revenue bill. One curious bill was that which created a number of counties—curious because, for remote locations, the area of the county was the immediate valley under settlement; hence, some of the counties appeared on the map as small detached irregular areas, inhabited islands which had no common boundary with other counties. Also significant were these items of the revenue law: (*a*) liquor was taxed at 50 per cent of the selling price; and (*b*) "iron, steel, castings, glass, nails, hardware, hollowware, paints, oils, dye-stuffs, tea, coffee, sugar, rice, molasses," and various other essentials were "exempted from all and any assessment, or tax whatever."

It appears that, whatever the constitutional requirements, the general assembly met from time to time whenever convenient or necessary, on call from its master, Brigham Young. For example, the assembly met on July 4, 1850, a public occasion when the governor made a speech. Then the people were blessed and dismissed, and the "Senate and House went into joint session."[11]

Another informal session of the general assembly convened in Salt Lake City on September 14, 1850, to pass an ordinance incorporating the Perpetual Emigrating Company, an agency already informally organized as the Perpetual Emigrating Fund Company. The purpose of the "P.E.F." was in part private, but it was also desired to give the agency a quasi-public character. Thereafter, certain ferry companies chartered to individuals by the general assembly were required to pay a portion of their net earnings, usually 10 per cent, to the P.E.F.

By September 9 Congress had taken action respecting the disposition of the Deseret plea for statehood. It required more than a month to get the news to Salt Lake City and must have required fast riding for the report to reach Brigham Young by October 15. The Mormons had been given not statehood but territorial status. Their commonwealth was to be called not "Deseret" but "Utah," a designation which was then in more popular use.

The third session of the general assembly, which met on December 2, 1850, passed an elaborate criminal code, of which two provisions may be noted: (*a*) Section 10 indicated that in case of murder, "he, she or they shall suffer death, by being shot, hung, or beheaded." None was ever beheaded. (*b*) Section 28 provided that, among other penalties (fine or imprisonment) a thief would be required to pay back fourfold. Whipping was abolished.

The general assembly met finally on March 26, 1851, to pass a resolution dissolving itself in favor of its successor, the territorial government of Utah, by which act the state of Deseret went informally of of existence. The actual disbanding took place two days later. Territorial officers appointed by the president, including Brigham Young as governor, had already been sworn in.[12]

The dream of Deseret did not pass when the Mormons failed to win statehood. They probably would have been surprised had the state of Deseret been created. That was a matter much less urgent in 1850 than the problems of producing food and of keeping the road open for emigration from the east. No problem was paramount to the growth of Zion.

In 1850 and 1851 the gold rush was on. For every person passing over the road to Utah, possibly ten were going to California and three or four to Oregon. This raised the problem of grass for the work animals pulling the Mormon wagon trains. Plans had to be devised to enable Mormon migrants to travel at different times or otherwise to time their movements so as not to be crowded off the roads. While the Mormons brought in no more than three to five thousand converts each year during the covered-wagon days, their task was difficult because of the large number of women and children.

The *Missouri Republican*, a St. Louis paper, reported the following as the volume of migration that passed Fort Kearny[13] during the summer of 1850:

Men	39,506	Oxen	36,116
Women	2,426	Horses	23,171
Children	609	Mules	7,548

Deaths before reaching Kearny, 316
Deaths between Kearny and Laramie, about 700

How many Mormon emigrants were included in the above number is not revealed. Reports of the period indicate that, while many died before passing over the South Pass, the greatest hazards were in the deserts between Great Salt Lake and the Sierras. Gentile casualties were great because some of the gold-rush companies were so eager to reach California that they equipped themselves carelessly. Some companies were poorly led and badly disciplined.

The road was long and heavy, the Indians bothersome, and gentile parties along the route often unfriendly to Mormon emigrants. The Mormons were well managed, but they were exceedingly poor and had to depend on help from the Saints in Utah.

Wagons loaded with food were sent to meet every emigrant train bound for Utah. Swift riders were dispatched to locate the companies and learn their needs respecting food, clothing, shoes, bedding, and medicine. While the impoverished Saints could not meet all these needs, they did make sacrifices to meet the most urgent. In the frontier states of California, Oregon, and Colorado there was no such organization of first-comers to extend aid and protection to newcomers. The forty-niners organized no wagon and pack trains loaded with food to meet the gold rushers crossing the desert in 1850 and after. Only Utah fostered the helping-hand emigration policy.

Recognizing the difficulties of maintaining from Salt Lake City the Deseret end of the Mormon life-line, Brigham Young began plans to establish a way station. Accordingly, in 1853 the church purchased from James Bridger what was thought to be a Spanish grant, the land claimed by him on the Green River. Here John Nebeker and Isaac Bullock with a company of ninety-two men established a community known as "Fort Supply." The location was immediately within the Utah line and became the center of Green River County. It is now the southwestern corner of Wyoming. Fort Supply had a double purpose, to aid Mormon emigrants and to guard Mormon ferries on the Green River against the "mountain men." Bridger, who had not given up his holdings, was unceremoniously driven out.[14]

Mormon policy called for control over the watering places at key points from the Green River to the Carson Valley. An approximate monopoly was thus also set up over all convenient herd grounds, and that was done by the Mormons through their government granting to themselves monopoly rights on the ferries at the crossings of the Green River as well as of the Bear River.

Typical of the ferry charters was that granted by the Utah legislature to Daniel H. Wells on January 17, 1853. Wells was required to conform to the following scale of prices, although it was claimed that Mormons never paid as high rates on these ferries as were extracted from the Gentiles.

$3.00 for each vehicle weighing not over 2,000 pounds
$4.00 for each vehicle weighing from 2,000 to 3,000 pounds
$5.00 for each vehicle weighing from 3,000 to 4,000 pounds
$6.00 for each vehicle weighing over 4,000 pounds
$0.50 for each mule, ox, or horse
$0.25 for each sheep, goat, or swine

Ten per cent of the ferry tolls had to be paid to the P.E.F. for the aid of the emigrants to Utah. Thus the emigrants to California and Oregon were taxed indirectly to help Mormon emigrants reach Zion.

The "mountain men" claimed priority rights for operating ferries, but they were men without rights, as far as the Mormons were concerned. They had no protection from Utah law, because Daniel H. Wells was the law. He was one of the inner circle of the church and high in public life. So they wrote to Lieutenant H. B. Fleming at Fort Laramie, who referred their grievance to the Commissioner of Indian Affairs.

Fleming wrote that the "mountain men" "have wives and children among the Snake Indians, and therefore claim the right to the Green River country in virtue of the grant given to them by the Indians to whom the country belongs, as no treaty has yet been made to extinguish this title." The Mormons claimed, so Fleming reported, that their territorial status took precedence over the Indian title. The lieutenant asked for information whether he should take action, and, if so, what action.[15]

There were demands that soldiers be placed along the road to protect emigrants against the Mormons. Stories were spread about the food and feed prices they charged. Mormon prices in 1849 and on to 1854 were high, but mainly because food and feed were scarce. Gentile prices were equally high.[16]

Food prices were high from Iowa to California because none but the Mormons were engaged in producing food. All were intent on getting gold—all but the Mormons, and they stood firm by their faith in the wealth of the land.

They believed with Brother Brigham that Zion's security was more precious than gold and insularity than rarest jewels. "Utah suits us," he explained to strangers, "merely because no other well-informed people can covet its possession." To the Saints who wished to be in California he gave the warning that from such a country, if persecution came, there would be no escape save to jump into the sea.

Concerning those who went against counsel, Brigham Young said: "Let such men remember that they are not wanted in our midst. Let such leave their carcasses where they do their work. We do not want our burial grounds polluted with such hypocrites."[17]

The choice that every Saint had to make, whether to follow the counsel of Brigham Young or to follow the gold rushers, involved a fundamental decision. It was a choice between two systems of life; one seeking security in the land by continuous hard labor, the other seeking security by a quick piling-up of metallic wealth. One was the way of quiet, pious, even-tempered living; the other was tense, daring, and turbulent. The one emphasized the domestic, neighborly way of life; the other sacrificed these values for immediate personal satisfaction.[18]

Brigham Young was against Mormons going to the California gold country, but he was not so unfavorable to southern California. He had been impressed by the reports of Jefferson Hunt and other members of the Mormon Battalion. That section of California just then was not so much in the public eye as the gold diggings to the north.

In the autumn of 1849 there was stranded in Salt Lake Valley a considerable number of California-bound emigrants. Church leaders were not anxious to have them remain for the winter. Jefferson Hunt was engaged to guide one of these companies over the southern route. Taking advantage of the occasion, Brigham Young assigned to this journey Apostle C. C. Rich and a number of other reliable Mormons. They would accompany the Gentiles to California, after which they were expected to look over the country for likely places to establish a colony. Apostle Amasa M. Lyman, as already mentioned, was in California on that special assignment, exploring the prospect of California and Deseret joining in statehood. The Rich-Hunt party would work with Lyman in contacting all Mormons on the coast to determine what plans could be made to settle them in southern California.

That journey of the gentile company might have been uneventful had it not been for the leadership of a certain "Captain Smith" who claimed he had information about a route called "Walker's Cutoff." This man Smith, with a few companions, had overtaken Hunt's company about 200 miles south of Salt Lake City. A forceful, self-promoting man, he very soon convinced the greater number of the Gentiles that they would be foolish to travel some 600 miles to the south and then double back about 700 miles to reach the diggings. He proposed a course due west from some point along the route.

Hunt advised against the proposal. He had never heard of anybody having traveled the cutoff. Smith would brook no disagreement, being so positive that he probably convinced himself. Besides, who was Hunt? A gentile-hating Mormon. About seven of the wagons remained with Hunt and took the long way. About a hundred, including Smith's party, took the short way. They encountered bare mountains and the worst of barren deserts.

A considerable number of the party died. They had to abandon all their wagons and resort to pack animals. Like the men who led them into that forbidding place, most of the animals died of hunger, thirst, and exhaustion. This is said to be incident from whence that area now called "Death Valley" got its name.[19]

Hunt's detachment reached California on December 22.

While, on the one hand, the Mormons could avoid the gold rush, they could not avoid the gold rushers, that motley brigade of individualists, ranging from upright men to fugitives from justice. Each winter of the gold-fever period a considerable number of men, arriving in Salt Lake Valley too late to journey safely over the mountains, would stop among the Mormons.

Probably it was the presence of the "Winter Saints," more than any other factor, that stimulated the Mormons to put their priesthood government aside and to set up for themselves the civil government already described. On January 3, 1851, a special session of the Salt Lake County Court was called for the purpose of handling a number of these gentile guests on charges of stealing.

Concerning that session of the county court, it was written in the general epistle of the presidency on April 7, 1851: "This was the first jury trial there had been in the state of Deseret since its organization, and the first occasion for the empaneling of a grand jury." About three hundred emigrants quartered in Salt Lake City that winter. Some were converted to Mormonism and proved their sincerity by their works. Others by their works "have made manifest their hypocrisy, and their sins remain on their own heads. Had it not been for such kind of characters, no jury would have been needed in Deseret to this day."

As good Saints, the Mormons were not anxious to have the gold rushers come among them, but as normal men of affairs they felt very differently. The strangers brought money to the settlements. They brought overloaded wagons and were glad to trade their merchandise for food. This accounts for a Mormon legend about Heber C. Kimball, who in 1848 prophesied in a public meeting that God was watching over them, that the day would soon come when goods would be sold in the streets of Salt Lake City at less than New York City prices. Some gentile merchants came to town with heavy loads and tired oxen. Some needed to trade their heavy wagons for lighter ones. Canny New Englanders among the Saints took advantage of the situation. They bought the goods cheap. The Gentiles called it robbery, but Brother Heber's prophecy was fulfilled."[20]

Brother Brigham's positive program suggests that he did not rest his case against the gold fields on condemning and forbidding. His opposition to joining the gold rush might have failed had he relied merely on damning those who fell as before a plague. The Saints did not have to wait long to realize that all the old bonanza stories about California were not true, since many Gentiles who went out in high hope came limping back later.

It was Brother Brigham's positive program of work and sacrifice, more than his fulminations against gold, that saved Zion from temptation. He was prepared each year to send out to settlements all the emigrant Saints that came over the long trail from the east. They wanted land, and he had land to give them. They wanted to make homes, and he told them where to go. He gave nothing but a place to work. He tendered nothing but sacrifice and social responsibility. For those people these were values against which California gold could not compete.

Brigham Young's settlement program expanded from the center, stride by stride. The first base community to be established after Salt Lake City was Ogden, fifty miles to the north. Captain James Brown, who upon advice of church counsel bought the Goodyear claim with Battalion funds, led the first settlers to that place in 1848. The Mormons believed they bought from Goodyear title to a Spanish grant, but the grant turned out to be nonexistent.[21] Ogden became a base community, or mother-town, for a number of smaller villages and towns between Ogden and Salt Lake City.

James Bridger, as previously noted, recommended the Utah Lake area as the most promising location for settlement, but he indicated that the Mormons would meet with Indian resistance. Brigham Young decided not to locate in the area just then, but Mormon exploring parties looked over the country soon after the pioneers arrived. In January, 1849, the first steps were taken to plant a settlement on Utah Lake "for the purpose of farming and fishing and of instructing the Indians in cultivating the earth and of teaching them civilization."[22]

The Indians were not favorable to the settlers; and, because of their resistance, the Mormons resorted to discipline. Four Indians were killed. Thus in the spring of 1849 a group of about thirty men, under the leadership of John S. Higbee, established Provo, which is about fifty miles south of Salt Lake City.

The Provo settlers continued to have Indian trouble. The natives made exorbitant demands and often behaved insolently. In August, 1849, an Indian, known as "Old Bishop," was killed in a scuffle for the possession of a shirt he was wearing. A Mormon claimed the shirt had been stolen from him. Old Bishop's body was weighted with rocks and placed in the river. When the tribes learned of Old Bishop's death, they demanded the men who had killed him. The men were not surrendered. They next demanded compensation in horses and cattle. Again they were refused. Thereafter they shot their arrows into horses and cattle as a warning.[23]

In spite of being harassed, the Mormons avoided open hostilities. They built their fort and their houses, harvested their 1849 crop, and carried on all essential activities. Indian delinquencies multiplied. On October 18 Brigham Young wrote to Higbee: "Take care of your corn, brethren, and grain of all kinds, and pursue the course proposed in our former letters and counsel to you. Stockade your fort and attend to your own affairs, and let the Indians stay out, but, while you mix with them promiscuously, you must continue to receive such treatment which they please to give."[24]

When winter set in, the Indians began to steal and kill Mormon stock. Possibly they mistook Mormon patience for fear. They called the settlers "cowards" and challenged them to come out and do battle. Mormon leaders took counsel with Captain Howard Stansbury, who was then in Salt Lake City in connection with the survey of the region. He advised discipline. A detachment of the Nauvoo Legion was sent against them on February 8 and 9, 1850. About forty Indians were killed. One Mormon was killed and eighteen wounded. This chastisement served to keep the tribes quiet for a while, but in 1853 they began their depredations again, under the leadership of Chief Walker.[25]

After Ogden and Provo, came the move inland. Isaac Morley with a company of 224 persons, including women and children, set out in October, 1849, to plant a colony in Sanpete Valley, a hundred miles southeast of Salt Lake City. The company arrived in Sanpete on November 22. This expedition, equipped to set up a community and go to work, was typical of others soon to follow.

Morley's settlement was called "Manti," named for a city mentioned in the Book of Mormon. The third epistle of the presidency, addressed to the "Saints scattered throughout the earth," was released on April 12, 1850, just after the annual conference of the church. These communications, which came out about one each year, contained instructions, exhortation, and news. One item of news concerned Patriarch Morley and his Sanpete Valley settlement. This report indicated that the colony comprised 60 families, which would approximate to the 224 persons mentioned above.

Concerning the achievement of Morley and his party, the epistle said:

They have suffered many inconveniences through the deep snows and severe frosts, for the want of houses and other necessaries common to old settlements, and have lost many of their cattle; but they have laid the foundation of a great and glorious work, and those who persevere to the end in following the counsel of heaven, will find themselves a thousand-fold richer than those who have made gold their counsellor, and worshipped it as their God.

In order to keep their cattle alive, the settlers had to shovel the snow from the grass. Thus was started the fourth base community, the other three, in order, being Salt Lake City, Ogden, and Provo, around which smaller settlements grew.[26]

While Morley was pitching his camp in the Sanpete, Apostle Parley P. Pratt, with a party of about fifty men, was starting on a winter exploration of the southern regions of Deseret to the "rim of the Great Basin" and beyond. This expedition, Pratt said, had been authorized by the legislature of the state of Deseret. Pratt's exploration was important because it approximated to a systematic survey of resources, streams, land locations, and timber supplies and made fairly correct measurements of the distances between places.[27]

Making a stop about two hundred miles south of Salt Lake City, in an area which he called "Little Salt Lake Valley," Pratt left part of his company to survey the location. With the rest of the party he pressed on, crossing the divide between the Great Basin and the drainage area of the Colorado River. Here he found the terrain sharply broken and the canyons steep. Following the water course, he came to the Rio Virgin. The altitude was low and the weather mild; and Pratt came away convinced that he had found a semitropical region with sufficient land area to support several communities.

Church leaders were impressed with the general report and favored the immediate development of the Little Salt Lake Valley. The *Deseret News* for July 27, 1850, carried the announcement that "50 or more good and effective men with teams and wagons, provisions and clothing, are wanted for one year." The call for "good and effective men" was repeated at the church conference of October 6. Within a few days a company was brought together, including 119 men, 30 women, and

9 children. The volunteers were organized by Apostle George A. Smith.

The Little Salt Lake Valley settlement was somewhat different from the other bases. Pratt in his explorations had found toward the interior of Deseret vast deposits of coal and iron. The Little Salt Lake Valley would be the agricultural area for the great industrial area just beyond. The "good and effective men" would go there for the winter as a work crew.

For all practical purposes, when Apostle Smith set out with his party of pioneers he was at once the head of a work crew and the captain of a military company, not to mention the head of a quorum of the priesthood. All the equipment, the livestock, the tools, the food—possibly everything but the bedding—was property that owners felt impelled to loan as if it were co-operative property.

Here is a partial inventory of what was taken along:

Food and Seed	Pounds	Livestock	
Flour	56,822	Oxen	368
Wheat	35,370	Cows	146
Corn	3,486	Chickens	121
Potatoes	3,240	Horses, mules	112
Oats	2,160	Beef cattle	20
Barley	1,267	Cats	16
Groceries	1,228	Dogs	14

Work Tools and Other Equipment			
Wagons	101	Stoves	55
Carriages	2	Axes	137
Iron for sawmill	1	Spades, shovels	110
Sets of carpenter tools	94	Hoes	97
Blacksmith outfits	33	Grass scythes	45
Plows	57	Grain scythes	72
Ship saws	3	Sickles	45
Windowpanes	436	Pounds of nails	190

In addition, each man carried his side arms or rifle and two hundred rounds of ammunition. Most of the men had saddle horses and saddles, and for each "ten" there was a quota of cooking utensils, work tools, and farm implements.

On January 13, 1851, Smith's company arrived and went to work, preparing for the spring: building a fort and houses, making roads to the timber, clearing land, digging ditches. They named the place "Fort Louisa" for Louisa Beeman, one of Brigham Young's wives, who died May 16, 1850. She had been a widow of the prophet, having married Joseph Smith on April 5, 1841, the first woman to enter polygamy.

The name was changed to "Parowan" when the general assembly on February 6, 1851, issued to the new colony a city charter. "Parowan" was the name of a local Indian chief.

Iron County, of which Parowan became the county seat, was created by the general assembly on December 4, 1850, more than a month before its inhabitants arrived. This area was also called the "Iron Mission." Parowan was the beginning of a plan for the Pittsburgh of Deseret. Brother Brigham, for all his opposition to gold-mining, was of different mind about iron-mining. He considered iron a civilizer.

When President Young visited Parowan in May, 1851, he talked about iron; but he also talked about Indians and about the slavery of Indians, which he was trying to stop.[28] Traders from New Mexico were in the habit of visiting the tribes of the region and buying children. Indian tribes waged raids on each other for the purpose of taking children, to be sold to the traders.

Although the Mormons had occasional conflict with the Indians, they did not depart from their basic policy of friendliness. They recognized that they were trespassing on Indian land but excused themselves with the argument that they were giving the Indian a superior civilization. "There is room for us all," they told the Indians. "We can work together and produce enough food so that you will have more than before we came." The plan would have succeeded, but the Indians would not work. They preferred the lazy way; and, if they could not survive on mendicancy, they tried stealing. Mrs. Thomas L. Kane remarked that they lingered about the kitchen doors of the Mormons like domesticated animals. She noted they had "the appetites of poor relatives and the touchiness of rich ones. They come in a swarm; their ponies eat down the golden grain."[29]

By 1851 there were in Utah five base communities around which were a total of possibly forty smaller communities. Except Salt Lake City, the other four places—Ogden, Provo, Manti, and Parowan—had already experienced some trouble with the Indians. In only one case, that near Provo, were strong measures used. In other places the mustering of military force was sufficient, up to 1851, to send the Indians hurrying into the mountains to hide or into the settlements to talk peace. After 1851 the tribes began to come under the sway of Chief Walker, who preached that the Mormons ("Mormone") were trespassers to be driven out.

It was true that the Saints were trespassers, but so had pioneer settlers been in other places on earlier frontiers. Previously the problem had been met by the government entering into treaty agreements with the Indians. In accordance with such treaties the Indians moved to reservations and received payment for their lands, which were then sold to settlers. The government was slow to work out such an arrangement in the Salt Lake Basin.

Indian relations in Mormon-occupied areas are pertinent at this point for two reasons: (*a*) Indian depredations were costly not only because of the livestock stolen but also because of the interruptions they imposed on the settlement program. Every community, however small, had to build a fort; and some men had to be on guard most of the time. (*b*) Indian depredations served as a basis for reports to the government by gentile officials of alleged Mormon encroachments on Indian rights. Although little was done by the government for these wards of the Great White Father, frequently, under the guise of Indian welfare, gentile Indian agents found occasion to report critically on the activities of the Mormons.

When Utah Territory was formed and Young was named governor, he also became Ex-Officio Superintendent of Indian Affairs. One of his Indian agents was Henry R. Day, a Gentile. Day was distinctly anti-Mormon. He considered the Mormons trespassers on Indian land and described their policy as one calculated to exterminate the Indians. He quit his job in a short while and was replaced by Major Jacob H. Holeman, also a Gentile.

Holeman, too, was unfriendly and he, too, was insubordinate to Brigham Young, his superior. He found a few Gentiles in Salt Lake City, some of them bitterly anti-Mormon; and because he fraternized with them and with the "mountain men," he was regarded with suspicion by the Mormons.

Holeman sent his reports not to Brigham Young but directly to Washington. He charged the Mormons with encroaching on Indian rights. In one of his first letters to the Commissioner of Indian Affairs he said that Young's "power and influence is so great, that no officer either of the Territory or the Government, who is a Mormon, will dare to disobey his will."[30] Here was the beginning of a new difficulty in building Zion, surveillance from Washington.

NOTES

1. The High Council, composed of president, two counselors, and twelve councilmen, all high priests, is the church governing unit for the stake. For a report on the actions of the High Council for Salt Lake Valley, see "The State of Deseret," *Utah Historical Quarterly*, VIII (April, July, October, 1940), 66–78, 234–39.

2. The relation between the Quorum of the Apostles and the High Council was settled in a case between Apostle John Taylor and Peregrine Sessions involving the possession of a horse. The decision of the High Council went against Taylor in a hearing on November 7, 1847. Taylor took "appeal to the Quorum of the Twelve." Brigham Young ruled that all members of the church are subject to the high council of the stake and to the bishops. There was no separate rule for apostles ("L.D.S. Journal History," February 16, 1849).

3. Robert S. Bliss was a member of the Mormon Battalion. His journal was published in the *Utah Historical Quarterly*, October, 1931, p. 128. Battalion members without families suffered neglect, according to the journal of John Steele, printed in the *Utah Historical Quarterly*, January, 1933, pp. 19–22. Brigham Young later expressed regret that these men had to suffer more than their brethren ("L.D.S. Journal History," September 24, 1848).

4. Mormon communities for years had no jails, and that may have been one reason for the whipping post. Mormons later discontinued the penalty for white men but used it for Indians. John Nebeker ("Early Justice in Utah," *Utah Historical Quarterly*, July, 1930, p. 88) describes a penalty which he was called to administer. For stealing a lariat a man was fined by the High Council $10 or was to be given ten lashes. He had no money and would not permit friends to pay his fine. "I proceeded to tie him, but he refused to be tied. C. C. Rich was appointed by the Council to see that the whipping was carried out in the spirit and meaning of the judgment. I appealed to him whether he should be tied or not. Rich decided that the decision did not mention it and the man didn't want

to be tied, it was his right to choose for himself, inasmuch as he would stand to be whipped. He was then asked to strip. He refused on the ground that it was not in the decision. But his refusal did not count. He stripped, and the lashes were administered in the presence of the people."

5. The Kirtland Safety Society Bank was organized on November 2, 1836. When appeal was made for a charter, Ohio state authorities refused. The organization then changed its name to the "Kirtland Safety Society Anti-banking Company" and proceeded to operate without a charter. Like many another frontier bank, it failed in 1837, leaving hundreds of people with worthless Kirtland notes on their hands. It is reported by Beardsley that the Saints believed the notes would ultimately be redeemed because Prophet Joseph had said: "The bank is of God and cannot fail." Saints carried these notes for many years, and they circulated even in Nauvoo. Smith issued a notice on June 6, 1844, which was published in the *Nauvoo Neighbor*, warning the Saints that most of the Kirtland notes being circulated had been forged. He said: "The bills are not collectable by law in an unchartered institution." See *History of the Church*, *Period* I, II, 467, 470; VI, 429; also Harry M. Beardsley, *Joseph Smith and His Mormon Empire*, pp. 166–70, 319.

6. "L.D.S. Journal History," October 10, 1848. Evan M. Greene, nephew of Brigham Young, in a letter of October 7 advised his uncle that two ways were open: either the Mormons could ask to be made a district of California, "or, if you would prefer it, send a judicious man to Congress to log roll with old coons of the White House a season."

7. The signing of the petition began on December 10 before the text of the memorial was written (*ibid.*, December 10, 11, 13, 1848; March 27 and April 30, 1849).

8. Babbitt was sent to be "delegate" to Congress in the event that Deseret gained statehood, after which senators and a representative would be sent. He was not seated because the "alleged state of Deseret" was not given existence. It was claimed by Woodruff and Bernhisel that Babbitt kept low company in Washington and tried to trade politically for his own gain. Orson Hyde said of him: "Brother Babbitt, I believe, is a good hand to manage a dirty law suit . . . . ," but he did not think him a good representative for the people. See *Utah Historical Quarterly*, Vol. VIII: *The State of Deseret*, for references to Babbitt and Bernhisel.

9. A quotation from the journal of Wilford Woodruff in "L.D.S. Journal History," November 26, 1849.

10. *Ibid.*, September 6, 1849. This letter was written a week after the arrival of Wilson; apparently Young was acting on his own. One of the concluding paragraphs stands out for its wisdom: "Don't get too much in the constitution, lest it tie your hands. This has been the grand difficulty with almost all constitution-makers. The grand desideratum of a constitution is to be unalterable by the power that grants it, i.e., perpetual, and that the people under the constitution can alter or amend the same at their election. But in the case of a constitutional state, the constitution must bona fide remain unalterable during the consolidation." President Taylor made a similar proposal to New Mexico, suggesting a joining with California to get statehood and then separating later. See H. H. Bancroft, *A History of Arizona and New Mexico*, pp. 446–47.

11. The record of this meeting is found in the *Deseret News*, July 6, 1850. The *News* was first issued June 15, 1850.

12. The general assembly on March 28, 1851, passed resolutions dissolving itself and transferring its functions and holdings to the Territory of Utah (*ibid.*, April 8, 1851)

13. The *Deseret News*, December 11, 1852, reported the following from Fort Kearny (later "Kearney") for persons and equipment passing that point: May 1 to October 6: 19,000 men, 4,400 women, 5,555 children, 74,538 cattle (including oxen), 7,800 horses,

5,000 mules, and 6,479 wagons. Along some sections of the road to the west grass was far too scarce to feed so many animals. Also, there were herds of sheep and beef cattle driven over the same route.

14. On August 27, 1853, Dr. Thomas Flint reached the Green River, driving a herd of about 2,000 sheep, oxen, cows, and horses for southern California. On that date Flint wrote in his journal (published in *Annual Publications of the Historical Society of Southern California*): "Moved to a small creek bottom with out sheep for feed, opposite to the fort and to avoid poisonous weeds that grow in the larger bottoms in which Hildreth lost 13 sheep just below our last camping place. White went to the Fort for ammunition but found the Fort in possession of a territorial officer. Mormons had 24 hours before driven old man Bridger out and taken possession. Fort made by setting in the ground two parallel lines of high posts and filling in between with gravelly clay. The location commanded quite an extensive view of surrounding country. Here Bridger had established his trading post many years before his fort had been taken by the Mormons, with a goodly supply of merchandise selected for the Indian trade."

Apparently, from Flint's report, the Mormons took Bridger's property and changed the name to "Fort Supply." In the spring of 1854 William A. Hickman and W. I. Appleby went to Green River to set up a county government. Appleby was judge and Hickman was sheriff, attorney, and assessor. They did not drive the "mountain men" out; they all but deprived them, however, of any means of livelihood. Hickman. who later left the church, wrote *Brigham Young's Destroying Angel* (1872), in which the Green River experience is reported on pp. 88–108.

15. Fleming's letter was dated August 15, 1854, which was four days prior to an uprising of the Sioux tribes in the vicinity of Fort Laramie. Fleming indicated that unless the proprietary rights of Mormons and "mountain men" at Green River were adjusted, conflict might ensue over possession of the ferries, which were profitable investments. The government took no action.

16. Dr. Flint, mentioned in n. 14 above, wrote in his journal, while buying sheep in Illinois and Iowa, that sheep were scarce. He reported paying $3.50 per head. In Utah he bought 210 sheep at $4.00 per head, possibly because he could pay cash. He bought them from a Gentile who had driven them from Illinois, but would accept any price. However, he bought oxen in Utah at from $30 to $45 per head. At Provo he bought flour at $6.00 per 100 pounds and dressed beef at $9.00 per 100 pounds. Some of his men had trouble at Nephi, where the Mormons drove their horses into the stray pound and charged $20 damages. They would not show the damage to their wheat stacks but informed Flint's assistant they would "double the amount *if he found fault or swore*."

Leaving Utah on October 25, Flint wrote: "We were not robbed or molested to an amount more than a set of horseshoes. With other trains the treatment was harrassing in most every conceivable manner, particularly if they were from Illinois or Missouri. Fines were imposed by the authorities for every infraction of their regulations, real or fictitious—enforced by men with rifles on their shoulders, making their demands more emphatic." Some Mormons joined Flint's company to go to southern California. They were in fear of the "Destroying Angels," and they "did not dare to venture away from the camp at night."

17. Church leaders wrote in the general epistle of April 12, 1850; "Gold is good in its place. It is good in the hands of good men to do good with, but in the hands of a wicked man it often proves a curse instead of a blessing. Gold is a good servant, but a miserable, blind and helpless god, and at last will have to be purified by fire, with all its followers."

18. Brigham Young said that, instead of gold, the people should have "iron and coal, good hard work, plenty to eat, good schools and good doctrine" ("History of

Brigham Young," September 28, 1849). "The true use of gold is for paving streets, covering houses and making culinary dishes; and when the Saints shall have preached the Gospel, raised grain, and built up cities enough, the Lord will open up the way for a supply of gold. . . . . "

19. In William Lewis Manly, *Death Valley in 1849*, (San Jose, California, 1849), is an account of the tragedy of the Smith party by a survivor. The company traveled eastward over the worst of rough deserts without food and water, arriving in Tulare Valley, California.

20. Kimball was a practical prophet. He gained a reputation for other prophecies than this one about the New York prices in Salt Lake City. Communities were started on the strength of Kimball's saying: "I see in vision a beautiful city in this valley." Once he met a neighbor who was in economic difficulty. He promised the neighbor. "Next year this time you will have a team and wagon of your own." Later, by twelve months, the neighbor called on Kimball. "You promised me in the name of the Lord I would have a team and wagon this year. I have worked hard, I have paid an honest tithe, I have done right by my brethren; yet I have, not a team, but only one horse." Kimball answered: "You have done all these things. I have been watching you. I'll tell you what you do. Go out in my stable and pick a horse to match yours; and take a set of harness. If the Lord will not fulfil my prophecies, I will myself."

21. Dale L. Morgan has delved into the question of Spanish land grants in Utah, of which there were three so alleged: The Goodyear case, the case of Bridger's holdings on Black's Fork of the Green River, and the case of a small holding purchased from a Mexican who claimed some land on the Jordan River near Salt Lake City. Morgan found no basis for any of these claims. See Historical Records Survey, "Inventory of the Archives of Weber County," pp. 172–80.

22. "History of Brigham Young," September 14, 1849. According to other letters contained in this documentary history, the Provo settlers were at one time almost out of powder for several days when the Indians might have attacked. The Indians were afraid of the small brass cannon that made such a big noise. According to the *Church Chronology*, on September 1, 1849, the cannon exploded prematurely, killing William Dayton and crippling for life George W. Bean, the only casualties from that cannon.

23. Historical Records Survey, "Inventory of the Archives of Utah County," pp. 12–13, taking the information from the journal of George W. Bean. Shortly thereafter the Indians were chastened by a plague of measles.

24. "L.D.S. Journal History," October 18, 1849, Young added: " . . . . and some of the brethren have spent too much time in smoking and chatting with them [the Indians], instead of teaching them to labor."

25. The Fort Utah battle is related in detail in "History of Provo," by E. W. Tullidge, in *Tullidge's Quarterly Magazine*, III, 235–40. See also Howard Stansbury, *Exploration and Survey of the Valley of the Great Salt Lake of Utah*, pp. 148–49.

26. The third epistle reported also: "They have been surrounded by a tribe of Indians who appear to be friendly, and who have suffered much from the measles since they have come among them, and many have died, as have most of the tribes in the mountains; and those who live urge the brethren to remain among them, and learn how to raise wheat and make bread; for having tasted a little during their afflictions, they want a full supply."

27. "History of Brigham Young," for November, 1849, shows that Pratt took with him 50 seasoned men, 12 wagons, 24 yoke of oxen, 38 horses, an odometer for measuring roads, a brass cannon, and food for about four months. The expedition was supposed to have been authorized by the state of Deseret, but there is no record of this. It was probably sent by Brigham Young, who was the real authority of Deseret.

28. *Ibid.*, May, 1851: "I spoke upon the importance of the Iron county mission, and the advantages of the brethren filling it. I advised them to buy up the Lamanite children as fast as they could, and educate them, and teach them in the Gospel, so that not many generations would pass ere they would become a white and delightsome people. . . . . I knew the Indians would dwindle away . . . . . I told the brethren to have the logs or pickets of their fort so close that the Indians could not shoot arrows through."

29. Mrs. Elizabeth Kane, *Twelve Mormon Homes* (Philadelphia, 1874). Sharing the friendly attitude of her husband, Colonel Thomas L. Kane, Mrs. Kane wrote of her observations on a trip to St. George in December, 1872, with Brigham Young. They returned two months later. This was Kane's last visit to Utah. He died in 1883.

30. In this letter written on December 28, 1851, Holeman also charged that Brigham Young was trying to buy the friendship of Indian chiefs with presents paid for by the government. He failed to recognize that presents were always given to Indians for that purpose; that he was distributing gifts himself to the Indians for the same purpose. He said that the Mormons "are a people who have no sympathy for our government or its institutions, and who are frequently heard cursing and abusing, not only the government, but all who are American citizens."

CHAPTER V

ZION GAINS PARTIAL SELF-GOVERNMENT

As PREVIOUSLY noted, the Mormons had three representatives in Washington in November, 1849. Dr. John M. Bernhisel was there in the capacity of special "agent." Almon W. Babbitt had been sent as "delegate" of the provisional state of Deseret. The third representative, Apostle Wilford Woodruff, was a sort of adviser.

The burden for presenting the case for Deseret rested on the shoulders of Dr. Bernhisel, a man of pleasing personality, dignified bearing, and tact. Babbitt tried to further the interest of Deseret, but his methods were different, since he was more of a political horse-trader. However, neither Bernhisel's approach on the higher plane nor Babbitt's on the lower resulted in much progress. Congressmen and senators were interested in many things, but Deseret was a subject too remote to excite them.

Many people, however, were incited to opposition when news got abroad that the Mormons were asking for statehood. For example, William Smith, younger brother of the late prophet Joseph, was on hand to spread the report that when the Mormons left Nauvoo they had vowed a lasting hatred of the United States government.[1] Bernhisel was able to head off some damaging publicity and managed to get some favorable notice in the press, but Smith got a wider hearing.

Senator Stephen A. Douglas of Illinois, chairman of the Senate Committee on Territories, an old acquaintance of the Mormons, presented a memorial in the Senate. He thought the Mormons should have some form of government, but he avoided assuming responsibility for deciding whether Deseret should have statehood or a territorial government. A similar memorial was presented in the House of Representatives. In his message to the Congress on January 21, 1850, President Zachary Taylor said: "No material inconvenience will result from the want for a short period of a government established by Congress over that part of the territory." Possibly the president was in favor of waiting until he received a report on his plan to have the entire area come into the Union as a Deseret-California state, which would be divided later to form two or three states.

Bernhisel and Babbitt did not see eye to eye on the course to be taken by Deseret. Babbitt would make the best trade possible and have the matter settled. Bernhisel stood out against anything but statehood. He wrote to the church presidency that under a territorial government the Mormons would have no control over the officers who might get appointed. "I feel entirely unwilling to run the risk of having a set of whipper-snappers or broken-down politicians to tyrannize over us, and 'make a man offender for a word,' by accepting the ordinary territorial government . . . . for I have every reason to apprehend that we should be constantly brought into collision with the Central Government, and be constantly involved in difficulties with them."[2]

While Bernhisel was trying to put Deseret through Congress, Babbitt was trying to put himself into Congress. The House Committee on Elections on April 4, 1850, reported on his case unfavorably, claiming a man could not be seated representing a nonexistent state. In July the House sustained the committee by a vote of 104 to 78, which shows that Babbitt did not lack friends.

On March 25 the Senate Committee on Territories reported two bills for passage. Both concerned the establishment of government over the territory acquired from Mexico. One bill gave statehood to that area known as California, and the other bill divided the rest of the accession into the Territory of Utah and the Territory of New Mexico. The Mormons by this arrangement would be deprived of the area requested below the thirty-seventh parallel of latitude, and their request to have their territory called "Deseret" was rejected.

This decision was not pleasing to the Mormon representatives, Bernhisel and Babbitt. Such reports as they were able to send home had been so discouraging that the general assembly of Deseret met on September 14 to consider a resolution declaring that, if Deseret could not get statehood, "it is far preferable for us to remain as we are in relation to governmental affairs, until Congress shall see proper to admit us as a state."[3]

Even before that resolution had been written, the decision had been made by Congress. Bernhisel had made every effort to in-

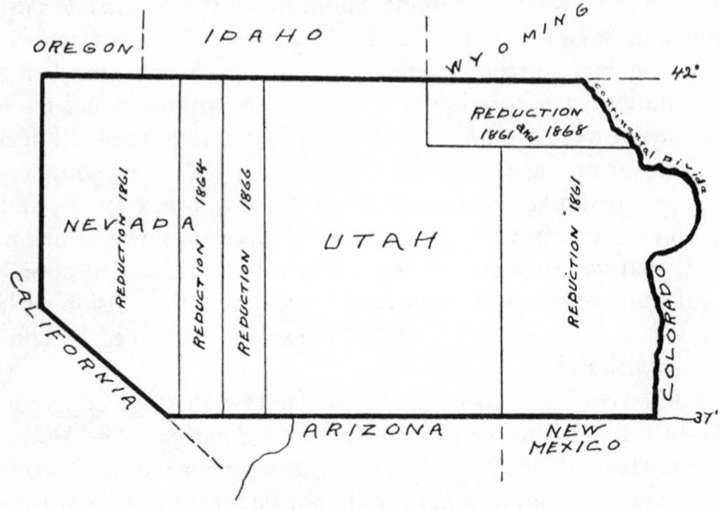

Source: From map by Historian's Office of the Church of Jesus Christ of Latter-Day Saints.

fluence President Zachary Taylor, but the president was not disposed to take any action. The decision, he said, rested on the "breast of Congress." But the breast of Congress was then heaving with political emotions, and Washington was, as ever, full of job-seekers. Hence, whatever the Mormons might wish, they were due for a territorial government; and some of the jobless politicians were due for jobs. Taylor died on July 9, 1850; and two months later, on September 9, President Millard Fillmore signed the bills making California a state and giving territorial status to Utah and New Mexico.[4]

Bernhisel failed to get statehood for Deseret. He could not prevent the clipping-off of all the territory claimed south of the present southern boundary of Utah or north of the present northernmost line of Utah. All the land between these lines from the top of the Sierras to the peaks of the Rockies was theirs, about 220,000 square miles.[5]

Dr. Bernhisel went to work with a right good will to salvage what he could. There would be a number of key officials appointed by the president. Bernhisel endeavored to have as many of these posts filled by Mormons as possible—not an easy task with every senator and congressman offering candidates for these jobs. He got:

Governor	Brigham Young	Mormon
Chief justice..................	Joseph Buffington	Gentile
Associate justice...............	Perry C. Brocchus	Gentile
Associate justice...............	Zerrubbabel Snow	Mormon
Secretary of state..............	Broughton D. Harris	Gentile
Attorney-general...............	Seth M. Blair	Mormon
Marshal	Joseph L. Haywood	Mormon

[Snow was then not living in Utah but in Ohio. Buffington, of Pennsylvania, refused to serve, and Lemuel G. Brandebury, of Pennsylvania, was appointed in his stead. Brocchus was from Alabama, and Harris from Vermont.]

Congress appropriated for Utah $20,000 for the erection of public buildings and $5,000 for the purchase of a library. The first amount had been intrusted to Almon W. Babbitt; the second, to Dr. Bernhisel. Harris brought to Utah $24,000 to pay the expenses of the forthcoming sessions of the legislature. Utah, then, started out with a federal appropriation of $49,000. Steps were taken at once to begin a "statehouse" at the new capital city, Fillmore, in Millard County, both named in honor of President Millard Fillmore.

All the newly appointed officials from the outside were at their posts in Utah by the end of August, 1851. The first meeting of the legislature convened on September 22, and one of its first acts was to adopt all laws passed by the provisional government of Deseret which were not in conflict with the organic act creating the territory.

Whatever form of government Congress might grant, the purposes of the church would remain the same. Brigham

Young was aiming at an isolated commonwealth. Zion needed isolation just then. Thousands of people were needed. The missionary program had to be expanded. The communities had to be developed so that Zion's birth-rate could increase to the maximum. Then more missionaries would be sent and more people brought in.

The Mormon frontier differed radically from other frontiers in its methods of recruiting population. Utah did not have an open-door policy, as did California, during the first decade of the westward rush. Utah used every device to discourage random migration. Just any individual migrant was not welcome in Zion, not even if he could pay his way. Missionaries were sent out to every "kindred, tongue and people" to select the emigrants Zion wanted and could use. They wanted emigrants who could accept the Mormon Gospel and make sacrifices to establish the new society.

Zion did not grow on the principle of individualism; in fact, it would have failed had it been built on the individualism of California. Had the emphasis been placed on such a principle, Brigham Young's following would have fled to California, even before the forty-niners. Zion had to be built by co-operative effort, and it was.

During the presidency of Joseph Smith, and afterward under Brigham Young, the church kept a body of missionaries continuously in the field. Going about, two by two, from town to village, along the highways from farm to farm, Mormon missionaries had been canvassing the states north of the Slave Belt since 1830, but the harvest was not so great as in certain countries of Europe, especially Great Britain. In June, 1837, Apostles Heber C. Kimball, Orson Hyde, and Elders Willard Richards and Joseph Fielding were set apart at Kirtland to preach the Gospel in England. It has been estimated that before 1851 about 50,000 Saints had been baptized in Great Britain and that between 1840 and 1846 about 17,000 had migrated.

The foreign mission field was not expanded greatly until 1849, when the leaders of the church determined to carry the message of Mormonism to other countries. The measure of missionary success is set forth in the *Church Chronology* for December 31, 1854.

Members in all foreign countries	32,627
Great Britain	29,441
Scandinavian (mostly Denmark)	2,447
Switzerland and Italy	299
France	326
Germany, Malta, Gibraltar	114

According to the 1850 census of the United States, there were in Utah 11,380 persons. In 1854 the number of Mormons in Utah probably did not exceed 30,000, with another 5,000–7,000 elsewhere in the United States.[6]

The missionary system could bring into the fold 4,000 converts each year. The task of the church was to get that many migrants yearly to Zion before too many grew cold in the faith. This was a great burden on the settlers, all the greater because of the bothersome Indian problem. Young wanted to move the Indians into the northern mountains. He proposed that the Indian land titles be extinguished and that the land be made available for purchase.[7]

The expedient of having the Indian titles extinguished and moving the Indians had been resorted to in many places, usually to the injury of the Indians. Young argued that the Indians could not work the land anyhow and that only the Mormons could make the barren country prosper. He said: "We can then devote more time to agriculture and raise more grain to feed the starving millions desirous of coming hither."

Young had in mind thousands of converts anxious to migrate to Zion. A greater number could be brought if the Indian problem were out of the way, making available more man-power to produce food, and more men, wagons, and teams to bring in more of "the starving millions." Most of those converts were from Great Britain's industrial centers, where factory workers were ground into poverty. In Zion they had the prospect of land and a chance to labor for themselves and to work for a cause.

To speed up this program the church established in 1849 the

Perpetual Emigration Fund Company, chartered by Deseret on September 14, 1850. The P.E.F. operated more than forty years as the emigration agency for the Zion-building program, bringing to Utah no less than 80,000 persons. This organization was a church-wide co-operative for shipping and settling convert Saints. It supervised the preparations of converts for leaving their homes abroad. It chartered ships and trains and organized handcart and wagon companies for crossing the plains. Its wagons were used for hauling freight, as well as food, for the emigrants. In the interest of these emigrants, it operated a banking and credit service. Those who received benefit from the P.E.F. were expected to pay it back and later, in addition, to make contributions. The P.E.F. harvested the fruits of the missionary program and was but an extension of that program. Those who gave their time to the P.E.F. were deemed to be on missions. They got no pay. It was just another service for the cause.

No service for the cause took precedence over the preaching of the Gospel. That was a sacrifice, not only to the missionary, but to his family. Brigham Young said to a group of departing missionaries in 1852: "Don't take anything with you but the Lord and yourselves. You will want horses to bear you over the plains, but don't carry your wives and your children in your hearts . . . . ; dedicate them to Lord God of Israel and leave them alone. . . . ."

That group of missionaries was the first publicly to preach polygamy. Young said to their wives and mothers: "Don't cling to them one particle, but let them go cheerfully. . . . ." Then, as afterward, many a good wife, to serve the Lord, sent her husband away only to meet him on his return two years later with one of his converts as a plural wife. That was her mission, to accept as a blessing whatever helped build Zion.

It was one kind of mission to preach the Gospel, but another to work in the service of the church. The men who joined the Mormon Battalion and gave their earnings to the church were on a mission. The 143 pioneers who comprised Brigham Young's 1847 advance company were on a mission. In 1849 and 1850 a company of men answered the "call" to found a settlement on Utah Lake. That same year Father Morley took a group of missionary settlers into Sanpete Valley. In the winter of 1850–51 the "Iron Mission" founded Parowan. Some years after that came the famous "Cotton Mission" to southern Utah.

For every thousand converts brought into the church by the missionary program and brought to Zion by the P.E.F. a thousand places had to be found. It was for promoting that home-finding service that the settlement missions were formed. In the autumn of 1850 several responsible men, including Apostles Amasa M. Lyman and Charles C. Rich, and Captain Jefferson Hunt, Battalion veteran, were sent over the southern route to California.

As already noted, some of the families arriving in California on the ship "Brooklyn" in 1846 were still in the state. The Lyman-Rich mission was given the task of gathering these families at some southern location. They reported favorably in January, 1851. Within a few weeks Brigham Young announced a plan to send a small company of settlers to California.

Although the organic act establishing the Territory of Utah wiped out the dream of a Deseret reaching to the southern border of the United States and set the limits of Utah at the thirty-seventh parallel, the Mormon plan of settlement still faced that direction. Brigham Young was determined that his economic empire should have an outlet to the sea. He would plant a settlement at some point south of the Cajon Pass and build a line of settlements between that location and Salt Lake Valley. Beyond that point he would plant communities to the sea. He would then have a broad highway from Salt Lake to the ocean, passing through that envisioned industrial center in Iron County and ending in the olive groves of southern California.[8]

Only a few people were wanted for the California mission; but the call of March, 1851, brought 570 persons and 152 wagons, the largest settlement company yet to volunteer. Such was the fascination of California's name. The emigrants set out about April 1 and arrived at the Cajon Pass on June 11. At that point they rested on the 37,509-acre rancho of the Lugo brothers, which had been offered for sale. They bought the land, with a considerable herd of cattle and certain other properties, for $77,500—all with a down payment of $700. They surveyed the townsite, which became San Bernardino, and laid out the surrounding land in tracts ranging from 5 to 90 acres. Each family got land according to its needs. They dug ditches for irrigation, built fences, put up dwellings, and made a road to the mountain, where they set up a sawmill. They built a flour mill and a meeting house.[9]

Since the land was being purchased by the people as a group, title to lots and fields was held by the church organization. San Bernardino started after the social ideal of communities in Utah. Californians were amazed at the speed and the order of the settlement. About 3,000 acres of grain were harvested the first year. Wheat sold for $5.00 a bushel, and flour for as much as $18 per hundred. They put in orchards and vineyards and extensive vegetable gardens. They proved by their industry Brother Brigham's maxim that land is better than gold.

Southern California had known the members of the Mormon Battalion, and they had a good reputation.[10] It was not long, however, before some began to speak ill of the settlement. Apostle Rich had three of his six wives with him. Apostle Lyman was there with his five wives. Perhaps there were other polygamists among them, but the presence of at least two pluralists encouraged the opposition of some Gentiles.

At the time of settlement the Mormon community was in Los Angeles County. Jefferson Hunt was elected as one of the county's two assemblymen to the California legislature. He was instrumental in getting a bill passed setting aside part of Los Angeles County as San Bernardino County, which gave the Mormons a political subdivision in which, as far as local government was concerned, they were supreme.[11]

There were in the county a number of Gentiles; but they were not happy with Mormon authoritarian control, which, behind the scenes, was dominated by the priesthood organization. They formed an organization called the "Independents," which eventually came into open conflict with the dominant group. Eventually they were instrumental in having the Mormons driven out.

Governor Young in his message to the general assembly of Deseret on December 2, 1850, called attention to the iron-ore deposits down south, in the region where Parowan was established a month later. He suggested the possibility of developing a great industry there and later building a railroad from Salt Lake City to the iron mines and on to southern California.

In November, 1851, after the first harvest in Little Salt Lake Valley, a company of 35 men set out from Parowan to build a fort near the iron deposits, some fifty miles to the south. The new location was named "Cedar City," and a hundred or more families were soon residing there. The men selected were mainly artisans, sent from the various other settlements—men who had worked in the iron and steel industry, coal-miners, coke-makers, masons, carpenters. They could even set up and operate a smelter, a task which they had to work at between those primary duties of raising food and guarding their homes and herds against the Indians.

These mechanics joined together to form the Pioneer Iron Company and went ahead experimenting and running the iron into molds. The settlements needed many things too heavy to be transported from the east: stoves, pots, rolls for squeezing the juice out of sugar cane, castings for sawmills, as well as mold boards for plows. Could they make these many items, it would be a great saving in the cost of freight, which was not less than $200 per ton from the Missouri.

Church leaders had great hopes for their "Deseret Pittsburg," and this enthusiasm was encouraged when, in October, 1852, George A. Smith, head of the Iron Mission, brought to Salt Lake City a number of articles that were made experimentally, on the basis of which he preached an "iron sermon."

When news of the Iron Mission reached England, the new vision of Zion's greatness led to the formation of the Deseret Iron Company, chartered in Liverpool on May 29, 1853. Apostles Erastus Snow and Franklin D. Richards were the prime movers of the new company. They succeeded in collecting a few thousand dollars and hastened back to expand the new industry. They bought out the investment of the pioneer company and secured an operating charter from the territorial legislature.

Many man-years of hard labor were invested in that primitive iron experiment before it was finally abandoned and Cedar City became just another outpost on the agricultural frontier around which a number of lesser communities were located.

For example, in the spring of 1852, John D. Lee, who had been active in establishing both Parowan and Cedar City, founded Harmony on Ash Creek, twenty-two miles to the south. Lee built a fort and from this location began his work as missionary to the Indians. When Washington County was established in 1852 as the southernmost county of Utah, his was the only community within its limits. It was, at the time, the longest political subdivision in the United States, being only fifty miles wide but extending from California to Kansas.

Lee was among the first of the frontiersmen called as missionary to the Indians. Following the Walker War, several missions were started, including one established in 1854 on the Santa Clara Creek by Jacob Hamblin and a group of five sturdy men with their families. For about four years Santa Clara was the most remote outpost beyond the rim of the Basin.

While one arm of the settlement program extended toward the south, the church was not neglecting its opportunities toward the west, for the spread of the Mormon domain embraced all the desert as far as the Sierra Nevadas. Along the Overland Trail from the Green River, past the Bear River, and around Great Salt Lake to the Humboldt were a number of watering places and grazing sites. Brigham Young was not willing to permit these to fall into gentile hands. From the Humboldt River to Carson Valley were a few settlement sites, some of which could be safely occupied without danger from Indian raids. Carson Valley was of greatest importance, and steps were taken to plant a colony there.

Gentiles were already ranging the mountains back of Carson

Valley; but they were gold-hunters, not farmers. John Reese was sent into the section in 1851. Three years later Apostle Orson Hyde, having closed the Iowa community, was set to strengthen and hold Carson Valley.

Orson Hyde went to the Carson mission with a probate judgeship from the legislature and with authority to establish Carson County. Although a man of force, Hyde was not tactful or tolerant, and the exclusiveness of his colony roused the opposition of the Gentiles. Carson-Valley Mormons did not like the wild and reckless ways of the outsiders and treated them accordingly. Feelings, about 1856, reached such a tension that hostilities seemed imminent. Hyde called for more settlers, but Young declined to send them. To avoid the prospect of open warfare the settlement was abandoned in 1857.

In 1851, the same year that John Reese took his stand in Carson Valley, a few Mormon families moved northward from Ogden to start the town of Willard. Other families started Brigham City. These communities and others near by formed the nucleus of Boxelder County, organized in 1856. This county encircled the northern half of Salt Lake and bordered on Oregon.[12]

South of Boxelder County, enveloping the southern half of Salt Lake, was Tooele County. While few emigrant trains went this way, the overland route for the mail and stage coaches circled the south shore of the lake, at which point were two or three meadows occupied by a few Mormon families. These in 1853, owing to danger from Indian raids, joined together and formed Grantsville, a walled town of two hundred and fifteen persons.

Jules Remy visited Grantsville in 1855 after a mule and horseback journey of more than four hundred miles from Carson. Here he saw his first wholly Mormon community. He found most of the families living in the "fort," a walled-in inclosure typical of several Utah fortified towns. The wall was nine feet high, made of mud and brush, and tapered from six feet thick at the bottom to about two feet at the top. Usually the wall was built by tamping layer upon layer of clay and brush into wooden forms. Often, when other lumber was not available, the sideboards of the wagons were used. In the Grantsville wall there were two gates, one the entrance and the other the exit for the road. Few of these defenses can be found in Utah today.

Remy was greatly disappointed with his first sight of a frontier Mormon settlement. He wrote that the houses were

> so mean as scarcely to give the idea of comfort. They consist of a ground floor with a loft over it, and are built of the trunks of trees laid one upon another, and plastered together with mud. Seventy-five families live in these small, low and obscure huts. We noticed a great number of children, apparently in full health. The impression of the men is stupid and coarse, that of the women is less common and less unpleasant.[13]

While Grantsville was never attacked by Indians, perhaps because of the fort, the Indians were bothersome. They were members of the Gosiutes, a lowly half-naked tribe, subsisting so near the animal stage that they scarcely aroused pity. The usual appeals to Indians were quite out of the question with them.

How much of a problem the Indians were to these settlements is illustrated in the case of Grantsville, where the Saints possibly expended more labor building a wall around their village than building their homes. The Indians in that vicinity offered an extreme example of native incapacity to rise above the primitive savage level. They did not, probably would not, and possibly could not, respond to the teachings of industry which the Mormons endeavored to impart.

Every Mormon community met with frustration in attempting to carry out Brigham Young's policy of enlightened Indian relations. In pursuance of this policy the Mormons stopped the Indian slave trade. Tribes had been in the habit of staging raids one against another solely for the purpose of capturing children for sale. Sometimes these little captives were dragged around for weeks, bound with thongs by day and tied to stakes at night, until many perished of hunger and exhaustion.[14]

The Utah legislature on March 7, 1852, passed a law which gave authority to probate judges to take in charge Indian women or children prisoners found in possession of Indians or traders. These would be indentured to "suitable" persons to be reared and educated. Children so disposed of by the courts were invariably assigned to "suitable" Mormons.

Whereas the antislavery law of 1852 was passed for the protection of the Indians, it proved to be offensive to them, which added to the already growing Indian problem faced by the settlers. The raiding tribes came to the Mormons saying: "You won't let the Mexican traders buy children from us. *You* must buy them." The Mormons answered: "It is not right to steal children and sell them." To the Indians this talk and advice was foolishness.

Brigham Young's Indian policy was justified by him on practical grounds. "It is cheaper," he said, "to feed the Indians than to fight them." He argued that the government policy of sending out units of the army to slaughter Indians indiscriminately in punishment for uprisings would incite the natives to retaliate. Had the Mormons followed such a policy, many of the small communities could not have been established. Many Mormons caught away from their communities would have been ambushed. Some of the settlers were killed; but the toll would have been greater had the Mormons followed a less tolerant policy, and a great many more Indians would have been killed.[15]

Young did not favor the government policy of keeping the Indians pacified by an occasional distribution of presents. He wrote to the Commissioner of Indian Affairs on March 30, 1853, reporting on uprisings against the settlers: "I, however, reiterate my former opinion that settlement would be far more productive of good, and better subserve the interests and purposes of the government than a military post. . . . ."

The Indians were frequently between two fires in the quarrels between Mormons and Gentiles. By both groups they were being dispossessed of their hunting grounds and game, and it made little material difference whether they were pushed back without mercy by the Gentiles or gently by the Mormons.

Around the settlements south of Utah Lake the communities faced an Indian problem which led to conflict. The Indians

INDIAN SHELTERS

Originally the Indians made them of brush; later they got tents from the white man. *Above*, wi-ki-up near Silver Reef, Utah, about twenty miles from St. George. *Below*, winter scene near Kanosh in central Utah. From photographs taken about 1883.

there did not starve, as some did in the deserts west of Great Salt Lake, where they were driven from the springs and streams by the gentile emigrant companies.

Indian tribes to the north and west of the Salt Lake Valley settlements had considerable association with the "mountain men," some of whom had Indian wives. Few of these men were friendly with the Mormons. Occasionally these "mountain men" joined the Indians in raids on gentile emigrant companies and freight trains. Reports got abroad that the white men associated with the Indians were Mormons, and these reports received wide acceptance.

Along the Overland Trail from Salt Lake to Carson Valley there were raids on emigrant trains by bands of outlaw whites, also alleged to be Mormons. In some cases the white men were associated with Indians in these robbing assaults, which frequently resulted in the murder of men, women, and children.

Major Jacob H. Holeman arrived in Utah early in 1852 to serve as Indian agent under Governor Young. He criticized Young and his Indian policy to the Commissioner of Indian Affairs.[16] On May 2, 1852, Holeman reported that information had come to his attention about a Mormon in Carson Valley who was leading a group of robbers, including whites and Indians. This man had written to a Mormon named Williams telling him that Mormon wagon trains would not be molested by his band but that they should identify themselves by painting the horns of their oxen red.

On May 8 Holeman wrote again to the commissioner, reporting that his first information was incorrect. Williams had received the letter, but it had been sent by a "notorious character by the name of Reading, and although he was once a member of the Mormon Church, he is now held by them in utter contempt, and looked upon as a great scoundrel, but in consequence of some act of friendship which was shown him by Williams previously, he has given him his warning."

Holeman confirmed the reports that some of the raids on the emigrant companies were led by white men. "The WHITE Indians, I apprehend, are much more dangerous than the RED."

He mentioned the "renegades, deserters and thieves who have had to fly from justice in California."

Reports continued to circulate along the trail that the Mormons were dangerous people, that they would kill the men of an emigrant train in order to capture their women. Holeman got reports from both sides—Mormons blaming the Gentiles, and Gentiles accusing the Mormons—each claiming that the other used the Indians as a screen.

Early in 1852, Holeman made a quick trip from Salt Lake City to Carson and back. He wrote to the commissioner on June 28 that certain white men in the emigrant trains had been in the habit of shooting Indians, or shooting at them, without provocation. Two months later Holeman wrote to the commissioner about the character of some of the emigrant companies bound for California. Some companies were badly led and poorly disciplined. There were frequent quarrels and occasional killings.[17]

William A. Hickman, known to the Gentiles as "the Danite chief of Utah," made a trip about 1854 to the California gold fields. He started in company with a few Mormons, but in northern Utah they joined forces with a number of gentile men waiting for reinforcements before crossing the desert to Carson. Altogether, the company included 42 men, 6 of whom had their families along. Hickman, because of his reputation as a scout and Indian fighter, was named captain.

Other men joined Hickman's company, until the number totaled 64. He described the men as "a first rate set of fellows." After about four hundred miles of travel, the company came upon the scene of a massacre, recently perpetrated. Around the ashes of the burned wagons they found the "skeletons of men, women and children, their long and beautiful hair hanging on the brush, and sometimes a head with as beautiful locks of hair as I ever saw. . . . . The wolves had eaten the flesh off their bones. . . . . They had been scalped."

Soon thereafter Hickman's company met a number of emigrants retreating after having given the Indians battle and losing several men. Three days later the Indians fell on Hickman's party, but the attack was no surprise. "The train halted; twenty-five of my men in less than a minute had their guns, about half of us mounted our horses, the balance on foot, and instead of waiting for them to circle and fight, we went for them." Unprepared for attack, the Indians scattered in all directions. Two of the company were wounded, but none were killed. More than thirty Indians were slain, and some of them had on their persons the dried scalps of whites they had slain.[18]

While the Indians from 1850 through 1853 were causing such trouble along the Overland Trail, the tribes of central Utah were committing depredations on the settlers. This was known as the "Walker War," for the militant Chief Walker, who was the leader. Governor Young called out the Nauvoo Legion. He had the armed forces move to and fro from one settlement to another, without attempting to hunt down the Indians or harass them. These tactics finally had the desired effect. The show of force stirred in the Indians "a strong desire to be at peace."[19] After the parade of the legionnaires between the settlements Brigham Young personally went to Manti, two hundred miles from Salt Lake City, for a peace conference. One issue was the slave trade, which the Mormons had stopped. The Indians demanded, without effect, that the Mormons should buy their captive children and furnish them with horses guns, and ammunition, as did the Mexican traders.[20]

The Pahvantes, a tribe near Fillmore, headed by Chief Kanosh, had not taken part in the depredations of Walker and his brother, Arapeen. Kanosh accepted the Mormon plan; and his Indians, under church guidance, were trying to farm. They did have trouble with some gentile companies passing through during the first week in October, 1853. These companies—the first led by a Colonel Hollister, the second by Captain Tom Hildreth, and the third by Dr. Thomas Flint—were driving herds of sheep and cattle to southern California. Pahvante Indians visited the camps to beg and were fed; but in Hildreth's company there was trouble, which resulted in the death of a white man and an Indian. Two Indians were wounded.[21]

Later in October, Captain John W. Gunnison, in charge of a

unit of the United States Topographical Survey, was in the same locality, surveying a route for the proposed Central Pacific Railroad. Three years earlier Gunnison had been a member of the party of engineers under Captain Howard Stansbury, who surveyed the Great Salt Lake Basin. Gunnison, like Stansbury, bore a good reputation among the Mormons. Residents of Fillmore told Gunnison of the incident between the Indians and Hildreth's company. He expressed the opinion that his relations with the Indians had been friendly and that his party would be safe.

On October 28 a number of Pahvante, to even the score for the Hildreth incident, attacked Gunnison's camp, killing him and seven of his men. The survivors escaped to Fillmore, leaving behind their camp equipment, instruments and records, and their extra horses. Mormons did not reach the spot until about four days after the event. They found the bodies of the victims eaten by wild beasts and the bones scattered. They brought in the property and the remains and then set about to collect from the Indians all the equipment and horses that could be located.[22]

The Gunnison murder brought down upon the Mormons a flood of criticism. The murdered men were employees, and, some of them, officers of the United States government. The offending Indians belonged to the one tribe in Utah that maintained friendly relations with the Mormons. There was this serious question: Since the Mormons could find the killers, to recover from them all stolen records, instruments, and other items of equipment, why had they not taken action to punish them?

The settlers understood the Indian side of the case. Relatives and friends of the Indian who had been killed by Hildreth's company had sworn to get revenge. Chief Kanosh advised against it, but they would not heed. The tribal tradition prevailed. The "Mericats," not the Mormons, had committed the offense; and they would take toll from the first "Americans" to come within gunshot. That happened to be Captain Gunnison's party. They trusted the Mormons, and for that reason the Mormons took no action against them. Had the settlers followed any other course, the result would have been more bloodshed.

For this reason no action was taken on the Gunnison case until two years later. Colonel E. J. Steptoe arrived in Utah in August, 1854, with a detachment of soldiers. One of his assignments was to apprehend and bring to trial the murderers of Gunnison. Everyone knew, or suspected, that he also had a political assignment, to become governor at the end of Young's term of office. Steptoe did not get around to catching the Indians until the next spring. They were brought to trial in April, 1855. Of the five Indians brought to trial, three were found guilty of manslaughter and given prison terms of three years each. The trial before Chief Justice John F. Kinney, gentile friend of the Mormons, was described by Steptoe as abortive. The Indians later escaped.

Outsiders, then and later, tried to link the church leaders to the Gunnison case. Public opinion against Brigham Young had been rising since 1852, when he publicly announced that polygamy was an admitted doctrine of the church. Around this issue public sentiment was beginning to crystallize. Previously the Saints responded with straight-faced denials to all charges,[23] but on August 29, 1852, the church sent out one hundred and nine missionaries to teach the Doctrine.

It was now claimed that Smith had recorded the polygamy revelation in 1843; but it was learned later that the prophet had taken his first plural wife in 1841. How the church carried on during those years without many internal conflicts has not been reported, but the issue never came into the open. Priesthood control was so all-embracing that polygamy was taken in the same stride as other mandates from heaven.

When H. H. Bancroft, author of a *History of Utah*, a church-sponsored book, was visiting Utah in 1880, he tried to learn what Mormon women thought about polygamy. He asked Wife No. 1 of a leading apostle how she adapted herself to the celestial principle. The woman answered:

> I went into the cellar and prayed, but it seemed that the more I prayed, the more my feelings became wrought up. But I did not give up. I stayed there. First I'd weep; then I'd rage in anger and then I'd pray. So I struggled until

I was about exhausted. When I was about to give up the effort a great calm settled on my soul. Then I knew that polygamy was a true principle of the Lord.

In such mood this good wife approached her apostle-husband and gave her consent for him to enter polygamy. That finished, her weakness took possession of her. She said to him: "I know I will not be able to control myself. If I see any of your children running around, I'll feel like wringing their necks." But she overcame this attitude and eventually became mother superior to all the children of all her husband's other wives.

The public announcement of polygamy in 1852 placed the church in a new light before the world. It made a difference in Mormon-gentile relations. Polygamists thereafter openly claimed their plural wives—not only in Utah, but in outlying places.

It may then be said that by the end of 1853 the newly established Territory of Utah, what with Indian troubles and polygamy, had begun its political history as a commonwealth of ill-repute. The Saints were dedicated to a cause and a course bound to bring them in conflict with the general government. And, whereas the organic act placed local government under slight federal surveillance, there was no way in which the federal authorities could exercise that control without collision with the church.

As in other territories, the president held the power of appointing certain officers of the territory. As elsewhere, some of these appointees were local men, and some were sent in from the older places. That meant the appointment of some Gentiles to official posts in Utah, some of whom would be objectionable. If they were acceptable to the Mormons, they could not be to the Gentiles; and the opposite would also be true.

President Millard Fillmore, considering the pressure on him from political office-seekers, seems to have tried to be fair with the Mormons in making the first Utah appointments. He named Brigham Young governor, a courageous selection, considering the opposition to Young. Two of the three judges were Gentiles; the third, a Mormon in good standing. The secretary of state, Broghton D. Harris of Vermont, a Gentile, was intrusted with $24,000 of federal funds to pay the cost of the first Utah legislature. The two law-enforcing officers, the attorney-general and the marshal, were Mormons. Still the church was not satisfied.

The legislature convened on September 22, 1851. On September 24 a resolution was passed calling on Joseph L. Haywood, United States marshal, to take possession of all funds and documents in the keeping of Secretary of State Harris. Clearly the legislature had no authority to issue such an order to place Harris in custody "until he shall comply with the foregoing resolution." Harris appealed to the gentile chief justice of the territory, Lemuel C. Brandebury, for a restraining order, which was granted at once.[24]

On September 28, less than a week after the legislature had convened, four of the carpetbag Gentiles—Harris, Brocchus, Brandebury, and Indian Agent Day—departed for the East, taking with them the funds to pay the legislature. These "runaway officials" reported that they could not administer their offices because of priesthood domination.[25]

Utah, then, was left with four vacancies in the key offices. The Gentiles had been smoked out, and the Mormons sang:

> Though Brocchus and Brandebury
> And Harris, too, the Secretary
> Have gone. They went. And when they left us
> They only of themselves bereft us.

Brigham Young, as governor, appointed acting officials, high church brethren, to replace the runaways. President Fillmore, harassed with the coming election, did not get around to appointing new officials for Utah until August, 1852. In the meantime, without benefit of federal funds, Brother Brigham and his brethren continued to govern as if Utah were the state of Deseret.

The territorial legislature convened again on January 5, 1852, without the gentile officials. In his message Governor Young planted in a sentence this cryptic array of words, often quoted against him: "Free, sovereign and independent government." In that session they granted a charter for Fillmore City, which had been settled the year before, to be Utah's capital. They still had the $20,000 for the building of the capitol and the $5,000 for a library. Construction was started on Utah's statehouse.

UTAH'S FIRST CAPITOL

Built at Fillmore, near central Utah, from funds appropriated by Congress and from supplementary funds from the territorial legislature. The legislature met here in 1855 and again in 1856. It was reported by one gentile visitor that when the Mormon lawmakers were in session they represented an average of four wives each.

In place of Harris as secretary of state, Benjamin G. Ferris was named. His stay in Utah was brief, only long enough to gather material for a book, which has been described as "a semi-charitable history of the Mormons."[26] Lazarus H. Reed, of New York, was named chief justice; Leonidas Shaver, associate justice. These appointees arrived in the autumn of 1852. They were moderate men, who managed to hold their jobs without raising issues.

The year that Utah was without gentile federal officials was a busy one for the Saints. It was during this period, when Mormons were in full control, that polygamy was publicly proclaimed. It was the period of new impetus to the missionary program. Church leaders realized that the quiet would not last. The federal gentiles would come again, and soon.

Also, during this year of relative quiet the program of domestic industry got under way. The principal reason for this development was the presence among the new Mormon converts of many craftsmen and industrial mechanics. There was need for the things they could produce. Brigham Young wrote in the *Deseret News* for December 25, 1852, of pottery, which they were getting and needed badly; of leather works starting up; of the iron industry starting in Iron County; of a woolen factory already under way; and of a sugar factory about to be established.

This sugar factory was a daring enterprise. A corporation, the Deseret Manufacturing Company, had been formed with a capital stock of $50,000. The machinery was purchased in England for $12,500. It was landed at New Orleans, where an import duty of $5,000 had to be paid. It was taken up the Mississippi and Missouri rivers to Leavenworth, where it was loaded on forty special "sugar wagons," drawn by two hundred yoke of oxen. It required five months to drag this heavy equipment to Salt Lake Valley. In 1853 the plant was ready to make sugar out of beets. The attempt was a failure, but the idea did not die. The experimenting went ahead, and years later there developed from it one of Utah's most profitable industries.[27]

NOTES

1. "L.D.S. Journal History," March 31, 1850, letter from John M. Bernhisel to the first presidency.

2. *Ibid.*, March 5, 1850, letter from John M. Bernhisel to the first presidency. This letter asked for advice as to whether Deseret's application should be withdrawn if statehood could not be secured.

3. The resolution was published in the *Deseret News*, September 14, 1850.

4. Letter from Wilford Woodruff to Orson Pratt in England, dated January 26, 1850 (*Millennial Star*, XII, 75): "All parties have now ceased ridiculing the idea of dissolving

the American Union, but the two great parties, North and South, are rushing into it with all possible speed." In the "L.D.S. Journal History," July 7, 1850, a letter written on this day by Babbitt to Brigham Young indicated that President Taylor was opposed to any separate government for the Mormons. He did not think they had the ability to govern themselves.

5. The following areas in square miles were later taken from Utah: to Colorado in 1861, 29,500 square miles; to Nebraska in 1861, what is part of Wyoming, 10,740 square miles; to Nevada in 1861, 73,574 square miles, and in 1864 and 1866 two slices totaling 18,326 square miles; to Wyoming in 1868, 3,580 square miles. No other state suffered so many raids on its territory. See Andrew L. Neff, *History of Utah*, p. 691.

6. On file in the office of the church historian are the returns of a census taken in 1856 showing in Utah 37,277 males and 39,058 females, a total of 76,335 persons.

7. "L.D.S. Journal History," November 20, 1850, letter from Brigham Young to Dr. John M. Bernhisel in Washington. Young said that the natural vegetation had been reduced in the region and that not much was left "save the naked rocks and soil, naked Indians and wolves. The first two we can use to good advantage; the last two are annoying and destructive to property and peace, by night and day; and while we are trying to shoot, trap and poison the wolves on the one hand, the Indians come and drive off, butcher our cattle, steal our corn on the other, which leaves us little time between the wolves and Indians to fence and cultivate our farms. . . . ." He wished the Indians well and that was the reason he proposed moving them to a place where they would have better hunting and fishing.

8. "History of Brigham Young," March 23, 1851. President Young indicated that twenty men had been called for this mission. "They were instructed by letter to select the site for a city or station, as a nucleus for a settlement near the Cajon Pass, in the vicinity of the seacoast, for a continuation of the route already commenced from this place to the Pacific; to gather around them the Saints in California, to search out their route and establish, as far as possible, the best locations for stations between Iron County and California, in view of a mail route to the Pacific; to cultivate the olive and manufacture olive oil, and also to cultivate grapes, sugar cane, cotton and other desirable fruits and products; to obtain information concerning the Tehuantepec Route, or any other across the Isthmus, or a passage around Cape Horn with a view to gathering the Saints from Europe; to plant the standard of salvation in every country and kingdom, city and village on the Pacific and the world over as fast as God should give the ability."

9. Accounts of the San Bernardino colony are found in H. H. Bancroft, *History of California;* Z. S. Eldridge, *History of California;* L. A. Ingersol, *Ingersol's Century Annals*.

10. *Los Angeles Star*, May 31, 1851: "We learn that 150 Mormon families are at Cajon Pass, sixty miles south of this city, on their way from Deseret. The families, it is said, intend to settle in this valley, and make it their permanent home. We cannot yet give full credit to these statements, because they do not come to us authenticated, but if it is true that Mormons are coming in such numbers to settle among us, we shall, as good and industrious citizens, extend them a friendly welcome."

11. *Millennial Star* on November 3, 1855, reprinted an item from the *Southern Californian* regarding the Mormons at San Bernardino: "They propose to sell lots and farms at fair prices to those who desire them, and for this purpose have sent out their members to every portion of the State to preach the faith and represent their difficulties." However much people may differ on the subject of Mormonism, no umbrage can be taken against the settlers at San Bernardino as citizens and neighbors." The lots for sale, of course, were for Mormons only. It was their determination to keep others out that helped start trouble.

12. "Inventory of the Archives of Boxelder County," by the Historical Records Survey of the Utah W.P.A., contains a historical sketch of these settlements.

13. Jules Remy and Julius Brenchley, *A Journey to Great Salt Lake City*, I, 177. Remy was a friendly observer who reported on many phases of Mormon frontier life. Also see "Inventory of the Archives of Tooele County," Historical Records Survey, Utah W.P.A.

14. Daniel W. Jones, *Forty Years among the Indians*, pp. 52–53, reports on some experiences with this slave trade. He related a story about the anger of Arapeen, brother of Chief Walker, because the Mormons would not buy captive children in his possession. Arapeen would not release the captives. "Several of us were present when he took one of these children by the heels and dashed its brains out on the hard ground, after which he threw the body towards us, telling us we had no hearts, or we would have bought it and saved its life."

15. Brigham Young wrote the Commissioner of Indian Affairs, September 30, 1853, asking payment for losses due to Indian depredations. Letters to or from the commissioner are filed in the National Archives. His appeal for payment mentioned several lives lost, about four hundred cattle and some horses stolen, the cost of abandoning most small settlements, and the labor of building forts and standing guard. This request for federal aid was ignored.

16. In a letter to the Commissioner of Indian Affairs dated February 29, 1852, Holeman reported much destruction of life on the Overland Trail the previous season. He predicted a big emigration in the spring. He asked if he had authority to prevent Young from issuing permits to Mormons to trade with Indians. He made no mention of gentile traders who had been active in the slave trade.

17. Holeman wrote a number of reports to the Commissioner of Indian Affairs. From his letter of June 28, 1852: "It is my painful duty to report to you, that from all the information I can get from whites and Indians, the great, and almost sole cause of all the difficulties, the destruction of life and property on this route is owing to the bad conduct of the whites who were the first to commence it; and in many instances the whites are the sole depredators of it. They manage to have it charged to the Indians."

On August 30, 1852, Holeman wrote: "There are a great many outbreaks and difficulties between the emigrants themselves; companies have quarreled, killed each other, and broken up, some from their bad conduct have been driven from their companies. Many of these are scattered over the road, without means, living on the charity of others. They also steal and commit other depredations, which they endeavor to lay upon the Indians."

18. William A. Hickman, *Brigham's Destroying Angel*, pp. 70–80. In connection with this journey across the desert Hickman also related the story of a company quarrel and killing which led to a hanging. It illustrates how each emigrating company, like a ship at sea, had to be its own law while crossing the desert, where there was no law. One man of the company, Watson, who had crossed that desert with Kit Carson years before, was killed by a man named Hensley. Watson was much liked; Hensley was a crank and bully. No action was taken at once, but Hickman detected that his company was tense. The day after the killing he had Hensley seized before he could draw his gun. Some men from another company camped near by were invited over to assist in the trial. Men from both companies were selected to the court. There were judge, attorneys, jury. The jury found Hensley guilty. He was given thirty minutes to say or write anything. He spent the time swearing, weeping, cursing this man and that, and promising to haunt all of them. They hanged him on the only tree that was near, then rolled him in a blanket and buried him at the foot of the tree. Some years later Hickman left the church and thereafter was hated by the Mormons as much as Gentiles dreaded him before. It is hard to believe that he had not been a killer for the Mormon cause; but

when he turned against them, Gentiles never brought him to trial. He died a natural death in Lander, Wyoming, in 1883.

19. Holeman wrote to the Commissioner of Indian Affairs on March 29, 1852, telling of the Nauvoo Legion drilling weekly. He reported that a commanding officer "has been heard to say that they were in the habit of drilling punctually while in Nauvoo, when they had but one state to oppose them, but now they have the whole United States, they should be properly drilled and equipped. Others say they do not fear the United States. They have neither respect for her or her citizens, and should they want assistance to defend themselves against the government they can easily get it from England."

20. Young stated in his report of June 28, 1853, to the Commissioner of Indian Affairs: "I told them we wished to do them good, and counseled them to raise their own children, and to refrain from stealing any from other tribes, and that ammunition sufficient for hunting would be traded to them for skins and peltry as soon as it could be produced or procured." Again Young made his plea that the Indians be placed on reservations and be paid annuities. Otherwise the Indians either would "fade rapidly from the earth by starvation and neglect, or on the other [hand] be induced to plunder our citizens, or become an onerous burden to our sparse population. . . . ." No response was received to this plea.

21. Diary of Dr. Thomas Flint, *Annual Publications of the Historical Society of Southern California*. Flint wrote on October 7, 1853: "Took a late and leisurely start and drove to Corn Creek or Willow Flat, 4 miles. As Mr. Burnap and I were selecting a place for camp an Indian came up and showed us water and feed. He soon left us and returning brought in Capt. Connuse and party of about a dozen Indians. Next move they sent for their squaws. All of whom we out of friendship had to feed. This same party had killed one of Hildreth's men who was trying to disarm the Captain. Hildreth's men in turn killed an Indian and wounded two, camped near the Indian *wickeups*." Hildreth was traveling a day or two ahead. The Indians had not yet taken the vow of vengeance. "Connuse" may have been Kanosh.

22. Governor Young's report, a long and convincing document, was written to the Commissioner of Indian Affairs on November 30, 1853. It covered the details of the massacre and the events before the following. The bodies had been so eaten and torn by animals that it was not possible to identify even the bones. One of the victims was a Mormon from Manti, William Potter—a fact which would not support the story that Mormons had been active behind the scenes. Young reported that Gunnison had refused to take Potter's advice to camp in an open space easily guarded but had camped in a sheltered place easily attacked. Young also criticized Captain Morris for running away when he could have returned from Fillmore and recovered the bodies. Later Morris refused to approve the bill presented by the men who spent several days finding the bodies and collecting the property.

23. "L.D.S. Journal History," August 29, 1852, contains a report on the conference. The revelation claimed to have been written by Prophet Joseph on July 12, 1843, is found in Section 132 of the Doctrine and Covenants.

24. The clash began on September 8, 1851, when Brocchus was invited to speak to the Saints at a conference in Salt Lake City. In the course of this speech he said that he had a request from the Washington Memorial Association for a stone from Utah to be placed in the Washington Monument. The stone was later sent in the name of the "State of Deseret" and was placed in the monument, where it still may be seen. Brocchus then proceeded to lecture the Saints on morals and patriotism. Brother Brigham rose after him and said that the judge was "either profoundly ignorant or wilfully wicked." He said that if discussion were permitted it might result in "a pulling of hair or a cutting of throats." He then damned the rascals "who administer the government."

The stone for the monument had been authorized by the legislature months earlier, on February 12, 1851 (Neff, *op. cit.*, p. 171).

25. The runaway officers had difficulty collecting their pay when they got to Washington. Brocchus on July 2, 1858, wrote to President Buchanan that the women of Utah "are held in a state of miserable bondage, and are treated as slaves rather than wives." Correspondence is found in the Utah territorial papers at the National Archives.

26. Ferris and his wife boarded in a Mormon home. His book, *Utah and the Mormons*, was published in 1854. *Mormons at Home*, by Mrs. Benjamin G. Ferris, was published in 1856. It was largely a collection of letters which she wrote while in Utah.

27. "The Romance of Sugar" is told by Neff (*op. cit.*, pp. 292–301), who indicates that the general interest in manufacturing gained impetus from this unsuccessful effort, which cost five years of labor and about $100,000 cash outlay.

CHAPTER VI

ZION GIRDS FOR THE BATTLE

IN MORMON history the period from about 1850 to 1857 stands out distinctly as one of industrious preparation, diligent organization, persistent expansion, and unrelenting morale-building. During this period five separate appeals were made for statehood for Deseret; in 1850, 1852, 1853, and again in 1854 memorials were sent by the legislature of Utah to Congress. In 1856 a constitutional convention was held and a memorial prepared. This memorial, because of the hostility in Washington, was not presented to Congress.

This urgent desire of the Mormons for statehood was based upon the fears of church leaders for the future of Utah's self-government. Carpetbag officials would surely come to rule them roughly, and restrictive legislation might be passed to harass them. Could Utah attain statehood before the onslaught of legally established opposition, much of the impending persecution might be averted.

The struggle for political independence started with the church at the zenith of political control and ended with the church all but defeated. Between 1850 and 1857, however, the church was in a distinctly unique position. Weak in numbers, poor in material resources, and without sufficient tools or equipment, Zion was yet strong in spiritual unity.

By the summer of 1857, after a decade in their mountain valleys, the Mormons had already established the more important communities of Utah, and brave attempts had been made to push the frontier to more remote places—into Oregon, into Carson Valley, and into southern California.

The United States census of 1850 reported for Deseret, 11,330 persons, but the leaders claimed a greater number. In 1853, when statehood was again sought, Orson Pratt, rated by the

Mormons a scientist and philosopher, estimated 30,000 persons in Utah. The Gentiles estimated a maximum of 25,000 for that year.

In 1856 the political leaders of Utah, their previous petitions to Congress having been ignored, proceeded to call a constitutional convention. Delegates met at Salt Lake City from March 17 to 27.[1] Prior to this convention the legislature caused a census to be taken, about which we have little information except the totals, sworn to on March 1, 1856, as "a true estimate," by Census Agent Leonard W. Hardy. This census, as

Counties	Males	Females	Total
Salt Lake	12,730	13,074	25,804
Utah	6,951	7,614	14,565
Davis	4,765	4,575	9,340
Weber	3,486	3,585	7,071
Iron	2,474	2,943	5,417
Tooele	1,315	1,673	2,988
Eleven other counties	5,556	5,594	11,150
Total	37,277	39,058	76,335

shown in the accompanying table, had the appearance of validity, if the absence of round numbers is any criterion.

The 76,335 population claimed for 1856 was probably double the true number. When church leaders sent a petition to Congress in 1849 asking for statehood, they secured signatures of the Saints in Iowa as well as in the Salt Lake Valley. Is it possible that in 1856 they prorated to the several counties the thousands of Saints then in Europe, most of whom would eventually be in Utah? The church historian has the record of this census.

In 1860 the United States census for Utah may have been a short count, since the counting was done by Gentiles. They found that year in Utah a total of 40,295 persons, which may not have been as much below as the 1856 census was over the real figure.

Whatever the true population figures may have been, church leaders tried every means to bring in more people each year.

Between 1851 and 1861 the church moved 21,195 persons from England. These included persons from other places who gathered in England for passage on chartered ships. Foreign emigrants for the year ending July, 1856, totaled 4,395 persons. The principal countries contributing to this influx were: England, 2,611; Wales, 667; Denmark, 505; and Scotland, 367.[2] Besides the foreign Saints gathered to Utah each year, there were others from points in the United States. Many of these formed small companies and came on their own initiative. Possibly the total emigration in that peak year, 1856, was between 4,000 and 5,000.

The distribution of emigrants after their arrival in the valley required careful home-finding and competent personal guidance. Quite a few were industrial workers from large cities. Many, however willing, were not qualified for the work of a frontier settlement. There are stories of cobblers who could not hitch their oxen, of millers who were baffled by the plow, and of musicians not able to wrangle cattle. Care had to be taken that no community received too great a portion of inexperienced persons. On the positive side, every effort had to be made to distribute fairly the mechanics—blacksmiths, masons, potters, and carpenters.[3]

Among the newcomers were many unattached women—widows, spinsters, and younger single women. We have heard how they were forced into marriage. It is possible that some of the leaders had their pick of the young, pretty emigrants; but it is probably not true that these women were forced to go to places against their will or to marry into polygamy against their wishes.[4]

Having among his new converts workers from such a variety of manufacturing industries, Brigham Young was encouraged in his plan to make of Zion a self-contained commonwealth. He prayed that the bars of their isolation should be raised high, so that the Saints would be forced to turn with diligence to manufacturing.[5] It was in keeping with this program that such effort was put forth to carry out the "Iron Mission." The mission failed, but the experiment illustrates how workers of different occupations were distributed so that their skills would be put to the greatest use.[6]

Brigham Young's strategy called for the possession of all land within reach before the Gentiles were tempted to compete with the Mormons in farming. The expansion program faced southward, across the deserts and mountains to southern California and to the sea. Expansion in this direction was thought to be safest from gentile interference, but it was blocked by the Gentiles in 1857.[7]

No movement for settlement north of the Utah boundary was initiated until 1855, because the hostility of the Bannock, Snake, and Shoshone tribes discouraged any plans. Oregon, which until 1863 included Idaho, was the trading ground of fur companies. Agricultural and herding communities had not been encouraged by the traders and other white men who lived among the Indians of the north. These "squaw men," or "free men," were generally bitter toward the Mormons because they had been excluded from trading with Indians in Utah.

Until 1855 the country north of the border had not attracted Brigham Young. "The farther we go north, the less good characteristics are connected with the valleys." This opinion was based neither on personal observation nor on responsible report, but the Saints believed Brother Brigham when belief served a purpose and until the church changed its policy.

A company of twenty-six men from the Ogden area, led by Thomas S. Smith of Ogden, ventured over the Oregon line and made their way a distance of three hundred and fifty miles northward to the Salmon River. Here they found a new kind of country, where grass was plenty and timber tall. They struck camp, set up a stockade, and called the place "Fort Limhi" (after a king in the Book of Mormon).

The second summer of the Salmon River settlement was encouraging to the missionaries. Some of the men returned to Utah for their families, and their reports were so optimistic that Brigham Young, with a party, visited the settlement during April and May, 1857.

It is not clear in what capacity Young visited that section of

Oregon territory, whether as head of his church or as governor. He went with one hundred and fifteen men, most of them members of Utah's militia, the Nauvoo Legion. Daniel H. Wells, head of the Legion, was in command. Also there were three apostles and Heber C. Kimball, all of them prominent in the political life of the Territory of Utah. It is known that Brigham Young tried to charge the cost of the trip to the Commission of Indian Affairs, but the bill was rejected because he had gone outside his territory to deal with tribes not under his supervision.[8]

In the interest of good Indian relations Brigham Young did have reason to meet with the chiefs of the north. Two years before his journey he had met with Chief Walker, that wily "Napoleon of the desert," with results that were satisfactory to both sides. Since that time, Walker had passed to his reward, and his brother, Chief Arapeen, had become leader of the Utah tribes. Arapeen accompanied Young on that expedition to Limhi, where they hoped to establish the same friendly understanding. He sat with Young in a council with the Bannock and Shoshone chiefs, and he testified that the Mormons were not bad people. A year later the tribes of the north came under gentile influence.[9]

Young's conference with Chief Walker in the spring of 1854 had been the beginning of his Indian program. He had journeyed to Nephi in Juab County as soon as he learned that Walker wished to see him. Walker was worried because he thought the Mormons wanted to kill him for his leadership of the recent hostilities.[10] However, when Young's party neared the Indian camp, word was sent to him that Walker was sad and would not come out of his wickiup. But Young went to Walker's tent. Walker asked Young to come back in a little while, perhaps then he would be in good spirits.

When Young returned, he learned that Walker was grieving because one of his children was sick.[11] He feared the child would die, in which event, he said, a white man would also have to die so that the child would have company.[12] Young took up the sick child, "administered to it," and went away. Later he returned to find the child improved. Walker was pleased and said that Young had the power of the Great Spirit. Walker then traded for horses, and a peace pact with the Mormons was made: but the Indian problem soon reappeared in other forms.

As superintendent of Indian affairs, Governor Young made out fairly well until 1855, when Dr. Garland Hurt arrived to serve as a subagent under his supervision. Like his gentile predecessor, Major Jacob Holeman, Hurt was unfriendly toward the Mormons, but he lacked Holeman's sense of fairness. Hurt was zealous, and he imagined some evil purpose behind even the most sincere Mormon approaches to the Indian problem.

Dr. Hurt misinterpreted the Mormon program for the Indians which was launched after the Walker War. Groups of men were sent to the various Indian tribes as missionaries. The expedition sent to the Salmon River in Oregon was in line with this program. A similar mission had been intrusted to Jacob Hamblin, who settled on the Santa Clara. At Las Vegas (then New Mexico, now Nevada), William Bringhurst attempted another mission. These missionaries were expected to work with the Indians and, by a policy of patience and kindness, teach them the arts of agriculture.

Except that the religion taught was different, the Mormon missions were not different from similar experiments carried on elsewhere by missionaries of other churches. Garland Hurt knew about such missionary efforts, but he viewed with alarm the same program when initiated by the Mormons.

It was at the April, 1855, conference of the church that these missionaries were designated. On May 2, Hurt wrote to the Commissioner of Indian Affairs charging that the real purpose of the missionaries was to prejudice the minds of the savages against all non-Mormons. He pleaded with the commissioner to warn all government officials and "other loyal citizens residing or sojourning in the Indian country" to be on the watch lest the missionaries should succeed in their diabolical purposes.

In fairness to Dr. Hurt, there was this element of truth in his report: the Mormons were making a strong effort to gain the friendship of all Indians with whom the settlers had to live.

The missions were established to win good will, so that settlements could be planted without warfare. If the Mormons did not secure the confidence of the Indians, these same Lamanites might be turned against them by the Gentiles.

Governor Young paid little attention to Dr. Hurt except to have him watched. Without supervision Dr. Hurt wandered from tribe to tribe, passing out presents and telling the Indians about patriotism. He spent $12,000 of the $20,000 allocated to the Utah agency. Three times during 1855 and 1856 the Commissioner of Indian Affairs reminded Hurt that he should limit himself to a reasonable share of the Utah allocation, leaving a proper amount for Young and other agents.

In his zeal to counteract the missionary program of the Mormons, Hurt planned to start several Indian farms in Utah, one of them on the Overland Trail. His plan differed from the Mormon program in two particulars. He would preach loyalty to the Great White Father rather than to Brigham Young. He would isolate the Indians on farms, whereas the Mormons would work with them and teach them by example until they could associate with them on equal terms.

Young once said: "If a white man steals, shoot him. If an Indian steals teach him better." He did not favor hunting down and killing Indians. He did not, for example, offer support to gentiles who wished to avenge Gunnison's murder. While regretting the affair, he took into consideration the mitigating circumstances. In that case the Mormons may have taken a hand in frustrating the effort to punish the killers. Three Indians were finally caught and sentenced to three years in prison, but all three escaped.[13] Since Mormon officials were holding them in custody, they could not have escaped if these officials wanted to keep them. There is no record that these officials tried to retake them, although it was known that they returned immediately to their tribe.

Gentile federal officials, a class of which Dr. Hurt was a typical specimen, either could not understand Mormon Indian policy or sincerely suspected some sinister motive behind it.

They continued to report the Mormon approach to the Indian problem as being out of harmony with the policy of the federal government, if not inimical to it.

The same suspicion was directed to Brigham Young's doctrine of civil government. He would have the Saints govern themselves by the same direct rules that he offered for dealing with Indians. In his annual message of December 13, 1853, he proposed such a simple code for Utah. He said: "The greatest simplicity which can be attained in the formation of a code of laws, tends to lessen litigation. . . . . Strip a judge of justice of all the legal mists and fog which surround him in this day and age; leave him no nook or corner of precedent, or common law ambiguous enactments, the accumulation of the ages, wherein to shelter, and it is my opinion that unrighteous decisions would seldom be given."

Young's term as governor was due to terminate with the close of 1854. Even before the end of his first term Young had reason to fear about his reappointment. President Franklin Pierce was not friendly. Among the political job-seekers, however, there were apparently few applicants for Young's job.

There were reports that Colonel Steptoe came to Utah with a secret commission to replace Brigham Young as governor. Information about the president's purpose was transmitted by Dr. John M. Bernhisel, Utah's delegate in Congress, to Franklin D. Richards, on January 4, 1854. "The President finally declined," he wrote, "to reappoint Governor Young to the office he now holds. Lieutenant Steptoe is the appointee." Bernhisel added that the colonel was held in high esteem but that he doubted whether he would accept the assignment.

Although Colonel Steptoe arrived in Salt Lake City in August, 1854, he did not get around to the business of capturing Gunnison's murderers until the following spring. He remained in the valley and kept his troops there. Relations between the soldiers and the Mormons were reasonably cordial except when the soldiers became friendly with the Mormon women.[14]

Brigham Young, more or less outwardly resigned to the appointment of Colonel Steptoe, went to the colonel's quarters on

Christmas Day to pay a courtesy call. He found a wild party in progress. A number of Mormon women were present, making whoopee with the officers. There was drinking and singing. He rebuked the girls and sent them home. Perhaps the colonel was embarrassed. A few days later a petition was sent to the president of the United States asking that Brigham Young be reappointed. This petition was sent on the eve of the close of Young's first term. Mormons were much relieved when, later, Steptoe and his soldiers departed, after nearly ten months in Utah.

There may be no basis for the story that Colonel Steptoe had been placed in an embarrassing position by Brigham Young, because of which he signed the petition for Young's reappointment. Moreover, it may not be true that Brigham Young arranged to have the ladies present in the officers' quarters at the time he called. It may have been merely coincidental. In any case, the Lord seems to have been on Brother Brigham's side, and Brother Brigham was shrewd enough to make the most of a situation which may have put Colonel Steptoe at a disadvantage.[15]

During 1855 several new federal appointees took up their posts in Utah. Almon W. Babbitt replaced Benjamin G. Ferris as secretary of state. Zarubbabel Snow, associate justice, was replaced by former Mormon, George P. Stiles. Neither Babbitt nor Stiles was popular. The friendly associate justice, Leonidas Shaver, who died at Salt Lake City in June, 1855, was succeeded by the soon-to-be-hated W. W. Drummond. Late in 1854 John F. Kinney, of Iowa, arrived in Utah to take the post of chief justice, vacated by the resignation of Lazarus H. Reed.

This was the line-up of Young's official family in 1855: Babbitt and Stiles, apostate Mormons; Drummond, a Gentile opposed to the Mormons; Hurt, whose status as Mormon-hater has already been described; and Kinney, a Gentile friendly to the Mormons. It has been reported that when Kinney came to Utah he had a wagonload of goods which he managed to sell at a good profit. Later he started a boarding house to which the Mormons sent customers. Brigham Young's problem was one of running the government his way with the help of these gentlemen if their co-operation could be had and, if not, in spite of their opposition.

Judge Drummond teamed up with Judge Stiles in pushing a lively attempt to dispute the jurisdiction of the probate courts. He finally left Utah in a huff and a fright, reporting there was no law in the territory save Brigham Young. The Mormons made an issue of Drummond's private life. It was charged that he left his family in Illinois and brought a harlot with him to Utah. They were furious because he permitted this alleged wife to sit on the bench beside him.

As an added complication, in July, 1855, David H. Burr, appointed surveyor-general for Utah, arrived in Salt Lake City to begin the survey of the occupied areas. Whether the Mormons were opposed to the survey or did not like Burr is not known. At any rate, the survey met with considerable opposition. Perhaps the difficulties arose because Burr openly criticized the Utah legislative practice of granting monopoly charters to individuals for choice timber and grazing lands.

On August 30, 1856, General Burr wrote to his chief, Thomas A. Hendricks, Commissioner of the General Land Office in Washington, that one of his deputies, a Mr. Troskolowski, had been "assaulted and severely beaten by three men under the direction of one Hickman, a noted member of the so-called 'Danite band.'" The beating had been administered, it was alleged, by order of higher-ups in the church.[16]

Burr tried without effect to get the Utah civil authorities to take action against the offenders. He was told that the beating was probably deserved because the men of Burr's party had been "talking and railing against their religion." He concluded: "We Gentiles feel that we cannot rely upon the laws for protection and are permitted to live here at the pleasure of the rulers."

A month later Burr wrote another letter to Hendricks, reporting that he had made a contract with a man named Mogo to survey Sanpete Valley. When Mogo got ready to leave the city, he found that ten of his oxen had been stolen. "Suspicion falls on a noted character who stands high in the councils of the

Church, but to convict or punish him would be impossible, and it is but another instance that the laws afford no protection to life or property." Burr advised that two persons who could testify feared to talk lest their lives should be in danger.

Burr did not indicate what, if any, reasons the Mormons had for their opposition to him. Had he cared to search for the answer, he would have found it in their feelings of insecurity about the probable consequences of the land survey. Would the survey result in extinguishing the Indian rights and throw the land open for purchase? Would outsiders buy land beside them or even have prior purchase claim on the land occupied by them? Would the new survey result in a different division of the land from that then in effect in all the villages? These were practical worries not mentioned by the surveyor-general.[17]

Whether Burr was motivated by political considerations is not clear, but his opposition to the timber, grazing, and millsite grants by the legislature reflected the views of Gentiles in Utah. By these grants the Mormons were able to exclude Gentiles from using various natural resources which were public property.

Burr reported to Hendricks on February 15, 1857, that because of his opposition to legislative grants he had been threatened by Acting District Attorney Hosea Stout and Territorial Marshal Alexander McRay. "They did not deny the truth of the charges I had made, but asserted the *right* of doing what they did, stating that *the country was theirs*, that they would not permit this interference with their rights, and this writing of letters about them would be put a stop to."

Burr also critized the Mormon doctrine of consecration of individual property, including land, to Brigham Young as trustee in trust for the church. It was thought that such consecration would secure the land against federal encroachment in the event of the survey later presenting a problem of ownership.[18]

The next available letter by Burr to the Commissioner of the General Land Office was dated March 28, 1857. He reported that his friends were pleading with him to leave for his safety but that he would stay at his post, adding that, even if he wished to leave, he could not, because snow was deep in the mountains. He said that lately several houses of Gentiles had been pulled down by rowdies. All were anxious for the mail to get through. "If it should bring us no tidings of protection from the United States every Gentile officer may be compelled to leave the Territory."

Burr was disliked, and the tense hostility against him could not have continued long without some overt expression. The final letter from Burr to Hendricks was written at Washington on June 11, 1857. He had been able to leave Utah and expressed gratitude that no harm had befallen him. "Demonstrations of mob violence and inflamatory [*sic*] appeals by the leaders to the worst feelings of the people were frequently made."

Conditions reported by General Burr reflected the spirit of the "Reformation," called by Roberts a period of "much-needed moral and spiritual awakening." It might be described also as a searching religious inventory. In the midst of building their industries, speeding up the settlement program, bringing in more emigrants, and establishing peaceful relations with the Indians the leaders became concerned with the religious integrity of the people.

Church leaders felt the need of revival and reform. Some Saints were thought to be too friendly with the Gentiles. Some were complaining about the hard way of life in Zion and talked of going to Oregon or California. There were complaints about immorality, gambling, and of drunkenness in Zion. These conditions caused Jedediah M. Grant, second counselor to Brigham Young, to raise a hue and cry about Zion's virtue.

On Saturday, September 13, Grant was scheduled to speak to the Saints at Kaysville. It was this speech that touched off the great drive for pentecostal revival which was carried with grim intensity to such extremes that it threatened to get out of control.

The "Reformation" was an occasion for every Saint to purge his soul and to be rebaptized, to rededicate himself to the church. The leaders, possibly sensing tense times ahead, set out to bring about a unity which no persecution from without could shake. Also, the issue of polygamy was involved. Some of the women were not accepting the doctrine "in the right spirit."

The *Deseret News* for September 21, 1856, reported a speech by Jedediah M. Grant. He said: "We have women here who like everything but the Celestial Law of God; and if they could, would break asunder the cable of the Church of Christ; there is scarcely a mother in Israel but would do it this day." Brigham Young said on the same occasion, speaking to the women: "I am going to give you from this time to the 6th of October next for reflection, that you may determine whether you wish to stay with your husbands or not, and then I am going to set every woman at liberty and say to them, '*Now go your way, my women with the rest; go your way*. . . . . I will not have them about me. I will go to heaven alone rather than have scratching and fighting around me."

A speech by Heber C. Kimball was reported in the *Deseret News* for November 9, 1856. He declared that no wife or child of his had a right to rebel. "It is the duty of a woman to be obedient to her husband, and unless she is, I would not give a damn for all her queenly right and authority, nor for her either."

Sinners had to confess; Saints had to stand up and be counted. Those who would do neither were cast out of the church. Thousands were rebaptized.[19] Repentant backsliders confessed and begged forgiveness of the congregations. There were allegations that many were dragged from their homes and beaten and their property destroyed. Burr did not exaggerate. Some of the Gentiles were in danger.

An example of reformation zeal was reported in a letter sent by Dr. Garland Hurt, sometime in the autumn of 1856, to Brigham Young. With General Burr and other members of the land survey he had visited central Utah. They were on their way to Corn Creek, near Fillmore, to visit the government farm of the Pahvante tribe. As they approached the farm, they noticed two men riding full speed ahead of them. They noticed also, on reaching the farm, that some Indians were riding away in the opposite direction. Later they learned that the riders were Mormons going to warn the Indians that the "Americans were coming to their camp to arrest the murderers of Captain Gunnison." As previously mentioned, some of the Indians of this tribe had been tried and convicted for the murder of Gunnison, but they escaped and were still at large.

Hurt and his party returned to Fillmore and stopped during the evening at the home of a Mr. Peter Robison. In the course of the evening a Mr. Edwin Pugh, a neighbor, stepped in and invited two young men of the party to visit at his house. No sooner did they enter Pugh's house than some persons began to stone the place. "Mr. Pugh ran out and asked what they meant. They asked what he was doing with those damned Americans about his house." Apparently the two men visiting with Mr. Pugh, although working for Hurt or Burr, were not "Americans," but Mormons. Pugh so stated. The voices of the attackers responded from the darkness: "They are no better than Americans, or they would not be with them."[20]

The incident reported by Hurt reflected the prevailing attitude of the Saints toward the Gentiles. There were other reports of stoning at night the houses of Gentiles and apostates. Thus Utah Mormons in 1856 were conducting themselves like Missouri Gentiles in 1833, when Mormon houses were stoned in Jackson County.

Brigham Young on September 21, 1856, made a speech upon which enemies of the church built a harsh case. He said there were some sins that could not be expiated by repentance; that, if sinners guilty of such acts could see their true condition, "they would be perfectly willing to have their blood spilt upon the ground, that the smoke thereof might ascend to heaven as an offering for their sins."[21] Thus the idea got around that some sinners could only be saved by spilling their blood. As the idea spread, the stories began to travel that men had been slain; that "destroying angels" went about at night on their missions of death, thus to save the souls of Saints who had sinned. That was "blood atonement."

In August, 1856, Almon W. Babbitt, secretary of state for Utah, was on his way from Omaha with a load of supplies for the territorial offices. He and two of the party were killed by Indians near Fort Laramie. It was charged that Babbitt was a marked man, that he had been killed by "destroying angels." There was no basis in fact for the charge, but it served to link his death with the atonement mania.[22]

In March, 1857, three men were killed in Springville: W. R.

Parish; Benson Parish, his son; and G. G. Potter. The Parish family, against advice of counsel, planned to leave for California. Priesthood leaders, it was alleged, thought such a migration would do them no good and might be an evil example for others. Two years later Associate Justice John Cradlebaugh attempted to apprehend the murderers of the Springville brethren. Mormon leaders bitterly opposed him and denied all the allegations, but the fact remains that the Mormons in charge of the local government did nothing to find the murderers.

When the "Reformation" is viewed in relation to its social antecedents, it turns out to have a logical evolution. Zion, from 1850 to 1857, was girding itself for a great struggle—a struggle for statehood, for population increase, for economic self-sufficiency. The ordeal of faith was being faced every day, with great zeal by some, casually by others. Challenging times were ahead. A toning-up was needed. Here it was: a revival to search the hearts of all, to fortify the strong, to hearten the weak, and to purge the wicked.

The ordeal of faith was severely applied in the sacrifices demanded to bring the emigrants over the plains and mountains to Zion. It was the burden of the missionaries seeking new converts to stimulate also in the heart of every convert a burning desire to migrate. The missionaries did the job so well that many of the older converts, obsessed with the idea of the "gathering," would pray that, if they might not live in "the Valley," their bones at least might be buried in Zion.

It was a laudable courage, but too often the kind of courage that does not respect the limitations of inexperience. Many a brave convert permitted himself to believe he could travel to Zion in a broken-down wagon and have less trouble on the roads than a Gentile with a new one. Thus the idea grew that a man could make his own vehicle for crossing the plains, and the original stimulus for this idea came from the fountainhead of priesthood authority. The sixth general epistle of the presidency, dated September 22, 1851, begged the Saints in all the earth to hasten to Zion.

The sixth epistle was, by suggestion, a challenge of faith.

"Some of the children of the world have crossed the mountains and plains from Missouri to California, with a pack on their back to worship their god—gold! Some have performed the same journey with a wheelbarrow; some have accomplished the same with a pack on a cow."[23]

Brigham Young's word in that epistle had an uplifting effect. During the following two years plans were discussed of organizing the emigrants into handcart companies and of having them come to Zion by their own motive power. In October, 1855, more instructions about the handcart plan were sent out. The emigrants were to gather in Iowa City. They were to make their handcarts, starting as early in the spring as possible. Said the epistle: "We are sanguine that such a train will out-travel any ox team."[24]

Three handcart companies started from Iowa City early in June. They averaged about 200 persons, 50 handcarts, and 5 ox-team wagons to the company. They took along cows to have milk for the children, or for meat if other food ran low. These companies traveled from 10 to 15 miles a day. Each handcart was loaded with about 300 pounds of food and clothing. Extra food was hauled in the wagons. The first two companies reached Salt Lake City on September 26, having made the journey of 1,200 miles in 108 days. The third company arrived a week later. Apart from general fatigue, hunger due to short rations, trouble with handcarts breaking down, inconvenience crossing streams, and exposure without tents in stormy weather, these companies had a successful journey.

The fourth company, under command of James G. Willie, and the fifth, under command of Edward Martin, numbered together more than 900 persons. These began preparations late in June. There was a shortage of equipment. In great haste additional handcarts were made, and some were made badly. Wheels were made without iron for tires, but that did not deter the emigrants. Had not Brother Brigham assured them that carts made entirely of wood would stand the journey?

These companies did not reach the Missouri River until August 11, when they should have been several hundred miles

A DRAWING, BY WILLIAM H. JACKSON, OF A MORMON HANDCART COMPANY ENTERING THE MOUNTAIN REGIONS EN ROUTE TO UTAH

There are no photographs of the handcart companies

on their way. Some feared that the handcarts would not hold out. A number of families dropped out. They were roundly condemned for exchanging the glories of Zion for "the leeks and onions" of Iowa. Captain Willie's company left Florence on August 19, and on the twenty-fifth the Martin company started.

According to Captain Willie's report to Brigham Young, his company had been on rations from the start: 10½ ounces of food for the men, 9 ounces for the women, 6 ounces for the children, and 3 ounces for the infants. It was less than a marching diet. From the fresh meat they killed en route dysentery broke out in the camp. Before the companies reached Fort Laramie they encountered storms and freezing weather, with the worse half of the journey ahead. They had not sufficient clothing, and some members of the party were already without shoes.

The Willie company reached Salt Lake Valley on November 9, having lost from exposure about 70 of its 400 members. Three children were born on the trip, and three couples were married. The Martin company, with about 580 members, did not arrive until November 30, but the casualties of this party are not known. Based on various reports, B. H. Roberts places the number of deaths of the Martin company at 145. Yet these handcart emigrants came into Zion rejoicing.

John Chislett, who later left the church, wrote his recollections of the sufferings of the Willie company. He related that, while at Florence, the leaders and members of both companies debated the advisability of attempting the journey so late in the season. One leader, Levi Savage, thought the hazards were too great. He was rebuked as a man of weak faith. In reply, according to Chislett, Savage said: "What I have said I know to be true; but seeing you are to go forward, I will go with you, will suffer with you, will rest with you, will die with you. May God in mercy bless and preserve us."[25]

Altogether the first year of the handcart experiment brought to Utah between 1,600 and 1,700 souls who might not have reached Zion that year had they waited for teams and wagons. Counting those who came during 1856 with wagon trains, the total emigration to Utah was possibly in excess of 4,000, several hundred fewer than the 1855 emigration. In 1857 emigration dropped off because of political troubles; however, in that year there were two small handcart companies, but they were better equipped and they started in time to reach Utah with a minimum of inconvenience. The two handcart companies of 1857 had an anxious march getting to Utah ahead of the advance unit of Johnston's Army. Because of the Utah War there was no emigration in 1858. In 1859 and 1860 there was some handcart travel, but none after that.[26]

The sacrifices of the handcart pioneers bear witness to their determination to reach the Great Salt Lake Valley. The spirit of those people is felt in the following verses of the "Handcart Song," which took its place with "Come, Come, Ye Saints" around the fire.

Ye Saints who dwell on Britain's shore,
Prepare yourselves with many more,
To leave behind your native land,
For sure God's judgments are at hand.
But you must cross the raging main
Before the Promised Land you gain,
And with the faithful make a start
To cross the plains with your handcart.

As on the way the carts are pulled,
'Twould very much surprise the world
To see the old and feeble dame
Thus lend her hand to push the same;
And maidens, too, will dance and sing,
Young men more happy than a king;
And children, they will laugh and play
Their strength increasing day by day.

That some of the aged and even of the young and hearty died of overwork and exposure made no difference. Nor was the spirit dampened at all because the children cried for food which was not to be had, for the handcart scheme was "designed by the Gods above."

Such expressions of faith created in Zion the illusion of might. In 1856 Brigham Young said: "We are bound to become a sovereign state in the Union, or an independent nation by ourselves, and let them drive us from this place if they can. If they get rid of polygamy they will have to expend $3,000,000 for a prison, and roof it over from the summit of the Rock Mountains to the Sierra Nevadas."

When the federal officials, including the judges in 1851, ran away from their posts in Utah, the Mormons charged that the government had left them without the protection of a judicial system. The legislature met in February, 1852, and enacted a law to meet the situation. Re-reading the organic act for the territory, the brethren discovered that the district courts over which the federally appointed judges would preside were to exercise "original jurisdiction, both in civil and criminal cases, *when not otherwise provided by law*." That was an invitation to pass a law creating a territorial court system which would "otherwise provide" the machinery for handling such cases. The same district courts were to have supervision over the inferior courts, to prevent and correct abuses "*where no other remedy is provided*."

The legislature passed an act vesting the probate or county courts with "original jurisdiction both civil and criminal, and as well in chancery as at common law, when not prohibited by legislative enactments." Technically, the law was constitutional and could be annulled only by Congress, from whence came the organic act.

To assist the probate judge, who would be named by the legislature and commissioned by the governor, there was created the office of county prosecuting attorney, who would "attend to all legal business in the county, in which the territory is a party, and prosecute before the probate court of his county all individuals accused of crimes."

The legislature also created the office of territorial marshal, vested with authority "to execute all orders or processes of the supreme or district court, in all cases arising under the laws of the territory, and such other duties as the executive may direct, or may be required by law pertaining to the duties as the executive may direct, or may be required by law pertaining to the duties of his office." The law also created the offices of territorial attorney-general and territorial marshal, appointed by the legislature.[27]

When the new federal judges arrived in Utah, they found

themselves holding offices with little work to do. Under the circumstances, no judge but a Mormon could be named to a county probate court. Probate courts had jurisdiction in all matters except issues in which the federal government was a party. Chief Justice John F. Kinney, twice appointed to that position from 1854 to 1863, when he was removed by Lincoln, was not opposed to the Utah court law. Lazarus H. Reed, who was chief justice during two years preceding 1854, found no fault with the law, nor did Associate Justice Leonidas Shaver. These three judges were Gentiles. Associate Justice Zerubbabel Snow, a Mormon, was a strong defender of Utah's judiciary law. Approval or disapproval was determined by like or dislike of the Mormons.

Associate Justice W. W. Drummond, who arrived in September, 1855, found himself very much inconvenienced by the judiciary law of Utah. The law did not please Associate Justice George P. Stiles, who had been a faithful Mormon when he received his appointment in 1855 but who, in 1856, had been cut off the church for immoral conduct. After his excommunication Stiles was much less popular than if he had never enjoyed the Gospel light. He was the first federal judge to come into conflict with the territorial judiciary system.

Stiles took the position that the United States marshal and not the territorial marshal should have jurisdiction over serving writs and impaneling juries. The former officer was usually a Gentile; the latter, a Mormon, an important factor in selecting jurors. Because of his opposition, three Mormon lawyers—James Ferguson, J. C. Little, and Hosea Stout—in February, 1857, created a disturbance in the court of Judge Stiles. Not satisfied with breaking up the court and forcing its adjournment, these lawyer-Saints raided the office of Judge Stiles, took possession of some of his books, and carried some of his documents and papers to an outhouse and burned them.

Drummond set out to ignore the county court law of Utah. He was able, being a Gentile and a federal justice, to secure a favorable audience in the press of the country. He attended the sessions of the Utah legislature in 1856 at Fillmore, where he saw the priesthood at work.[28] Young, as governor, dispensed with all formalities and met both houses of his legislature together in the same circle—senators, representatives, and county judges all joining in the discussion. All voted as if all were members of the two lawmaking bodies. This New England town-hall method of legislation offended Drummond.

Being practical jokers, some of the Mormons present at Fillmore maneuvered to have a local Jewish storekeeper named Abrahamson say something that offended Drummond. Abrahamson was one of the few Jewish Mormons. Drummond had his Negro servant attack Abrahamson. The judge was arrested. The case was dropped, but not until Drummond had been greatly embarrassed. Soon afterward he went to Carson Valley, ostensibly to hold court; but he took the occasion to flee to California, from whence he went to Washington by way of Panama, spoiling for revenge, and he proved to be a damaging witness.[29]

On reaching Washington, Drummond resigned; and on March 30, 1856, he submitted to the United States attorney-general six charges, alleging—

1. That Brigham Young is absolute dictator in Utah.
2. That male members of the Church are bound to Young by secret oaths.
3. That a group of men have been set apart as "destroying angels" to take the lives and property of those who question Young's authority.
4. That Federal officials are insulted, harassed and annoyed, and have no redress; that they are forced to listen to Mormons condemning the Government.
5. That records of the court have been destroyed with the knowledge and approval of Young.
6. That laws are administered differently against Gentiles and against the Mormons.

The judge also blamed the Mormons for the murder of Captain J. W. Gunnison and Almon W. Babbitt; and he intimated that they had poisoned Judge Leonidas Shaver, Drummond's predecessor, who died in Utah.[30]

Federal officials had already come to the conclusion that an expedition should be sent to Utah, but Drummond's report added fuel to the fire and served to speed the disciplinary action to be taken against the church.

NOTES

1. According to the journal of Leonard E. Harrington, in the *Utah Historical Quarterly*, January, 1940, p. 21, when George A. Smith and John Taylor arrived in Washington with the memorial for the proposed state of Deseret "they found the prejudices so strong against us, they did not present their credentials or documents."

2. This information was given by church officials to Richard F. Burton and was reported by him in *The City of the Saints*, p. 300.

3. Among the emigrant converts were a considerable number of Danes and Swedes, some Swiss, and a few French and Italian Saints. English-speaking Saints who were familiar with the language and customs of the special groups were sent along to assist them in establishing their own communities. The church then followed through with a program of education for the non-English-speaking groups. All were encouraged to become citizens as rapidly as they could qualify under the law.

4. Mrs. LeRoy Cox, of St. George, told the writer about her grandfather, a Dane living at Parowan. He had two Danish wives. A Danish emigrant woman was brought to town. The bishop said: "Brother Bayles, take this sister to your house where she will have someone to talk to. I suggest that you marry her." Brother Bayles "obeyed counsel" and took a third Danish wife. Some time later, under similar circumstances, another Danish woman had been sent to Parowan. The bishop sent her to Brother Bayles, where some months later she became Wife No. 4

5. Andrew L. Neff (*History of Utah*, p. 278) quotes the following from one of Governor Young's messages: "Produce what you consume; draw from the native elements the necessities of life; permit no vitiated taste to lead you into the indulgence of expensive luxuries, which can only be obtained by involving yourself in debt; let home industry produce every article of home consumption."

6. When William R. Palmer of Cedar City spoke before the Utah Trails and Landmarks Association on September 4, 1933, he said, in part: "The women made candles and tallow bitches, for the works had to be lighted, and when greases or tar ran low, either for lights or lubrication, the butter supply of the colony was commandeered. The men built roads to the coal mines and to the iron, constructed bridges, hauled ore. . . . . Sometimes they were paid for their services in the produce of the country, but the big end of it was done without charge for the building of the Church and the Kingdom of God." A report on the iron experiment is found in Neff, *ibid.*, pp. 301–10.

7. By dint of industry and co-operation the San Bernardino colony prospered. Z. S. Eldridge, in his *History of California*, reported that in 1856 San Bernardino Mormons owned 14,357 head of cattle, 1,786 horses and mules, 4,417 sheep and goats, and 437 hogs. During that year they produced 50,000 bushels of corn, wheat, and other grains.

8. James W. Denver, commissioner of Indian affairs, wrote Brigham Young on November 11, 1857, that he had overspent his allowed funds by $31,380.60 and had made an unauthorized trip to visit Indians outside his territory.

9. Brigham Young's party included 115 men, 22 women, 5 children, 26 wagons, and 28 carriages. They took along light boats to cross the rivers. Leonard E. Harrington wrote in his journal, printed in the *Utah Historical Quarterly*, January, 1940, that Young stopped on the return trip to visit Captain Grant in charge of the Hudson's Bay Company's station at Fort Hall. Grant was married to a squaw and had several half-breed children. An account of the Salmon River mission by Lewis W. Shurtliff was published in the *Utah Historical Quarterly*, January, 1932.

10. Young wrote to Walker on July 25, 1853: "I send you some tobacco to smoke in the mountains when you get lonesome. You are a fool for fighting your best friends, for we are the best friends, and the only friends that you have in the world. Everybody else

would kill you if they could get a chance. If you get hungry send some friendly Indians down to the settlements and we will give you some beef cattle and flour" (B. H. Roberts, *Comprehensive History of the Church*, IV, 49).

11. This meeting was reported by Anson Call in his journal for May, 1854 (quoted by Roberts, *op. cit.*, p. 36). Walker "began to beat the mother of the sick child. The president stopped him and reprimanded him severely and asked him why he abused his squaw that way. He answered that he did not want the child to suffer alone." Walker also said that if the child died it would not die alone. Some Mormon would have to die with it, so the child would "have company and some horses to ride" in the next life. At this point Young blessed the child.

12. This item is taken from Hurt's letter of May 2, 1855, to the Commissioner of Indian Affairs. He said of the missionaries: "The character of many of those who have been nominated is calculated to confirm this view of the case. They embrace a class of rude and lawless young men, such as might be regarded as a curse in any community—But I do not wish to excite prejudice, or encourage feelings of hostility against these people; on the contrary I think that such a course would be unwise and impolitic. They have always and always will thrive on persecution."

13. Colonel Steptoe on April 5, 1855, wrote to the Commissioner of Indian Affairs: "The trial was abortive, but it will, notwithstanding, have two good effects—one upon the savages, the other upon the general government which will now understand the undue sympathy felt by the Mormons for the Indians." He did not think there was evidence that the Mormons would "aid or countenance active hostilities by the government against the Utahs. . . . ."

14. Neff (*op. cit.*, p. 185) quotes from a letter dated March 22, 1855, printed in the *New Haven Journal:* "No sooner did the officers arrive here last fall than they began to inquire about women. And because they were rebuked openly they took offense. It is all the mothers can do to keep them away from their daughters."

15. The writer heard this story from Lyman L. Woods, Mormon pioneer of Clover Valley. He did not believe that Brother Brigham sent the girls to compromise the officers. The story first appeared in print in the book by Mrs. C. V. Waite, *The Mormon Prophet and His Harem*. It was repeated in J. H. Beadle's *Life in Utah*.

16. Burr's letters are found in the annual reports of the General Land Office for 1856 and 1857. The Hickman referred to was William A. Hickman, who later turned against the Mormons.

17. Neff (*op. cit.*, pp. 678–80) reports that the survey was carelessly done and not properly supervised. Brigham Young said in a letter on July 1, 1856: "The surveying is a great humbug, they have got their own party and surveyors imported for that purpose. . . . ." Later official reports proved that much of the work had to be done over.

18. *Millennial Star* of September 27, 1856, contained an editorial on consecration: "Latter-day Saints, we must consecrate ourselves, our lives, energies, wealth, talents, wives, families and all that we are or have unto Him who has thrice purchased us—by creation, by preservation, and by the blood of His Only Begotten. . . . . Objectors should step aside and become candidates for a lower glory."

19. Joseph Fish, of Parowan, wrote in his journal for November 15, 1856: "Everyone was rebaptized and they were catechised by the bishop and where they had done wrong required to make it right." Fish said that some would not bow the knee and were cut off the church.

20. Hurt's letter is found in the correspondence of the Commission of Indian Affairs, National Archives. Hurt protested against the practice of Mormons designating themselves as "Mormons" to create a distinction between them and non-Mormons,

called "Americans." He charged that Indians were led to believe that "Americans" were bad people.

21. In this speech *Journal of Discourses*, IV, 53) Brigham Young also said: "I do know that there are sins committed of such a nature that if the people did understand the doctrine of salvation, they would tremble because of their situation. And furthermore, I know that there are transgressors, who, if they knew themselves and the only condition upon which they can obtain forgiveness, would beg of their brethren to shed their blood . . . . to appease the wrath that is kindled against them, and that the law might have its course. I will say further: I have had men come to me and offer their lives to atone for their sins."

22. Utah's first murder trial was that of Howard Egan in 1851, for killing James Monroe, a former Mormon, for seducing one of his wives. George A. Smith, who defended Egan, said: "I argue that in this Territory it is a principle of mountain common law that no man can seduce the wife of another without endangering his own life." He argued that had Egan not killed Monroe he would have shared Monroe's guilt, according to the "style of old Israel." Egan was released with honor. This case was later cited as an example of the blood-atonement doctrine. See Neff, *op. cit.*, pp. 193–94.

23. This letter appeared in the *Millennial Star*, XIV, 17–25. "Some of the Saints, now in our midst, came hither with wagons or carts made of wood, without a particle of iron, hooping their wheels with hickory, or rawhide or ropes, and has as good and safe a journey as any in the camps, with their well wrought iron wagons; and can you not do the same? Families might start from the Missouri River with cows, handcarts, wheelbarrows, with little flour and no unnecessaries, and come to this place quicker, and with less fatigue, than by following the heavy trains with their cumbrous herds. . . . ."

24. *Deseret News*, October 31, 1855. Emigrants were advised to take cows for milk and beef cattle for meat. It was suggested that handcarts would obviate "the expense, risk, loss and perplexity of teams."

25. A report on the journey of the Willie company, written by John Chislett, was included by T. B. H. Stenhouse in his *The Rocky Mountain Saints*, pp. 309–38. John Jacques wrote a series of articles about the Martin company, which appeared in the Sunday issues of the *Salt Lake Herald*, beginning December 1, 1878. Apparently Brigham Young did not think the companies would start so late in the season.

In April, 1857, as a demonstration of what could be done with handcarts, 75 missionaries set out from Salt Lake City with 25 handcarts. Each cart was loaded with about 300 pounds. The trip to Florence, 1,031 miles, was covered in 48 days. The men arrived in good physical condition. It was believed that men, women, and children could make the same trip in 70 days. Most companies required 80 days or more. This report is from the mimeographed "History of Robert Gardner Jr.," pp. 56–61.

26. William E. Waters, an officer in Johnston's Army (in *Life among the Mormons*, pp. 170–71), noted that the wagons, several to each company, were used only to carry baggage and rations and could not accommodate even those who were sick. "They have no tents nor any protection from the storm. It is a sad sight to see the road lined with these people laboring to get along in a severe snow storm, as I have seen them. Old and decrepit men and women; some with their wooden shoes, others without any, totter along in the rear of the slow-moving ox trains; but slow as they move it is too fast for some of these. . . . . Notwithstanding all their hardships and privations, murmuring is not heard because it is not allowed. . . . . Then in addition they are urged to a contented and hopeful state of mind, by frequent allusions at their religious services, to that beautiful land flowing with milk and honey, which they will soon possess."

Waters related a report given him by a lady at Fort Bridger who informed him that it "was one of the most sickening sights she ever beheld. Men and women had lashed themselves with cords to their carts like beasts, and without shoes their mangled and bleeding feet trod the rough ground as they toiled over it with their load. One of the men was wheeling his wife who had become exhausted. . . . ."

27. The legislative act of February 4, 1852, which gave such powers to the courts, also vested the courts with control over the natural resources.

28. The *New York Herald*, September 15, 1856, reported some figures received from its correspondent at Fillmore to the effect that the 39 members in the legislature and 4 other officials had a reputed total of 328 wives. Of more than 40 men in elective office in Utah, not half a dozen were monogamists.

29. Jules Remy reported in *A Journey to Great Salt Lake City*, I, 469, his interview with Drummond. He found him not an "estimable character." The Mormons learned that the woman with Drummond was Ada Caroll, who had been the wife of Charles Fletcher, a Baltimore schoolteacher. The *Deseret News*, May 20, 1857, printed a letter from Drummond's wife denying she had been divorced. Much of this scandal was spread on the record in the trial of Drummond instigated by William A. Hickman and others. See Hickman's *Brigham's Destroying Angel*, p. 112.

30. Drummond's charges are recorded in *House Executive Document No. 71* (35th Cong., 1st sess.), X, 212–14. In spite of answers by the Mormons, this report, brought so officially to the attention of the government, led to the military expedition. In 1885 Mormons heard with satisfaction that Drummond was sentenced to the Chicago House of Correction for stealing postage stamps. The *Church Chronology* reports for November 20, 1887, that he died in a Chicago grog shop, a pauper.

CHAPTER VII

ZION "INVADED BY A HOSTILE FORCE"

PRIOR to the Civil War, Mormon polygamy was politically linked with the slavery issue. Both issues were involved in the question of popular sovereignty. Proponents of popular, or squatter, sovereignty took the stand that the people in a new territory should themselves decide whether slavery would prevail with them.

The Mormons argued that the popular-sovereignty doctrine should also apply to the polygamy issue. In still another way the polygamy and slavery issues were linked. Political leaders from the southern states opposed legislation against polygamy, believing that, if Congress should regulate by law the family system of the Mormons, then Congress might undertake to regulate the family relations of the slaves.

This political linkage between polygamy and slavery became a campaign issue in 1856. The Republican platform called it an "imperative duty of Congress to prohibit in the territories those twin relics of barbarism—polygamy and slavery." James Buchanan and the Democrats won on the popular-sovereignty doctrine, defeating John C. Fremont and the "twin-relics" issue. However, when Buchanan became president, he was placed in a difficult position with reference to one of the "relics of barbarism." He stood his ground on slavery but had to reverse himself on the polygamy question. He resorted to the prevailing belief that the Mormons had challenged the authority of the United States government.

While the Mormons and certain political enemies of Buchanan called the Utah problem one of popular sovereignty, the government took the stand that the issue was not polygamy but rebellion. It was a question of the federal control of the local government and would have arisen had there been no polygamy, although it was aggravated by polygamy.

Senator Stephen A. Douglas made a speech on June 12, 1857, at Springfield, Illinois. He spoke with authority of reports which indicated that the Mormons were not loyal to the government. He charged that nine out of ten of Utah's inhabitants were aliens, that Mormons were bound to their leader by "horrid oaths," that the church was inciting the Indians to acts of hostility, and that the Danites, or "Destroying Angels," were robbing and killing American citizens.[1]

On June 26 Lincoln made a speech, also at Springfield; and he also touched the Mormon question. He ventured the opinion that perhaps territorial status should be repealed and Utah placed under the judicial control of neighboring states. The Mormons, he said, "ought somehow [to] be called into obedience."

The rumors and reports mentioned by Douglas were not new, but it was new for the Mormons to hear such talk from a man who had befriended them. Church leaders responded with defiance. According to the *Deseret News* for December 5, 1855, Heber C. Kimball said in a speech: "Now, if any persons wish to begin another scrape and desire again to break us up, and corrupt this people, and to bring death, hell and the devil in our midst, come on, for God Almighty knows that I will strive to slay the man who undertakes it."

Jedediah M. Grant, said on March 2, 1856: "Who is afraid to die? None but the wicked. If they want to send troops here, let them come to those who have imported filth and whores, though we can attend to that class without so much expense to the government. . . . . If we were to establish a whorehouse on every corner of our streets, as in nearly all other cities outside of Utah, either by law or otherwise, we should doubtless then be considered good fellows."[2]

President Buchanan felt impelled to take action against the Mormons, although such action appeared to violate his squatter-sovereignty campaign pledge. He met the situation by calling the Mormon problem one of civil disobedience. He asked for advice about the means of calling the Saints to obedience. On May 26 General Winfield Scott wrote to the Secretary of

War regarding a proposed garrison for Salt Lake City "to enforce obedience."

General Scott reported that Utah's population was about 40,000, with possibly 8,000 males capable of bearing arms. He suggested that the united front of the Mormons might offer a challenge, for "fanaticism has often proved itself to be an overmatch for military discipline." He suggested that there was in Utah a party of "*American* men in favor of Christianity, law and order" and that the women of Utah might be induced to rise against the church if proper leadership were provided.

General Scott warned against any plan to send a small force against the Mormons. He recommended about 4,000 troops. "It is certain that if the occupation is attempted with an inadequate force and consequently cut off or destroyed, the United States, after suffering the deep mortification, would be obliged to employ double the force that would originally have been necessary. The disgrace ought not to be risked by too great a parsimony in the means first employed." He advised against sending an expedition too late in the season.[3]

On June 29 General Scott dispatched orders to General W. S. Harney at Fort Leavenworth, instructing him to outfit a detachment of 2,600 men and officers for garrison service in Utah to restore order and support civil authority. He described the mission as a "delicate function of the military power." Harney would co-operate with Utah's governor, Brigham Young, but was instructed to "conform your action to his requests and views in all cases where your military judgment and prudence do not forbid, nor compel you to modify."[4]

Rumors leaked through to Utah about Harney's assignment. The Mormons knew about Harney, for he had been active in punishing the Sioux Indians along the emigrant trail. They called him "Squaw-killer," and it was not long before his name in Utah was symbolic of ill-repute.

Definite news did not reach the Saints until July 24, 1857, when nearly 3,000 people, with several brass bands and with uniformed drill units of the Nauvoo Legion, were having a picnic in one of the canyons. Ten years prior to that day the pioneers entered the valley. Three messengers rode into camp bearing the report that an army was marching against Utah. Dancing and merrymaking carried on until the break of day on July 25.

After the celebration rumors began again to circulate. "Harney boasted he would hang Brigham Young and the apostles." "He has a wagon load of ropes for a necktie party." Harney said he "would winter in Utah or in hell." Whatever Harney said or thought, the fact is he had no wish to go to Utah. While with one hand he made preparations to go, he also drummed up political pressure to be relieved of the assignment. It was decided that he was "needed in Kansas."

The idea of defending Zion had been growing. For example, on July 5, 1857, Brigham Young and Heber C. Kimball made speeches to the Saints at Salt Lake City. Both speeches were reported by the *Deseret News*. Young remarked about the rumors of 2,000 troops to be sent to Utah. "You will see that they will ask us to make their soldiers behave themselves, until they can get out of this place, which will be as soon as possible." He wished that, instead of sending the poor soldiers, they would send "those here that mobbed us in days gone by. . . . . But no, the priests and some editors and politicians wish to have innocent soldiers sent here to fight us."

Kimball told the parable of the mustard seed that was once kicked about, but in the mountains it multiplied to "make ten thousand more little mustard trees." "We have some big mountains between us and them." It would make no difference if he and Brother Brigham and all the apostles were killed. Other elders would rise to replace them.[5]

According to the *Deseret News* for August 12, Kimball declared that he had wives enough to whip the oncoming soldiers. He spoke of 700 wagons of food being sent to supply the soldiers, 2 tons on each wagon; of the 7,000 oxen; and of the wagons containing ample quantities of clothing. He said with a wink that possibly the troops would not reach Utah; but, if the supplies did, "they would be a mighty help to us." He damned the president and other "poor rotten curses," and he did it "in the name of Jesus Christ and by the authority of the Holy Priesthood."

It was this spirit that found expression in song. One of the war songs carried on for many years. It was a parody on Stephen Foster's "Camptown Races."

There's seven hundred wagons on the way,
Du dah!
And their cattle are numerous, so they say,
Du dah; Du dah day!
Now, to let them perish would be a sin,
Du dah!
So we'll take all they got for bringing them in,
Du dah; du dah day!

Chorus: Then let us be on hand
By Brigham Young to stand;
And if our enemies do appear
We'll sweep them off the land.

Old Sam has sent, I understand
Du dah!
A Missouri ass to rule our land,
Du dah; Du dah day!
But if he comes we'll have some fun,
Du dah!
To see him and his juries run,
Du dah; Du dah day!

Old Squaw-Killer Harney is on his way,
Du dah!
The Mormon People for to slay,
Du dah; Du dah day!
Now, if he comes, the truth I'll tell
Du dah!
Our boys will drive him down to hell,
Du dah; Du dah day!

The Nauvoo Legion had a standing strength of 2,000 and included all able-bodied men between the ages of 18 and 45 years. This army was led by Lieutenant General Daniel H. Wells, "Tartar of the Mountains." Wells, on August 1, informed the Legion that Utah was about to be "invaded by a hostile force." He knew of no reason for sending an army against a people who stood for the Constitution and against mob rule; therefore, every Legion member was to prepare to defend the homeland.[6]

On August 7 the church, through the *Deseret News* announced that remote settlements would be abandoned. Missionaries were advised to return home. Church leaders decided to "leave the world go to the devil." Plans went ahead to build defenses and cache food in the fastnesses of the mountains. These orders were followed so strictly that gentile companies traveling through Utah had difficulty purchasing supplies.

While the Mormons were hastening their defense, a messenger from General Harney was on his way. On July 28 Harney dispatched Captain Stewart Van Vliet with a small detachment to visit Utah. He did not arrive in Utah until September 8.

Van Vliet's letter of instructions contained this unfortunate sentence: "The General Commanding has deemed it proper and courteous to inform President Young of the Society of the Mormons of the object of your visit." He carried a letter to Governor Young similarly addressed. To Brother Brigham the title given him was accepted as a studied insult.

The instructions given to Van Vliet were tolerant and moderate:

> You will explain freely and fully the objects of your mission and the steps you propose to take for its accomplishment. . . . . You will impress upon the officer in charge of your escort the imperious necessity of a very careful circumspection of conduct in his command. The men shall not only be carefully selected for this service, but they shall be repeatedly admonished never to comment upon, or ridicule anything they see or hear. . . . .[7]

Van Vliet was tactful. He left his military escort on the Green River and continued to Salt Lake City with a small guard, which somewhat counteracted Harney's patronizing message to Young. The message assured the Mormons that the soldiers were sent on a peaceful mission, that they would pay "liberal prices for all the supplies needed." The Mormons were by that time too aroused to be reassured, and they were not tempted by the prospect of a market for their produce.

Captain Van Vliet was given an opportunity to speak to the people in a public meeting on September 13. Brigham Young introduced him as a man of honor for whom soldiers have respect. In the course of the meeting Apostle John Taylor put this question to the congregation: "All of you that are willing to set fire to your property and lay it in ashes, rather than submit to their military rule and oppression, manifest it by raising your hands." All hands went up with a loud "Amen."[8]

When Captain Van Vliet met with the church leaders, he could give no assurances regarding the conduct of the army. He made it clear that the army would come and that resistance would be futile. He advised against resistance because it would strengthen the popular belief that the Mormons were not worthy of self-government.

On September 14, the day following the public meeting, Van Vliet left Salt Lake City. Two days later, at Green River, he wrote his report. He indicated that the Mormons expected the worst from the army, believing that the coming of the soldiers would be the beginning of such persecutions as they had experienced in Missouri and Illinois.[9] He believed the Saints would resist to the last man and were capable of stiff opposition. Apparently his superior officers did not take the report seriously.

A Mormon express was sent to Carson Valley with orders for the settlers to come home. Within three weeks the families had sold out and about 450 persons with 123 wagons were en route eastward. Of this number, 160, according to Roberts, were males able to bear arms. These brethren brought to Utah from California 2,700 pounds of ammunition. Beginning late in November and continuing until the spring of 1858, the entire San Bernardino colony of about a thousand persons migrated. Most of these people located in southern Utah.[10]

On September 15, the day after Captain Van Vliet left Salt Lake City, Governor Young issued his famous proclamation, announcing: "We are invaded by a hostile force who are evidently assailing us to accomplish our overthrow and destruction." In his next sentence he spoke as a church official: "For the last twenty-five years we have trusted officials of the Government, from Constables and Justices to Judges, Governors and Presidents, only to be scorned, held in derision, insulted and betrayed."

The document recited the suffering and sacrifices of the people. It ended with "Therefore I, Brigham Young, Governor, etc.,

PROCLAMATION

BY THE GOVERNOR.

CITIZENS OF UTAH—

We are invaded by a hostile force who are evidently assailing us to accomplish our overthrow and destruction.

For the last twenty five years we have trusted officials of the Government, from Constables and Justices to Judges, Governors, and Presidents, only to be scorned, held in derision, insulted and betrayed. Our houses have been plundered and then burned, our fields laid waste, our principal men butchered while under the pledged faith of the government for their safety, and our families driven from their homes to find that shelter in the barren wilderness and that protection among hostile savages which were denied them in the boasted abodes of Christianity and civilization.

The Constitution of our common country guarantees unto us all that we do now or have ever claimed.

If the Constitutional rights which pertain unto us as American citizens were extended to Utah, according to the spirit and meaning thereof, and fairly and impartially administered, it is all that we could ask, all that we have ever asked.

Our opponents have availed themselves of prejudice existing against us because of our religious faith, to send out a formidable host to accomplish our destruction. We have had no privilege, no opportunity of defending ourselves from the false, foul, and unjust aspersions against us before the nation. The Government has not condescended to cause an investigating committee or other person to be sent to inquire into and ascertain the truth, as is customary in such cases.

We know those aspersions to be false, but that avails us nothing. We are condemned unheard and forced to an issue with an armed, mercenary mob, which has been sent against us at the instigation of anonymous letter writers ashamed to father the base, slanderous falsehoods which they have given to the public; of corrupt officials who have brought false accusation against us to screen themselves in their own infamy; and of hireling priests and howling editors who prostitute the truth for filthy lucre's sake.

The issue which has been thus forced upon us compels us to resort to the great first law of self preservation and stand in our own defence, a right guaranteed unto us by the genius of the institutions of our country, and upon which the Government is based.

Our duty to ourselves, to our families, requires us not to tamely submit to be driven and slain, without an attempt to preserve ourselves. Our duty to our country, our holy religion, our God, to freedom and liberty, requires that we should not quietly stand still and see those fetters forging around, which are calculated to enslave and bring us in subjection to an unlawful military despotism such as can only emanate [in a country of Constitutional law] from usurpation, tyranny, and oppression.

Therefore I, Brigham Young, Governor and Superintendent of Indian Affairs for the Territory of Utah, in the name of the People of the United States in the Territory of Utah,

1st:—Forbid all armed forces, of every description, from coming into this Territory under any pretence whatever.

2d:—That all the forces in said Territory hold themselves in readiness to march, at a moment's notice, to repel any and all such invasion.

3d:—Martial law is hereby declared to exist in this Territory, from and after the publication of this Proclamation; and no person shall be allowed to pass or repass into, or through, or from this Territory, without a permit from the proper officer.

{ L. S. }

Given under my hand and seal at Great Salt Lake City, Territory of Utah, this fifteenth day of September, A. D. Eighteen hundred and fifty seven and of the Independence of the United States of America the eighty second.

BRIGHAM YOUNG.

1. Forbid all armed forces, of every description, from coming into this Territory under any pretense whatever.
2. That all the forces in said Territory hold themselves in readiness to march, at a moment's notice, to repel any and all such invasion.
3. Martial law is hereby declared to exist in this Territory, from and after the publication of this Proclamation; and no person shall be allowed to pass or repass into, or through, or from this Territory, without a permit from the proper officer.

On August 15, just a month before the issue of the proclamation of defiance, a detail of the Nauvoo Legion was sent out on the trail to protect the Utah-bound emigrant trains. About 1,200 of these converts were en route in several companies, most of them traveling with handcarts. Legion members met these companies to help speed their safe entry to Salt Lake Valley. This scouting and aid service was carried out under the guidance of Colonel Robert T. Burton.

When General Harney was assigned to other duty, command of Utah expedition was given to General Penifor F. Smith, who died a few days afterward. Next to be assigned to the task was Colonel Albert Sidney Johnston, then stationed in Washington. An advance cavalry detachment of about 500 men under Colonel E. B. Alexander had already begun the westward march. Johnston took over "all the orders and instructions" given to General Harney."[11]

As Colonel Alexander's detchment approached the mountain region, the Mormon scouts were there to watch him. Some information about Alexander is obtained from a letter by Captain Jesse A. Gove, written on August 2, 1857. He indicated that the colonel was not on good terms with his subordinates, that he was constantly interfering with discipline, and that "no one calls on him or treats him with hardly the common courtesies of life."[12] In another letter written on September 27 Captain Gove spoke of the possibility of getting the Shoshone and Snake Indians to fight the Mormons. He thought that some Indians should be hired as guides and hunters. He referred to the colonel as "the old woman" because he would not consider such a proposal.

Toward the end of September, General Daniel H. Wells took

the field to direct the defense. Legionnaires were ordered to annoy the enemy without spilling blood or risking their own lives. Provisions were removed from the Mormon emigrant depot at Fort Supply, and all buildings or improvements that might be used by the enemy were put to the torch. Wherever possible, the grass was burned. Obstructions were set up in the roads.

Such was the mode of defense: strike and retreat, but take no life; beat the enemy with fire and hunger; let him freeze in the mountains, as had the handcart companies the previous winter.[13] If the enemy kept on advancing, he would get the same reception after crossing the mountains to the valleys. That was the theme of one Mormon war song, of which we quote the first three verses:

> If Uncle Sam's determined
> On his very foolish plan,
> The Lord will fight our battles
> And we'll help Him if we can.
>
> If what they now propose to do
> Should ever come to pass,
> We'll burn up every inch of wood
> And every blade of grass.
>
> We'll throw down all our houses,
> Every soul shall emigrate.
> And we'll organize ourselves
> Into a roving mountain state.

If Colonel Alexander underrated the threatened Mormon resistance, he was rudely shocked when he learned on October 4 that three of his supply trains had been burned. Major Lot Smith with a few of his scouts came on the trains in the night. He ordered the teamsters to remove their personal effects, permitted them to hold out 2 wagons for their own supplies, then forced the drivers to set fire to their own trains. Thus 74 wagons went in flames, and Smith made away with most of the oxen. The loss totaled about 420,00 pounds of foodstuffs, enough to amply sustain the expedition in winter quarters about sixty days. Only the nearness of the supply trains to Colonel Alexander's troops prevented the Mormons bringing the wagons on into Utah.[14]

Upon receiving news of Lot Smith's exploit Brigham Young sent word to Colonel Alexander, warning him against bringing the military into Utah. He advised the colonel that if the lateness of the season did not permit him to return to the states he might winter on the Green River, but he would be required to surrender his arms.

Colonel Alexander replied to Governor Young on October 12 that he had been sent to Utah by the government but that he had met resistance of an unbecoming character. He added, and this was irritating to the Mormons:

> You have resorted to open warfare, and of a kind, permit me to say, far beneath the usages of civilized warfare, and only resorted to by those who are conscious of inability to resist by more honorable means, by authorizing persons under your control, some of the very citizens, doubtless, whom you have called to arms, to burn the grass, apparently with the intent of starving a few beasts, and hoping the men would starve after them.

Such a letter General Braddock might have written to the French and Indians at the time his redcoats had to be rescued by George Washington, who was practical enough to employ the means of warfare that the situation called for. The colonel warned Young that the blame for any bloodshed due to Mormon resistance would be on his head.

When Brigham Young received Colonel Alexander's letter of October 12, he was stirred to anger. He replied on October 16. If the army was coming on a peaceful mission, why had it not been sent four years earlier, when the Saints were in a death struggle with the Indians? To the colonel's warning that the contest would be unequal for the Mormons, Young replied: "We have counted the cost it may be to us; we look for the United States to attempt to swallow us up, and we are prepared for the contest, if you wish to forego the constitution in your insane efforts to crush out all human rights. . . . It is now the Kingdom of God and the kingdom of the Devil."

This letter ended with a warning and a taunt. "If you undertake to come in here and build forts," wrote Young, "rest assured that you will be opposed, and that you will need all the force now under your command and much more." And the taunt: "Inasmuch as you consider your force amply sufficient to enable you to come to this city, why have you unwisely dallied so long at Ham's Fork at this late season of the year?"

Colonel Alexander replied to Brigham Young in two letters, on October 18 and 19. In the first he was conciliatory, "but my troops have the same right of self-defense that you claim, and it rests entirely with you whether they are driven to the exercise of it." The second letter was firm. The colonel would not argue the points advanced by Brigham Young. His troops would not molest Utah citizens. Regarding Young's mandate to leave the territory, he said it was "illegal and beyond your authority to issue, or power to enforce, I shall not obey it."[15]

During late October or early November, Colonel Johnston arrived on the Green River, where the army went into winter quarters. By that time the weather did not permit much harassing by the Mormon defenders, nor was it convenient for the loads of supplies to get over the mountains. Rations were short. The Mormons knew that the army lacked supplies, and it was fully expected that starvation would force Johnston to surrender before spring.

News reached the valley that the army had no salt. On November 26 Brigham Young sent two men with 800 pounds of salt and a message to Colonel Johnston. He said that the salt was a gift but that, if the colonel could not accept the gift, he was at liberty to pay for it. It the colonel was suspicious of the salt, he could try it on the messengers or the Mormon prisoners in his charge. Johnston read the message, refused the salt, and drove the messengers out.[16]

Young took the occasion to again remind the army officers that the demonstrations against their supply trains were carried out in all earnestness to prove that the Mormons would stand on their rights. "I have further to inform you that by ordering you here upon pretexts solely founded upon lies, all of which have long since been exploded, the President has no more regard for the Constitution and laws of the United States and the welfare of her legal citizens than he has for the constitution, laws and subjects of the Kingdom of Beelzebub." He added that he had in his stable a small white mule belonging to Colonel

Alexander. The mule arrived in poor condition, but he would care for it until spring, when the colonel might need a mount for his return to the East.

In Zion there was rejoicing and some boasting that the army had been stopped and was eating mule meat on the Green River. But church leaders knew that the end of this rebellion was yet to be faced.

In August of the previous summer Brigham Young had sent Samuel W. Richards to call home the missionaries. En route to Europe, Richards visited that friend of the Mormons, Colonel Thomas L. Kane, leaving a message for the president. Kane was on friendly terms with Buchanan, but his friendship was not sufficient to stem the tide of political expediency.[17]

Buchanan had to justify the expedition and explain its failure. The first was easy. Buchanan said in his message to Congress on December 8, 1857: "This is the first rebellion which has existed in our territories, and humanity itself requires that we should put it down in such a manner that it shall be the last." The irony of this resolve was that his chief adviser was Secretary of War John B. Floyd, one of the leaders in the rebellion over slavery four years later. Also, Colonel Johnston, so strong for punishing the Mormons on the polygamy issue, later left his post to join the southern rebellion and died for the slavery issue.

On January 11, 1858, General Winfield Scott, issued an order regarding reinforcements. He indicated that Colonel Johnston's command would need 850 men and 44 officers to bring it to the limit of 118 officers and 2,470 men. These, with the additional force to be sent, would have aggregated 251 officers and 5,355 men. The standing army of the United States then was about 13,000.

Such were the plans that could have gone forward had there not been so much criticism from Congress. Most of the opposition was political, but not all of it. Senator Sam Houston of Texas thought the entire issue had been bungled. He called it a waste of money to carry on war against Utah. He said it would require a force of 50,000 to maintain and supply, at so great a distance, sufficient soldiers to overcome the Mormon army. Some newspapers asked what legal evidence existed against the people of Utah and whether the issue could not be settled otherwise.[18]

In the meanwhile Colonel Kane prevailed on Buchanan to intrust him with the mission of peacemaker. On December 31, 1857, the president gave Kane his unofficial blessing. Kane left at once by way of Panama.[19] From Los Angeles, traveling as "Dr. Osborne," Kane hastened to Salt Lake City over the southern route, arriving on February 25. This was a remarkably fast trip by clipper ship and stage. En route from San Bernardino he passed one of the companies of Saints returning to Utah from that place and Apostle Amasa M. Lyman, who accompanied him to Utah.

Kane's first task was to impress upon Brigham Young that, if the Mormons did not accept peace, the army would devastate Utah. Brigham's answer was defiance. In the long run, so Kane argued, the church organization would be destroyed. To this, Brother Brigham answered that such a thing would come to pass only if God wished it. He told Kane that the cessation or resumption of hostilities depended entirely on the assurances he could get from the government and the army.

After a few days in Salt Lake City, Colonel Kane went on to Camp Scott, the temporary headquarters of the army on the Green River, arriving in Colonel Johnston's hostile presence on March 12. There he met Alfred Cumming, sent to succeed Young as governor. Cumming was a governor whose authority had been ignored by the Mormons and was not quite recognized by Colonel Johnston. The colonel was abiding by his army orders to co-operate with the civil authorities or not, as seemed best in his military judgment. Johnston was not interested in Kane's peace talk. He rejected an offer of beef cattle from Brigham Young through Kane. He insulted Kane, who responded with a challenge to a duel, which was stopped by Cumming.

Kane's mission did serve to pave the way for amicable relations between Young and Cumming, who later, on several occasions, defended the Mormons against Colonel Johnston. It is possible that Kane's visit indirectly brought Brigham Young to the conclusion that he would not fight the army as he had threatened but would burn everything and retreat. Such tactics might have left the army in difficult straits.

Colonel Johnston and Governor Cumming were not in agreement about the next step to be taken. The one would move with his troops and let the Mormons take the consequences.[20] The other favored a more conciliatory course. Delaney R. Eckles, also in the camp as the new chief justice for Utah, wanted the courts to call for civil obedience. He would use the military only to enforce orders of the court as an aid to the new United States marshal, P. K. Dotson, also at Camp Scott. He seemed to be of the opinion that "loyal" citizens of Utah would rally around him and the governor.

Kane proposed that the new civil officers should go with him to Utah without the army, so that they could establish peace by friendly discussion with the Mormon leaders. Only Cumming would accept this proposal. On April 3 Cumming and Kane, without military escort, started for Salt Lake City. They were passed through the Mormon defense lines and arrived two days later. Eckles, following his own course, opened court at Camp Scott, which was just inside the Utah line. He called a grand jury and heard complaints against the Mormon leaders.[21]

Alfred Cumming had been appointed to the governorship of Utah on July 30, 1857, by Secretary of State Lewis Cass. He arrived in Utah at Camp Scott on November 19. Two days later he issued a proclamation that he had established a temporary seat of government. He ordered all armed forces in Utah to disband and go home or suffer "the punishment due to traitors." He assured the Mormons that he hoped to "command their confidence."[22]

Although the people would not recognize Cumming, his presence in the territory gave Utah two governments—one in Salt Lake City and the other at the Camp Scott military headquarters. Hostility to Cumming found expression in a line of their "Du Dah" song about Uncle Sam sending a "Missouri ass to rule our land." Cumming had been transferred from a post in the Indian service at St. Louis. Formerly he had been mayor of Augusta, Georgia. It helped the Mormons to hate him the the more when the mark of Missouri was placed on him. In

LIEUTENANT GENERAL DANIEL H. WELLS

Head of the Nauvoo Legion, Lieutenant General Wells was in charge of the resistance to Johnston's Army.

view of this attitude, it was an act of courage for Cumming to go alone with Kane among the Mormons, who held him in such contempt.

Governor Cumming took up his duties in Salt Lake City with

the promise from Colonel Johnston that the army would not march from Camp Scott until such a move was agreeable to both. On the strength of this undertaking Cumming made pledges to Brigham Young, although he could not promise that the army would not march, nor could he promise that the law would not be invoked against Mormon leaders for their opposition to the government.

Brigham Young indicated that he expected the worst. Preparations continued to abandon all towns which might become occupied territory. In spite of Cumming's order of the previous November, the Nauvoo Legion had not disbanded, nor would the Legion submit to his authority. The Legion was in charge of the evacuation.

To the credit of Cumming, he remained patient when his authority was not recognized. As he went about telling the people they were foolish to move away, he was not offended if they were not impressed. He set up his headquarters in Salt Lake City and notified all persons who wished that they would be given safe conduct out of Utah. Ostensibly for his protection, Major Howard Egan was put in charge of the guard stationed at the governor's headquarters, but the guard also served to frighten people away. On April 24, after two weeks, Cumming learned the real purpose of the guard and posted another notice. Only 50 men, 33 women, and 71 children came to him and were certified for safe exodus. Cumming protested this military surveillance, and the guard was removed.

Cumming made a journey south in the direction of Provo. On his return he wrote to the Secretary of State, as of May 12, that the road was congested with large numbers of families on the move. "I have reasons to hope that my intercourse with with these persons has contributed to allay fears on their part which are perhaps unreasonable. I regret to have been an eye witness however to scenes of great trial and suffering."[23]

On May 2, before making the journey just mentioned, Cumming wrote the Secretary of State of the fears which prompted the people to move. "Our military force could overwhelm most of these poor people involving men, women and children in a common fate: but there are among the Mormons many brave men accustomed to arms and to horses—men who would fight desperately as guerrillas, and, if the settlements are destroyed, will subject the country to an expensive and protracted war, without any compensating results."

While Governor Cumming was on his way to Salt Lake City, President Buchanan in Washington was meditating a change in policy. He may have been moved to action by criticism in Congress. On April 6, 1858 the birthday of the Mormon church, he issued a proclamation of pardon. He appointed two men to bear this proclamation to Utah and there to act as a peace commission." The commissioners were Senator-Elect L. W. Powell, former governor of Kentucky, and Major Ben McCulloch, of Texas.

The peace commission reached Camp Scott about May 29 and Salt Lake City on June 8.[24] Conferences did not begin until June 11, possibly because a number of the Mormon leaders were in hiding. Judge Eckles had issued warrants for the arrest of Brigham Young and sixty-six others. News of the pardon brought them together at the "Old Council House."[25]

While the Mormon leaders were relieved by the presence of the commission, they were offended with the contents of the president's proclamation. They objected to such terms as "treason" and "rebellion," and they took exception to the following:

> Fellow citizens of Utah, this is rebellion against the Government to which you owe allegiance; it is levying war against the United States, and involves you in the guilt of treason. Persistence in it will bring you to condign punishment, to ruin, and to shame; for it is mere madness to suppose that with your limited resources you can successfully resist the force of this great and powerful nation.
>
> If you have calculated upon the forbearance of the United States, if you have permitted yourselves to suppose that this Government will fail to put forth its strength and bring you to submission, you have fallen into a grave mistake. You have settled upon territory which lies geographically in the heart of the Union. The land you live upon was purchased by the United States and paid for out of their Treasury; the proprietary right and title to it is in them, and not in you. Utah is bounded on every side by States and Territories whose people are true to the Union. It is absurd to believe that they will or can permit you to erect in their very midst a government of your own, not only independent of the authority which they all acknowledge, but hostile to them and their interests.

Do not deceive yourselves nor try to mislead others by propagating the idea that this is a crusade against your religion. The Constitution and laws of this country can take no notice of your creed, whether it be true or false. That is a question between your God and yourselves, in which I disclaim all right to interfere.

The Saints were not willing to be treated as spoiled children due for presidential chiding. The chief executive was telling them in straight talk what Lincoln later had to tell the South—that they had to remain in the Union and they had to behave. Here were southerners—the governor, two commissioners, the commanding officers of the troops, and even the marshal—all joining to enforce the proclamation. Brigham Young and the brethren argued, telling of their sacrifices and their love for the Constitution, but in the end they accepted the conditions of the pardon.

News was taken to Colonel Johnston (lately promoted to brevet brigadier general). On being told that the Mormons agreed to offer no further resistance, he issued, on June 14, a reassuring proclamation. It was not for him to address the people, and his proclamation was evidence of his unwillingness to let Governor Cumming speak for him in civil matters.[26]

The Commission made its final report to the Secretary of War on June 26, 1858, having remained in Utah long enough to assist in putting the peace agreement into effect and observing its acceptance by the Mormon people.

The march of Johnston through abandoned Salt Lake City on June 26 was described by a writer in the *Atlantic Monthly* for April, 1859, as "most extraordinary." Houses were empty. Flags on public buildings had been struck. Along the streets were a few Gentiles, for the day was theirs. Lined along the route of the march were a scattering of Mormon men but no women or children. The army did not stop.[27] The march continued through town and on to Cedar Valley, west of Utah Lake and 36 miles south of Salt Lake City. At this place General Johnston established Camp Floyd, named for Secretary of War John B. Floyd. Gentile camp followers trailed along and set up their own community, Fairfield, adjacent to the camp.

Peace brought less than the illusion of victory to either side. Failing to reach their objective, the troops were forced to winter in the mountains and to live on short rations. Some of the officers were anxious to even the score with Brigham Young. They did not like the peace proclamation. Arriving in Salt Lake Valley, they were shunted off to an isolated spot, remote from the city they had hoped to occupy.

As for the Mormons, the brave front they showed to their invaders was nothing if not deceiving. Zion was no longer theirs alone, and they knew it. The army had come to uphold the Gentiles sent to run their government. The Mormons had saved their self-respect; they had demonstrated their unity and courage; yet they had to swallow their pride and submit to a pardon that branded them traitors and rebels.[28]

The settlement program suffered a severe setback. The colony in California had to be abandoned; so, also, the settlement in Carson Valley. The Salmon River Mission in Oregon had been forced to retreat. On February 28, 1858, a war party of 200 Shosone and Bannock Indians attacked the Limhi settlers, killing 2 men and wounding several others. The attackers made away with 29 horses and 250 head of cattle. A company of 150 men was sent out to relieve the outpost and cover the retreat of the settlers. Mormons blamed white agitators.[29]

On the military front it had been a bloodless war, for which the credit is due the Mormon policy of striking and running. The most serious consequence by far was the massacre of a company of emigrants in September, 1857, at Mountain Meadows. Concerning this tragedy little was said during the period of hostilities because Gentiles could not get into the region and the Mormons were not talking.

About the time that news reached Utah of the punitive expedition there came into the territory an emigrant train bound from Arkansas to California. This group, known as the "Fancher company," after Charles Fancher its captain, included about 140 persons; and its equipment included 40 wagons, about 800 head of cattle, and 60 horses and mules. As the emigrant company moved south, heading for California, the Mormons began the speak of them as "Missourians." The emigrants encountered hostility. War preparations were on. An order had just gone out to conserve food; so none was sold to these strangers. In some cases when they approached towns, they were not permitted to pass through but had to break a road around. Perhaps the Mormons were afraid of attack, perhaps only antagonized by the presence of people from Babylon.

There were stories that the emigrants taunted the Mormons, saying that the army would hang Brother Brigham and the apostles, that they told coarse jokes about Mormon religion, perhaps repeating some of the then current waggish remarks about polygamy. We do not know the truth of these charges.

Brigham Young, learning of the emigrant train moving southward and sensing the tensions that prevailed, sent, on September 10, an order to Isaac C. Haight at Cedar City, an officer of the Nauvoo Legion: "In regard to the emigration trains passing through our settlements, we must not interfere with them until they are first notified to keep away. You must not meddle with them. The Indians, we expect will do as they please, but you should try and preserve good feelings with them. There are no other trains going south that I know of."[30]

The above message had been sent while Captain Van Vliet was in Salt Lake City. There was probably no thought in Young's mind that any harm would befall the emigrants, although he indicated cryptically that the Mormons could not be held responsible if the Indians got out of hand. The message came too late. On the day it was written Indians and whites were gathering at Mountain Meadows near the southern boundary of Utah. The emigrants defended themselves behind their wagons. Three days later, on September 13, the white leaders of the attackers, under a flag of truce, induced the company to surrender. Why the company surrendered and on what terms is not clear, but the people came out from their barricades. Indians and whites fell on them, killing all but a few small children, too young to have very definite memories of the tragedy.

There had been other frontier massacres, other cases where

white men joined with the Indians; but this was the only case of the kind in the settled part of Utah. In most of the other massacres robbery was the primary motive; here it was probably but incidental, although some $30,000 worth of loot was seized. In this case all property was taken—household equipment, even wagons and livestock. Indian Agent John D. Lee must have gained some of the booty.[31]

The first official report of the massacre appears to have been sent to Brigham Young by Indian Agent George W. Armstrong, a Mormon, on September 30, which was nineteen days after the event. This report alleged the ill treatment of the Indians by a group of emigrants. The emigrants had given poisoned beef to the Indians. Four died, and many were sick. They followed the emigrants to Mountain Meadows, "where they attacked the camp and after a desperate fight, they killed 57 men and nine women"—a masterpiece of understatement and inaccuracy, but Brigham Young was content officially to accept this report.

Feverishly preparing to resist a force threatening their own destruction, the Mormons were too occupied for shock, though they did sense the seriousness of the massacre. They were content to believe statements such as that recorded by Wilford Woodruff in his journal on September 29, 1857: "Brother Lee said that he did not think there was a drop of innocent blood in their camp, for he had two of the children in his house, and he could not get but one to kneel down in prayer time, and the other would laugh at her for doing it, and they would swear like pirates."

Officials of the army, once the soldiers had been comfortably settled in Cedar Valley, began to concern themselves about civil affairs in Utah and to give moral support to the new gentile civil officials. These civil officials, as will be seen in the following chapter, were determined to put things right in Zion. They were horrified at reports of the massacre, but the scene was far away and evidence hard to get. They directed their attention to the more immediate details of their judicial purge.

Chief Justice Eckles, as already noted, gathered about him at Camp Scott enough non-Mormons to form a grand jury. He took evidence from sundry persons on the basis of which he indicted some sixty-six church leaders for treason. It was expected there would be wholesale arrests as soon as the soldiers arrived in Salt Lake Valley. This plan was frustrated by the receipt of the president's proclamation of pardon.

A new drive was launched to indict other Mormons on other charges. Certain of the Gentiles previously feared to speak up; but with the army on hand to protect them, they stepped forward with all the fanaticism that Mormons had demonstrated in their Reformation, which flourished up to the arrival of news about the army en route.

The crusade of 1856, which lasted through the winter until the summer of 1857, might have gone to embarrassing lengths. The punitive military expedition against Utah probably saved the Mormons from themselves, but it brought them face to face with a group of federal officials fired with a similar zeal of their own and determined to bring the Mormons to judgment for such crimes as the Springville murders and the Mountain Meadows massacre.

NOTES

1. The speech by Douglas was reported in the *Missouri Republican* (St. Louis), June 18, 1857. Lincoln's speech was reported in the *Illinois State Journal* (Springfield), July 1, 1857. Mormons took comfort in recalling a prediction made to Douglas by Joseph Smith that if he ever raised his voice against the Mormons the hand of the Lord would rest heavily on him. The prophet told him he would aspire for the presidency but would fail if he opposed the Saints. Douglas did aspire, and he did fail.

2. *Journal of Discourses*, III, 234. Grant's reference to prostitution had a basis in his efforts as mayor to close certain brothels, gambling halls, and other gentile resorts on "Whiskey Street" in Salt Lake City.

3. The letters quoted in this chapter are on file at the National Archives in the letter books of the Commission of Indian Affairs for the Territory of Utah.

4. For a recent and complete summary of the Utah War from the Mormon viewpoint see Andrew L. Neff, *History of Utah*, pp. 456–84.

5. During the reformation of 1856 (*Journal of Discourses*, IV, 77) Brigham Young made a speech from which the following much-quoted item is taken: "I have many a time on this stand dared the world to produce as mean devils as we can. We can beat them at anything; we have the greatest and smoothest liars in the world; the cunningest and most adroit thieves, and any other shade of character you can mention. We can pick out elders in Israel right here who can beat the world at gambling, who can handle cards, cut and shuffle them with the smartest rogues on the face of God's footstool. I can produce elders who can shave the smartest shavers, and take their money from them. . . . . We can pray the best, preach the best, and sing the best. We are the best-

looking and finest set of people on the face of the earth; and they can begin any game they please, and we will be on hand to beat them at anything they have a mind to begin. They may make sharp their two-edged swords, and I will turn out the elders of Israel with greased feathers and whip them to death."

6. Reprinted in a church publication, the *Contributor*, III, 177. Also see B. H. Roberts, *Comprehensive History of the Church*, Vol. IV, chap. cv.

7. Captain Van Vliet had been in contact with the Mormons some years earlier when they were in camp at Winter Quarters in 1846–47. His relations with them then had been pleasant. Other letters regarding the expedition are found in *House Executive Document No. 71* (35th Cong., 1st sess.), X, 24–26.

8. Regarding preparations James G. Bleak wrote in the "Manuscript History of St. George," August 19, 1857: "Apostle George A. Smith, Colonel Wm. H. Dame, James H. Martineau and others visited the settlements of Southern Utah. He informed the Saints that the United States Army was on the way to Utah. He advised the Saints to be saving of their grain, and not to sell it to travelers to feed to animals, for the teams could live on the grass better than our women and children. He said all we could afford to do under the circumstances was to furnish the travelers with bread."

Joseph Fish, of Parowan, wrote in his journal, August 16, 1857, that men were in the mountains looking for places of retreat in case the Saints would be forced to abandon their homes; that the people were prepared, if necessary, "to apply the torch and burn everything and leave the country as they found it, a barren desert."

9. Roberts (*op. cit.*, Vol. IV, chap. cvi) cites charges that Mormon women had been tempted to leave Utah with the soldiers of Colonel E. J. Steptoe's command. These charges, strangely enough, had not been given publicity before the threat of another army of occupation.

10. *Ibid.*, chap. cv, quotes the "History of Brigham Young" for November, 1857, referring to an undated article in the *Los Angeles Star* regretting the departure of the Saints from San Bernardino. Saints leaving Carson Valley and San Bernardino were unable to sell. Gentiles were not willing to buy what they would be able to take later. Orson Hyde was obliged to leave a flour mill. It was reported that he cursed the mill so that no Gentile would profit by it. Gentiles took possession, but soon thereafter a flood washed the mill away.

11. Albert Sidney Johnston was a Kentuckian and a West Point graduate. He resigned from the army to join the army of the republic of Texas. In the war with Mexico he apparently found favor with Zachary Taylor; and when Taylor became president, Johnston got a political appointment as army paymaster. He returned to army service after Taylor's death. In the Civil War he was one of the southern generals and achieved considerable distinction. He was killed in action in 1862.

12. *The Utah Expedition* by Captain Jesse A. Gove is a collection of letters written by Captain Gove to his wife and to certain newspapers. It is clear from these letters that the officers were not favorably moved by the views of Captain Van Vliet. They wanted action against the Mormons. Gove wrote on September 18: "If the Mormons will only fight their days are numbered. We shall sweep them from the face of the earth and Mormonism in Utah will cease."

13. Captain Gove (*ibid.*, October 15, 1857) remarked that a "Major Taylor had been captured. This was Joseph Taylor, who had on his person a copy of the order from Wells, dated October 4, which instructed him to annoy the troops in every possible way. "Use every exertion to stampede their animals and set fire to their trains. Burn the whole country before them, and on their flanks. Keep them from sleeping, by night surprises; blockade the road by felling trees or destroying river fords where you can. Watch for opportunities to set fire to grass before them that can be burned. Keep your

men concealed as much as possible, and on guard against surprise. Keep scouts out at all times, and communications open with Colonel Burton, Major McAllister and O.P. Rockwell, who are operating in the same way. Keep me advised daily of your movements, and every step the troops take and in what direction. God bless and give you success; Your brother in Christ, Daniel H. Wells." See Roberts, *op. cit.*, chaps. cvi and cvii.

14. Reports on the burning of the wagon trains are found in *House Executive Document No. 71* (35th Cong., 1st sess.). Lot Smith wrote a series of articles on "The Echo Canyon War," published in the *Contributor*, 1881–82. Smith reported that the captain in charge of the supply wagons tried to get his drivers to resist. They refused, saying they were "bullwhackers, not soldiers." Richard F. Burton (*The City of the Saints*, p. 215), relating the story, reported that he saw the half-circles of charcoal where the wagons burned, but the iron had been hauled away.

15. Captain Gove (*op. cit.*, October 20, 1857) wrote: "Last night Gov. Young sent to Colonel A. some *Deseret News*, a newspaper full of all sorts of nonsense about troops coming into the valley. An address in poetry is published by a Miss Snow to the ladies of this army of invasion; this means Mrs. Canby and Mrs. Burns, the only two ladies with us. It is very pathetic and warns them to persuade the army to go back." Captain Gove also noted a speech by Elder Kimball, saying: "No U.S. soldier shall set his foot in Salt Lake City so long as a drop of blood is in his veins." He noted in the same papers that Brigham Young had said that Colonel Alexander "was no gentleman. Right, for once." The younger officers were apparently angry that Alexander did not surge ahead and shoot it out with the Mormons.

16. Captain Gove, *ibid.*, December 4, 1857: "Brigham Young sent in to Col. Johnston some salt and an impudent letter; the Colonel told him [the messenger] to go back with his salt and tell Brigham not to attempt any more communication with him or his emissaries would hang; that he could not treat with him only under a white flag."

Concerning the salt episode, there was discussion in the United States Senate on February 25, 1858. Senator Sam Houston of Texas, who knew Colonel Johnston and did not think well of him, said: "What was the message the officer sent back? I believe the substance of it was that he would have no intercourse with a rebel, and that when they met they would fight. They will fight, and if they fight, he will get miserably whipped. That was a time to make peace with Brigham Young, because there is something potent in salt. With the Turk, who has similar habits and religion to the Mormons, it is a sacrament of perpetual friendship."

17. Richards carried messages to the president and any other government officials he could reach. A story of an interview with him was printed in the *New York Times* of September 12, 1857. Elder Richards met a contingent of the troops at Fort Kearny. He reported that some were pessimistic about the winter journey to Utah. Others were anticipating a good time in Utah, where "the women are as thick as blackberries." A statement by Richards is found in the *Millennial Star*, XIX, 670. Such expressions as this were good propaganda with the English: "Every dirty, foul-mouthed Dutchman and Irishman, of which many of the troops were composed, fully expected some 'Mormon' woman would jump into his arms upon his arrival in Utah. . . . ."

18. Such was the view of the *New York Times*, January 23, 1858. The *Times* said on November 12, 1857: "It would puzzle ordinary men, we suspect, to explain why a hostile army was sent to Utah at the outset. There were undoubted disorders in the affairs of the territory; but it has never yet been shown that they were such as could only be remedied by fire and sword."

19. Buchanan gave a letter to Kane describing his mission as "pacific and philanthropic." He commended Kane to all federal officials en route. In his annual message of December 6, 1858, Buchanan praised Kane for his part in settling the Utah War.

20. *House Executive Document No. 2* (35th Cong., 2d sess.), II, Part II, 44, contains a letter dated January 20, 1858, written by Johnston to Major Irvin McDowell, assistant adjutant general of the army. Johnston said, in part: "Knowing how repugnant it would be to force these people into unpleasant relations with the federal government, I would, in conformity with the views also of the commanding general, on all proper occasions have manifested in my intercourse with them a spirit of conciliation, but I do not believe that such consideration for them would be properly appreciated now, or rather would be wrongly interpreted; and, in view of the treasonable temper and feelings now pervading the leaders and a greater portion of the Mormons, I think that neither the honor nor the dignity of the government will allow the slightest concession being made to them."

21. Judge Eckles on June 4, 1858, wrote to the Secretary of State that his hearings confirmed his view that Brigham Young was the cornerstone of the "Mormon system"; that in him rested "all power, civil as well as ecclesiastical, in heaven, on earth and in hell. . . . . Any other government than his is sinful, wicked and illegitimate."

22 Instructions from the Secretary of State to Cumming at the time of his appointment were liberal. Regarding the Mormons, Secretary Lewis Cass wrote: "With any peculiar opinions of the inhabitants, however deplorable in themselves or revolting to the public sentiment of the country, the Executive Government has no legitimate concern, and no design to interfere. Our social and political institutions recognize the utmost freedom of discussion, and men are justly obnoxious to legal penalty for their actions only and not for their opinions."

23. At the instance of Judge Eckles, Marshal P. K. Dotson made a trip to Salt Lake Valley, apparently by stealth. He learned that a detachment of the Nauvoo Legion under Howard Egan was guarding Governor Cumming so closely that people were excluded from seeing him. Dotson wrote his report to the judge on April 27: "All of the settlements north of Ogden City and in Rush and Tooele Valleys have been entirely deserted, but the houses, fences, etc., have not been destroyed or injured. All the loose cattle have been driven south from the vicinity of Salt Lake City and from the northern settlements. The people in these places are moving as rapidly as possible and concentrating in the neighborhood of Provo City."

24. Captain Gove (*op. cit.*, May 22, 1858) wrote his wife that the proclamation fell like a thunderbolt. "It is a finely written document, and instead of sending it here at this late hour, it should have been sent nearly a year ago. I do not think Brigham Young will heed it. I hope not. If he does comply, or seem to, it will keep us here much longer."

25. Following the indictments by Judge Eckles, Governor Cumming wrote General Johnston asking for a posse of soldiers to assist Marshal Dotson to "serve writs on Brigham Young and sixty-six others indicated for treason and other felonies by the grand jury in Green River County." This was a jury of gentile refugees. The request was made on May 25, a few days before getting the president's proclamation of pardon. Johnston refused to furnish the posse "at this time."

26. Johnston and Cumming had an understanding, which the former did not keep. Johnston was to await word from Governor Cumming before beginning his march. On the basis of this understanding, Cumming made certain pledges to the Mormons. Johnston began marching as soon as he received word from the peace commission, ignoring Cumming. He explained that he was operating under his own orders, which required him to be governed by military reasons (*House Executive Document No. 2* [35th Cong., 2d sess.], II, Part II, 119).

27. When the army marched through Salt Lake City, a group of men from the Navuoo Legion stood on the side lines. Among them were some members of the Mormon Battalion who had served under Colonel Philip St. George Cooke in 1846–47.

When Colonel Cooke rode past these Battalion veterans and recognized them, he uncovered his head.

28. M. Hamlin Cannon wrote a Master's thesis (George Washington University, 1938): "The Mormon War: A Study in Territorial Rebellion." One conclusion is pertinent: "In the first place, it was part of the tendency toward secession in the United States which culminated in the Civil War. Some of the constitutional questions discussed in connection with it may well have clarified the thinking of some at the time when, shortly thereafter, the southern states attempted to secede."

29. "L.D.S. Journal History," March 31, 1858, quotes Brigham Young on "tempering" with the Indians: "Whether the massacre and robbery by the Indians at Fort Limhi on Salmon River, February 25; the killing of cattle and stealing of horses in Scull, Rush, and Tooele Valleys; the late killing and robbing on Bannock Creek; the threatened Indian foray from Uinta Valley; and the current rumor that the army have offered the Indians $150 for every Mormon they bring into Colonel Johnston's camp, can be proved in court to be part of the 'civilized mode of warfare' to be pursued by government officers against the Mormons is uncertain, for witnesses may absent themselves, keep back the truth, or be excused from testifying, on the plea that they would incriminate themselves. But it is certain that no trouble had hitherto occurred at Fort Limhi, and that a certain J. W. Powell was most actively engaged with the Indians in the massacre and robbery perpetrated at that fort; and it is reported that soldiers from Colonel Johnston's camp wintered at Beaver Head, a short distance from Fort Limhi."

30. One of the latest non-Mormon accounts of the massacre is found in Hoffman Birney's *Zealots of Zion* (1931), chaps. vii–x. The latest account from the Mormon viewpoint is Neff, *op. cit.*, pp. 410–32. Church officials did attempt for years to block all investigation, principally because most investigators were not so much interested in the facts as in using the incident to indict Brigham Young.

31. The writer examined the census books at the United States Bureau of the Census for 1850 and 1860. In 1850 John D. Lee was living at Parowan with two of his wives. His property was valued at $3,000. In 1860 he was living at Harmony with ten of his wives, and his property was valued at $49,500, making him several times richer than any other man in southern Utah. There was no way, except by miracle or loot, for any man to gain that much property, since no man on the frontier of that region could gain wealth except by his own labor. Few church leaders in those parts reported more than $4,000 of property in the census of 1860.

CHAPTER VIII

CARPETBAG GOVERNMENT IN UTAH

BRIGHAM YOUNG went into retirement, apparently for more than a year. No sooner were the people back in their homes than he closed his own, the "Beehive" and the "Lion House." A strong guard was posted. Month after month he held his silence, although keeping in communication with trusted associates. He did receive some visitors, but appointments were carefully made.

This retirement may have been a form of passive resistance which put the gentile officials on notice: "Try to run things here without our co-operation." Gentile observers began to realize that, whoever held the office of governor, Brigham Young was leader of his people. His silence was more effective than any proclamation of Governor Cumming.

This retirement of President Young was also a safety measure, probably demanded of him by his brethren. Gentiles were in the saddle, and some were not averse to riding down those in church control. Many Gentiles, free of speech, were wont to utter threats. There was boasting that Brigham Young would be captured and "done up."[1]

At Camp Floyd there were about three thousand soldiers, probably the largest single garrison in the nation. Normally the soldiers spent their leisure at Fairfield, a civilian auxiliary community peopled by hangers-on who lived by trade with the military or by other gentile affiliations. To the Mormons, Fairfield was "Frog Town"; and its reputation for evil compared with that of "Whiskey Street," the area of gentile cosmopolitanism in Salt Lake City.

If soldiers took leave, they generally went to Salt Lake City to rendezvous on "Whiskey Street." The *Deseret News* for September 15, 1858, complained of the "rapidly increasing profanity and drunkenness, of the progress of gambling, whoredoms, etc." In that area were street fights every night and killings almost ever week. On army payday there was rowdyism and brawling, which was not always confined to the restricted area.

Enlistments sometimes expired in groups of from fifty to more than a hundred soldiers. For the army to turn so many men loose in Utah, where they had no economic opportunities, created a considerable problem. Moreover, a hardship was imposed on the discharged men. Eventually the army officers recognized the problem and made arrangements to send the men in groups to the eastern states or west to the mining camps. A few preferred to remain in Utah, where they sought employment as teamsters with the gentile freighting companies.

Church leaders contemplated the change wrought by the army's presence and asked if such was the "Christian civilization" that force of arms would establish. While the leaders did not speak out in public, they did go quietly from place to place exhorting the people to maintain a dignified aloofness. Possibly any other tactics than polite, passive silence might have stirred numerous forays.[2]

In other respects the people were instructed on their conduct with strangers: "Be wise as serpents, but harmless as doves." The good Saint would confide in no stranger. Children were taught to meet direct questions with indirect or indefinite answers, or to reply innocently: "I don't know."

This policy of telling the Gentiles nothing and holding aloof was a mandate from Brother Brigham. When United States Attorney Alexander Wilson called on him to bid goodbye, he sent this message to the world outside: "I wish you would tell them that I am here, watching the progress of civilization." Wilson was one of the gentile office-holders who took issue with the gentile reform group.

Not all Mormons viewed the presence of the army with alarm. There were some who found the camp a good cash customer for feed and foodstuff. Not all the soldiers shared the prevalent antagonism of the Gentiles. A few got on well with the Mormons. Some remained in Utah on friendly relations with the Saints. An occasional one joined the church.

The gentile office-holders installed in Utah after the arrival of the army were not of a single mind. One faction, led by Governor Alfred Cumming, favored tolerance. It offended the opposing faction when Cumming, on July 26, 1858, joined Brigham Young and other church leaders on a picnic in Big Cottonwood Canyon. United States Attorney Wilson was also a member of the party. Superintendent of Indian Affairs Jacob Forney was allied with the governor's faction. He was subjected to considerable criticism because he did not join the crusade to fix blame on Brigham Young for the Mountain Meadows massacre and other charges. Hostile Gentiles believed that evidence was obtainable to hang Brigham Young.

The other faction was led by Chief Justice D. R. Eckles and the two associate justices, Charles E. Sinclair and John Cradlebaugh. Closely allied with the judges was United States Marshal Peter K. Dotson and Indian Agent Garland Hurt, concerning whom enough has already been said to indicate his dislike of the Mormons.[3] Another of the anti-Mormon group was Forney's other subagent, Columbus L. Craig, a rough fellow with a propensity for brawling when intoxicated. Craig engaged one of the judges, presumably Sinclair, in a knife and gun duel, which resulted in his suspension and later dismissal by Forney.

The feud between the Governor Cumming faction and the Judge Eckles faction of Utah's carpetbag government is traced to the poison-pen letters of the latter. On July 9, 1858, Eckles wrote to Secretary of State Lewis Cass that "Brigham Young is de facto governor of Utah, whatever Governor Cumming may be de jure. His reign is one of terror. His unbridled will is king. Every apostate Mormon and every Gentile here, who has hitherto lived in the Territory is in constant fear of personal violence. To me the future is dark and gloomy."[4] In this letter Eckles expressed regret that all the federal officials in Utah were not united in what he considered the proper course in dealing with the Mormons.

Utah law, as already reported, had assumed for the territorial courts jurisdiction over criminal and civil cases. These courts were clothed with the powers of state courts. Although a stickler for law in other things, Judge Eckles elected to ignore the claims of the probate courts and to take cases from these courts on the slightest pretext. His lead was followed by his associate judges, Sinclair and Cradlebaugh.[5] All three judges busied themselves with cases of long standing, some of which had been heard by the probate courts. In some cases they assumed jurisdiction after the probate courts had taken action.

Efforts were made to bring prominent Mormons to trial on various old charges. For example, Judge Sinclair in Salt Lake City had charges filed against James Ferguson, Hosea Stout, and other Mormon lawyers for the alleged burning of court records in February, 1857. These lawyers had raided the office of Judge George P. Stiles, a purged Mormon, described by Church Historian B. H. Roberts as a "disreputable character" for whom "disgust for the man led up to contempt for the judge."

This trial dragged for several weeks during the autumn of 1858 and was used by the prosecution as an excuse for bringing before the court, for questioning, various Mormon leaders, including Brigham Young. Recognizing the purpose of the review, Governor Cumming added to his unpopularity by offering personally to escort Brigham Young before the bar. Young appeared but was not placed on the witness stand. Court sessions were so irregular that Mormons charged the judges with operating on the principle of "loaferism," primarily to enlarge the costs of operation and to prolong the jobs of various gentile hangers-on. It was claimed that the cost of operating any one of the federal district courts was greater than the territorial budget.[6]

In the spring of 1859 came an open break between the governor and the courts. The occasion was an encroachment on local authority at Provo by Judge Cradlebaugh, aided by detachments of soldiers supplied by General Johnston. There was a threat of using troops to support the court at Salt Lake City. The latter episode involved a plot to arrest Brigham Young on a charge of counterfeiting. Two men at Camp Floyd had been arrested for counterfeiting, not money but United States quartermaster orders. The culprits reported that the plates which they used had been engraved by a young Mormon in Salt Lake City. When the police raided the engraver's plant, they found the plates used for printing church tithing scrip. While scrip was not money, it offered an occasion for bringing the head of the church in as a defendant.

When Marshal Peter K. Dotson raided the engraver's plant and found the plates for making Deseret currency, the token money used by the tithing offices, the findings were extremely satisfactory to the group at Camp Floyd headed by Judge Eckles. They concluded and hoped that President Young would resist arrest. Then they could call on the soldiers.

Governor Cumming heard of the plan and sent for the planners. They admitted their purpose: to bring cannon and blast a hole in the wall around Young's premises. Stenhouse reported in his book, *The Rocky Mountain Saints*, the governor's answer as told him by Cumming: "I was indignant, sir, and I told them, 'By God, gentlemen, you can't do it! When you have a right to take Brigham Young, gentlemen, you shall have him without creeping through walls. You shall enter by the door with heads erect as becomes representatives of your government, but until that time, gentlemen, you can't touch Brigham Young while I live, by God!' "

While General Johnston was too careful to put himself on record, his attitude toward Mormon authorities was evidenced by his failure to meet personally any of them. Apparently, he was willing to make his soldiers available on request from the judges. He did send troops to Provo upon request from Judge Cradlebaugh and without conferring with Governor Cumming.[7]

There is a report that Judge Cradlebaugh was an eccentric who came riding into Salt Lake City in November, 1878, on a load of wood. He came as far as Hank's Station on the stagecoach but refused to finish the journey in such style and accepted a ride with a farmer who was taking a load of firewood to town. He was assigned to the southern Utah district, for which court headquarters were at Nephi. Instead, he elected to open court at Provo, to which place he went on March 8, 1859, flanked and supported by a military guard. He announced that he was prepared to bring to justice all Mormons involved in the Springville murders, the Mountain Meadows massacre, and various other crimes, already too long neglected.

Provo residents were offended because the judge feared to come among them without his military escort. The judge was apparently of the opinion that soldiers were needed to guard prisoners and keep order in the court. The troops were not detailed for making arrests or hunting fugitives from justice.

Residents of Provo and other towns in Utah County brought to Judge Cradlebaugh a petition protesting against the use of troops in dealing with civil problems and claiming "that standing armies in time of peace are dangerous to liberty, especially when placed in proximity to the judicial bench." The judge was assured that the citizens of the county were prepared to discharge their duties in the interest of justice, a matter which the judge had not taken the trouble to discover previously. They made bold to remind Cradlebaugh that his action was a "high-handed violation of the rights and constitutional liberties of free men, unprecedented in our great republic, and never tamely submitted to by the Anglo Saxon race."

The judge was not moved by this petition, nor was he dissuaded from his course, even though reports came to him that the presence of the troops was demoralizing to the community. He took no action on complaints that the soldiers, while intoxicated, had terrorized Provo residents. Instead of disciplining the fractious soldiers, Cradlebaugh concluded that the people had become rebellious. He requested more soldiers. The request was honored by General Johnston, with the result that within a few days there were some nine hundred troops in Provo to guard less than half a dozen prisoners.

General Johnston wrote Judge Cradlebaugh on March 19 that he hoped the presence of the soldiers would "prevent that portion of the population who may be disaffected from involving the better-disposed citizens in an outburst against the authority of the government."[8] Johnston probably did not realize that the so-called "disaffected" part of the population included almost all the inhabitants. The rest were hovering around the camp of the soldiers and dreading the day when the troops would leave. Apparently, neither Johnston or Cradlebaugh could understand that their expedition into Utah County had alienated the loyalty even of the moderate Mormons. When the mayor of Provo was arrested on some charge, every able-bodied man in town immediately became a member of the police force, and the judge found himself confronted with a civilian army of his own indirect creation. The report of Captain Henry Heth for March 18 reads like a bulletin from the front: "The position I now occupy is such that I can, should matters be brought to an issue, hold out against any force that might be brought against me. . . . ."

At this point Governor Cumming took a hand, arriving in Provo on March 20, about two weeks after the beginning of the fiasco. He found the army and citizens at the point of open hostilities. Respectfully, although apologetically, Captain Heth informed him that he was not at liberty to take orders from the governor. Cumming wrote to Johnston: "I am satisfied that the presence of a military force in this place is unnecessary."

Under protest General Johnston complied with Cumming's request, indicating that he was free, according to his orders, to co-operate with the governor or not, as seemed best from the military point of view. He assumed that, so long as the orders originally given to General Harney and later transferred to him had not been changed, he was expected to be governed by them. These orders had been issued when Brigham Young was governor, but Johnston would not veer from them.[9]

Three appeals were sent to Washington. Both Cumming and Cradlebaugh wrote to Secretary of State Lewis Cass. Johnston wrote to the adjutant general of the army. Said Cumming: "I respectfully request that the discrepancy which exists between the instructions given to the civil and military departments in this territory may be removed by some further action on the part of the government, and I would further request that all requisitions for troops be made through the governor of the territory. . . . ."

Judge Cradlebaugh found himself unable to carry on court,

such was the drop in morale. He had lost face in the community. The grand jury did not share his zeal to indict leading Mormons. He dismissed the jury, but not without using the occasion to read a speech which caused wide comment. He told the jurors: "You are the tools, the dupes, the instruments of a tyrannical Church despotism. The heads of your Church order and direct you. You are taught to obey their orders and commit these horrid murders. Deprived of your liberty, you have lost your manhood, and become the willing instruments of bad men."[10]

Cradlebaugh declared there was in Utah a conspiracy to obstruct justice, "to cover up and conceal crimes committed by Mormons." He charged that witnesses had been intimidated, that the grand jury would join him in indicting Indians or Gentiles, but not Mormons. As a sort of personal reprisal he released two Indians awaiting trial for rape.

On May 17, 1859, Attorney General Jeremiah S. Black wrote to the federal judges in Utah that they had exceeded their authority to become public accusers. Concerning the Provo episode he wrote the following opinion, concurred in by the president:

1. That the governor of the territory alone has power to issue a requisition upon the commanding general for the whole or a part of the army.
2. That there was no apparent occasion for the presence of the troops at Provo.
3. That if the rescue of the prisoners in custody had been attempted, it was the duty of the marshal and not of the judge to summon the force that might be necessary to prevent it.
4. That the troops ought not to have been sent to Provo without the concurrence of the governor, nor kept there against his remonstrance.
5. That the disregard of these principles and rules of action has been in many ways extremely unfortunate.[11]

By the same mail Secretary of War John B. Floyd sent an order to General Johnston: "You will, therefore, only order the troops under your command to assist as a *posse comitatus* in the execution of the laws only upon the written application of the governor of the territory, and not otherwise."

Frustrated by this rebuke, Judge Cradlebaugh went away to Carson Valley to hold court. When the Territory of Nevada was formed in 1860, he was named its first delegate to Congress. It should be added that, before going to Carson Valley and immediately after his Provo experience, he made a trip with a military escort to the scene of the Mountain Meadows massacre. While the evidence he gathered on this expedition was not used by him as a judge, it was used in speeches against the Mormons. One such speech was made on February 7, 1863, but the Civil War was on and Congress was occupied with other matters.

The division on authority and policy in the matter of the courts in Utah was also present in the handling of Indian affairs. During the Utah War period the Commissioner of Indian Affairs joined in a general program against the Mormons. Indian agents working with the tribes surrounding Utah were authorized to be liberal in giving presents and to impress upon the Indians that the Great White Father was angry with the Mormons, who were "misguided and badly disposed persons." On November 25, 1857, Commissioner J. W. Denver authorized the agencies in New Mexico to expend from $10,000 to $14,000 to win the good will of the Navajo and other tribes along the southern border of Utah, where Mormon missionaries were active.[12]

In dispatching this order General Denver added significantly: "Should you fail in your efforts to keep the Indians in a state of peace and quiet, then your aim should be to array them against such other Indians as may be found on the side of the enemies of the government." The agents were to go about this mission "with great caution and delicacy."

When Jacob Forney reached army headquarters at Camp Scott in November, 1857, to assume his duties as superintendent of Indian affairs in Utah, succeeding Brigham Young, he found that the Snake and Shoshone tribes were already hostile to the Mormons. This hostility had been previously engendered by the "mountain men" living among them. He met the chiefs of several tribes and in return for presents received their pledge of friendly co-operation. He reported on February 10, 1858: "I am assured by reliable persons that the tribes in this Territory, with the exception of those in and about Carson Valley, have been uniformly peacable, and never molested any of our people and the government, although frequently importuned by the Mormons to steal from and murder emigrants."

On March 11, 1858, Forney reported that Colonel Johnston had requested him to get the co-operation of the Indians in the army's operations. "The intention is not to engage Indians for actual fighting, but as scouting parties. . . . . I have concluded that it is my duty to render the army all the aid in my power."

Forney's well-intentioned co-operation resulted in trouble for him later. The Indians came to believe that the "big soldiers" would support them in any action against the Mormons. Later when hostilities ceased, Forney failed to advise them that the Great White Father was no longer angry. The redskins continued their depredations against Mormons and others.

Federal officials, while inciting the Indians against the Mormons, were charging the Mormons with "tampering with the Indians." Young answered in a letter to the Commissioner of Indian Affairs sent on April 8, 1858: "Our enemies have no scruples in exciting the Indians against [us] and, especially when taken in connection with actual hostilities and depredations on their part, and the boasted 'allies of Utah Indians' in the camp of United States troops, as stated in their correspondence and published in the eastern papers, leaves but little room to doubt the complicity of the army in these hostilities." Young asked sarcastically if these methods were in line with what the army officers would describe as a "civilized mode of warfare."[13]

After hostilities ended, Forney soon learned that the Indian problem was far different from the reports received by him while at Camp Scott. He learned that most of the time some of the tribes were on the verge of starvation. He learned, as had Major Holeman six years before, that the Mormons were not in league with the Indians to waylay and rob gentile emigrant trains. And while Dr. Forney was learning these facts, the conclusion was being forced upon him that there was no solution of Utah's Indian problem except to put the Indians to work on farms. But he lacked the funds to start a farm program.

Along the Oregon-Utah border the tribes were especially delinquent during 1858 and the early part of 1859. On July 24 of the latter year a party of Indians, and some whites, who were alleged to be their leaders, attacked an emigrant train at Sublett's Cutoff. Seven persons were killed and eight wounded. At Forney's request a company of dragoons was sent to discipline the offenders. When the redskins learned that the soldiers were coming, they fled to the mountains. This experience was disillusioning to the Indians, who had rested securely on the Fort Scott pledge of the army that the Indians and soldiers would be allies.

Forney's farm plan was not new. Garland Hurt had already started some Indian farms, but his program was interrupted by his flight in the autumn of 1857. He tried to put the Indians to work, but the farms were a luxury. Hurt had to hire white labor or he would not have had any crops. The Indians were lazy; interested in the harvest but not in the tilling.[14]

Owing to war conditions, the agency farms during 1858 fell into neglect, and the Indians were not interested in assembling later to make a new start. Forney and Hurt found the tribes demoralized and perhaps confused about the contradictions in authority. Before the war they were aware of two groups of whites, the "Mericats" and the "Mormone." After the war the Mormons were out of power, whereas the Americans were in power but much divided. It was confusing to the simple savage mind.

Forney discovered that most of the property on the Indian farms had been carried off, obviously by the Mormons, because the Indians had no need for farming equipment. Apparently, the Indians did take the stores of food, after which they left the farms and were roaming promiscuously among the settlements, begging from the Mormons. Forney reported to the commissioner on June 18, 1858:

> These Indians have recently taken away several yoke of oxen to eat. They also enter the farmhouse almost daily, the farmer informs me, and carry away oats and barley and wheat. They did not leave potatoes enough for seed.

These Indians tell the farmer that the farm and everything on it is theirs, and if any opposition is made, they threaten the farmer, and say that Agent Hurt told them to take away anything that may be of service to them.

This concerned the Spanish Fork farm, and such were the instructions which Hurt gave when he fled for his own safety the previous autumn.

In the same letter Forney reported that the Indians in central Utah, who before the war had been peaceful, were now "troublesome and hostile," harassing travelers and residents. He resorted to the expedient of visiting the tribes and giving presents in exchange for pledges of peace which could not be kept.[15]

Superintendent Forney operated under the added disadvantage of being alone. He was merely tolerated by the Mormons, who were following through with their own Indian program. He was suspected by the Judge Eckles faction of the federal officials and other members of the court, and the confidence of the Governor Cumming faction was of little help to him. Dr. Hurt, his subordinate, instead of working with him, was actively opposed to him. He finally requested Hurt's removal.[16]

The removal of Dr. Hurt was based on his mishandling of an incident involving the misconduct of certain Indians at the Spanish Fork agency. On September 10, 1858, a number of Indians from the agency entered a Spanish Fork home and assaulted two women, a mother and daughter. The Mormons demanded that the culprits be arrested; but they fled to Camp Floyd, believing that they would be protected by the soldiers. Four days later Hurt, in a discouraged state of mind, wrote Forney: "The process of redeeming these wretched creatures from savage indolence to habits of industry and morality has been greatly interrupted during the past season. . . . "

Hurt was further distracted a few days later to receive an order from Governor Cumming to demand that the chiefs deliver the men who had assaulted the women. If the demand was refused, he was told to secure a posse from the inhabitants. Wrote the governor: "It is my desire to avoid resorting to the military posse until other means have been unsuccessfully tried, yet if it is finally necessary you will please communicate with

a

b

INDIANS AT HOME

These pictures were taken by Major J. W. Powell about 1870 at the time of his survey of the Colorado River. The Indians in both pictures were photographed somewhere near St. George. (*a*) An old woman weaving a basket. (*b*) A girl grinding meal on a flat stone.

me promptly and I will take the necessary action." Forney was then in Carson Valley, and the governor was acting in his stead.

Hurt issued his demand to the chiefs, but they would not co-operate. The offenders had returned from Camp Floyd and were then under the protection of the chiefs. The Indians argued that no arrests were necessary, since the two women had not died. Without calling for a civilian posse Hurt reported to the governor the reply of the chiefs. Cumming ordered that Hurt should call another council and again demand the offenders. "If they hesitate or refuse, you will break up the council, and without advising anyone of your intention, proceed to Camp Floyd and deliver to the general in command the enclosed requisition for two hundred mounted men."

The council was called. The chiefs did not understand why "Mericats" wanted to "tie" (i.e., arrest) Indians for attacking "Mormone squaws," since they had been told that the Mormons were "bad people." When Hurt arrived with his military posse, he found that all but a few of the Indians had fled into the mountains. Two of the wanted Indians—Pintuts and Tintic—were still on the farm but would not submit to arrest. Tintic escaped, but Pintuts was shot in the attempt. Most of the others were arrested.

Angered by the raid and sorrowed by the loss of one of their leaders, the Indians swore to be avenged. It was soon reported that Arapeen, brother of Chief Walker, had taken to the warpath. A party of Indians ambushed two white men at Chicken Creek, south of Nephi, thus taking toll for the death of Pintuts. Some Indians claimed they thought the white men were Gentiles; but they were Mormons—Samuel Brown and Josiah Call, of Fillmore. One Indian was killed in this affray.

The report that the Utahs had taken the warpath was not entirely true. Bands of Indians did circulate through the country stealing livestock, but no settlements were attacked. Although angry about the action of the soldiers, Arapeen was too wise to create a situation that would bring the soldiers out against his tribes. According to B. H. Roberts, an appeal was made by Arapeen to Brigham Young offering the help of the Indians to drive the soldiers out. "Brigham Young wrote to the chief that there must be no war on the Americans." Arapeen accepted the advice.[17]

At the time the soldiers raided the Spanish Fork farm, they took into custody two Indians who had been involved in the assault on the women. These Indians, Pangunts, known as "Moze," and Namowah, known as "Looking Glass," were taken to Salt Lake City before Judge Sinclair, who ordered that they should be returned to Provo and held for trial.

These Indians, after being confined the whole winter, would have appeared for trial before Judge Cradlebaugh in March, 1859. But the judge, as mentioned above, became involved in a controversy with the citizens over the use of a military guard. When Cradlebaugh was defeated in his program, he became angry and dismissed the grand jury. He said: "When this people come to their reason, and manifest a disposition to punish their own high offenders, it will be time to enforce the law for their protection. If this court cannot bring you to a proper sense of your duty, it can at least turn the savages in custody loose upon you." The Indians were taken by the court's order to Camp Floyd, where they could be safely discharged.[18]

The rebuke administered to the federal judges in Utah by the Attorney General early in 1859 did not have the chastening effect that might be expected. There were no more calls from the judges for military aid in holding court, but they continued to operate as if the Mormons were a conquered people to be hunted down.

Judge Eckles wrote from Camp Floyd on September 27, 1859, to Secretary of State Lewis Cass, reporting his attempt to hold court at Nephi. As he entered the place from one direction with his retinue, "a third of the male population fled from it" in the opposite direction. Considering the known opinions of the judge and the purpose for which he came to town with his train of followers, the behavior of the people was not surprising.

Eckles wrote of the flight from Nephi: "Some alleged that they did so for fear of being summoned on juries, and others that they feared being apprehended for crime, which version of the matter is true, it is not now my purpose to decide." The judge was not altogether displeased when he could find no Mormons to serve as talesmen. He then selected jurors from the followers who came with him from Camp Floyd, Cedar County, and from others who came later from the same place.

After a few days of holding court, the judge discovered that he had no funds available to pay either jurors or witnesses. "Neither the United States nor the Territory had provided one cent to pay my expense. . . . . If the marshal had funds, as I presume he had, he declined to pay out any until his vouchers had first been sent to Washington and allowed. The Territory never has, and as I believe never will provide any means to support the district courts."

The territory would not support the district courts, for the very good reason that the Mormon officials of Utah did not believe the federal judges had jurisdiction over civil, criminal, or chancery cases. Eckles charged that many of the crimes he wanted to investigate which involved Mormons were being ignored by the probate courts. Mormons charged that Eckles and his fellow-judges were determined to try Mormons only and were winking at gentile criminals, many of whom were their friends and associates. Eckles also complained that there were no jails in the Mormon towns and that, if he had Mormon culprits arrested, there were no means for holding them. For that reason he wanted the right to have all prisoners detained at the army garrison, and he would hold court at Camp Floyd. By this device he would be able to maintain the type of military tribunal that Cradlebaugh tried to set up at Provo.

In the above-quoted letter of Eckles to the Secretary of State reference was made to a proposal of the territorial marshal to aid the United States marshal in making arrests and selecting jurors. This offer he would not countenance because he "could make no terms with criminals." The judge believed that to accept such an offer of co-operation would result in the Mormons packing the juries and the witness stand.

Eckles also paid his respects to the church and the Saints:

Here the people are nearly destitute of the civilizing effects of commerce, Christianity and government. They are drawn here from the hard-working but ignorant classes of foreign countries, whose want of intellectual culture made them an easy prey to Mormon delusion, and when here, governed in everything by designing knaves from the states whose love of plunder and gratification of the animal appetites, have been induced to quit the society of home for its good, and seek seclusion in this inhospitable region.[19]

Secretary Cass, on receiving the report of Chief Justice Eckles, sent portions of it to Governor Cumming for comment. The governor's response has often been cited by church leaders and was quoted by Roberts in his *Comprehensive History of the Church.*

By implication Cumming's response made it clear that Judge Eckles was under the influence of the most rabid of Mormon-baiters at Camp Floyd. The Gentiles at Camp Floyd and Fairfield included in their number many who "were banded together for rapine and acts of violence. They have stolen large herds of horses and mules. Many of these men, maddened by intemperance, or rendered desperate by losses at the gaming table, or by various other causes, have shed each other's blood in frequent conflicts and secret assassinations."

The record reveals no effort having been made by the federal judges to bring such culprits to justice. On the contrary, they did use the power of office to free some of these Gentiles, who were brought before the probate courts and sentenced by Mormon judges.[20]

When Eckles reported that he was forced to adjourn court at Nephi because there was no money to pay the costs, he was referring to cases involving the violation of territorial law. In his reply Cumming indicated that the annual revenue of the territory did not exceed $13,000 and that, were territorial officers so disposed, they did not have funds to pay court costs. The United States marshal had funds to pay the cost of hearing cases involving federal offenses, but he would not expend these moneys without specific authorization from Washington on each claim. This procedure required three or four months at the least. The report of the governor further indicated a stalemate between the federal and probate courts, each claiming exclusive jurisdiction over criminal cases. While the fight continued for control of the courts, certain classes of criminals were running wild. "Lawless and desperate men" had been emboldened to the extreme.

Governor Cumming added this observation: "One of the strongest reasons which prevents the administration of law in Utah is the conviction generally held by the people of this Territory that the minds of the United States judges are so blinded with prejudice against them that Mormons can hardly expect a fair and impartial decision in any case where they are concerned." He pointed to the experience of Judge Eckles at Nephi, where the people went into hiding when he approached. Cumming argued that Eckles was not justified in bringing gentile jurors from another county. He suggested that all the soldiers should be withdrawn from Utah, except possibly five hundred, to deal with Indian troubles; and he hinted that new judges should be appointed.

In justice to the soldiers at Camp Floyd, it should be said that theirs was a life of monotomy. They were stranded in a desert place with no social outlets save the tenderloin of Fairfield, crowded with saloons, gambling halls, and houses of vice. If they left Fairfield to visit Salt Lake City, they were shunned by the Mormons.

Some soldiers with other interests published a small weekly sheet, called *Valley Tan*, which was ardently anti-Mormon.[21] The columns of this paper carried notices of various social activities. There was a military dramatic association which produced plays in a little theater built and decorated by the soldiers. In this place there were frequent home-talent concerts and musical entertainments. Before the passing of the camp there was some social intercourse between these talent groups and similar groups among the Mormons in Salt Lake City.[22]

Whatever the social life, the soldiers lived well, with a full commissary of fruits and vegetables from the valley. A steady stream of freight trains brought supplies from the eastern states. The quantities of goods brought in by the contractors was a subject of no small scandal. Reference was made to these army contracts by Horace Greeley, who visited Utah in the summer of 1859. In his *Overland Journey* he remarked on questions asked by the soldiers: "Why were we sent here? and why are we kept here? What good can our remaining do?" He described the army as "fettered, suspected, watched, distrusted." He concluded that the army was kept in Utah because of the fat contracts given to freighting companies. He observed that the cost of hauling a pound of freight from the Missouri was twenty-two cents and that some of the goods could have been bought in Utah at less than the cost of hauling.[23]

The beginning of the end came in March, 1860, when orders were sent to General Johnston to reduce his command. Johnston had already acted on his discretionary orders and turned his command over to a subordinate. With a small detachment he left by the southern route for California, from whence he sailed by way of Panama for Washington. He later joined the forces of the Southern Confederacy, and he lost his life at the Battle of Shiloh, April 6, 1862, the thirty-second anniversary of the Mormon church.[24]

Two months after Johnston's departure, a detachment of troops left Camp Floyd for occupation service in New Mexico. Away with the troops went most of the civilian population living at Fairfield. With the soldiers away, they would have had difficulty earning a living in Utah. The Mormons were glad to see them go. The *Deseret News* on May 23, 1860, said that it was a source of "great joy to the citizens" that the "blacklegs, thieves and murderers are not so plenty hereabouts by half as they were two weeks ago, with a fair and increasing prospect that their numbers will grow less. . . . ."[25]

From May, 1860, until July, 1861, the troops at Camp Floyd were under command of Colonel Philip St. George Cooke, who led the Mormon Battalion from Sante Fe to California during the war with Mexico. He changed the name of the post from "Camp Floyd" to "Fort Crittenden," since former Secretary of War John B. Floyd, a southern Democrat, had joined the Confederacy. Apparently the new name was for Senator J. J.

Crittenden of Kentucky. The task was left with Colonel Cooke to close the post and dispose of all properties that could not be hauled away.

Then followed a military auction which made history, when about $4,000,000 worth of goods were sold for no more than $100,000. Brother Brigham sent his agents to the sale, and they spent for him or the church about $40,000. He secured 25 tons of flour at $10 per ton. The government took a loss on each ton of more than $500.[26] Russell, Majors, and Waddell, army contractors who kept the garrison supplied, freighted this flour from the Missouri Valley for $570 per ton.

Mormons were permitted to buy livestock, wagons, harness, utensils, food stores, and building material; but powder, guns, and other ordnance were not for sale to them or Gentiles either. Cannon were dismantled and thrown into a pit, whence later they were extricated by the Nauvoo Legion and used for ceremonial purposes. Kegs of black powder and other munitions were heaped in a pile and burned. Mormons came around later and picked up the iron, which served the needs of the blacksmiths.

The story is told that some enterprising Mormons gathered several wagonloads of empty cannon balls. These were hauled to Cedar City, where the Deseret Iron Company was still experimenting in connection with the Iron Mission. The cannon balls were cast into the furnace and melted. The iron was drawn off in molds to make various utilities—bells to call people to church, rollers to squeeze the juice out of sugar cane, stove parts, flatirons, and other castings.

When the last of the troops marched from Cedar Valley, Colonel Cooke presented Brigham Young with the garrison flagstaff. Here was a symbol of personal victory for Brother Brigham. He planted the pole on his own property near the Beehive and the Lion House.[27] In these buildings were domiciled his wives, and here was his office.

After the withdrawal of the troops it became evident that some provision was necessary to guard the mails. In May, 1862, the government ordered Colonel Patrick E. Connor, of Cali-

EAST SOUTH TEMPLE STREET, SALT LAKE CITY, ABOUT 1870

This was Brigham Young's property. Note the surrounding wall, which General Connor threatened to batter down with his cannon. The "House of Gables" in the foreground is the "Lion House." Next is the "Beehive House." The flagpole beyond this building is the famous pole that was brought from Camp Floyd after the departure of Johnston's Army in 1861.

fornia, to proceed to Utah with several hundred volunteers from that state.[28]

Colonel Connor did not arrive with his troops until November, 1862. While his command was en route over the desert west of Salt Lake, within a hundred miles of Salt Lake City, Connor hastened ahead to select a camp site. He learned that the Mormons wanted him to locate, as did Johnston, in the isolated Cedar Valley. He concluded that his assignment did not permit him to garrison his soldiers so remotely. He would set up camp within gunshot of Salt Lake City. The site which he selected on the bench above the city he named "Camp Douglas," in honor of Senator Stephen A. Douglas.

In making this decision Colonel Connor did not discuss his plans with church leaders. William A. Hickman, who later became friendly with the colonel, wrote that word had been sent to Connor "by the head men that he would not be allowed to cross the Jordan River . . . . but this did not stop him; he kept up his march, crossed the river, and encamped within eight miles of the city. A delegation was sent to him to apologize, or rather to deny any such word had been sent to him by Mormon authority."[29]

Soon after arriving Colonel Connor served notice on the Mormons that he would tolerate no disloyal talk. He would arrest anyone "guilty of uttering treasonable statements against the government." He had no authority to carry out such a threat, but that was a matter which did not bother this Irish emigrant, who had worked his way up from the ranks. His finger-shaking was greeted with frigid silence.

Such an order was resented, naturally; but the Mormons had been called traitors before. They had been labeled traitors by President Buchanan when they resisted Johnston's army. They had been called traitors in 1846 when they were being driven from Illinois. On that occasion the apostles stood up and protested: "Our patriotism has not been overcome by fire, by sword, by daylight or midnight assassinations which we have endured."

But here again they had to listen when their patriotism was

MAIN STREET, SALT LAKE CITY, ABOUT 1870

Here is shown the office of the Deseret Telegraph Company, where the people came to learn the news. The buildings in the picture are examples of a type of colonial architecture adapted by the Mormons. The typical house was built with adobe walls, over which a coating of plaster was spread.

called into question. After Colonel Connor there came to Utah a governor, Stephen S. Harding, who openly doubted the loyalty of the Mormons to the government. He was amazed that the Saints should have so little concern about the outcome of the Civil War.

Harding wrote to Secretary of State William H. Seward on August 3, 1862: "Brigham Young and the other teachers are constantly inculcating in the minds of the crowded audiences who sit beneath their teachings every Sabbath, that the government of the United States is of no consequence, that it lies in ruins."[30]

Mormons like to believe that they helped in the Civil War, that they furnished soldiers to guard the mail and the telegraph lines. This call came from the adjutant general of the army to Brigham Young on April 28, 1862, asking the services of about ninety men for three months "to protect the property of the telegraph and overland mail service between Forts Bridger and Laramie, to continue in service until the United States troops shall reach the point where their services are needed."

Church leaders accepted this as a call from President Lincoln, and it should be noted that the call had not been sent to the acting governor of Utah, Frank Fuller, but to the head of the church. Administratively this may have been an error on Lincoln's part. His issuing of such a call to the head of the priesthood was tantamount to his recognizing that Utah's Nauvoo Legion was, in fact, an army of the church, with the result that Gentiles were offended.[31]

The Nauvoo Legion proceeded to carry out the order, and ninety-three men were placed in the service under the leadership of Captain Lot Smith, who in 1857 led the raids against the army supply trains and burned about seventy wagons loaded with rations. The Legion guard was relieved upon the arrival of Colonel Connor and his California volunteers.

NOTES

1. Regarding Brother Brigham and his aides, Samuel W. Richards on July 23, 1858, wrote E. W. Tullidge, then in England (*Millennial Star*, XX, 620). "The presidency is quite retired and [they] are seldom seen. The people are in a great measure left to themselves. There are no public meetings and consequently no public sacraments. The word

of the Lord is seldom heard through his prophets by the people." Richard F. Burton, who visited Utah in 1860, wrote in *The City of the Saints* (p. 276) that he heard Gentiles say what they would like to do to the "big Mormon."

2. B. H. Roberts (*Comprehensive History of the Church*, IV, 467) reports a letter of January 12, 1859, from Apostle John Taylor to Apostle George Q. Cannon, then at Florence, Nebraska, in charge of emigration: "There has been a very riotous, obstreperous and vindictive spirit manifested by our missionary civilizers; who while they are utterly regardless of common decency themselves, seek to embroil us in difficulties and trouble; and provoke us if possible to commit some overt act to reopen the wounds that have so far been healed, and cause a renewal of hostilities in the diabolical hope of fattening themselves upon the prey of their victims."

3. Before the hostilities with the army Hurt fled from Utah. He met Colonel Alexander's advance company and on October 27, 1857, wrote to Colonel Johnston regarding his escape, how the Mormons tried to catch him, and how the Indians helped him. He wandered in the mountains for days, wading through snow. His Indian escort nearly froze. They were short of food. Hurt indicated that his escape was a surprise to the Mormons. In the files of the Commissioner of Indian Affairs, besides Hurt's letter, is one from Brigham Young, written on September 26, the day that Hurt escaped. Young wrote: "I am informed that you propose going to the States by some unfrequented route, and in company with certain Indians as pilots and traveling companions. Such a course is very unsafe and highly improper for an officer of our government." Young offered to give him a carriage and safe transportation. On October 7 Young wrote the Commissioner of Indian Affairs of Hurt's flight, calling it "an occasionless and unwise movement."

4. This letter from Eckles, found in Department of State papers in the National Archives, mentioned a possible Mormon migration to Central America. Eckles added: "I am informed that a petition signed by Mormons and mailed by Governor Cumming, has or will be presented to the President, asking among others for my removal. I am informed that the cause assigned is my opposition to polygamy. . . . ."

5. William A. Hickman (*Brigham's Destroying Angel*, p. 132) noted that Eckles came from Indiana and was "a fine, clever old gentleman." Hickman claimed that he "got seven or eight cases out of the probate court jurisdiction and placed them before his honor; gained my case every time. . . . ." This was the beginning of Hickman's break with Brigham Young.

6. "History of Brigham Young," January, 1859, contains a letter from George A. Smith to Colonel Thomas L. Kane stating that the district court in Salt Lake City had 38 sitting days in a period of 100 days and that only 6 days were occupied with United States business. Sessions rarely lasted more than an hour. This was done, it was alleged, to enable the marshal "to deplete the treasury and sustain some of the strangers who are in the country. . . . ."

7. The following episode was typical of a number which influenced General Johnston in his attitude. The story is taken from items listed for the dates in the *Church Chronology*. In 1855 Colonel E. J. Steptoe set aside an area in Rush Valley for a government military reservation for grazing and hay. Johnston took the area over. Some Mormons had been using the land as a ranch. On March 22, 1859, occurred a clash between Mormons and soldiers. Sergeant Ralph Pike struck a young Mormon, Howard O. Spencer, on the head. Spencer was given surgical treatment at Camp Floyd. He recovered. On August 11 Pike and other soldiers were in Salt Lake City for the trial. Spencer shot Pike and escaped. Pike died. All attempts to locate Spencer failed. He had gone to southern Utah in the service of the church. He became a bishop and was later in charge of the Orderville community. In 1877 he was made president of the Kanab Stake. In 1888 he was arrested for polygamy and was also taken into custody

for the murder of Pike. Almost thirty years had passed. Witnesses could not be found. The case was dismissed May 15, 1889.

8. Correspondence on this issue is found in *House Executive Document No. 78* (36th Cong., 1st sess.). Also see Roberts, *op. cit.*, Vol. IV, chap. cxvii.

9. Cradlebaugh was determined to bring local church leaders into court, believing they were all implicated in the Parrish and Potter murders. At his request Marshal Dotson on March 24 wrote General Johnston, asking for a posse of 200 soldiers to help arrest 14 Mormons who were hiding in the canyons. Johnston refused the request. He was willing to furnish soldiers to guard prisoners but not to hunt down wanted men.

10. While the Provo incident was in process, Judge Sinclair in Salt Lake City was occupied with the arrest of Brigham Young on the counterfeiting charges mentioned in the text. Although Governor Cumming denounced the scheme, word reached Salt Lake City on April 17 of two regiments of soldiers making a night march to the city. Cumming called on General Daniel H. Wells, head of the Nauvoo Legion, to prepare for resistance. The preparations were made, but the troops did not come. A report on this near battle was sent to the *New York Herald* and appeared on April 23, 1859. The counterfeiters were tried and sentenced. Later Brigham Young collected $2,600 for church property seized by Marshal Dotson. The marshal resigned in disgust on August 1, 1859. While not friendly with the Mormons, he was opposed to judicial persecution, which, he thought, consolidated them.

11. These letters are found in the papers of the Territory of Utah for the dates and are on file in the National Archives.

12. General Denver probably knew that the Navajo were ancient enemies of the Hopi and the Utah Indians. For the Great White Father to encourage this enmity was bound to cause trouble later. The Navajo felt they had the blessing of Gentiles in New Mexico if they raided Mormon territory. It took years of effort before the Navajo were brought to realize that the government did not approve such raiding.

13. With this letter from Brigham Young to the Commissioner of Indian Affairs was submitted an affidavit dated March 24, 1858, by Joshua K. Whitney, sworn before Probate Judge Elias Smith, declaring that on March 18, 1858, a Goshute named Dick Mooneye told him that "Naracuts, a Weber Ute and one of the party lately engaged in stealing horses from our settlements, had come to him and told him that a 'big man' named Forney in the Soldier's Camp at Bridger, told the Weber Utes that the Soldiers were coming with their big guns to kill all the Mormons, all through the mountains; that Brigham had put a charm on Naracuts' children that made them die, and Naracuts believed it and was mad; that Forney told him they could make medicine for Brigham and would kill him; that a long time ago he, Forney, had killed Joseph Smith very easy, and that he was a great deal bigger man than Brigham, and that he could kill Brigham much easier. Naracuts said that Forney gave them a heap of powder for a buckskin, and also gave them guns and hats and clothing. Forney further told the Weber Utes that he wanted them to steal the Mormons' horses, not a few, but lots of them. . . . ."

14. On June 30, 1857, Garland Hurt sent to the Commissioner of Indian Affairs an estimate of the crops he expected to produce on the four farms, comprising about 700 acres: 11,155 bushels of wheat, 5,500 bushels of potatoes, 2,000 bushels of oats, 360 bushels of corn, and several tons of garden and other products. He estimated the value of the crops to be harvested a few months hence at $24,752.75; however, he expected to hire all the labor for cultivating these crops. Indian labor would not respond. The war spoiled the plans and possibly only a small part of the hoped-for crop materialized.

15. On October 7, 1857, while yet at Green River, Forney sent the following estimate of expenditures for the fiscal year beginning July 1, 1858: his own salary, $2,000; three agents, $4,000; clerk and three interpreters, $2,500; agency expenses, $3,000; con-

tingencies and travel, $18,000; "presents to Indians," $50,000; total, $79,500. Although the budget was not granted, it evidences Forney's notion of how the agency should be operated.

16. Forney was a Democrat from Pennsylvania, appointed by Buchanan. When the Republicans came to power in 1861, Forney's expenditures were investigated. It was charged that he purchased from Salt Lake City stores great quantities of whiskey and had the store bill him for blankets. He was accused of buying goods at wholesale prices and of charging the government retail prices or having the stores so bill him. None of these charges could be proved.

17. Roberts (*op. cit.*, IV, 520) quotes items from the "History of Brigham Young" to the effect that Hurt's blunder resulted in restoring good Mormon-Indian relations. The incident demonstrated that in a crisis the Indians had confidence in Brigham Young.

18. *Ibid.*, p. 495, expresses the Mormon belief that Cradlebaugh's release of the Indians evidenced a type of insanity they ascribed to him. Judge Eckles also vilified the Mormons from the bench.

19. Including naturalized persons, probably one-half of Utah's adult population was foreign-born. The alien converts came mostly from the British Isles and the Scandinavian countries. Most of these converts could read and write, as was almost necessary to be converted. Mormon proselyting was done largely by the printed page. Missionaries gave out literature asking prospects to read and pray.

20. Cumming wrote to the Secretary of State, March 1, 1860, that five Gentiles had been convicted by the probate court in Salt Lake County. While serving their sentences, an order was received from Judge Eckles at Camp Floyd asking that the prisoners be brought to his presence. When the men arrived at Camp Floyd under guard, Judge Eckles read a prepared statement to the effect that the probate court had no authority over them. He released the men without further review of the charges against them. Later two of the men were shot by Mormon officers when avoiding arrest for alleged horse-stealing.

21. "Valley tan" was a term used to describe leather tanned in Salt Lake Valley. Later the term was given wider application for any "homemade" goods. When the church was pressing for a wider use of Mormon made goods, there was a type of dress called the "valley-tan costume." It was also called the "Deseret costume." It was thought that, if the women would wear a simple uniform type of dress, they would spend less money on the flimsy things brought from the east. The plan did not work. Mormon women would not submit, as would women of other religious cults, to a uniform dress.

22. See George D. Pyper, *Romance of an Old Playhouse*, chap. vi, for a report on recreational activities at Camp Floyd. Pyper's book is the story of the famous Salt Lake Theatre, completed in 1862 and torn down in 1928.

23. See Horace Greeley, *An Overland Journey*, pp. 253–57, for revelations on army contracts; for example: "There have recently been received here 30,000 bushels of corn from the states at a net cost, including transportation of $340,000, or over $11 per bushel. No requisition was ever made for this corn, which could have been bought here, delivered, for two dollars per bushel, or $60,000 in all. The dead loss to the treasury on this corn is $280,000. Somebody makes a good thing of wagoning this corn from the Missouri at over $10 a bushel."

24. While Johnston was in Washington, army headquarters issued orders on November 22, 1860, directing him to a post in the Department of the Pacific, headquarters at San Francisco. "He will repair [to that place] by the steamer of the 21st of December next." Apparently he did not accept the assignment.

25. Some bitter Mormon-baiters followed this detachment of soldiers. Evidence of their feelings is indicated in the following incident: While the soldiers were in camp at

the head of Echo Canyon, they were overtaken by two Mormons, William and James Hennifer. The brothers had a supply of eggs and butter to sell. The assistant surgeon, Dr. Edward Covey, recognized William Hennifer as a former member of the Salt Lake City police force by whom he had been arrested for disorderly conduct in November, 1858. In company with Lieutenant Ebenezer N. Gay and a number of soldiers, Covey ordered the seizure of William Hennifer. James escaped. William was stripped of his clothing, tied to a wagon wheel and lashed with a blacksnake whip. His load of produce was destroyed and he was driven naked and bleeding from the camp. Covey shouted after his victim: "Go and tell Brigham Young that it was I who whipped you, and that if he had been here I would have whipped him also" (*Deseret News*, June 6, 1860).

26. One of Utah's gentile pioneers, Alexander Toponce, wrote (*Reminiscences*, p. 39) that he had charge of one of the army supply trains and was present at the great auction of army goods. He wrote that contractors Russell, Majors, and Waddell used about 3,000 wagons and hauled about 16,000,000 pounds of freight from Nebraska City to Camp Floyd. At the sale, "Colonel Carter, a storekeeper at Fort Bridger, bid on 200,000 pounds of side meat at a quarter of a cent a pound. One man contracted to deliver 30,000 sacks of flour at 30 cents a pound. He did actually deliver 2,000 sacks, but the department paid him for 30,000 sacks, and then advertised it for sale again, and he bought the 30,000 at auction, paying only one cent a pound. The 28,000 sacks he never saw at all." Toponce said that fully equipped government wagons sold for $6.50 each. He bought mules at $40 per span, which he sold later at $500 per span. See Andrew L. Neff, *History of Utah*, p. 515.

27. The charges of graft by army contractors might have become a national scandal had it not been for the Civil War. Estimates of the total cost of the expedition and occupation reached as much as $40,000,000. The "History of Brigham Young," December, 1858, contains an estimate of sending the army and of maintenance the first several months, which was $9,000,000. See Roberts, *op. cit.*, Vol. VI, final chapter.

28. Samuel Bowles (*Across the Continent*, pp. 25–28) gives some personal information about Patrick E. Connor, then brigadier general. Bowles met Connor after the Civil War, when he was in command of the District of the Plains, his headquarters at Fort Leavenworth. His troops were guarding the mails as far west as the South Pass. About 1840 Connor, an Irish emigrant, had served his first enlistment at Fort Leavenworth. He was a captain in the Mexican War. After the war he settled in California and prospered in business. When the Civil War began, he was appointed as a colonel over the volunteers sent to Utah. Connor later left his command of the District of the Plains and returned to Salt Lake City to engage in mining activities.

29. Hickman (*op. cit.*, pp. 158 ff.) reports friendly relations with Colonel Connor and Governor Harding. Hickman was later useful to Connor in his mining interests. He was also useful to Harding in his opposition to church leaders.

30. This conviction that the Mormons would some day return to Jackson County was based on prophecies of Joseph Smith. It was believed by all good Saints, and all preparations for other undertakings were carried out subject to change if the Mormons should be called back to Jackson County. Brigham Young in his instructions for his burial attached this conditional clause.

31. Prior to sending the California volunteers, the Secretary of War authorized James D. Doty, superintendent of Indian affairs for Utah, to raise a company of volunteers to guard the mails. The Mormons resented this action, claiming that the territory had its militia, which was available. Lincoln met the situation by wiring Brigham Young, who had no official status; and Young arranged for the use of the Nauvoo Legion, over which officially he had no control (*Deseret News*, April 30, May 7, and August 13, 1862). See also Neff, *op. cit.*, pp. 623–24.

CHAPTER IX

BABYLON WARRED AND ZION GREW

PRESIDENT LINCOLN tried to deal tolerantly with the Mormons. They enjoyed under his administration a brief respite during which they had no outside supervision. Later, as already noted, came Colonel Connor and his soldiers to bother them. Still later they had, for a while, Governor Harding; but on July 4, 1861, they had the field to themselves.

On that occasion John Taylor was orator of the day. His speech, reported in the *Deseret News*, was a declaration of Mormon patriotism, but not in support of the war. He asked: "What part shall we take in the present difficulty?" He recalled Joseph Smith's prophecy, saying that a "rebellion" would begin in South Carolina. "And it shall come to pass, after many days, slaves shall rise up against their masters, who shall be marshalled and disciplined for war." Here was that war over the slavery issue. What part, if any, should the Mormons take in a war between gentile factions—a war which had to come? Apostle Taylor declared: "We cannot pervert the laws of Nature, nor alter the decrees of God." The Gentiles would have to find their own solution.

For this occasion Eliza R. Snow wrote a song which hailed the birth of the nation; hailed the flag; hailed freedom, truth, and liberty; hailed the Constitution, which Mormons would defend. The song told of a bloodless victory over Babylon. The army came into Zion, and the army went away. They still had the Constitution, and she added: "Every law from lawful powers we've loyally obeyed." Here are two verses from that song of triumph:

> The patriot's wreath we proudly wear
> Around our temples now,
> Unholy hands have sought to tear
> Ignobly from our brow.

Foul politicians basely left
Truth, law, and justice, too;
With their own hands the Union cleft,
And war and blood ensue.

Six weeks prior to this celebration, on May 17, Governor Alfred Cumming resigned his office. He carried with him Mormon good will; but soon afterward, being a southerner, he was taken into custody as a prisoner of war.[1] Secretary of State Francis H. Wooten became acting governor; but he, too, was a southerner, and very soon he was on his way to join the Confederacy. Frank Fuller, a Mormon, who was acting secretary of state under Wooten, then became acting governor, holding the position until the arrival of John W. Dawson on December 9, 1861.

Dawson met with the legislature the next day and delivered his message, which reflected the friendly tolerance of Lincoln. However, he fell from grace on two counts a few days later. The first count was that he vetoed an act of the legislature calling an election for a constitutional convention. Dawson did not oppose the convention, but he believed such an action should first receive the approval of the Congress.

The second count came in the midst of this disagreement. Whether true or not, the story circulated that Dawson had made improper advances to a Mormon lady. On the last day of December, three weeks after arriving, he took the stage for Indiana, a sudden, unheralded exit. At Mountain Dell, a relay station near Salt Lake City, he was waylaid by several men and soundly beaten. Some say he was emasculated. Although glad to see him go, the Mormons did not hesitate to punish his attackers.[2]

Frank Fuller again became acting governor, remaining so until relieved on July 7, 1862, by the new appointee, General Stephen S. Harding. In the previous chapter it was mentioned that Harding joined hands with Colonel Connor in assuming for Utah a military police supervision. This control was applied mainly in the northern areas, where the Gentiles resided. Little attention was paid to the remote Mormon communities; aid was not even sent when they were harassed by Indian raids.

Upon his arrival in Utah, Harding found Mormons and Gentiles in a tension over the pending trial of the "Morrisites." These were a group of dissenters led by Joseph Morris, who attempted to establish a new church. They had been subjected to a persecuting discipline reminiscent of the gentile treatment of Mormons during the Missouri period.

Morris had espoused Mormonism in England. He migrated to Utah in 1853 and the next year settled in Sanpete County. In 1857 he moved to Provo, where he was caught up in the fervor of the reformation. He began to receive "revelations" and regarded himself as a man of destiny. He appealed to Brigham Young for inclusion to the inner councils of the church.[3] No action was taken. He was not disciplined, perhaps because the army was in Utah and the Gentiles were in control.

A few years earlier, Morris might have fared as Gladden Bishop, a man who lead a movement against polygamy. Brigham Young, head of church and state, preached at the tabernacle on March 27, 1853, calling Gladden Bishop "a poor, dirty curse." Young shouted: "Now you Gladdenites, keep your tongues still, lest sudden destruction comes to you." The movement of Gladden Bishop heeded Brother Brigham's "bowie-knife" threat.

But Joseph Morris continued to receive what he called the "Word of the Lord." William A. Hickman reported that the Morrisites sold their holdings elsewhere and, with their movables, gathered in 1860 at a place called "Slaterville," near Ogden,

> to prepare for great blessings that were to be given them from heaven through their prophet. They increased very fast and were bold in advocating their doctrine. They were peaceable and ignorant, as a general thing; but had some smart men amongst them, who seemed as steadfast in their belief as those of more ordinary talent. They were hissed and hooted at by those who wanted mischief, and some of them occasionally beaten. Some were arrested under pretense of being guilty of crime, and got misused and turned loose.[4]

In February, 1861, the church caused an investigation to be made by Apostles John Taylor and Wilford Woodruff. They held hearings in the Morrisite community, and sixteen Morrisites were disfellowshiped; but Morris himself was not disturbed, though he was preaching that the apologists for Brigham Young had lost the right to lead the Saints.

The Morrisites tried to revive the United Order, and all who joined had to give their property to the combine. Those who broke away were not permitted to take any of their property. They appealed to the courts, but Morris would not heed the courts, which he claimed were under domination of the "erring" leaders of the Mormon church. Here was a legal reason for action against the group. It came in the spring of 1862.

A military posse of about two-hundred legionnaires, under the lead of Captain Robert T. Burton, was sent to assist the territorial marshal in arresting Morris and several of his aides. The Morrisites, about ninety men and three hundred women and children, took refuge in an old fort. Followed a three-day siege with rifle and cannon fire. On June 15 the Morrisites surrendered. Two of them had been killed. It was after the surrender that Morris, John Banks, and two women were shot down, apparently in the spirit of revenge, because two of the posse had been killed and others wounded by Morrisite fire.

In July of 1862, a month after the Morrisite episode, Stephen S. Harding arrived to take his post as governor of Utah. Colonel Connor and his California volunteers did not arrive until six months after the affair, which means that Mormon authorities had been in complete control. It was shocking to Governor Harding to find the Mormons involved in a religious war and not at all exercised about the Civil War. This affair gave substance to his conviction that the Saints were opposed to the federal government.

Harding sent his first report to the Secretary of State on August 3. He indicated that the Mormons took it for granted that

> the United States as a Nation is to be destroyed, that the Gentiles will continue to fight each other until they are exhausted, and then the Saints are to step in and quietly enjoy possession of the land, and also what is left of the ruined cities and desolate fields; and that Zion will be built up, not here in the valleys of the mountains, but the great center of their power and glory is to be in Missouri where the Saints under the head of their prophet were expelled many years since.

When the trial of the Morrisites opened in March, 1863, which was nine months after the arrests, Harding watched with a critical interest. Seven of the cultists, found guilty of second degree murder, were sentenced to prison terms ranging from seven to fifteen years. Gentiles charged that they were forced to work on a road for Brigham Young. Sixty-six other Morrisites were fined $100 each, which took about all the property of the entire group. Chief Justice John F. Kinney, gentile friend of the Mormons, was on the bench.

Most of the Gentiles of Utah and some of the Mormons were so aroused over the handling of the Morrisite cases that they appealed to Governor Harding to take a hand. The governor had already offended the Mormons. Some of the leaders were still smarting under a lecture he had administered to the legislature in his message of December, 1862. On the score of patriotism Harding said: "I am sorry to say that since my sojourn amongst you, I have heard no sentiments, either publicly or privately expressed, that would lead me to believe that much sympathy is felt by any number of your people in favor of the Government of the United States, now struggling for its very existence."

The gentlemen of the legislature, most of them church leaders and polygamists, might have overlooked this jibe at their patriotism; but they took umbrage when Harding lectured them on morals. He called plurality a wicked institution, and he likened the marriage of one man to a mother and daughter "no less a marvel in morals than in matters of taste." The *Deseret News* made no mention of the speech. After listening in silence the legislature retaliated by refusing to order the customary printing of the message of the governor.

That message was still a bitter memory when Governor Harding decided to act in the Morrisite affair. He issued a full pardon to all members of the cult who had been convicted, and he remitted the fines. He then authorized Colonel Connor to provide a military escort to assist some of the dissenters in moving to a location near Soda Springs, Oregon, now Idaho.

Following this action, there was a great furor in Utah: Mormons demanding the removal of Harding for interfering with local government, and Gentiles demanding the removal of Judge Kinney because he was thought to be under the thumb of Brigham Young. Lincoln met the situation by granting both demands. He transferred Harding to another job, making him chief justice for Colorado. Kinney was removed, and his place was taken by John Titus, of Pennsylvania, an unknown who remained unknown. The Mormons retaliated by selecting Kinney to be Utah's delegate to Congress.

The governorship was bestowed by Lincoln upon James D. Doty, who was already serving in Utah as superintendent of Indian affairs.

The constitutional convention, which Governor Dawson had vetoed, was opened in Salt Lake City on January 20, 1862. Church political leaders believed that with the Civil War in progress the government would be happy to have Utah in the Union. They would be willing to support the Union cause in return for statehood.

Within three days after the delegates convened, a constitution was framed and adopted. The name "Deseret" was again applied. Then the convention named candidates for three elective offices and set March 3, 1862, as election day. It was a "yes" or "no" election, with only one candidate named for each of the elective offices. Here are the returns from all but three counties (opposition votes were obviously not counted, and apparently Gentiles did not vote):

For Brigham Young, candidate for governor	9,880
For Heber C. Kimball, candidate for lieutenant-governor	9,880
For John M. Bernhisel, to be member of Congress	9,862
In favor of the proposed constitution	9,878

In this same election the people voted for representatives to the general assembly, in the event of Deseret gaining statehood. The *Deseret News* of April 16 reported the names of the ten senators and twenty-two representatives elected, and every name on the list was that of a prominent church official. Seven were those of apostles. On March 17 Governor-Elect Young issued a proclamation calling the general assembly of Deseret-to-be for a session, which convened on April 14.[5]

Here was a strange procedure, not paralleled in any other state or territory. The general assembly met as ordered. Brigham Young made his speech as "governor," and the members settled to the business of naming and confirming men for the various appointive offices of the ghost government. Deseret would be ready to function when news came of her statehood status. William H. Hopper and Apostle George Q. Cannon were named senators. They set out at once for Washington with the proposed constitution and the memorial from the general assembly.[6]

This first meeting of the government of Deseret carried on a four-day session. Ten laws were passed for the future state, and the laws of the Territory of Utah were decreed "in force in the State of Deseret." Mormons were encouraged by moves already afoot to grant statehood to Colorado, Nevada, and Nebraska.

Instead of the Mormons winning their plea for statehood, Congress took action against polygamy in a bill sponsored by Congressman Justin R. Morrill of Vermont, which became law on July 8, 1862. Mormons thought the bill had been inspired by Governor Harding, who had been in Washington when the act was under discussion and who arrived in Utah about the time the bill was passed. He also opposed the Deseret statehood bill.[7]

The dream of Deseret was not abandoned. Each year until 1870 the ghost government went into a one-day session immediately after the adjournment of the legislature, adopting the laws passed in that session. At each meeting of Deseret's ghost government appointments would be made to the nonfunctioning offices.

In his "message" as "governor" of Deseret, delivered on January 19, 1863, Brigham Young likened the ghost government to the Kingdom of God on earth. It was the perfect priesthood civil body. He reminded the members of the assembly that events were moving fast. God was taking over control and whipping the Gentiles with scorpions.

> Our Government is going to pieces, and it will be like water that is split upon the ground that cannot be gathered. If we do not take care of ourselves,

no one will take care of us. . . . . I do not care whether you sit one day or not, but I do not want you to lose any part of this government which you have organized. For the time will come when we will give laws to the nations of the earth.[8]

Not until 1865, after the fourth annual meeting of the ghost government, was there any gentile opposition. Previously there had been fun-poking at this half-civil, half-ecclesiastical assembly, which aspired to represent Mormons in places beyond the borders as well as in Utah. On January 28, 1865, Governor James D. Doty wrote Secretary of State William H. Seward: "There are three distinct governments in this Territory, the Church, the Military and the Civil. In the exercise of their several powers, collisions cannot always be avoided." Doty indicated amusement and some concern over the antics of the ghost government. He inclosed with his letter a copy of the *Salt Lake Daily Telegraph* for January 24, reporting the proceedings of the latest session of the Deseret officials. All but two of the apostles were officially present at this session.

Colonel (now General) Connor, head of the military government mentioned by Doty, through his paper, the *Daily Union Vedette*, began to denounce the ghost government. The *Vedette* for January 26, 1865, referred to Brigham Young as playing a comic role as "governor," in "that immensely funny affair, the farce entitled 'The State of Deseret.' " After the 1866 session of the ghost government the *Vedette* stood up in wrath and damned the church leaders as traitors and the people as benighted serfs.

With the Civil War over and the government of the United States still intact, with other interests pressing for attention, the ideal of Deseret gradually faded. The ghost legislature did not meet after 1870. Brigham Young was wise enough to abandon any venture that failed to serve a desired objective.

Although the Mormons gave up their ghost government, they were slow to surrender their dream of sometime being the state of Deseret. Nor did they abandon the ideals for which the ghost government stood. For that reason they made every effort to push their settlement program during the war period.

This was a time to bring in their convert emigrants and to think of security against the possibility of another army of occupation. Interest developed in a plan to provide Utah with a broad road and a steamboat service to the sea. It was then thought that the Colorado River was navigable and that somewhere along the Colorado were beautiful valleys waiting colonization.

It was Brigham Young's vision of a southern expansion that prompted the sending of missionaries to the Indians. Central Utah was to have great industries near the iron deposits. From that point to the Mexican border would be a string of farming settlements. To that end Jacob Hamblin and four other men with their families settled Santa Clara in 1854. Hamblin and other missionaries carried on their labor with the Indians, a work of education and peace. Plans were already afoot when Hamblin opened the Colorado slope for settlement to plant in that region a number of communities devoted to producing semi-tropical products. In 1857 a company of fifty families was sent into that "Dixie" section to experiment with cotton. They were called "cotton missionaries." The war stimulated interest in cotton.[9]

At the October, 1861, conference of the church three hundred families were called to join the Cotton Mission. Some of these were volunteers, the rest selectees. This mission was enveloped in an aura of service and sacrifice, a sort of substitute for the patriotism of war.

Such enthusiasm was aroused for the Dixie expedition that it assumed an importance not unlike that of the gold rush. It was an honor to be among the first three hundred families. Utah's Dixie was extolled as a great opportunity to sacrifice for the good of Zion. Significantly, nothing was promised those who went but years of toil and deprivation, but in the end they would develop in that scorched region a choice settlement. Perhaps not even Brigham Young realized the limitations of the area.[10]

The Cotton Mission was headed by Apostles Eratus Snow and Orson Pratt, the same who in 1847 led the advance company of pioneers into Salt Lake Valley. Although teamed together by their file leader, these apostles were temperamentally the opposite of each other in every trait of personality. Pratt was a dreamer and a delver into the universal mysteries. Snow was a man of action, few of words and halting of speech; whereas Pratt was a facile orator. Snow was in the apostolate at Brigham Young's choosing. Pratt had been one of the first apostles selected by Joseph Smith. Snow was Young's type. In his relations with Pratt he sat in the driver's seat.

For more than twenty years Snow was head of the Southern Mission, which included all settlements over the rim of the Great Salt Lake Basin. His rule in this domain was as absolute as the reign of Brother Brigham in the larger sphere. Snow's field of operations expanded with each new settlement on the southern border of Mormondom. It finally embraced settlements throughout Arizona and some in Nevada, New Mexico, and over the boundary. No problem was too great for him to handle or too small to invite his attention.

The role that Snow played was not out of line with the priesthood duties of his office. He told people what to do or what not to do, and they were expected to obey. Those under him in authority had the same powers in more limited spheres. They obeyed Brother Snow, just as Snow obeyed Brother Brigham. That was how communities were settled, how irrigation projects were realized, and how co-operatives were formed. Snow assumed a protective custody of the natural resources of his region, and he watched the use of these. He supervised the civil government in the counties and towns. He judged disputes between neighbors and settled domestic difficulties. His judgment was generally good, and the evidence was that people did bring their problems to him.

It was not surprising that the people went to this man, for they were selected settlers, schooled in the priesthood way of government. They had been tested in other places and proved true. Some had crossed the plains with the handcart companies. Some had served with the Mormon Battalion. Many had been active in church affairs since the exodus from Nauvoo. Some even dated back to Missouri and to Zion's Camp.

PIONEERS OF DIXIE

Pictures taken about 1900. *Above*, some of the high priests, and among them members of the High Council of the St. George Stake. *Below*, some pioneer sisters engaged in work at the St. George Temple performing ceremonies for the living and the dead.

One of the cotton missionaries was Robert Gardner, who operated a sawmill near Salt Lake City, where he lived happily with three wives and sixteen children under one roof. Gardner heard that his name has been placed on the list as a "volunteer." He went to church headquarters, where, as related in his autobiography, he met Apostle George A. Smith, who confirmed the rumor. Gardner wrote:

"I looked and spat, took off my hat, scratched my head, thought and said 'All right.' "

"Don't blame anyone but me," said the apostle, "The president asked me to get a list of names for this mission, so I thought of you for one, and thought you would be willing to go, if called; so I put your name down. If you don't want to go, step into the president's office and ask him to take your name off the list, and he will do it."

"I expect he would, but I shan't try him. I have come out to find out what kind of an outfit is wanted, and when we go."

Gardner took only one wife and two daughters, leaving the other wives to manage his place and prepare to follow later. He said to those left behind: "We go where we are told to go, and make a track, and we have always been glad to do so."

When the company came to the Black Ridge, which divides the Great Salt Lake Basin from the Colorado slope, they confronted the steep and hazardous canyon of Ash Creek, where the road followed the steep boulder-strewn creek bed. The nakedness of the scene was depressing to Gardner. He noted that, when a cow plucked a mouthful of grass, "she had to range a great way to get another."

So down the canyon to the narrow valleys of the Virgin River, where they came to the Washington settlement. Gardner was appalled when he noted the sickly appearance of the people. They were dressed in homespun cotton, colored with home dyes. "Their clothes and their faces were all of a color, being blue with chills. It tried me harder than anything I had seen in all my Mormon experiences, thinking my wives and children from the nature of the climate, would have to look as sickly."[11]

Among the many personal accounts of the pioneer company is one by Ann Prior Jarvis, who with her husband migrated from England in 1860, bringing four small children over the plains, walking all the way and pulling a handcart. A few weeks after arriving in the valley her fifth child was born. Jarvis, a ship carpenter, went to work helping build the Salt Lake Theater, then being completed.

Mrs. Jarvis wrote many years later: "My husband was one of the volunteers. He had no wagon and he had always said he would never travel again without a team." Jarvis bought an old wagon, and Brigham Young gave him as part pay for his work on the theater a "steady" yoke of oxen. Neither Jarvis nor his wife knew about frontier ways. She wrote: "I didn't even know how to sit in the dirt." They arrived in "Dixie" on schedule, December 5, 1861. "The first meal we had on my city lot was some flax seed." They had bran meal for dinner on Christmas Day.

Some who went on the Cotton Mission were men of special skills. One was sent because he knew about sawmills.[12] Another was selected for his knowledge about cultivating and curing tobacco. Several knew about wine-making. The second year there was need of a potter, and John Eardley was sent, so that the women would have churns and crocks. Some were blacksmiths; others carpenters. Then there was Joseph Orton, one of several men who could make shoes.[13] He was a recent arrival from England, a bachelor who knew nothing about the tools and implements of other crafts. When he learned his name was among those called, Orton hastened to buy himself a "fit out"—a rickety wagon and two footsore oxen.

Orton wrote of his preparation: "Just the evening before, having gathered together my traps, wagon standing in front of my house. Bishop Jacob Weller of my ward seeing it said, 'Joseph, is this the wagon you propose starting to Dixie with?' Answering yes, 'Well,' he said, referring to the togglings, 'I am used to teaming, but I wouldn't chance it.' I said, 'I have done my best to get a fit out. I feel satisfied. I am going on my mission.' "

Orton was to make shoes, so that other men could produce what Brother Brigham wanted: "cotton, sugar, grapes, tobacco, figs, almonds, olive oil, and such other articles as the Lord has shown us places for garden spots."[14] The first cotton produced in Dixie in 1857 cost $3.50 per pound. By 1860 the cost had come down to a dollar a pound. The 1863 crop was 56,094 pounds, but even that represented cotton at almost a dollar per pound.

St. George became the base community for the entire southern area, from the hot grassless Virgin River to the grazing sections.[15] In 1863 Zera Pulsipher, with his sons, daughters, their families, and a few others, were sent to occupy the grazing country to the westward. They settled Shoal Creek and devoted themselves to raising cattle and producing dairy products. The place, because it was far removed, as was a remote town in the Bible, was called "Hebron." Other groups of families were sent to the west and south from St. George to hold Clover Valley, Panaca, Ruby Valley.[16]

Snow realized that the Muddy River Valley on the California road south of St. George should be occupied lest the Gentiles move in. In the autumn of 1864 the church called one hundred and fifty families to settle the "Muddy." Within three months they were packed and moved, ready on the site to begin work, holding for Zion that branch of the Virgin River. Some of the land they occupied is now submerged by the waters of the Boulder Dam.

Occupying the Muddy Valley proved to be an ordeal beyond compare. In all the domain of Mormondom there was not to be found a more forbidding habitat. Even the scorching summer heat at St. George was mild by comparison. Nature seemed to have abandoned the place, for on the hills surrounding there was no grass to feed stock or trees for fuel; but the land in the valley was fertile and productive, if irrigated. It was difficult for the settlers to find feed for cows; so milk was scarce for their children during those first years. But they could grow cotton.

In the autumn of 1862 Brigham Young with his staff of church leaders paid a visit to St. George. He found his settlers in dire need but willing to remain on the job. He ordered them to start building a great tabernacle. He would send foodstuffs from the established settlements to pay those who worked on

THE ST. GEORGE TABERNACLE

Completed about 1871. The walls are of hand-tooled red sandstone, and the woodwork is all hand fashioned. This is a remarkable example of pioneer craftsmanship. The clock in the tower was one of the first of its kind in the West.

the tabernacle, making the structure a sort of public-works project. They went to work on a large edifice that would seat about three thousand persons—three times the population of the Cotton Mission. Such was Brother Brigham's vision of Dixie's future, a vision related to his plan to establish, by way of the Colorado, a route to the sea.

In line with this plan for a road to the sea the church in 1864 sent Anson Call, former bishop of Fillmore, to build a landing on the Colorado River, somewhere near the present Boulder Dam. From the point where the warehouse was erected, two small vessels had already found a landing. These were private ventures of Gentiles who likewise believed the Colorado would carry river boats. But the plans came to naught.[17] The river boats, the "Nina Tilden" and the "Esmeralda," proved to be unprofitable.

Another factor in changing the river transportation plan was the final realization that along the Colorado were no broad valleys suitable for agriculture. This was the evidence brought to Brigham Young from the various exploring parties. He turned his attention to other possibilities, for he did not surrender the idea that Zion must expand southward into all the area that once had been envisioned as part of Deseret.

After the Cotton Mission the next important settlement during the Civil War period was a group of communities on the northern border of Utah. To this projected extension of Mormon settlement the chief obstacle had been the northern Indian tribes. But the Indians had been subdued by the raids of the troops under command of Colonel Connor, whose job it was to make the overland roads safe for the mail and the emigrant trains bound for Oregon and California. In 1864 Apostle Charles C. Rich, previously associated with the San Bernardino colony, was placed in charge of the settlements near the Idaho border in the vicinity of Bear Lake.

As already indicated, Mormon expansion into northern Utah and beyond the Utah boundary had been discouraged because of the enmity of the Indian tribes. A daring attempt had been made in 1855 to plant an outpost on the Salmon River, but the

Fort Limhi mission had to be abandoned in 1858 because of Indian raids. It was Colonel Patrick E. Connor and his California volunteers who disciplined the Indians in January, 1863. This action had been brought on because on numerous occasions the Indians had waylaid emigrant trains, robbing the wagons and killing the travelers. White men, living with the Indians, were frequently involved in these assaults.

Colonel Connor, with a force of about two hundred soldiers, marched into the Bear River and Bear Lake area, where they found a large concentration of Snake and Bannock Indians in camp for the winter. He surrounded the camp and began battle on January 29, although it was less of a battle and more of a slaughter than Connor's report would indicate. Upward of three hundred Indians—men, women, and children—were slain. Only a few escaped. Some hid in the frozen stream. Some little children "played dead" and were passed by when the soldiers went over the camp ground shooting the wounded. Fourteen soldiers were killed, and seventy-nine were wounded in the fray.

Connor's men found the guns, wagon covers, utensils, and quantities of clothing that the Indians had stolen in their raids. Connor was elevated to the rank of brigadier general. In his report he charged that, instead of helping him, the Mormons made his task harder because they would divulge no information about the Indians; moreover, they "charged enormous prices for every article furnished my command."[18]

Under the circumstances, probably Connor's method of dealing with the Snakes and Bannocks was the only one that could have been applied. These tribes had been spoiled by association with white men who taught them the gentile hatred of Mormons; and, because they were on the border, moving to and fro between Utah and Idaho, they had no opportunity of being constructively influenced by either Gentiles or Mormons. They were more able than other tribes to subsist on fishing and hunting and were rarely forced to the necessity of going to the settlers begging for food. They usually had horses to ride and had more access than other tribes to guns and ammunition. Like the Navajos, south of the Colorado, they were associated with adventurous white men, which may have encouraged them to be raiders and robbers.[19] If the Indians of the Nevada deserts assaulted traveling companies, their proverty and starvation were the compelling factors. The Snakes, Bannocks, and Shoshones were not starved, but they did become bad Indians. Because of their chronic badness in raiding and robbing emigrants, soldiers had been sent against them before. For example, in 1859 General Johnston dispatched a troop of cavalry to hunt down some of these marauders.[20]

While gentile military discipline cleared the way for Mormon expansion toward the north, no such help was offered to open the way for Mormon settlement on the southern border. Indian resistance in those wholly Mormon areas did not menace the Gentiles; hence the job of protecting the settlers had to be assumed by the Nauvoo Legion. Mormons had to furnish their own military guard for all of Utah south of the settlements on a line from Utah Lake to the northern points, a day or two from Salt Lake City, where most of the Gentiles lived.

Beginning about 1864, the tribes of central and southern Utah showed signs of hostility, which took the form mainly of stealing cattle and sheep for food or horses for riding. In a few cases the settlers were robbed or intimidated. This behavior was a repetition of the Walker War of 1852 and 1853.

When trouble was manifest, the Mormons called on General Connor for military aid. He replied that his force had to be used to guard the mail. The settlers regarded his attitude as a rebuke for what he regarded as Mormon indifference to the Union cause in the Civil War. He implied that people who did not care for the government had no right to call on that government for protection.[21]

Daniel H. Wells, in command of the Legion, placed all the units of his organization in a state of war readiness. We quote from a letter sent by him to Colonel William H. Dame, commanding the "Iron Military District," with headquarters at Parowan. This order, dated April 5, 1864, was typical of communications sent to other military districts of Utah. The letter follows:

Dear Brother:

You will hold musters and inspection of arms of forces in your district; it is also deemed wisdom for each settlement to keep a guard night and day, for the present, that houses, stables, corrals, pastures and ranges may not be robbed, nor men, women and children carried off in the night time, nor in the day time, and none but the sufferers know of it until it is too late to help it.

In addition to the guard, the brethren must be ready and on hand to come to the rescue, at a moment's notice, whenever a hostile intention or demonstration should manifest itself, either night or day. Have, therefore, your appointments and places of rendezvous, and every necessary arrangements made for a quick movement in any direction, as the emergency of the case may seem to require.

For this purpose you will not neglect to have good horses with the necessary equipment, wagons or carriages with the teamsters and drivers selected, where you know you can put your hand upon them at a moment's notice, and depend upon their going. Let every arrangement be quietly and perfectly made, and not wait until wanted; and then have to hunt up bullet-moulds, saddles, wagon hammers, linch pins, harness or anything else; but be minute men in fact, and let all these arrangements be made immediately upon receipt of this letter.

Several such letters of instruction are found in Bleak's "Manuscript History of St. George," some of them being chiding letters advising not to appoint lazy men to stand guard or men who would sleep in the shade and be killed by Indians and admonishing against putting playful youths in charge of the livestock. Workers were to go in groups to the fields, and one of the number was to be on the lookout. It was forbidden that persons go riding about alone.

Two men from St. George, Dr. James M. Whitmore and Robert McIntire, in December, 1865, went with a herd of sheep to Pipe Springs, in the Arizona "strip," which is east of St. George. Early in January, 1866, word came that both sheepmen had been killed by a party of raiding Navajo who had crossed the Colorado when the water was low.

Captain Daniel D. McArthur with a company of the Legion went after the Indians and caught two of them. Both professed ignorance about the killings. When they were threatened with hanging, one of the captives remembered he had had a dream about a group of Indians camped ten miles distant. The camp was found, but the Navajo would not surrender. Two Indians were killed, and five were taken prisoners. Some escaped. From the Indian who told of his dream, they readily located the bodies of Whitmore and McIntire, shot full of arrows and stripped of clothing. Quoting in part from McArthur's report:

> A wagon was sent out and whilst those with the wagon were taking up the bodies, the five prisoners were brought up to the place, in charge of eleven men. Among the Indians taken were found the clothes of the murdered men, some money, fresh sheepskins, and a few other things which stood as evidence against them of their guilt. This meeting was too much for the brethren to stand, so they turned the Indians loose and shot them on the ground where the murdered bodies lay. Thus did retribution overtake them on the scene of their crime. This makes seven Indians killed. We have one prisoner in camp from whom we hope to get more information.[22]

The Black Hawk War was a series of such Indian depredations, each followed with a swift attack by the Legion. An effort was made in each case to capture and punish the leaders. Some were killed, but others were released after being publicly whipped. It was not the General Connor type of discipline. The Legion did not raid Indian villages and indiscriminately shoot men, women, and children. In the entire war, which lasted three years, about twenty-five Mormons were killed and some seventy-five Indians lost their lives.

For many years the Mormons pressed a claim for payment from the federal government, urging that the burden and the cost of the affair was one which the settlers should not have carried alone. For the work of the Nauvoo Legion, guarding and going on expeditions, the outlay was estimated at $1,190,000. The cost of horses, cattle, and sheep stolen by the Indians was placed at $170,000. It was claimed that twenty small villages had to be abandoned for two or three years, and for this loss the settlers asked $175,000. This made a total bill of $1,535,000, which may have been overstated in some details; but the cost would have been greater had the federal troops been assigned to the task, and more Indians would have died.[23]

The greatest cost, and one which cannot be measured, was the part the Black Hawk War played in slowing up the Mormon program of emigration and settlement. These were the years when the missionary program was fruitful and when the migration of converts was the great imperative of the church program. Indian hostilities delayed by at least three years the founding of a number of smaller settlements.

In order to put the missionary and migration service on a sound and dependable basis and to speed up the church program, a new policy of missionary support was adopted. It was reported in the *Deseret News* of September 19, 1860, that henceforth the church expected families and communities "to fit out their own missionaries, to clothe them and give them money to take them to their destined fields of labor, and in all cases where it is necessary, to sustain their families while they were absent." Previous to this fixing of responsibility, the man called on a mission got to his field of labor as best he could. His family got along as they could, with the help of neighbors. This order made the missionary a representative of his community as well as his church. Thus the missionaries out in the world would be better sustained and able to give more time to saving souls.

As a companion policy, the church decided that handcart migration should be discontinued after 1860. Wagons loaded with food would be sent to meet the poor. Convert emigrants would still have to walk to Zion, but no longer were they required to carry burdens or pull loads or forced to trudge through inclement weather without shelter. Brigham Young concluded it was no credit to Zion for the emigrants to travel on half-rations or to toil mile after mile without shoes.[24]

According to the new plan, an assessment was imposed upon each ward, calling for wagons, teams, men, and supplies. The outfits were assembled in Salt Lake City for inspection and loading by the presiding bishop. The first of such emigrant-aid companies to be formed was in the spring of 1861, when 200 wagons, each pulled by 4 yoke of oxen and all loaded with about 150,000 pounds of flour, assembled to "bring in the poor." These outfits left as soon as the canyons were free of snow and the roads free of mud—that year, April 23. They were formed in four companies. These companies returned late in September from the Missouri, bringing an unreported number of Saints.

In 1862 the number of outfits sent to the Missouri was much greater, including 262 wagons, 239 men acting as guards and

Milton H. Hardy Joseph Birch Pr. Donaldson Brigham Carrington Robert McQuarrie Elijah A. Box John Neff

Samuel S. Jones George Crismon John B. Fairbanks Erastus Snow David O. Calder George F. Gibbs David George Calder

A GROUP OF MORMON MISSIONARIES OF THE GLASGOW CONFERENCE IN 1873

Most of the men in this picture were veteran missionaries and frontiersmen. Apostle Erastus Snow, sitting in the center on the cushioned chair with his feet on the cushioned footstool, was founder of the Southern Mission.

teamsters, 2,880 oxen, and a food load of 143,315 pounds of flour. That much flour, expended at a pound per day per person, was sufficient to feed the crew for the round trip and to bring back about 2,000 emigrants. It was sufficient for a much larger emigration if meats and vegetables were added, but such foods had to be procured at the other end of the route. Possibly the number of emigrants brought in during 1862 was in excess of 3,000 since there were many who migrated with their own teams.[25]

Ten companies of teams were sent back to the Missouri in 1863. This was the record year for this type of program and affords a measure of Mormon sacrifice for Zion when the rest of the country was spending its energy on the Civil War. This caravan included 384 wagons, 488 teamsters and guards, 3,604 oxen, and 235,969 pounds of flour. The Perpetual Emigration Fund Company, in addition to supervising the team outfits, had the responsibility for chartering ships and trains. It was a service that involved year-around planning, and there had to be a proper timing of the various steps involved.

For example, the ship "Electric" left Hamburg on April 18, 1863, with 336 Scandinavian Saints on board. About the same day the church teams were leaving Salt Lake City for the Missouri River. The "Electric" reached New York on June 5. After a few days' rest the Saints were loaded on an emigrant train, and on June 19 they arrived at the Missouri. On about the same schedule in the same month two ships left Liverpool; one, the "John J. Boyd" carried 766 Saints, and the other, the "B. S. Kimball," carried 657. The passengers from both these chartered ships arrived at Florence on June 20, a day following the arrival of the Scandinavians. Within a few days all were organized into companies, the wagons were loaded, and the crossing of the plains begun.

Such sacrifices were made in 1861 and the next two years that the settlements in 1864 were unable to send more than 170 outfits. In 1865 no church teams could be sent at all. There had been a drought in some parts of Utah, which began in 1864 and continued through to 1866. This was also the period of the

Black Hawk Indian War, which suggests that the Indians were cramped in their food supply by the same drought that throttled the emigration service. Conditions in southern Utah, after a winter without snow and a summer without much rain, were indicated by Apostle Erastus Snow in a letter sent on March 20, 1864, to Presiding Bishop Edward Hunter. Bishop Hunter had sent out his usual February call for wagons, teams, men, and provisions for the emigration service.

Snow replied that Dixie's livestock had been starved to the point that it was hard to find horses or oxen able to pull a load.[26] He had visited the settlements in that region, and he found depressing poverty. "The winter has been dry and cold, and little or no grass for our stock. No rain or snow to wet the ground since last September. Hay and grain for our horses have been entirely out of the question."

Concerning the scarcity of food, Snow wrote that the people of St. George had met in public meeting. Every householder was asked to report the pounds of food on hand. The report was appalling: "It was ascertained that the whole supply of foodstuffs is about 25 pounds, 15 ounces per person." Yet Dixie agreed to send its quota of teams, although in making this pledge Snow did not hesitate to complain that Dixie in previous years had been discriminated against.

> Our teams travel 700 miles farther than the teams in and around Salt Lake, for which we have hitherto received no additional compensation. Last year our teams, being compelled to wait seven weeks at Florence for their loading, were seven months making the trip, while some other trains made it in four months and received the same compensation. These well-known facts produce their effects upon the minds of the people and somewhat quench the ardor of their zeal.

The reference to "compensation" concerned payment not in cash or kind but in credit for service rendered.

By this method of donated service the poor were brought in until 1868, after which the railroad displaced the wagon trains. All that energy could then be applied to other work, and there was much to be done with the expansion of industry and other developments in Utah after 1868. There was great rivalry in commerce and industry between Gentiles and Mormons.

Gentile industry, most of it mining, was led by such men as General Patrick E. Connor, who had left the military life about 1866. Many of the soldiers who had served under Connor at Camp Douglas joined the throngs roaming Utah's hills looking for precious metal. Connor was not primarily an army man. Even while soldiering, he gave much of his time to scouting around for gold deposits. It was apparently to promote this interest that he started his newspaper, the *Union Vedette*, which invited prospectors and promoters to Utah.[27] The issue of November 30, 1863, averred the "strongest evidence that the mountains and canyons of the territory of Utah abound in rich veins of gold, silver, copper and other minerals." Connor thought the prospect would invite a "hardy and industrious" population.

On July 21, 1864, General Connor reported to the assistant adjutant general of the army, stationed at San Franscisco:

> My policy in this territory has been to invite hither a large Gentile and loyal population, sufficient by peaceful means and through the ballot box to overwhelm the Mormons by mere force of numbers, and thus wrest from the Church—disloyal and traitorous to the core—the absolute and tyrannical control of temporal and civil affairs, or at least a population numerous enough to put a check on the Mormon authorities, and give countenance to those who are striving to loosen the bonds by which they have been so long oppressed.[28]

This immediate objective was not untainted by political ambition.

Connor's plan was to be achieved by developing Utah's mines. On March 1, 1864, he issued from Camp Douglas a circular telling all Gentiles on the lines and all Mormons between the lines that "the mines are thrown open to the hardy and industrious, and it is announced that they will receive the amplest protection in life, property and rights against aggression from whatsoever source, Indian or white."

This handbill continued:

> In giving assurance of entire protection to all who may come hither to prospect for mines, the undersigned wishes at this time most earnestly, and yet firmly, to warn all, whether permanent residents or not of this territory, that should violence be offered, or attempted to be offered to miners in the pursuit of their lawful occupation, the offender or offenders, one or many, will be tried as public enemies, and punished to the utmost extent of martial law.

Thus Connor would use the army to promote the mining industry. He would try offenders by martial law, which he had no legal power to declare. Here was a Gentile talking in the spring of 1864 as the Mormon leaders talked in the spring of 1858.[29]

For the next several years, until he found himself out of sympathy with President Grant's carpetbag appointees, Connor was leader of a movement to expand the mines and take Utah captive. He was the gentile answer to Brigham Young's doctrine that land is better than gold. Said Young: "We want an abundance of wheat and fine flour, or wine and oil; and of every choice fruit that will grow in our climate; we want silk, wool, cotton, flax and other textile substances of which cloth can be made." He added that nations grow great on iron and coal but that with gold civilization perishes.

Connor answered in substance: "Give us the gold and silver and before long all the Mormons will be working for us."

Before ten years had passed Connor was out in front. The Gentiles were getting rich. They brought in cosmopolitanism. The Mormons had no choice, eventually, but to join hands with them.

NOTES

1. Cumming was among a number of prisoners exchanged by the Union forces with the Confederacy in 1864. Among the Confederacy prisoners exchanged on that occasion was Colonel Thomas L. Kane, who had been captured by the forces of General "Stonewall" Jackson. Cumming and Kane, who had gone to Salt Lake City in 1858 under a flag of truce, met again under a flag of truce near Richmond but under strangely different circumstances.

2. This story, recorded by Charles L. Walker in his journal on January 3, 1862, was told everywhere: "Our new governor, Mr. Dawson, in trying to practice some of his devilish civilization on the widow of T. S. Williams, met with a violent resistance from her. He offered her a large sum of money to say nothing about it, but to no purpose. He feigned to be sick and left for the States a day or two ago." Walker, a pioneer of St. George, was then living in Salt Lake City. B. H. Roberts (*Comprehensive History of the Church*, Vol. V, chap. cxxii) reported that Dawson at Mountain Dell had been "cruelly beaten and robbed." Two of the assailants were killed by officers when they avoided arrest (*Deseret News*, January 22, 1862).

3. L.D.S. Journal History," September 1, 1859; also "A History of Ogden" (Historical Records Survey Project), pp. 40–45. A good version of the affair from the Mormon viewpoint is given by Roberts, *op. cit.*, Vol. V. Two contemporary anti-Mormon reports are John H. Beadle, *Life in Utah*, pp. 402–34, and William A. Hickman, *Brigham's Destroying Angel.*

4. *Op. cit.* Former Governor Harding (*ibid.*, Appen. K) wrote: "Some men they had sent to a distant mill with grain were arrested and kept prisoners. Fines were assessed against them for refusing to drill in the Utah militia; some of their cattle were seized on execution, and others stampeded and driven off. Some of them found their way to the Church corral. It was carried so far that the last cow of many a poor man was taken. . . . ."

5. See "The State of Deseret," *Utah Historical Quarterly*, Vol. VIII, of which the issues of April, July, and October, 1940, appeared as a monograph, written by Dale L. Morgan, as a Historical Records Survey Project of the Utah W.P.A.

6. The *Desert News* of February 19, 1862, reported some remarks by Brigham Young to the church membership in Salt Lake City on January 19: "We are about to constitutionally organize a state government, and to again petition for admission into the family of States, to secure to ourselves the inalienable rights of American citizens. This we do to please ourselves and our God. If we please our heavenly Father, our elder brother, Jesus Christ, and the holy angels and the saints that have lived and died, and please ourselves in righteousness, then we ask no odds of all hell and their abettors. . . . ." Then followed damnation of Buchanan and the "treasoners." "I can tell all the world that we mean to sustain the Constitution of the United States and all righteous laws. We are not by any means treasoners, secessionists, nor abolitionists. We are neither Negro drivers nor Negro worshippers. We belong to the family of heaven. . . . ."

7. The ghost government of Deseret was a shock to Governor Harding. On August 3, 1862, he sent a copy of the *Deseret News* of January 29, 1862, to the Secretary of State. He marked the following item in an editorial about the constitutional convention: "There was a determination of purpose manifested by the delegates, collectively and individually, to carry out the designs and wishes of the people in the institution of a state government to supersede the territorial form of rule, unconstitutionally imposed upon them by Congress, as all who were present will testify, and, that in the event the request for admission to the family of states should be refused, they feared not the consequences of throwing off the federal yoke and assuming the right of self-government, of which they have so long been deprived."

8. "L.D.S. Journal History," January 19, 1863. The state of Deseret was to be held in readiness, in case the national government failed.

9. The altitude of Dixie ranges from 1,000 to about 2,500 feet above the sea. Rainfall average is 9 inches per year. Mean temperature is 37° F. for January, 49° for March, 76° for June; and the average temperature for the year is 59°. This refers to St. George, which has an average of 300 days of sunshine per year. At some points the mid-day summer heat reaches 110°.

10. In 1856 there were about 5,000 persons in the southern half of Utah. In 1860 there were less than 700 persons in Cedar City and eight other communities from that point to Santa Clara, and about 400 of these persons were under 15 years of age.

11. Gardner became a bishop in St. George. He operated a sawmill at Pine Valley and later on Mount Trumbull, where he helped cut lumber for the St. George Temple. His autobiography (mimeographed) was published by his family in 1934. His four wives bore him thirty-seven children.

12. William Carter, one of the pioneers of 1847, who plowed the first furrow in Salt Lake Valley under the guidance of Apostles Orson Pratt and Erastus Snow, also plowed, under the direction of these men, the first irrigated furrow in St. George. Many years later, at some western irrigation congress, he received a gold medal for pioneering in irrigation. The honor came in his sixty-seventh year, when he was serving a prison term for polygamy. He had three wives and twenty children.

13. Orton's brief typewritten autobiography, on file at the St. George Library, re-

ports some of the practical jokes played on him. Once he was permitted to yoke the wrong oxen to his wagon (his steers looked much like certain others). The chief practical joker asked him to make a pair of boots. He suggested that the joker could pay him by whittling a quart of shoe pegs. The man thought it an easy trade. He spent hours on the task and broke his knife in the effort. Cobbler Orton said the pegs could not be used. Some were too small, others too long or too thick or too thin. Orton had two wives but no children.

14. "History of Brigham Young," October 13, 1861, a letter written by Young to Orson Hyde. Tobacco was included among the products desired from Dixie, but tobacco was a taboo article under the Word of Wisdom, the Mormon dietary code. Very little was produced.

15. The legislature granted the St. George charter on January 17, 1862, about a month after the first settlers came on the location. The city was given 25 square miles of land, enough to include the fields within the municipal limits.

16. About the same time settlers had been sent to take up land at Panaca and other places on the Meadow Valley Wash. When the Nevada line was moved eastward in 1866, taking these settlements from Utah, the Mormons protested and did not pay taxes until the federal survey definitely established the line in 1870.

17. Roberts (*op. cit.*, V, 127–28) reviews the effort of the church to establish the Colorado River route. It was believed at the time that the river would float boats of 700 tons capacity.

18. On Connor's punitive expedition see J. H. Martineau, *Military History of Cache County;* the *Deseret News*, January 28, 1863; Roberts, *op. cit.*, V, 30–37. Connor indicated that the Mormons had been supporting the Indians because he took from them several thousands of bushels of wheat and 175 ponies.

19. The government service was not geared to deal with the poverty of the Indians. They still had to get most of their subsistence from the environment. Concerning the desert Indians west of Great Salt Lake, Forney wrote on November 5, 1859, to the Commissioner of Indian Affairs: "Like every other portion of this territory, with which I am acquainted, Humboldt Valley is devoid of game, with the exception of a few antelope and rabbits. The Indians there, like those I met in Raft Creek Valley, and many others in this territory, are obliged, to sustain life, to eat, besides the usual game, snakes, lizards, swifts, wolves, grasshoppers, crickets, ants and their eggs, etc. . . . ."

Poverty among some southern tribes was as great. Price W. Nelson, in a sketch of his life on file at the St. George Library and with the Utah State Historical Society, wrote of the Muddy Valley about 1866: "I remember once when we were clearing land, burning brush, an old Indian came to our fire. He looked nearly starved and was naked, all but his britch clout. He had a big rat which he threw into the coals to roast. When it was done, he skinned it and ate the skin. The head came next, then the entrails, and then the legs and meaty parts. He ate every bit of it. . . . ." Nelson wrote that they ate snakes, lizards, and grasshoppers. They shook the seeds off the grass. They would beg for the carcasses of animals that died in the settlement. "They would catch the locust as they came out of the ground in the spring and eat them alive, though sometimes they roasted them and kept them."

20. The territory of Utah papers at the National Archives contain a report from Judge Eckles sent from Camp Floyd on September 23, 1859, charging that the Mormons were leading Snake and Bannock Indians in raids on emigrant trains. The truth of this statement may be doubted, because these tribes were not at that time friendly with the Mormons but they were under the influence of certain gentile whites. He reported a raid on a small company, under Captain Mintmore. White men, painted like Indians, took part in the raid. Five persons were killed and three missing. One child, "about five

years old was found with her legs and ears cut off; her eyes gouged out and scalped." Eckles tried to fix blame on the Mormons.

21. *Annual Report of the Secretary of the Interior, 1865–1866*, p. 314, gives the account of the peace conference between the Indian chiefs and Colonel O. H. Irish, superintendent of Indian affairs for Utah, with Brigham Young present. This was held on June 7, 8, and 9, 1865. It was proposed that the tribes move to the new Uintah Valley reservation. The government would pay them $25,000 annually the first ten years and $20,000 annually the next twenty years. Some of the Indians moved, but the Great White Father did not keep his part of the bargain.

22. James G. Bleak, "Manuscript History of St. George," Book A, pp. 225–28. On pp. 311–14 of the same book is a report dated March 29, 1866, about the handling of some Indian killers by a gentile posse from Pioche. A miner named Rogers had been robbed and killed. The Gentiles blamed the Mormons. The Mormons found an Indian named Okus who confessed a part in the murder. Okus was delivered to the gentile group, led by a Mr. Woodman. He gave the names of two other Indians who were implicated. Okus, a chain about his neck, was forced to trot some ten miles to the location, where they found in camp three Indians and some women and children. They shot all three, although one of them "had bourne good character."

They returned to Panaca. "Okus saw by the preparations, that he was to be killed. He said through the interpreter that he knew he had bad blood in him and that it ought to be poured out, but he asked to be shot instead of hanged. His request was not granted. He was hanged and died without a struggle." Before his death Okus indicated that Bush Head, an Indian in Moroni's camp at Clover Valley, had also been implicated in the murder of Rogers. Woodman and his party went to Clover Valley, about fifteen miles, where they caught Bush Head and hanged him in the presence of the entire group of Indians.

The writer also heard this story from Lyman L. Woods, then in charge of the Clover Valley community. He told that, when Bush Head was placed on the top of a barrel with the rope about his neck, he was given a chance to speak. He boasted of his crimes against the whites. He called the whites bad. While boasting about what he would like to do to them, the barrel was kicked from under him.

23. A report on the Black Hawk War is found in Roberts, *op. cit.*, Vol. V, chap. cxxix. The number of lives lost in this war might have been much greater had the church not imposed such a strict program of caution.

24. John S. Stucki, of Santa Clara, in his *Family History Journal*, pp. 42–43, recorded his recollections of crossing the plains as a child of 9 years with the Martin company in 1860. This company of fifty families, pulling handcarts, had along four wagons and ox teams. They were placed on half-rations soon after starting. "My dear Mother had a little baby to nurse, and only half enough to eat, and to pull on the handcart all day long, day after day, she soon got so weak and worn out that she could not help father any more." He wrote that some days she would be far behind when the company went into camp at night. Stucki added: "Father let mother have a little bigger part of the half-ration. This shortage of food, together with having the three children with everything else we had on the handcart, made it too heavy for him to pull alone." The hunger was hard for the children to bear. One day they had a piece of buffalo meat, from which he cut off a few bits by stealth. He was surprised that his father did not punish him when the theft was discovered. His parents only wept.

25. Roberts (*op. cit.*, V, 109) gives some information about these companies, but the source seems to be the *Church Chronology*. Full information has not been taken from the records.

26. Bleak, *op. cit.*, Book A, pp. 177–79. Hunter's letter, dated February 16, 1864,

began: "President Young has called upon us to furnish 300 teams and wagons to send to Florence for freight and the poor this spring." He called for strong wagons to carry 3,000 pounds, also good oxen and horses; or communities could send the money and good "Chicago wagons" would be purchased in the east. Dixie teams would take to Salt Lake City cotton, molasses, and other offerings. Dixie would furnish twenty-eight outfits with guards and teamsters. These men and teams would be fully supplied with clothing, medicine, and tools. "You will be as careful as possible and select honest, temperate, good upright and responsible men for teamsters and guards; men who will conduct themselves properly on all occasions, as they would on missions preaching the Gospel. . . . . If teamsters and guards use obscene language or get intoxicated, or otherwise conduct themselves improperly, the captain of the company will be authorized to try them for fellowship and discharge them."

27. The *Union Vedette*, a Union sentry on guard, was the voice of the Gentiles. T. B. H. Stenhouse on July 4, 1864, began publishing the *Salt Lake Daily Telegraph*. These papers were foils to each other. They differed first on the mining issue. Later Stenhouse changed his mind and, in doing so, offended Brigham Young, for which he was excommunicated.

28. For a discussion on the mining issue see Roberts, *op. cit.*, V, 63; Edward W. Tullidge, "Mines of the West, I: Utah Mines," *Western Galaxy*, March, 1888; also by Tullidge, *History of Salt Lake City*, p. 328.

29. Tullidge (*History of Salt Lake City*, p. 327) quotes this handbill. Concerning Connor's mining activities, the following was written in the record of the High Council of the St. George Stake, June 11, 1864: "Brother Snow stated to the Council that in his recent visit to the settlements of Clover and Meadow Valleys, he was satisfied it was the intention of General Connor and Gentiles to settle in there and not only claim the mines of silver in that vicinity, but also the farming lands, water privileges, etc., in these and surrounding valleys." It was deemed wise to send a prudent man there to take charge of the Mormon settlers. He selected John Nebeker. "Brother Nebeker said that while it was very repugnant to his feelings to mingle in such society as would probably be gathered in those valleys . . . . nonetheless he would go." After about five years Nebeker was relieved of this assignment. General Connor later became more friendly with Brigham Young; and in 1870, when Young was arrested, he offered $100,000 bail.

CHAPTER X

REVIVAL OF GENTILE OPPOSITION

BEFORE the Civil War and during that struggle church leaders almost fiercely promoted their ideal of isolation. Possibly the leaders sensed it during the war, but certainly after the war they realized that Utah was in the path of change. Economic forces were already at work, and the tempo of these increased rapidly after 1865. Brigham Young and his associates became concerned with defending their insularism, while at the same time they were equally concerned with taking advantage of the economic changes in store for Utah.

Prior to the arrival of Johnston's army the urge for isolation was so dominant that when certain brethren brought to Brigham Young a proposal for a new alphabet he was impressed. The legislature, with his approval, on December 28, 1855, appropriated $2,500 to buy type for the strange characters of the Deseret alphabet. Responsibility was given to the regents of the University of Deseret for teaching the hieroglyphics, some of which had the appearance of Greek letters. Others were suggestive of Pittman's stenographic symbols.[1]

Some books, including the Book of Mormon and primary textbooks, were printed; but the Deseret alphabet languished until after the Civil War, when some more books were printed. The only importance in Mormon history of the Deseret-alphabet effort was the example it affords of the Mormon wish for isolation. They wanted to exclude the rising generation from the printed page of the Gentiles. The plan was abandoned when it proved impracticable.

Most potent of the invading influences was the mining industry, already mentioned. Mining served to raise certain problems about the ownership of land, which did not exist when land was used mainly by the Mormons and for agriculture only.

3

Long Sounds.

Name.		Sound.
e	as in	eat.
a	"	ate.
ah	"	art.
aw	"	aught.
o	"	oat.
oo	"	ooze.

Short Sounds of the above.

	Sound.
as in	it.
"	et.
"	at.
"	ot.
"	ut.
"	book.

Double Sounds.

Name.		Sound.
i	as in	ice.
ow	"	owl.
ye		
woo		
h		

Name.	Sound.
p	
b	
t	
d	
che	as in cheese.
g	
k	
ga	as in gate.
f	
v	
eth	as in thigh.
the	" thy
s	
z	
esh	as in flesh.
zhe	" vision.
ur	" burn.
l	
m	
n	
eng	as in length.

BRIGHAM YOUNG'S CURIOUS EXPERIMENT, THE DESERET ALPHABET

This alphabet was invented about 1854 in order to bring about perfect isolation. Some textbooks and the Book of Mormon were translated into the new script. The title-page on the left reads: "The Deseret First Book by the Regents of the Deseret University," now the University of Utah. Page 3 (*right*) shows the characters of the alphabet.

Also, the mining industry had the effect of placing certain sections of Utah on a cash basis, and this new enterprise made it possible for gentile mercantile firms to flourish in Salt Lake City.

Another force for cosmopolitanism was the coming of the railroad. Had it not been for the mining industry and the railroad, Utah's baffling land problem might not have been brought to a solution until much later.

As previously noted, Mormon settlers were squatters on Indian land; and, for all their memorials to Congress, nothing was done to enable these pioneer farmers to get title to the land they had been irrigating and tilling so many years. Land in Utah could not be bought or sold legally, which did not worry federal officials greatly until it was brought to their attention that Gentiles were also being inconvenienced.

In other territories the government arranged to buy the Indian rights, and the land was made available for private purchase under the Pre-emption Act of 1841. This law permitted settlers to buy tracts ranging from 40 to 160 acres at $1.25 per acre. In 1862 the Homestead Act was passed. This law permitted settlers to lay claim to tracts of 160 acres or less and receive title by developing the land and living thereon. Utah lands were not opened for homesteading until late in 1868.

Utah pioneers resorted to a legislative device which, at the time, was legal. The legislature, having power to incorporate communities, would give municipal charters to settlements, calling them "cities." Several such charters were granted in 1851, including Salt Lake City,[2] Ogden, Manti, Provo, and Parowan. Each of these communities received an area from 20 to 36 or more square miles, sufficient to include the land that would be cultivated. The land was distributed by the prospective owner, each according to the size of the family drawing the location. Each family head would draw from a hat the number of his plot in the "field," and by the same method he would determine the location of his lot in town.[3] Necessity forced upon the communities a type of co-operative ownership of the land as well as of the water used for irrigation.

This method of owning land went well until after the Civil War, when the promise of new enterprise brought to Utah numerous Gentiles looking for opportunity or easy money. Among them were many lawyers. They began to examine titles to the land held by the Mormons. They found flaws, loopholes, temptation.

On general principles, Mormons did not like lawyers. Brigham Young opposed using lawyers for any function the priesthood could perform. He wrote on August 11, 1866:

> Like the birds of prey, they snuff the carcass from afar. Business is poor where they have been; but they imagine that with the land claims and other business the enemies of truth promise them here, they will reap an abundant harvest. Armies have not been found to operate well in breaking us up, but it is now hoped that vexatious law suits and setting up and enforcing claims for our land, may do it.[4]

Land-jumpers became active in Salt Lake City in August, 1866. In September the squatters were busy placing "improvements" on such public properties as the parade ground and the race track. The Mormons broke down the squatter shanties and ducked the trespassers in the river until they begged for their lives and promised to leave the country.[5] In California in 1853 there had been mob action against land-jumpers, but those collisions scarcely attracted notice, compared with the national scandal that flared up when the Mormons in 1866 resorted to similar methods.

One of the jumpers was Dr. J. King Robinson, a young physician, who in October, 1866, was assaulted and so manhandled that he died. A native of Maine, Robinson went to Utah in 1866 as assistant surgeon at Camp Douglas. He married the daughter of a Mormon and began professional practice in Salt Lake City. He opened a saloon and bowling alley, a sort of gentile night-life center, at the Warm Spring within the city limits. A lawsuit for possession of the property was in process at the time Robinson was killed.

There followed an inquest, which endured many days. John B. Weller, former governor of California, and other gentile lawyers waged legal duel with such Mormon lawyers as Seth M. Blair and Hosea Stout. The Gentiles tried to trace responsibility for the killing to Brigham Young. They charged a campaign of terror to drive out honest men. Rewards were offered by both Mormons and Gentiles, but the killers were not apprehended.

Publicity in the Robinson murder case attracted attention to the Utah land problem. The Gentiles received a more favorable hearing from the outside press. They complained against the excessive tracts of land given to Utah's "cities" and called attention to a recently enacted federal statute, the Townsite Act of 1864, which limited the land within an incorporated community to 320 acres for a population of less than 200. Places of from 200 to 1,000 inhabitants were entitled to 640 acres, and for each additional 1,000 inhabitants another 320 acres could be added. Another Townsite Act was passed by Congress in 1867 which permitted municipalities to purchase occupied public land. These acts could not be applied to Utah until the Indian title to the lands had been extinguished.

In 1868 the Indians of northern Utah were removed to reservations, and considerable land previously held for them was made available for homesteading under the law of 1862 or for purchase under the law of 1841. Mormons rushed to get their land titles, but in some cases they found the land-jumpers were ahead of them. Here are two cases which illustrate the methods resorted to by the land-jumpers:[6]

On November 9, 1874, Samuel L. Baker, transient, bachelor, and miner, filed a homestead claim on 160 acres of meadow land within the limits of Grantsville. This land had been used by residents of the town for many years as a hay meadow. None of the co-operative users lived on the location. On behalf of the people, Mayor William C. Rydalch contested the claim. Baker met the technical requirements of the law by erecting on the land a small shanty. He hired another transient Gentile to occupy the property while he went away, seeking employment. The residents went ahead, according to custom, and removed the hay. They burned Baker's shanty. He demanded damages to the extent of $9,000 and charged through his lawyer that he had been threatened with bodily harm.

Possibly Baker had been threatened, since the Mormons regarded him as a thieving jumper. His charge had reference to a statement made by George Q. Cannon at Grantsville on July 20, 1875: "God has given us this land, and if any outsider shall come in to take land which we claim, a piece six by two is all they are entitled to, and that will last them to all eternity."

On March 15, 1877, Maurice M. Kaighan, a Salt Lake City lawyer, wrote to Mayor Rydalch offering to mediate between Baker and the people of Grantsville. He said that Baker wanted to do the "right thing." Would Grantsville make him a fair offer for his claim? "He seems confident that he will soon get his patent for the land, and between us, I think he will, and when he does, he will, of course, ask more for the land than he does now." If Mr. Rydalch would visit Salt Lake City, "I think we could get Mr. Baker into my back office and we could fix it all up in a little while." This, too obvious, offer was not accepted.

Grantsville people appealed the case to the General Land Office in Washington, but the appeal was denied because none of the users had built a residence on the property. The land was ruled unoccupied.

The second Grantsville case involved the apparent bad faith of a Mormon, Thomas McBride, who in 1869 filed a homestead claim on 160 acres of land which was also within the town limits but was occupied by a number of original settlers. In some towns where land was so occupied, the residents would join together and select one of their number to enter a homestead claim. After receiving title to the land, the homesteader would divide the acrage among the residents. They would share the costs in proportion. McBride went ahead apparently without entering into such an agreement with his neighbors; or, if he had such an agreement, he failed to respect it.[7]

McBride's claim was also contested and appealed to the General Land Office. Had he been given the rights of homestead, he might have dispossessed fifteen families. The commissioner ruled that the land was occupied and could not be homesteaded, that the facts were not similar to those in the Baker case. This decision was not reached until 1879 and was about the last of the land-jumping cases. While the experience was costly to the settlers, most of the pioneers by 1879 had acquired title to their land.[8]

The railroad reached Utah in 1868. The next year the Union Pacific and the Central Pacific were joined at Promontory Summit near the northern shore of Salt Lake. The golden spike was driven by Governor Leland Stanford of California on May 10. Thus, "with the iron of the east and the gold of the west" the two oceans were linked for commerce.[9] The railroad did not reach Salt Lake City but touched Utah at Ogden, circled the northern shore of Salt Lake, and crossed the Nevada deserts to California.

Brigham Young favored the railroad, and he was shrewd enough to turn its coming to the economic advantage of himself and the Saints. This meant a compromise with his ideal of economic isolation, for which he prayed in 1860. In 1869 he said that the Mormon religion was weak, indeed, if it "cannot stand one railroad."[10] The Mormons caught the railroad-building fever and formed a contracting company which aided in building the Union Pacific roadbed. Brigham Young took in pay rails and equipment for a branch line which connected Salt Lake City with Ogden in 1870.[11]

Church leaders called the railroad a blessing, although they were concerned about the social problems that would come in its wake. It might easily place Utah's Gentiles in a favored position. It would speed the opening of the mines and bring wealth to gentile pockets. With the cash in pocket, Gentiles would open up stores, banks, and factories.

Joseph Fish at Parowan wrote in his journal on December 8, 1867: "There has been considerable preaching of late about the Saints trading with and supporting our enemies, especially the apostates. We have one very bitter apostate in our place, James McGuffie." The boycott policy was in vogue before the arrival of the railroad, but in 1868 there began an organized drive to persuade, even force, Mormons not to "trade with the enemies of our Church who would seek to destroy us."[12]

This boycott had to be implemented by some positive devices

in order to be effective. If the gentile merchants in Utah had better credit in the East and could undersell the Mormon merchants, a boycott could not be effective. Church leaders met this possibility by laying plans to start a large co-operative store to serve all Mormon communities. On March 1, 1869, Zion's Co-operative Mercantile Institution (Z.C.M.I.) began operating. The opening of the establishment was preceded with a wave of preaching. The boycott was the major topic at the church conference of October, 1868. Esias Edwards, a Dixie pioneer, wrote in his journal on November 22, 1868:

> I attended conference at Salt Lake City with my wife on the 6th of October and had a very comfortable and happy time. We fared sumptously on peaches, apples, plums and so forth. We had a good instruction. There were measures entered into to cease supporting the Gentile merchants that was in our midst that was endeavoring to lay a foundation for our overthrow and destruction. The plan was to cease to trade with them and let them alone severely. That plan has been carried out so far by all of the true honest hearted Saints. But there a few that thinks they are at liberty to do as they please and will suffer themselves to be severed from the Church before they will obey the priesthood. Therefore, there is a dividing line about to be drawn by which the Saints will be tryed whether they will serve.

Such was the moral program paving the way for Z.C.M.I. There is available a report of Z.C.M.I., released on July 10, 1875, which indicates that the amount of business carried on during the first five years reached the total of $15,000,000. Branches had been established in most communities, and for these the parent-store maintained a wholesale service. In practically every ward there was a "co-op" branch, of which the bishop was president and in which practically every Mormon family had invested funds.

In the development of this co-operative store the profit motive was not entirely neglected. To quote from the Z.C.M.I. report of 1875: "What firm in all this broad land can point to a brighter and more honorable record than this. During the first four years and a half of its existence it paid to the stockholders a dividend in cash of 78 per cent, and 52 per cent as a reserve to be added to the capital stock, making in all a dividend of 130 per cent." This was an argument to persuade more Saints to invest more money in Z.C.M.I. stores.[13]

With more capital, Z.C.M.I. could could obtain credit with

eastern firms, giving Mormons new strength in the mercantile field. Previously the big stores in Salt Lake City were owned by outsiders who had the cash and who could risk bringing in wagon trains loaded with goods. Frequently, if they had on hand the only available supply of goods, they would use the situation to run prices up. After the arrival of the railroad it was no longer easy for merchants to corner goods of any class. The growth of Z.C.M.I. further blocked such price-fixing practices. As a service agency, Z.C.M.I. became useful as an outlet for Utah-made commodities.[14]

With their own well-stocked stores church leaders had in their hands an effective weapon for promoting the boycott of gentile merchants. This program of exclusion stimulated gentile businessmen to adopt measures for defense. A condition of conflict developed which was detrimental to both groups. There was a third group, comprising a number of men in Salt Lake City known as the "Godbeites," for their leader, William S. Godbe.[15] Godbe joined the church in England and migrated to Utah, where he became a leader and a loyal supporter of Brigham Young. He began as a druggist and later became a general merchant.

Among the men around Godbe were Eli B. Kelsey, who had been active in the state-of-Deseret movement; E. L. T. Harrison and E. W. Tullidge, coeditors of the *Utah Magazine*, a literary journal which eventually became the *Salt Lake Tribune;* T. B. H. Stenhouse, publisher of the *Salt Lake Telegraph*, a pro-Mormon newspaper; and W. H. Lawrence, who, like Godbe, was a polygamist and a successful businessman. Lawrence was a founding director of Z.C.M.I.

These men saw the future of Utah in terms of more tolerant relations between Mormons and Gentiles, but they were ahead of their time. The church was not prepared to divorce itself from a management relation to business and politics. The Godbeites opposed the boycott doctrine and regarded such ventures as the Deseret alphabet as foolish, if not antisocial. They opposed the all-Mormon co-operatives, believing that such activities stimulated all-gentile retaliation.

The Godbeites were called "reformers" by those who considered them dangerous. They started their opposition with a respectful presentation of their views but were rebuffed more sternly than if they had been Gentiles. Any concession to their position would have detracted from the control held by Brigham Young, and it would have been a retreat from total priesthood guidance. Stenhouse wrote: "Mormonism demands perfect submission—total dethronement of individuality—blind obedience. There is no middle path."[16]

Godbeites were polite rebels determined to stimulate business by encouraging cosmopolitan thinking in Utah. To this end the *Utah Magazine* published "broadening" articles designed to take the Saints upon a high hill where they might view the gentile world, which was not so bad as church authorities claimed. They were the "appeasers" of their time.

Brigham Young's group was stronger. The Godbeites were tried for heresy or apostacy and were excommunicated, but their explusion was not the example it might have been ten years earlier. The leaders were not simple poor folks like the Morrisites. They could speak their minds and write their views. They were men of means; and, although out of their church, they continued to work loyally for the interests of their people, the Saints.[17]

Church leaders confronted a practical obstacle in their home-industry program, because the high wage rates of the West did not permit Utah industries to compete with eastern industries. Moreover, eastern industries were more efficiently organized and better equipped. These matters were discussed by the brethren at the School of the Prophets in Salt Lake City. Schools such as this were inner forums where church leaders met to discuss spiritual and temporal problems. One of the apostles made the proposal that Utah workers accept lower wages. The Godbeites who were present, not yet having been excommunicated, opposed the suggestion. Defenders of the proposal argued that, if Utah workers would not lower their wages, Chinese workers should be brought in.[18]

When news of this proposal passed around, it turned out to be so unpopular that no move was made to import Chinese.

The church then pressed its program of co-operation and sacrifice. Charles L. Walker, of St. George, wrote in his journal on January 1, 1869: "The people are driving with all their might to sustain themselves by uniting together in cooperation, in mercantile and stock raising associations." Dixie's cotton textile mill was a typical home industry. It could not compete with outside mills, since the cost of cotton was too high, reaching sometimes a dollar a pound. But the Mormon plan closed its eyes to costs in this urge for economic self-sufficiency.

It should be added that the polygamy issue was also involved in this drive for self-sufficiency. The church would be the better able to defend itself on other fronts if the Saints could achieve economic security in commerce, industry, and finance as well as in agriculture. Economic power was imperative to political power; and, unless the Mormons could hold political control of local government, they could not resist pressure against their cherished institutions. To get and hold such power naturally served the private interests of certain leaders. It was that issue which brought the dominant priesthood inner-group into conflict with the Godbeites.

That issue opened anew with the arrival of each freshly appointed federal official from the outside. Every carpetbag governor was regarded with suspicion if he tried to assert the authority of his office; so was every federal judge and United States attorney. As far as the Mormons were concerned, the ideal federal official was one who did nothing but draw his salary, leaving to Mormon local officials the responsibility for handling local problems.

Governor Harding, for example, made the mistake of lecturing the legislature about Mormon morals and patriotism. He was succeeded in June, 1863, by James D. Doty, who had been superintendent of Indian affairs in Utah and who previously had served as governor of Wisconsin Territory and once was Wisconsin's delegate to Congress. Doty was a moderate man, willing to follow Lincoln's "let-them-alone" policy. He died in Utah in June, 1865. Utah was suddenly left without a governor; and the logical successor to the governor, the secretary of state, was also out of the territory. O. H. Irish, superintendent of Indian affairs, took over the duties of the two offices. The Mormons attempted to instal Apostle George A. Smith, president of the Legislative Council; but Irish held the position until the arrival of the new governor, Charles Durkee, of Wisconsin.[19] Durkee, too, was a moderate man, who did not get involved in disputes. He resigned in 1869 and was succeeded by his secretary of state, S. A. Mann.

In 1866, during Durkee's incumbency, the trouble with the land-jumpers began. The murder of Dr. Robinson in connection with the land-jumping efforts has already been mentioned. At the same time, Utah was stirred to the core by another murder case, that of Newton Brassfield, a Gentile of unknown origin but ill repute.

Brassfield courted and married the plural wife of a Mormon who was absent from Salt Lake City as a missionary for the church. The action was abhorrent to the Saints, although amusing to the Gentiles. Neighbors of the woman claimed the marriage was illegal and would not permit Brassfield to remove household goods from the home of his bride. On the occasion of this interference, Brassfield drew a revolver. He was brought before the court; and, while the trial was in progress, he was shot by an unidentified person. Gentiles offered a reward, but the murderer could not be found. Mormons called Brassfield a common seducer and wife-stealer and would not aid in apprehending the killer.

This incident gave rise to reports that Gentiles were not safe in Utah. The federal judge, Solomon P. McCurdy, who performed the marriage, reported that he had been threatened. When these reports reached General William T. Sherman, chief of the army, he telegraphed to Brigham Young, April 10, 1866: "I am bound to give protection to all citizens, regardless of religious faith, and shall do so." He warned, if "your people resort to measures of intimidation," troops would be sent to Utah. This message, the general indicated, was sent not as a threat "but as a caution that a sensible man should heed."

What reason Sherman had for sending a warning to a church

official when the message should have been communicated from the president through proper channels to civil authorities in Utah is not clear. Brigham Young made the most of Sherman's blunder. He advised the general that Gentiles were safe in Utah, but added: "There are a few speculators here who are anxious to make it appear that American citizens' lives are in danger through religious fanaticism, hoping thereby to have troops sent here to make money out of contracts."[20]

Also, during the period of Durkee's governorship began the crusade to pass anti-Mormon restrictive legislation. Utah Gentiles had an active lobby in Washington. At their prompting, various senators and congressmen offered bills to curb the church. Three of these are mentioned as typical:

Senator Benjamin F. Wade of Ohio in June, 1866, offered a bill which aimed at certain basic changes, including (*a*) placing the Nauvoo Legion under full control of the governor, who would appoint its officers (this would have deprived the militia units of the traditional right to choose their officers); (*b*) forbidding officers of the Mormon church to solemnize marriages; (*c*) giving authority to the United States marshal to select all jurors and the authority to the governor to appoint county judges; and (*d*) taxing all church property in excess of $20,000. The Wade bill failed, but most of its features were incorporated in a bill presented by Senator Aaron H. Cragin of New Hampshire in December, 1867. The Cragin bill also included a provision for hearing polygamy cases without a jury.[21]

While the Cragin bill was being debated and delayed in the Senate, Congressman Shelby M. Cullom of Illinois proposed a bill which was given precedence in both houses. This measure proposed to place in the hands of the United States marshal and the United States attorney all responsibility for selecting jurors—an important change, since these officials were usually Gentiles. Moreover, polygamy cases would have been confined to the exclusive jurisdiction of the federal judges. Plural wives would have been deprived of immunity as witnesses in cases involving their husbands. The bill proposed a definition of cohabitation, distinguishing that offense, as a misdemeanor, from polygamy, the felony, defined in the Morrill bill of 1862. The Cullom bill also proposed to abolish Utah's "marked ballot," by which it was possible to determine how each person voted.

There was still another bill being considered at the time the Cullom bill was being debated. This was a measure offered in January, 1869, by Congressman James M. Ashley of Ohio, proposing that slices of Utah be transferred to Nevada, to Wyoming, and to Colorado. These territorial deletions would have deprived Utah of about thirty-five thousand people and no less than half of her present area.[22]

While none of these bills became law, they indicated popular feeling on the Mormon question. It was a vindictive state of mind, else Vice-President Schuyler Colfax would not have journeyed to Utah in 1869 on a reconciliation mission. As speaker of the House of Representatives, he had made a similar visit in 1865. He tried to persuade church leaders to make concessions to public opinion. These proposals were politely but firmly rejected. There was some speculation about open resistance in the event the Cullom bill became law.[23] "This bill means war," declared the *New York World*. "Its terms and its provisions are in the nature of preparations for war. Its execution will assuredly be followed by war."[24] The suggestion followed that the federal government should not meddle with a problem that would eventually be adjusted locally.

In Washington were many who believed the Cullom bill would start war. Some Gentiles, apparently hoping the Mormons would resist, favored sending troops at once. President Grant appointed as Utah's governor an acquaintance from Illinois, General J. M. Shaffer, to replace Acting-Governor S. A. Mann, who had angered many in Utah because he approved a legislative act granting suffrage to Utah women. Shaffer reached Utah in March, 1870, and proceeded to carry out his duties in a strict military manner. He was a sick man, who for that reason needed a job in a mountain habitat; he was too sick to recover and too bitter for tolerant relations with the Saints.[25]

Concerning the possible uprising of the Mormons, Grant followed the wise course and sent General Philip Sheridan to Utah to review the situation. Sheridan was advised to meet Governor

Shaffer and the various factions and, especially, to learn the views of the Godbeites. The "Little General" concluded that no military expedition was needed except, perhaps, a few troops "to act as a moral force upon the public mind, convincing the Mormons that the government intended to carry out its policy."[26]

This drive for legislation was part of a general campaign to unhorse the church leaders. It was not merely coincidental that the laws, as finally passed, were not primarily antipolygamy measures but were designed to deal with the court system, the election system, female suffrage, naturalization of aliens, church ownership of property, and the militia.

Public opinion elsewhere was concerned mainly with polygamy. Churches sent missionaries to Utah to "rescue people" from the Mormon leaders. Gentiles in Utah were more realistic. They talked about polygamy, but they wanted political power. In this state of affairs General Shaffer became governor, and soon he was the dominating figure of a group called the "Gentile Ring."

Other members of the "Ring" were Secretary of State Vernon H. Vaughan, of Alabama; Chief Justice James B. McKean, of New York; and two associate justices, O. F. Strickland, of Michigan, and C. M. Hawley, of Illinois. Soon after his arrival Governor Shaffer requested the removal of Chief Justice Charles C. Wilson, thought to be too friendly with the Mormons. McKean was then selected to take Wilson's place. It was reported that he was a former Methodist minister and that he got the appointment at the suggestion of another Methodist, Dr. J. P. Newman, chaplain of the Senate. This was the same Dr. Newman who journeyed to Utah in 1870 to debate the polygamy issue with Apostle Orson Pratt.

President Grant's Utah appointments, when rank politicians were not named, seemed to include stern military men, such as General Shaffer, or pious men, such as Judge McKean. For the Indian service Grant appointed a minister, George W. Dodge, apparently reasoning that a superintendent of Indian affairs should be a kindly man.

Upon reaching Salt Lake City, Governor Shaffer made his

home at the boarding-house of William H. McKay. Thereafter the McKay house became the rendezvous of various other Gentiles, some of whom proved to be persons of shady character.[27] He associated not at all with the Mormons and very little with those moderates, the Godbeites. The spring conference of the church in 1870 began on May 5. Brigham Young invited the governor to attend and to speak. Shaffer attended but refused to address the people. He had already confidentially expressed his opinion of Brigham Young in a letter to Congressman Cullom:

> I find that my office is no mere sinecure. By the artful legislation of the dominant power, a most miserable skeleton of it only remains. As affairs now stand, the oath of office I have taken to execute the laws is nothing more than a useless form, a mockery, a farce. For without the enactment by Congress of a statute containing the main features of the bill which you introduced on the subject of Utah, I am rendered most powerless, and the laws, for all that I or other officers of the government can do to prevent it, may continue to be violated with impunity, and the federal authority openly defied and ridiculed. It is hard to be nominally the governor of Utah if Brigham Young is permitted to exercise the power of law-giver and autocrat of the Territory. As the leader of the Mormon Church, he arrogates to himself power and control of spiritual, temporal and political affairs.[28]

Shaffer probably honestly believed that the Mormons were foolish people, wickedly led. He was so dominated by this view that he failed to see the faults of the Gentiles close to him. A seasoned politican would have seen the badness in both groups and, while favoring his own group, would have been tolerant toward the other. Lacking political experience and striving for political virtue, he became a political tool of the ring. On April 1, a week after arriving in Utah, he wrote to Hamilton Fish, secretary of state: "I am fully satisfied that the people are worse than their enemies ever charged; of course, I speak of the leaders, but with a good strong law every trouble can be settled without the aid of a single soldier."

In 1867 William H. Hooper became Utah's delegate to Congress, the first candidate for the office to have opposition at the polls. His opponent, William McGrorty, received 105 votes. Hooper received 15,068 votes. McGrorty unsuccessfully contested the election. In this contest the Gentiles realized that they had in these protests an irritating weapon against the dominant group.

Before the general election of 1870 the Godbeites joined with certain Gentiles in a plan for an opposition party. They held a convention at Corinne, a tent town on the Bear River. This meeting gave birth to the Liberal party and nominated General George R. Maxwell, registrar of the land office in Utah, to oppose Hooper in the election for delegate to Congress. In response to this movement the Mormons formed the People's party, which supported Hooper. Maxwell received 1,444 votes, while Hooper garnered a total of 21,656. The Liberals contested the election, but again the effort was unsuccessful.[29]

Governor Shaffer was active in this election. He wrote to Secretary of State Hamilton Fish on July 22, complaining about Mormon control of the polling places. The control, he charged, was so managed that Gentiles employed in the mining camps were obliged, in some cases, to travel as much as fifty miles to vote. Many of them, upon arriving at the polls, would have their votes challenged.

Shaffer's letter to Fish helped lay the groundwork for an attack on Utah's probate court system. The issue was tested in the case of Paul Englebrecht and others, who operated a liquor store in Salt Lake City. Apparently this establishment had a permit to sell liquors wholesale; but a retail business was also being conducted, for which Englebrecht refused to take a special license. Local authorities arrested Englebrecht three times. He refused to pay the fine, and each time appealed his case from the probate court to the federal district court. The Salt Lake City police raided the place and destroyed most of the liquor stock.[30]

Englebrecht, aided by the gentile opposition, sued the city officials for $59,063.25, the alleged value of the liquor and property destroyed. The case was taken to the federal, not the probate, court—a direct challenge to the jurisdiction of the latter. The second challenge concerned the Utah law that jurors would be selected by territorial officers. The federal judge ruled that the United States marshal, Colonel M. T. Patrick, would select jurors from a list in his possession. While this was not a polygamy case, it was a good issue on which to test the right of the federal courts in Utah to take jurisdiction over criminal cases from the probate courts.

Naturally, the judge, being a promoter of the idea, found the city marshal and other local officials guilty of "wilful and malicious destruction of property." The case was appealed finally to the United States Supreme Court. In the meanwhile, heartened by this appearance of victory, the Gentile Ring set out to bring a number of prominent polygamists to trial for violation of the antipolygamy law of 1862.[31] They were heartened still more when Congress on January 10, 1871, approved a bill to transfer responsibility for the Utah penitentiary from the control of the territorial officials to the United States marshal. Warden A. P. Rockwood, a Mormon, refused to surrender the prison, but the federal judge ruled in favor of the United States marshal. This gave the gentile political group another victory and another coterie of jobs, and later placed in their control the incarceration of polygamists, a responsibility which Mormons could not have assumed.

Governor Shaffer died of consumption in October, 1870. His incumbency had been as stormy as it was brief. Apparently he had been closely surrounded by office-seekers, all of whom knew his time was short and wished to be on hand when again the offices would be shuffled. His secretary of state, Vernon H. Vaughan, was named governor, and his former private secretary was given Vaughan's job.

Although a member of the Gentile Ring, Vaughan was not an extremist, and he was not popular with the Mormon-baiters. The *Chicago Post* said: "He was a rebel throughout the war; engaged in a couple of duels after the war; his name is euphonious enough for a ten-cent novel; his record is sufficiently like Brigham Young's to render him an easy prey to the latter. . . . ." The *Salt Lake Herald* of December 3 indicated strong gentile feeling against Vaughan.

Mormon leaders went with a brass band to serenade Vaughan, who responded with a speech promising to deal justly with them. President Grant yielded to the opposition, and Vaughan's name was not presented to the Senate for confirmation. In January, 1871, he appointed George L. Woods, former Missourian, who had just finished an elected term as governor of Oregon. Woods missed no opportunity to impress upon the Mormons his dislike for them and their system. He arrived in time to join the plan to bring some of the polygamists to trail.[32]

On October 2, 1871, United States Marshal Patrick arrested Brigham Young on a charge of "lascivious cohabitation." Apostle George Q. Cannon, Counselor Daniel H. Wells, and one of the Godbeites, Henry W. Lawrence, were also arrested. The prosecution was mainly interested in Young. He was "dragged into court" on October 9, the day of the great Chicago fire, and the Mormons saw a connection between the events.[33] The occasion was a great day for Judge McKean, who attracted national notice for his prepared statement, which was reported in the *Deseret News* for October 18. The following item has become historic:

> It is therefore proper to say that while the case at bar is called *The People versus Brigham Young*, its other and real title is *Federal Authority versus Polygamic Theocracy*. The government of the United States, founded upon a written Constitution, finds within its jurisdiction another government—claiming to come from God—*imperium in imperio*—whose policy and practice, in grave particulars, are at variance with its own. The one government arrests the other in the person of its chief, and arraigns it at his bar. A system is on trial in the person of Brigham Young. Let all concerned keep this fact steadily in view; and let that government rule without a rival which shall prove to be in the right.

But to bring the Lion of the Lord into court proved to be less of a victory than was hoped. In 1859 an attempt had been made to convict him on a charge of counterfeiting. That failed. Now he was being tried for polygamy, of which he was the authoritative symbol. But the lion did not roar, as was expected. He placed his opponents at a disadvantage by his quiet dignity. The anti-Mormon *Salt Lake Tribune* lamented:

> It will divide the people in his favor and bring many Gentiles to the help of Israel, even as it has already brought two of their lawyers to the defense of the prophet. Perhaps there was more respect and sympathy felt for Brigham

Young, when he left the court room, feeble and tottering from his recent sickness, having respectfully sat in the presence of his judge three-quarters of an hour, after bail had been taken, than ever there was before in the minds of the same men.

One of Brother Brigham's attorneys was Major Charles H. Hemstead, former editor of the anti-Mormon *Union Vedette.* Hemstead, although opposed to Mormon domination, was more opposed to the power-politics of the Gentile Ring. Previous to becoming Young's attorney, Hemstead resigned as United States attorney. McKean then appointed Robert N. Baskin, who was quite in sympathy with his views. George R. Maxwell, Liberal party leader, assisted Baskin.

Because of his weak condition, Brigham Young asked permission of the court to make his usual winter visit to St. George. Judge McKean set the date of the trial for the following spring, in March, 1872. Young started for St. George on October 24, visiting the settlements en route. He had no sooner arrived at his Dixie winter retreat when word came by telegraph that Baskin had persuaded the judge to start the trial on December 4. It would have been impossible for Young to get back in time to appear in court, a fact which Baskin knew. He also knew that, if trial was called when Young was not present, then the court could brand Brother Brigham a fugitive from justice.

Although the Lion of the Lord did not appear in court, the judge did not forfeit the bond. Another date was set; and when court convened on January 2, 1872, Young was there. He made the trip from St. George through deep snow and severe weather—a considerable effort and hazardous to his health. Apparently Baskin had another reason for wanting to hasten Young's trial. A new United States attorney, George C. Bates, had been appointed to replace him. Bates was on hand when the trial began on January 2. Bates asked that bail be set at the unreasonable figure of $500,000, when Young could have been released on his word of honor. It is of interest that the former enemy of Brigham Young, General Patrick E. Connor, offered to share the bail. The judge finally decided to hold Young in custody, although he was permitted to remain at home under guard of the United States marshal. He was required to pay the guard $10 per day, and the guard was there 120 days.

On April 15, 1872, before Young's case came to trial, the United States Supreme Court reversed the Englebrecht decision, ruling that the local court had exceeded its authority by assuming a function that belonged by law to the territorial government. A number of polygamists and other cases, most of them out on bail, had to be released.[34] Among the pending cases were a number of men charged with murder. For example, Hosea Stout and W. H. Kimball had been arrested for the murder of Richard Yates during the resistance to Johnston's army in 1857. Two Salt Lake City policemen had been arrested, charged with the murder of Dr. J. King Robinson in 1866.

In making these arrests for murder and polygamy, the carpetbag cabal did not conceal its purposes.[35] These gentlemen wanted to capture control of local government, after which they would apply for statehood for Utah with themselves in key positions. Here was a prize worth the struggle, even if it had to be gained at the risk of civil war. Mention has been made of the fear that the Mormons would resist openly if the Cullom bill passed. It was the expectation of such resistance that caused Governor Shaffer to issue orders disarming the Nauvoo Legion. Technically the Legion was under control of the governor, but actually it was a church-dominated body under command of Lieutenant General Daniel H. Wells, who had been in charge since about 1850.[36]

On August 16, 1870, Wells issued his usual annual muster call for encampments, inspections, etc. A month later, on September 15, Governor Shaffer released an order forbidding "all musters, drills or gatherings of any nature, kind or description of armed persons within the Territory, except by my order or by the order of the United States marshal, should he need a *posse comitatus* to execute any order of the court." The Legion would surrender "all arms and munitions of war, belonging either to the United States or the Territory of Utah."

Ignoring General Wells, Shaffer commissioned General Patrick E. Connor as major general in charge of the Legion. The vindictive character and phrasing of the order caused Mormons to wonder what was afoot. Charles L. Walker of St. George wrote in his journal on September 17: "It is quite evident that our foes are bent on mischief toward us, and are trying every plan to bring us in collision with them to spill our blood."

Wells answered Shaffer on October 20, at which time he requested that the compliance date be moved to November 20. The ailing Shaffer answered immediately and caustically, this being a week before his demise. He poked fun at Wells, referring to him each time as "Mr. Wells." He called the Legion "an unlawful military system, which was originally organized in Nauvoo." He called Brigham Young the real head of the Legion and charged that Young and his aides thought themselves "more powerful than the federal government." He informed Wells that the Legion would take its orders from the governor. Wells responded at once, taking issue with Shaffer on all points—but too late, the governor was dying.[37]

During the next two years the Nauvoo Legion issue was the subject of a number of disputes. Three weeks after Shaffer died, a unit of the Legion in Salt Lake City assembled by a vague order for drill in one of the schoolhouses. The officers "just happened" to be there and took charge of the drill. Eight of the officers were arrested for violating a federal statute of July 17, 1862, by which it was illegal to set on foot or engage in any "rebellion or insurrection against the authority of the United States."

The catch in the statute was in the penalty clause, only the first part of which was read by the prosecution. Persons convicted could be sentenced to imprisonment not exceeding ten years, or subjected to a fine not exceeding $10,000. And the guilty person would also be punished "by the liberation of all his slaves, if any he have." It was a law aimed at the southern states. Some days later the eight officers were released. This was called by Mormons the "wooden-gun rebellion," for the homemade weapons carried by the legionnaires.

It was planned that the Legion in Salt Lake City should march without guns in the celebration of the Fourth of July,

1871. Governor Woods was in Washington on a political mission. Secretary of State George A. Black, the acting governor, ordered the Legion to take no part in the ceremonies, claiming that even to march was a violation of Shaffer's order.

Black called on Colonel R. De Trobriand of Camp Douglas to be on hand with his soldiers. If the Legion marched in the parade, it would be fired on by the soldiers. De Trobriand assured Black that he would make his troops available. He would line up his soldiers; and, if the Legion attempted to march, he would tell his soldiers to "take aim," but the order to fire "must be given by the acting governor." Black did not appear. The Legion paraded, much to the pleasure of the Mormons and the irritation of the Gentiles. Elsewhere in Utah the Legion paraded with gusto to the accompaniment of brass bands and the patriotic firing of cannon.[38]

In this issue Shaffer and his cohorts, and later Woods with his allies, attempted to make it appear that the Nauvoo Legion was a threat to gentile security. The question came up two years later, when Woods on June 21, 1873, wrote to Secretary of State Fish proposing the suppression of the Legion parades on July Fourth. Fish took a common-sense view, saying that the people in any community should celebrate the national anniversary as they wished, provided the manner was orderly. "The President desires to refer the whole matter to your judgment and wise discretion." The governor stopped the Legion marching in parades, but the Mormons were no longer interested.

It should be added that there is no evidence that the Mormons entertained any idea of using the Legion to resist the administration of any law or the jurisdiction of any court. Nonetheless, the Gentiles did not feel secure with an army of thirteen thousand under control of the priesthood.

NOTES

1. Andrew L. Neff, *History of Utah*, pp. 850–55. This alphabet had thirty-eight symbols or sounds, which were used phonetically with good effect. In 1868 the Utah legislature appropriated $10,000 "to the University of the State of Deseret" to procure books for the schools. With this public money the regents printed in the Deseret characters 20,000 first and second readers and 8,000 copies of the first part of the Book of

Mormon. Altogether, from 1855 to 1870 the legislature spent on the venture about $20,000.

2. The area of Salt Lake City lay within these landmarks: from a point near the hot spring to the west bank of the Jordan, to the west corner "of the five-acre lots south of this city," to the "southwest corner of the Church Pasture; thence to the place of beginning." Within this area of more than 40 square miles the city had control over the distribution of all the land.

3. Cedar City, incorporated in 1851, embraced 36 square miles and had 455 inhabitants in 1853 and 622 in 1870. Fillmore, chartered also in 1851, embraced 36 square miles and in 1853 included only 304 inhabitants. This town, planned to be Utah's capital city, had 905 inhabitants in 1870. Farms in these cities were generally small. The "L.D.S. Journal History," for September 13, 1865, and March 9, 1866, shows that the average farm in central and southern counties was: Sanpete, 10 acres; Beaver, 13 acres; Iron, 6 acres; Washington, 5 acres.

4. Letter written by Young to his sons, Brigham, Jr., and John W., missionaries in England, published in the *Millennial Star*, XXVIII, 604.

5. Some land-jumpers were former soldiers who had served under General Connor. A report on these raids is found in "History of Brigham Young," 1866, p. 752. See B. H. Roberts, *Comprehensive History of the Church*, Vol. V, chap. cxxi.

6. The report of the Commissioner of the General Land Office for 1871 indicated that the land contests in Utah were sometimes due to normal adverse interests, "but a large number of them are initiated by parties who have no interest in the land. . . . ." They endeavor to take advantage of "some alleged defect in the proceedings for the purpose of appropriating for their own use and benefit the labor and improvements of the parties who have made the claim."

7. Neff, *op. cit.*, pp. 687–89. The land office in Utah opened during January, 1869.

8. Cases of land-jumping involving Saints faithful to their religion were handled by the priesthood. For a discussion of priesthood procedure see below, chap. xiii. For a report on the Grantsville cases see *Senate Document No. 181* (46th Cong., 2d sess.).

9. Alexander Toponce, who witnessed the ceremonies, wrote in his *Reminiscences*, p. 178: "California furnished the golden spike. Governor Tuttle of Nevada furnished one of silver. General Stanford presented one of gold, silver and iron from Arizona. The last tie was of California laurel. When they came to drive the last spike, Governor Stanford, president of the Central Pacific, took the sledge and the first time he struck he missed the spike and hit the rail. What a howl went up! Irish, Chinese, Mexicans, and everybody yelled with delight. Everybody slapped everybody else on the back and yelled, 'He missed it. Yee!' The engineers blew the whistles and rang their bells." Telegraph instruments were attached to the rail, so that the driving of the spike was communicated to all parts of the United States. "When the connection was finally made, the U. P. and the C. P. engineers ran their engines up until their pilots touched. Then the engineers shook hands and had their pictures taken, and each broke a bottle of champagne on the other's engine."

10. Major General Grenville M. Dodge, chief engineer of the construction of the Union Pacific Railroad, reported the co-operation of the Mormons except for one issue, in which Brigham Young tried to force the railroad to pass through Salt Lake City and around the southern, instead of the northern, end of Great Salt Lake. Dodge would not change his survey. "Brigham Young would not have this, and appealed over my head to the board of directors, who referred the question to the government directors, who fully sustained me. Then Brigham Young gave his allegiance and aid to the Central Pacific, hoping to bring them around the south end of the lake and force us to connect with them there. He even went so far as to deliver in the tabernacle a great sermon denouncing

me, and stating a road could not be built or run without the aid of the Mormons. When the Central Pacific engineers made their survey they, too, were forced to adopt a line north of the lake. Then President Young returned to his first love, the Union Pacific, and turned all his forces and aid to that road" (*Senate Document No. 447* [61st Cong., 2d sess.], p. 136).

The *Deseret News*, June 17, 1868, reported a mass meeting on June 10 in Salt Lake City. Mormons and Gentiles made speeches blessing the railroad. George Q. Cannon said that the Mormons were turning from their isolation policy, "but today we court contact, if it is of the right kind."

11. Brigham Young, with Bishop John Sharp and others, took a contract for grading 90 miles of railroad. For the $2,125,000 earned on this contract he took from the Union Pacific rails, locomotives, etc., which were used in constructing the Mormon-owned Central Utah Railroad. By 1875 the Mormon railroad lines in Utah included 282 miles of track.

12. The editorial of the *Deseret News* of July 12, 1866, "Plain Hints to Merchants and Others," charged that certain traders were "open and avowed enemies of the people among whom they resided and from whom they drew their wealth. . . . ." It was proposed that such merchants should not be patronized. The *Salt Lake Daily Telegraph* on December 20, 1866, printed the reply of twenty-two merchants, addressed to the "Leaders of the Mormon Church," offering to sell to the Mormons. Brigham Young answered on December 21, saying the Gentiles could move or stay; but he charged again that some of them were "avowed enemies of the community. . . . missionaries of evil" (Neff, *op. cit.*, pp. 815–21).

13. The same Z.C.M.I. report contains the following socialistic item: "The very liberties for which our fathers contended so steadfastly and courageously, and which they bequeathed to us as a priceless legacy, are endangered by the monstrous power which this accumulation of wealth gives to a few individuals and a few powerful corporations. By its seductive influence results are accomplished which, were it more equally distributed, would be impossible under our form of government." See Edward W. Tullidge, *History of Salt Lake City*, pp. 728–32.

14. Section 20 of the constitution of Z.C.M.I. provided that no person would be eligible to hold stock or membership "except they be of good moral character and have paid their tithing according to the rules of the Church of Jesus Christ of Latter-Day Saints."

15. The records of the High Council for the St. George Stake, July 17, 1869, report the case of a Brother Maxwell who operated a small store in Pine Valley. He sold goods bought from Gentiles. Saints were warned not to trade with him. Maxwell did not heed the order to buy only from Mormon merchants. The first decision was to confiscate his goods, but that could not be done since he was selling on commission. Therefore, he was ordered to pay $300, the estimated value of the goods. The ecclesiastical fine was ordered paid to the St. George Tithing Office, to be used in the construction of the new tabernacle. Erastus Snow said the action was needed to discourage "these wicked men that come amongst us."

16. T. B. H. Stenhouse, *Rocky Mountain Saints*, p. 11. Stenhouse wrote this book after he was cut off from the church. Although he was prejudiced against Brigham Young, he has given a fairly complete account of the Godbeite movement. He reported that some of the Godbeites, once they rebelled, also became doubters on religious matters (*ibid.*, p. 630).

17. The Godbeites were excommunicated in October, 1869. *Tullidge's Quarterly Magazine*, October, 1880, p. 35, reported this statement from Godbe and Harrison: "We claim the right of respectfully but freely discussing all measures upon which we are

called to act. And if we are cut off the church for asserting this right, while our standing is dear to us, we will suffer it to be taken from us sooner than resign the liberties of thought."

18. The *Deseret News* of March 3, 1869, implied editorially that Utah labor should lower its wages unless it could produce with more efficiency. The matter was discussed later in the School of the Prophets, at which time an apostle suggested that Chinese labor should be brought in if the "working men did not come to terms." The *Deseret News* in an editorial of July 14, 1869, said that the Orientals would not injure Utah labor. The paper added that if Utah workers "act wisely, and in accordance with the counsel which is given, they can sustain themselves and be independent in any community in the world." Here is the first indication that leaders of the church were beginning to think of themselves as a class apart from the workers. See Roberts, *op. cit.*, V, 263–65.

19. Irish wrote the Commissioner of Indian Affairs, June 15, 1865, of a visit from "Hon. George A. Smith, President of the Legislative Council and Hon. John Taylor, Speaker of the House of Representatives, suggesting that the President of the Legislative Council would be Governor until the return of the Secretary of State." This visit was made an hour after the funeral of Governor Doty. Irish replied that he had been with the governor when he died, and had been charged with the duties of that office, that until other appointments were made he would act as governor and secretary of state.

20. Roberts (*op. cit.*, V, 185–93) gives various citations. He wrote: "One is tempted to ask when did military authority in Utah displace civil authority? . . . . Sherman was not on another march to the sea."

21. For discussion of the Wade, Cragin, and Cullom bills see Roberts, *op. cit.*, V 220, and Tullidge, *History of Salt Lake City*, chap. xlii. The *Deseret News* of January 8, 1868, said editorially of the Cragin bill: "No American citizen who is a Mormon has any rights; he is not a free man, but is a slave, to be tried, convicted, fined, sentenced, imprisoned, at the will of his masters; to be made to pay taxes but to have these taxes paid by his masters in persecuting and torturing him, and enriching them for the service. . . ."

22. The *Congressional Globe*, January 14, 1869, p. 363. Ashley would have distributed all of Utah, but it was feared that too many Mormons added to Colorado. Wyoming, and Nevada would have deprived the Gentiles there of political power.

23. Samuel Bowles, who accompanied Colfax on the first trip to Utah, later wrote a day-by-day journal of the trip, which he published as a book, *Across the Continent*. Bowles wrote (p. 83): "Mr. Colfax's reception in Utah was excessive, if not oppressive. There was an element of rivalry between Mormons and Gentiles in it, adding earnestness and energy to enthusiasm and hospitality."

24. The *Millennial Star* (XXXII, 193, 230, 243, 259) contained numerous quotations from eastern papers. The *Omaha Herald* of March 30, 1870, called the Cullom bill a measure that would persecute 150,000. "Omaha, and all this western country, have a deep stake in this matter, and the Union Pacific Railroad is also vitally concerned in it." Apparently, there was fear in Omaha that the bill would mean the "destruction of a vast and growing trade and business, which it would require twenty years to repair. . . ."

25. Acting Governor Mann signed the Utah female suffrage bill on February 12, 1870. Shaffer would have vetoed the bill. Wyoming granted female suffrage in 1869; but in Utah, because of an earlier election date, the women voted first. Congress abolished female suffrage in Utah by the Edmunds-Tucker Act of 1887. It was restored after Utah gained statehood.

26. Tullidge (*Tullidge's Quarterly Magazine*, October, 1880, pp. 61–66) indicated that President Grant had advised General Sheridan to be guided in his decision by the advice of Godbe.

27. This boarding-house was the meeting place of the gentile politicians. Probably when the governor died (October 31, 1870), he did not know that, on the same day or thereabout, William H. McKay, the proprietor, was arrested for holding up a stage near Chicken Creek. McKay and his gang took from the stage a Wells Fargo Company strongbox containing about $1,500 (reported in the *Deseret News*, November 2, 1870).

28. Papers of the secretary of state of Utah Territory, April 27, 1870, in the National Archives. Shaffer cited the following case, involving a Mormon merchant named Jennings, who "sent an agent to Chicago to purchase wagons, and gave him a letter to Peter Schuttler, a large manufacturer. . . . . Schuttler knew that Jennings was responsible, and as per direction of agent, Schuttler shipped 23 wagons to Jennings, which were received, stored and sold. Schuttler was compelled to sue for his pay in the U.S. district court. A jury was empaneled, selected by the county court and summoned by the territorial marshal, an officer elected here in violation of law. . . . . Jennings pled that inasmuch as another man, the agent, had bargained for and received the wagons, he, the agent, must pay for them. The court instructed the jury strongly on this point, almost to find for the plaintiff. They were out about five minutes and returned with a verdict, 'No cause for action.' Of course, the judge promptly set the verdict aside, but as matters stand, the second trial will be a repetition of the first." Shaffer may not have reported the facts correctly, but the case illustrates the inability of a gentile federal judge to hear cases involving Mormons with Mormons on the jury.

29. Toponce, *op. cit.*, p. 176: "In April and May of 1869, Corinne and Blue Creek were pretty lively places. At the latter place was a big construction camp known as 'Dead Fall' and spoken of by some as 'Hell's Half Acre.' It seemed for awhile as if all the toughs in the west had gathered there. Every form of vice was in evidence. Drunkenness and gambling were the mildest things they did. It was not uncommon for two or three men to be shot or knifed in a night. Back at Corinne, the 'Burg on the Bear,' it was every bit as bad. I saw there a tent 150 feet long and 50 feet wide crowded with gambling tables."

30. See Roberts, *op. cit.*, V, 383–386, 412, for a report and citations on the raid.

31. In September, 1870, and January, 1871, Chief Justice McKean struck another blow at the Mormons. He refused to naturalize John C. Sandburg, a Swede, and William Horsley, an Englishman. These men were not polygamists; but, since they would not condemn polygamy, the judge ruled they were not persons of moral character. The judge also refused citizenship to three polygamists who claimed that they entered polygamy before the antipolygamy law of 1862. See the *Deseret News*, October 26, 1870, and March 8, 1871.

32. Among the notes of H. H. Bancroft at the University of California, which were collected in the preparation of his *History of Utah*, is a life-sketch written December 9, 1880, by Phoebe W. Woodruff, wife of the apostle. She quoted a speech made by her in Salt Lake City, January 13, 1870, against the Cullom bill: "Shall we as wives and mothers sit still and see our husbands and sons, whom we know are obeying the highest behest of heaven, suffer for their religion without exerting ourselves to the extent of our power for their deliverance? No; verily No!" She added that if the men were sent to prison, "let them grant us this our last request, to make the prisons large enough to hold their wives, for where they go we will go also."

33. Orson W. Huntsman, of Hebron, wrote in his journal on October 2, 1871: "A telegram this afternoon tells us that Brigham Young was arrested in Salt Lake City by the United States marshals for cohabitation. About these times the United States of-

ficials of Utah act more like bigoted missionaries than administrators of the law. With their packed juries, they do about as the Lord suffers them. But here is an item of history worth remembering. The very day that this arrest of Brigham Young was made for polygamy, that great and terrible fire broke out in the city of Chicago. . . . ." The Mormons often claim a cause-and-effect relation between the arrest and the fire. Huntsman must have written the last two sentences of the October 2 entry at a later date, for the Chicago fire did not break out until October 8.

34. The Supreme Court decision, written by Mr. Chief Justice Chase, is found in *Clinton et al.* v. *Englebrecht*, 80 U.S. 434.

35. Roberts (*op. cit.*, V, 393) quotes from an editorial of the *San Francisco Examiner* regarding the "small fry, popinjay politicians and would-be statesmen" who are trying to capture court control in Utah. Their packed juries and prejudiced witnesses were condemned. "Having the judge and marshal they can pack the jury to suit themselves. If they can send Brigham to prison, and induce the people to rise up and liberate him, and thus produce a conflict, Utah will be at once admitted as a state, and under the protection of federal bayonets, these mischief makers can have themselves elected senators, congressmen, etc., just as the thieving carpetbaggers did in the South."

36. The Nauvoo Legion in 1870 included a lieutenant general, 2 major generals, 9 brigadier generals, 25 colonels, 112 majors, and 13,000 militiamen. Practically all the officers were high church officials. Orson W. Huntsman wrote in his journal for September 7, 1869, after attending an encampment near Harmony: "We arrived in camp in time to be enrolled and at eight oclock the bugle sounded and the hole armey were called out to prade under comand of Apostle Erastus Snow, Brigadier General, and marched all day long on foot, the next day on horseback and the next we charged on the great train of wagons just as though they were the foe, and the next two or three days we fought one armey against the other. We went right into battle and fought like valient soldiers. Could hardly see the enemy for the dust and smoke. The firing of rifles and canons and the great danger of being captured by the enemy made great excitement for man and beast."

37. The correspondence between Wells and Shaffer was published in the *Deseret News* on November 2, 1870.

38. Tullidge (*History of Salt Lake City*, p. 503) reports the double celebration of July 4, 1871. Gentiles and Mormons had separate parades with floats and different orators of the day. Tullidge wrote: "Each side in their notable celebration, ventilated its own special views and sentiments; but the grand day passed off peaceably, especially considering that Acting Governor Black had ordered out the troops to overawe the citizens."

CHAPTER XI

DECLINE OF ZION'S FRONTIER

IF IT is the test of a vigorous people that they multiply in spite of opposition, the Rocky Mountain Saints would qualify without reservation. In 1870 Utah had a population of 86,786, compared with 40,273 in 1860. Most of these—we know not the proportion—were Mormons. Nor do we know how many additional Mormons in 1860 or 1870 were living outside of Utah in eastern states or over the ocean.

From 1850 to 1870 Utah's population increased from 11,380 to 86,786. Gentiles were few in 1850, and in 1870 they probably did not exceed 5 per cent of the population even if disaffected Mormons were added to their number. In the election of 1870 the People's party, almost entirely Mormon, polled 21,656 votes; whereas the Liberal party, largely gentile, polled 1,444 votes.

Figures for Utah on the United States census of 1870 are enlightening when compared with those for another commonwealth of the West, Oregon. Utah and Oregon are compared, because in that year they were approximately similar in the number of population and not greatly dissimilar in agricultural and industrial organization.

In Utah there were 86,786 inhabitants; in Oregon, 90,923. Of Utah's people, 49.1 per cent were females, compared with 41.5 per cent in the population of Oregon. Utah's proportion of females was not only higher than Oregon's but was very high for a frontier territory. Could the figures for Mormons have been reported separately, the percentage of females would have been still higher.

Regarding age, Utah was in the hands of younger people. In Oregon there were 28,616 males 21 years of age or older, and that was 53.8 per cent of the male population. In Utah there were 18,042 males 21 years of age or older, which was 40.9 per cent of the total male population. This means that males under 21 years of age comprised 46.2 per cent of the total male population of Oregon, compared with 59.1 per cent in Utah.

	Oregon	Utah
Total population	90,923	86,786
Persons of foreign birth	11,600	30,702
Percentage of population foreign born	12.8	35.4
Percentage of citizens among male foreign born	86.0	51.7

Much was said in 1870 of Utah's foreign-born population, and much of it probably unfairly said. Utah had an ample proportion of alien born. As the above table shows, the percentage for Utah was better than double that for Oregon.

PRINCIPAL COUNTRIES OF ORIGIN OF FOREIGN-BORN PERSONS IN UTAH, 1870

Total foreign born	30,702
Principal countries of origin:	
England	16,073
Denmark	4,957
Scotland	2,391
Sweden	1,790
Wales	1,783
Norway	613
Canada	566
Switzerland	509
Ireland	502
China	466
Germany	358
South Africa	128
Holland	122

Out of each 100 persons in Utah, 35 were foreign born, compared with about 12 for Oregon. A higher percentage of the foreign-born males in Oregon were citizens. This lower percentage of citizenship among Utah's foreign born probably evidence only recency of immigration. To some it proved a lack of Utah's fitness for statehood.[1] It was claimed by Gentiles that aliens brought into Utah had too little opportunity to become acquainted with the American way of life.

The accompanying tables show for Oregon and Utah the principal countries of origin of the foreign-born persons in each commonwealth. The tables would be more informative if the sex distribution of the imigrants were given. We would have found a high percentage of males among the foreign born reported for Oregon, whereas for Utah the foreign-born females would have equaled the number of males and possibly exceeded the number of males from England.

PRINCIPAL COUNTRIES OF ORIGIN OF FOREIGN-BORN PERSONS IN OREGON, 1870

Total foreign born	11,600
Principal countries of origin:	
China	3,327
Ireland	1,967
Germany	1,875
England	1,347
Canada	877
Scotland	394
Sweden	205
Switzerland	160

The effects of Mormon evangelism are seen in the table for Utah; and the countries, in the order named, were in that proportion fertile fields of labor. The line-up for Oregon was quite in contrast.

Why did the Chinese in Oregon lead all the rest? Like the Irish, most of them had been imported to work on the railroad, in the lumber camps, or in the mines. Foreign-born persons in Oregon who did not go there at the behest of labor contractors went as individuals.

Utah's alien migrants joined a movement which was only incidentally economic. They might have moved on to Oregon with greater prospect of gain, but they were not bonanza-hunters. They were Zion-builders.

Of the 90,923 inhabitants reported for Oregon, 40.8 per cent were born there, whereas 47.6 per cent of the inhabitants of Utah in 1870 were Utah born. Although Utah had a larger percentage of foreign born, it also had a larger percentage of native sons and daughters, many of them children of the foreign born.

By 1870 the Mormons were fairly well rooted in their mountain habitat. Salt Lake City had a population of 12,846; Ogden, a population of 3,127; and there were twelve other communities with 1,000 or more inhabitants each. There were twenty-one communities with populations ranging from 500 to 1,000 inhabitants.

Practically every locality in Utah by 1870 that could be developed under irrigation had been inhabited. Every stream had already been put to the service of the husbandman, and the herdsman had taken possession of every spring and watering hole. Already the Mormons were crossing the borders into Wyoming and Idaho, and by 1875 the bounds of Mormon settlement extended over the Colorado River into Arizona.[2]

The Arizona development was projected in 1863, when Jacob Hamblin was sent with one hundred missionaries to lay out a road and build a ferry for crossing the Colorado, to erect forts, and to "take up a labor" with the Indians for the purpose of converting them and then teaching them to work the white man's way. This end achieved, it was hoped the way would be open for Mormon settlement.[3]

The Arizona mission was only a later phase of an earlier plan to expand southward and occupy the entire valley of the Colorado to the sea. To that end the Muddy Valley was settled and the Colorado water route opened in 1864 and 1865. Brigham Young said on January 23, 1865, in his message as "Governor of the State of Deseret," that the people were being "compelled to use and depend principally upon this route for the purposes of communication and commerce." He reported the organization of the Deseret Mercantile Association to build a warehouse and landing "at the head of navigation on the Colorado River."

The promise of a railroad and the participation of the Mormons in the construction of their own railway lines diverted attention from the river route. Two other reasons for dropping the scheme were the transfer of much of the area to the new state of Nevada and the final realization that there were no fertile agricultural lands along the Colorado. In 1863 one of his scouts, George W. Brimhall, had been sent with his wife and small children with wagon and oxen, to visit all the branch streams of the Colorado to which he might gain access with a vehicle. It was his job to locate roads and to spy out the land. His report was negative. Most of the side canyons were deep and difficult, and he found no land for settlement.[4]

Moving the Nevada line pleased the Gentiles in the mining camps. They did not like to be under Mormon local government. It was not a service to the Muddy Valley settlers, most of whom believed that they had not been included in the transfer. Thinking they were still located in Utah—and they were so included in the census of 1870—they refused to pay taxes to Nevada. In 1870 the line was surveyed, and the sheriff of Lincoln County, Nevada, demanded back taxes for the period of dispute. Church officials took action and released the Muddy Valley settlers to make homes elsewhere.[5]

At great sacrifice, one hundred and fifty families loaded their belongings in wagons and moved from the Muddy to a more inviting haven east of St. George, where in 1871 they formed the nucleus of Kane County. A number of gentile familes moved in, but they could not accomplish by individual methods what the Mormons could scarcely do by co-operative effort. One by one, these families moved away. By 1877 the Muddy was again reoccupied by the Mormons.[6]

Because of the drought in 1871, the Arizona mission had to be postponed, except for exploring, building roads, and making a ferry. The migration did not begin until March, 1876, when Lot Smith founded the co-operative community of Sunset on the Little Colorado. Within three years several other settlements were planted along the same river, and before two decades had passed the Mormons had a virtual monopoly of the irrigated land in Arizona.[7]

The Arizona mission was part of the second phase of Mormon settlement. This phase was more spontaneous in character than previous settlement and not so much under direct supervision of church headquarters, although just as much under priesthood supervision. In line with this secondary settlement there was, after 1875, a general expansion into the habitable areas of eastern Utah. Thus Escalante and other small places in Garfield County were started by groups of families moving on their own initiative.

In 1877 a group of seventy-five men, with their families, were chosen from the Sanpete Valley to move eastward and settle Castle Valley. Orange Seely was placed in charge of this project. Other pioneers in the Castle Valley settlement were Erastus Curtis, George H. Brunno, and Peter Anderson, not to speak of the Petersons, Jensons, Johnsons, Ottesons, and other whose names are prominent in the area today. While the church initiated this movement to the east from Sanpete, Carbon and Emery counties were really built up by a general migration of groups of families. Thus developed Huntington, Castle Dale, Orangeville, Price, Helper, and other communities. Such places might have been settled earlier had earlier efforts not been frustrated by Indian hostilities.

In the same secondary phase of the Mormon expansion new settlements were established in New Mexico, Colorado, Wyoming, and Idaho; groups of families moved from existing communities, and the church organization followed after them.

It should be noted that practically all the permanent key communities of the Mormon frontier had been established during the tense period prior to 1875. The settlement program of the church had been slowed up in places by Indian hostilities but not by the persecution from Gentiles. Such persecution may have been helpful, for, in spite of it, these communities thrived; and many reached the zenith of their growth and virility before 1870, others before 1880. Even the missionary system thrived more during that period of persecution than afterward. While the gentile world preached the horrors of Mormonism and the elders were preaching polygamy, Zion's missionary program was more productive—more productive than at any later date.[8]

There was a considerable influx of Gentiles during the decade preceding 1880, but we do not know how much they contributed to increase Utah's population from 86,786 in 1870 to 143,963 in 1880, when the census reported 74,509 males and 69,454 females. It is generally known that adult males predominated among the Gentiles. Most of the youth in the following distribution of Utah's 1880 population were children of Mormons.

AGE GROUPS OF UTAH POPULATION, 1880

Total population	143,963
Under 5 years of age	25,591
5–14 years	39,036
15–19 years	14,731
20–44 years	44,249
45 years of age and over	20,356

About 55 per cent of Utah's population in 1880 were youth under 20 years of age, and the number of persons under 15 years of age was almost exactly equal to the number 20 years of age and over: 64,627 in the younger group, and 64,605 in the older one. In this 1880 population of 143,963 the church had a loyal following of at least 100,000, against which gentile opposition could make little or no gain.

Although the Gentiles had on their side the federal public officials and the army, they were powerless against the vigorous social unity of the Saints. The soldiers were retained in Utah, and they afforded within Zion a few communities of refuge for the Gentiles, who tried in various ways to influence the values and interests of Mormon society. For example, Beaver was such a city of safety for outsiders. Near Beaver was Fort Cameron, at which were quartered federal soldiers. Joseph Fish wrote in his journal on January 9, 1874, that he visited Beaver and the military post. "In the evening I went to the Methodist Church and for the first time I heard a Methodist preach. Did not think much of it. It was all polish and show."

Beaver was home base for gentile public officials of the area, even some who resided in places like Cedar City, Parowan, or Fillmore. In the Dixie region the gentile community from about 1874 until 1885 was Silver Reef. In 1880 a Presbyterian missionary located in St. George. This gentleman, A. B. Cort, maintained active relations with the people at Silver Reef, where he received friendly support. In St. George the people had been told: "Let them make honey in their own hives."

In the election of 1880 the Rev. A. B. Cort joined hands with the "Reefers" in promoting a campaign for the Liberal party. He posted himself at the polls to watch that polygamists did not vote. He attempted to gather about him various lukewarm Saints in the town and got some support in his effort to start a school for small children.

The gentile home base of northern Utah was Corinne, where in 1870 the Liberal party was organized.[9] This movement was initially intended to be a coalition of Gentiles and certain Mormons who honestly favored a separation of priesthood and politics. Some very pious Saints were of the opinion that the gentile-Mormon issues would fade if the church detached itself entirely from politics. Antagonisms were too strong, and the Liberal party lost sight of its initial high objective. Instead of becoming the party opposing priesthood, it became a power-seeking party. As a party it scarcely got started for the election of 1870, but in 1872 it placed in nomination for delegate to Congress, George F. Maxwell, former director of the land office in Salt Lake City. General Maxwell was an ardent anti-Mormon, and the campaign was fought on religious lines. The Mormons through the People's party supported Apostle George Q. Cannon, a polygamist. Cannon received 20,969 votes; Maxwell, 1,942.

While the Liberal party could entertain no hope of electing a delegate to Congress, it did cherish hopes of capturing an occasional local election. It endeavored to obtain passage of the Cullom bill and other anti-Mormon legislation. It sought to capture by legal chicanery the domination of the courts, control in the selection of jurors, and control of the prison. It also sought control of election machinery. As already reported, the drive for such control was waged by the political group which was the core of the Liberal party. This group gambled on the successful outcome of the decision of the United States Supreme

Court in the Englebrecht case, which was reversed by that high body on April 15, 1872. This opposition group was disappointed but not discouraged.

Whereas the Gentiles had been frustrated in theii attempt to capture the judicial machinery, they were able to show their own strength on other issues. For example, in 1872 Utah tried again to gain statehood. The opposition could not prevent the initial steps being taken but it did call a halt in Washington, where the appeal received no consideration.

In January, 1872, the Utah legislature passed a bill authorizing a constitutional convention. Governor Woods vetoed the bill for the same reason that Governor Dawson in 1861 vetoed a like measure, claiming that such action should be authorized by Congress. The legislature found precedent in Arkansas, a state that held its constitutional convention in 1836 without approval of the governor or consent of the Congress. Michigan, in 1836, and California, in 1850, held such conventions with the approval of the governor, but without asking consent of Congress. The convention met on February 19, 1872.

This was the first constitutional convention in which Gentiles took part and the last in which the name "Deseret" was offered in the place of "Utah." The former was favored because it stood for an ideal, "while 'Utah' referred to a dirty, thieving, insect-infested, grasshopper-eating tribe of Indians," whose ill repute allegedly was the reason that Congress back in 1850 selected "Utah" when the Mormons wanted "Deseret."

The convention did not squarely face the polygamy question. Some of the delegates, including Mormons, argued that Congress would not accept any constitution which did not abolish polygamy, but the church would not yield. The question was disposed of in one of the clauses of an appended "ordinance," which provided that any changes suggested by Congress should become part of the constitution if ratified later by the people. This was a covert invitation for Congress to propose a compromise. Had this opening been accepted, the polygamy issue might have been settled, but the Gentiles wanted a full church surrender.[10]

After the approval of the constitution at a special popular election by 25,160 to 365 votes, at which time Frank Fuller was elected to be congressman in the event statehood were granted, two Mormons and a Gentile were named to carry the document to Washington. It was at this point the opposition showed strength. The appeal was ignored.

While the constitutional convention was deliberating, Utah was waiting for Supreme Court action on the Englebrecht case but the decision had not been reached when the convention closed on March 2. It had not been reached when the annual conference of the church convened on April 6, although favorable news was expected. The charges against Brigham Young rested on that decision, and he was still in the custody of the court. The conference met and passed a resolution that official adjournment would not be voted until Brigham Young could stand before the Saints a free man. Although the decision of the high court was given on April 15, Chief Justice McKean found various legal reasons for holding Young and other Mormons in his custody ten days longer.

Judge McKean did not permit the reversal in the Englebrecht case to halt his crusade against the church. He succeeded in getting control of the Godbeite paper, the *Mormon Tribune*. Later this paper became the *Salt Lake Tribune*, operating in close connection with the *New York Herald*. Oscar G. Sawyer, formerly of the *Herald* staff, was sent to Salt Lake City to take editorial charge of the *Tribune*. It was known that he worked closely with the judge and that he obtained from McKean exclusive advance stories about pending decisions of the court. The extreme conduct of Sawyer offended the Godbeites, and, because of their objections, he was permitted to resign.[11]

After the Godbeites turned, Judge McKean lost the support of United States Attorney George C. Bates, who charged that the courts were being used by the judges for private ends. Bates declared that President Grant had placed in office in Utah a gang of crooks who could not be trusted with the horse blankets in the executive stables. These charges appeared in the *Salt Lake Herald* of July 20, 1873. Bates accused Judge

Hawley of bigamy, Judge Strickland with having purchased his office, and Chief Justice McKean with having used his office for private gain. He charged that McKean and Strickland had contrived by court action to get possession of contested mining claims and had neglected to prosecute several mail-robbers. He also accused McKean and others of conspiracy to get possession of certain coal lands and of stripping the timber from other public lands.

Hawley and Strickland resigned. They were replaced in 1873 by P. H. Emerson, of Michigan, and Jacob S. Boreman, of West Virginia. McKean continued his crusade until removed in March, 1875.[12]

The methods used by the gentile politicians to gain power are well illustrated in the capture of the 1874 election in Tooele County by the Liberal party. Some time prior to the election the opposing groups agreed on a coalition ticket. Church leaders, through the People's party, rejected the plan; so each party named a ticket. The Mormons had a majority of votes, but the gentile Liberal party claimed the election. Without verifying the claims of either party, Governor George L. Woods issued commissions to the Liberal candidates. Judge McKean upheld the governor and issued a peremptory order installing the Liberals. Only one People's party candidate was elected, and his vote was similar to those of the rest. He had a majority of 402 votes out of a total of 2,200 cast. This candidate was George Atkin, legislative representative. The governor and chief justice who had decided the other cases did not have jurisdiction. The recount of votes in Atkin's case was made by the legislature.[13]

While Utah's statehood plea waited for a hearing in Washington, President Grant and other federal leaders were planning new legislation. Grant's message of December, 1872, asked Congress for a law which would bring about the "ultimate extinguishment of polygamy. He advised Congress the following February that military measures might be needed to enforce any kind of legislation against the Mormons.[14]

In response to Grant's request several punitive and regulatory measures were offered by senators and congressmen. They proposed in substance (*a*) that jurisdiction over criminal cases and the selection of jurors be placed in the hands of federal officials in Utah; (*b*) that proof of cohabitation be accepted as evidence of guilt in polygamy cases; and (*c*) that federal judges be empowered to appoint county commissioners in Utah.

These proposed bills were finally withdrawn in favor of a measure offered by Congressman Potter Poland of Vermont. The Poland Bill was passed on June 23, 1874. It (*a*) transferred to federal judges in Utah jurisdiction over criminal, civil, and chancery cases; (*b*) abolished the offices of territorial attorney-general and marshal and transferred their duties to the corresponding federal officials; and (*c*) gave federal court officials partial control in the selection of jurors. The basic object of the bill was to implement the antipolygamy law of 1862. The law permitted federal judges at last to try polygamy cases. It was now necessary to test in the courts the validity of the 1862 law.

In October, 1874, a number of polygamists were arrested. The case of George Reynolds, private secretary to Brigham Young, was accepted as one for testing the law. He was tried, convicted, and given a sentence of a year in prison and fined $500. The admitted facts were simply that Reynolds had married his first wife in accordance with the "law of the land" but that he had another wife "sealed to him" by church ordinance. Legally the second woman was not his wife in the prevailing sense but was a church-sanctioned consort. Was this a bigamous relationship?

When appealed to the supreme court of Utah, the Reynolds case, on June 18, 1875, was thrown out on a legal technicality. A second trail began the following October 30. This time the "friendly" aspect of the case was ignored, and Reynolds was given a sentence of two years at hard labor and fined $500. This time the supreme court of Utah upheld the district court and appeal was taken to the United States Supreme Court, where the real trial took place in November, 1878. Pending review by the high court, the women of Utah were active sending petitions to Congress, the president, and others. They were anxious that the world should know they were not slaves bound down by polygamy but were quite in favor of plurality. On January 6, 1879, the Supreme Court decided against Reynolds. He was taken to serve his sentence at Lincoln, Nebraska.[15]

The decision in the Reynolds case settled nothing, because he had been treated as a bigamist when actually his crime was of different character. He was cohabiting with a plural wife, but his marriage was not a civil union. Even the Gentiles had been forced to realize this distinction. The prosecution began to take up other cases.

In the meanwhile the prosecution had not failed to make the most of a private suit brought against Brigham Young by Wife No. 19, Mrs. Ann Eliza Webb Young, demanding separate maintenance. She asked $1,000 per month pending the hearing of the case, $6,000 lawyer's fee, a divorce with a payment of $14,000 when the decree was granted, and a final award of $200,000. She estimated, or her lawyers did for her, that Young's income was about $40,000 per month.

Judge McKean, when the case came before him in February, 1875, ordered Young to pay the estranged wife $500 per month and $3,000 to defray the cost of the trial. Young argued that the case did not come under the usual divorce-and-alimony category; that, when the alleged "marriage" took place, Ann Eliza Young, unknown to him, was the undivorced wife of another man; and that she knew he had a legal wife living. The defense was technical, on which point the *Deseret News* observed later on September 2, 1874: "Every technicality is taken advantage of to persecutingly prosecute and convict us, and it is our perfect right, if we choose to exercise it, to take advantage of every technicality that the law permits in defending ourselves."

Brother Brigham refused to pay the bill as ordered, for which Judge McKean ruled him in contempt of court. He was fined $25 and sentenced to a day in prison, a personal victory for the ardent McKean. March 11, 1875, the day of the sentence, was stormy and cold, but the aged Brother Brigham was taken to the penitentiary for the space of twenty-four hours.[16]

A few days after sentencing Young, Judge McKean was removed and his place taken by David B. Lowe of Kansas, who reached Utah in April. When he heard Young's case on April 24, the unpaid alimony debt had reached $9,500. Lowe ruled that there could be no legal alimony claim where there was no evidence of legal marriage. Later the case was brought into court by Judge Boreman, who reversed Lowe and ordered that Young be imprisoned until the bill was paid. He permitted the prisoner to be confined to his home in the custody of the marshal. Young did not yield; so the guard stood over him at his own expense until November 12, when Alexander White, the new chief justice, reviewed the case. White released Young from custody but took no action on the alimony debt, which had reached $18,000. Since White's appointment was not confirmed by the Senate, he left office; and his place was taken by Michael Schaeffer, the fifth judge to sit on the case. He suggested a compromise, and Young paid $3,600, a fifth of the alimony then due. The case was dismissed in April, 1877, a few months before Brigham Young's death.

The removal of Judge McKean was followed by that of George R. Maxwell as registrar of the land office in Salt Lake City. Already George L. Woods had been virtually removed, his term of office having expired in December, 1874; and he was not reappointed. In February, 1875, Samuel B. Axtell, of California, arrived to take up his duties as governor.

Axtell did not join the so-called "Gentile Ring," for which reason he was very soon the subject of attack. While not friendly with the Mormons, his aloofness to the Mormon-baiters caused them to dub him "bishop." After five months in office he was transferred to a judgeship in New Mexico. Gentiles said he had been called "to a mission in the land of the greaser."

Then came Governor George W. Emery, a Tennessean, who turned out to be a sane and fair administrator. He criticized the Mormons, even opposed the marked ballot used at the polls, but he was able to maintain cordial relations with them. The Saints named a county for him, an honor extended to no other federally appointed gentile official. It was during his administration that the initial drive against polygamists began, as well as the alimony case against Brigham Young. He was in office during the trial which ended in the execution of John D. Lee. He did not permit his office to become involved, and he could very easily have done so.

It was probably not a chance coincidence that the trial of John D. Lee was being prosecuted contemporaneously with Young's alimony suit, or that Judge Boreman, the trial judge in the Lee case, had at the same time arranged to keep Young in custody almost the entire period of that trial. Since the attempt of Judge Cradlebaugh in 1859, gentile federal officials had been pledging themselves to do something about the Mountain Meadows massacre. It was not until the passage of the Poland Bill in 1874 that the federal judges were in a position to fulfil these pledges.

Why had not local Mormon officials taken up the Meadows case when they had the authority up to 1874? They had taken church action against Lee to excommunicate him, but Brigham Young later extended favors to Lee, his adopted son by church rite. When Lee was finally arrested, no Mormon came forward to defend him. There were Mormons on hand to testify against Lee when he was arraigned in the federal court. They knew about the distribution of the property taken from the massacred emigrants, about the seventeen surviving children that had been gathered in 1859 and shipped back to Arkansas, and they knew a little more than hearsay about the persons involved.[17] Yet the Mormons did nothing about it, probably for the same reason that a family will not drag one of its own members into court, although they may cast him out of the house.

Lee lived at Harmony until about 1864, when he was asked to resign as presiding elder. Sometime after this date he disappeared from general view, and next he appeared in charge of the ferry at the point where the Mormon-made road to Arizona crossed the Colorado River. He could not have had this assignment without having been selected by Brigham Young. He called the place "Lonely Dell," and he called himself "Major Doyle." He was a major in the Nauvoo Legion, and his middle

EXECUTION OF JOHN D. LEE AT MOUNTAIN MEADOWS IN 1877 ON THE SCENE OF THE MASSACRE IN WHICH HE TOOK PART IN 1857

Soldiers brought Lee about a hundred miles from Beaver to the place of the massacre, an unusual procedure, but it served to get these pictures, showing the dramatic ending of the man whose life-story had just been written and needed this final touch. Lee sits on his coffin in the upper picture. He was shot by men concealed behind a blanket screen near the wagon at the right. Note some spectators on horseback in the distance. *Below, left*, John D. Lee; *lower right*, Lee in his coffin.

name was Doyle. A number of his wives remained loyal, although the church would not have required it of them. On November 9, 1874, while visting a branch of his family at Panguitch, he was arrested.

Other arrests were expected. Nobody knew how much information Lee could or would give, but it was known that the prosecution would arrest as many Mormon leaders as the occasion would warrant, although the primary interest of the prosecution was to fix guilt on Brigham Young.[18] Soon after Lee's arrest, William H. Dame, of Parowan, was arrested. Would Lee implicate others? The church had abandoned him to the buffetings of Satan. Would he retaliate, and what might he tell?[19]

Lee was kept in custody at the army post in Beaver, where his trial began July 23, 1875, before Judge Boreman. The prosecution set to work forging links to bind Lee with Young. The jury of eight Mormons, three Gentiles, and one "jack-Mormon" disagreed. A year passed before the new trial got under way. In the meantime Sumner Howard replaced William C. Carey as United States attorney. It was reported that, when he opened the second trial, he said: "We are going to try John D. Lee and not Brigham Young and the Mormon Church."[20] This time the jury included twelve Mormons. On September 20, 1876, the jury found Lee guilty of first-degree murder. He was sentenced to death on October 1; and, according to Utah law, he was permitted to choose whether he would be executed by hanging or shooting. Lee elected to be shot.[21]

Lee's appeal to the supreme court of Utah was denied. He was executed on March 27, 1877, five months after being sentenced, during which time he wrote his "confessions." This book, *Mormonism Unveiled*, was published under Lee's authorship in 1879, but the royalties apparently went to pay the fee of his lawyer, W. W. Bishop. Apparently, too, Lee's execution was utilized to give his book a sort of wild-West, bad-man ending. The marshal, with some soldiers as guards, a minister, a photographer, and newsmen, took Lee from Beaver to Mountain Meadows, about seventy-five miles. A plain board coffin was taken along. Lee was placed in a seated position at the end of the coffin and there photographed. He declined to be blindfolded. His only remark was: "All my life I have tried to be a good member of the Mormon Church from which I was expelled. This is what it gets me." His body was taken to Panguitch.[22]

The shots that killed Lee were, all the while, being aimed at Brigham Young. Many times the same end had been wished for him, and not a few would have been proud of an opportunity to hang "the big Mormon" or stand him against the wall. So real was the danger that Brother Brigham was under guard most of the time; and, in spite of the guard, attempts were made to do him harm.

Brother Brigham was spared the ignominious end wished for him by his enemies, the end to which Lee alone came. He died in bed of a natural cause. After a brief illness, due to cholera morbus, he passed to his reward on August 29, 1877. He had spent the winter in St. George, where he had gone frequently to enjoy the milder weather of Dixie. For him this was the most important winter of all, because the temple was being completed and he was much concerned about speeding the work so that the dedication could be carried through before his departure in the spring. To honor the occasion the annual conference of the church met in St. George on the day the temple was dedicated. There are legends about the occasion—for example, about the people hearing the angels sing after the dedication prayer had been read. Brother Brigham on that occasion went up on the high mountain, like Moses, and tasted the same glory which was for him also the beginning of the end.

No event in Mormon church history exceeded in spiritual importance the dedication of the St. George Temple. Here was the first sign that God's people had permanently established themselves in the valleys of the mountains. Other temples had been planned or begun, but here was one dedicated eternally. It was a kind of victory monument for thirty years of effort. To Brigham Young and some of the apostles the temple had a personal value. They were responsible for planning the temple ceremonies which thirty-three years before had been frustrated by their expulsion from Nauvoo. These ceremonies, complicated and secret, had been originally designed with a faith-promoting and educational purpose in mind. Some changes were in order. Moreover, there was the problem of getting the temple organized to carry out certain ceremonies for the redemption and confirmation of the souls of the dead. Brigham Young and his close associates were reaching the end of their days. They were anxious to finish up certain tasks which could be performed only in a temple.

From April 6 to August 26, 1877, three days before his passing, President Young was occupied with certain reorganization details of the church. Previously he had followed the policy of using his apostles as field marshals, as organizers, and as administrators over large areas of the frontier. Such had been the assignment of Erastus Snow over the Dixie Mission, of Orson Hyde in Spring Valley and, before that, in Carson Valley, and of Lorenzo Snow in the region around Brigham City.

In order to relieve the apostles from their special assignments, it was necessary first to set up the machinery of the stake organizations and put responsible local ecclesiastics in charge. Moreover, there were various local problems to be handled, some of them problems of Young's own making, for he had a way of dealing directly with local officials over the heads of stake officials. He visited dozens of communities, attending to these matters and putting affairs in order. He was so occupied until August 26.[23]

In many communities where the efforts to start units of the United Order had caused friction, it was necessary for Young to placate some and censure others. It was clear to him that in most communities the Order could not be established. Perhaps the local economy had passed the point when such a device for communal living was needed. On the whole, he found the communities of Zion in a fairly prosperous condition and the Saints in a good state of discipline. Here was doubtless a satisfying experience, to review in that last visit to his people the rough road over which he had brought them since he became their leader.

Together they had lived through famine. They had tested their wits against an invading army. They had solved the Indian problem with a minimum of bloodshed. They had moved into every locality ahead of the Gentiles and had pre-empted every acre of irrigation land. In short, they had developed under his leadership almost a culture of their own. Compared with these

A SECTION OF THE HURRICANE IRRIGATION DITCH WHICH TAKES WATER FROM THE VIRGIN RIVER

This view illustrates the great labor cost of irrigation systems in this region, and here is the chief reason why "Dixie" agriculture never was a profitable enterprise, especially for the pioneers, who had to expend so much toil on their ditches and dams.

great achievements, the final problems to which Brigham Young directed his attention were minor indeed.

Mormon frontier history would have closed at the death of Brigham Young had it not been for the polygamy issue. His genius and strategy had frustrated some of Zion's most unrelenting enemies, but he died at the beginning of another battle, which was not decided until more than a decade later. In his own way Young was an able politician, else he could not for over twenty years have withstood the gentile siege. He made no claim to being either sage or seer, but he counseled people well, and no man who followed his advice was the worse for it.

There was temporary confusion in the ranks when Joseph Smith died. There were rival factions. At Young's death confusion was expected. The Rev. De Witt Talmage in New York City paused in his sermon to make the following remark, which was reported in the *New York Times* on October 28, 1877, and was quoted by M. R. Werner in the conclusion of his book, *Brigham Young:*

> Now, my friends, at the death of the Mormon chieftain, is the time for the United States Government to strike. Let as much of their lands be confiscated as will pay for their subjugation. If the Government of the United States cannot stand the expense, let Salt Lake pay for it. Set Phil Sheridan after them. Give him enough troops and he will teach all of Utah that 40 wives is 39 too many. Now is the time, when they are less organized than they have been.

But it didn't come to pass that way. Three decades of priesthood discipline had had its effect. There was grief in Zion, but the organization went ahead without the expected confusion. Some believed there would be a contest for the headship of the church, since it had been noised about that Brother Brigham had been grooming his son Brigham Jr., already an apostle, to succeed him. Also, his son John W. had been his counselor. If the succession issue did arise, it must have been settled behind closed doors. That is the best evidence that the church had arrived at a stage of maturity.

After the death of Joseph Smith control of the church went automatically to the apostles, and the president of the quorum was acting president of the church for three years. There were probably inner-group reasons for not naming Brigham Young until 1847. There may have been equally potent inner-group reasons for not at once naming a successor to Brigham Young. Again for three years church control rested with the apostles. John Taylor, head of the quorum, served as acting president of the church. He was named president in October, 1880.

Perhaps the settlement of Brigham Young's estate figured in the delay in selecting the president. The administrators of the estate were George Q. Cannon, formerly his secretary; Brigham Young, Jr., his son, in whom he placed the greatest confidence; Albert Carrington, wielder of his pen and editor of the *Deseret News;* and John Taylor, senior apostle and his successor as trustee in trust for the church. These men faced a serious problem in adjusting accounts because it was not easy to distinguish between personal holdings of Brigham Young and church property which he held and managed.[24]

The settlement of the estate was a matter requiring patience —more patience than some of the heirs possessed. They appealed to the court, and Judge Boreman willingly granted an injunction, ordering the executors not to disburse certain moneys and imposing other restrictions which the executors ignored. For contempt of the order the executors were lodged in jail from August 4 to 28, 1879. The case was later settled out of court, by the estate paying the litigant heirs the aggregate of $75,000.[25]

At the close of his life Brigham Young was defending his dominion of Zion on three fronts:

1. On the political front, it was obvious that the Mormons were losing ground. Whether Young realized it or not, discouraging times were ahead.
2. On the polygamy front, the Mormons had suffered no defeat until after his demise, but the Reynolds case was moving slowly toward its conclusion in the United States Supreme Court.
3. On the economic front, Brother Brigham lived to see the failure of his dream of a united co-operative society. However, there were compensations. He knew that Zion was prospering, and he felt that a few units of the United Order held out promise.

The plan and purpose of the United Order needs only passing reference at this point, and that in relation to Mormon economic history. Since the exodus from Illinois, Brigham Young urged and preached co-operation. He envisioned a society of co-operating Saints, none of them rich and none in poverty. To that end he united them into groups, forced them to live in villages, and demanded the joining of their wealth in many undertakings. Thus they built roads and other public works. They shared the labor of clearing the land, digging the ditches, and damming the streams. They pooled their resources to form co-operative herds and took turns in defense against the Indians.

By co-operative effort the Saints had built factories, established a mercantile system, and constructed more than two hundred miles of railroad. Here was moving evidence that Zion was not only united but growing strong. But such efforts were not enough. They would all be more effective if united under a single control. The United Order of Enoch instituted by Smith was intended to supply this control.

Brigham Young by 1877 must have realized that the day was past when a whole people, however united in the spirit, could be welded into an economic unity. When they were all in poverty at the beginning of their frontier period, it was an easy matter to call for a sharing. They shared the last pound of flour. They loaned and borrowed tools and equipment. They exchanged work. At the dances a young man would sit on the bench in his stocking feet while his boots would be loaned to a friend who was dancing.

The United Order campaign was launched in St. George in 1874. During that year a great revival was staged, touching every community. The brethren were told to pool their resources, but they failed to follow through. For a year the Mormon co-operative plan limped along and was then pushed aside in all but a few remote places.

Zion's army in 1877, when Brigham Young passed from the scene, had become a mighty host, and the people were beginning to be conscious of their strength. The brethren no longer had to walk barefooted behind the plow. They had reached the level of relative economic security when every man had a Sunday suit and every family a house that did not leak. Every young man had a horse to ride. In the homes the women boasted board floors, stoves in their kitchens, and dishes in their cupboards. The day had passed when children lacked enough to eat.

The United Order of Enoch failed because the Saints in 1877 did not want an agency to lift up the poor and grade down the rich. However much they may have differed from the Gentiles in their social values, the Mormons were not substantially different in their economic values. No longer were their bellies against their backs or their backs against the wall. The youth of Zion in 1877 were looking into the future with confidence. At last the young man could feel that with reasonable effort and initiative he would be able to establish an economic security and a home of his own. To give up that dream of individualism was more than he was willing to surrender. But that same young man continued to identify himself with the co-operative social way of life which Brigham Young had fostered.

The real purpose of the United Order program was to be a weapon against economic encroachment by the Gentiles, many of whom by 1877 were beginning to become wealthy. These were the mine-owners, who since 1864 had been digging into Utah's canyons and finding rich deposits of gold, silver, lead, and copper. Brigham Young had tried mightily to discourage, and later obstruct, the mining movement in Utah. Once it began, he realized that gentile wealth from that source would far exceed Mormon wealth in agriculture, livestock, and minor industries. It became apparent by 1877 that the Mormon United Order would not prevent the growth of that industry; so Mormons did the sensible thing and turned attention to mining on their own account.

From 1864 to the turn of the century Utah mines produced precious metals at a rate which would average for the period from $25,000,000 to $30,000,000 per year. Most of that was gentile money. So the Gentiles, too, by 1877 were on their way to wealth, which speeded cosmopolitanism in Utah. Against such a development the United Order insularism was important.

NOTES

1. On June 22, 1878, J. C. Hemingray, of the Liberal party of Utah, told the House Committee on Territories, in support of a bill to regulate elections in Utah, that nine-tenths of the adult females in Utah were aliens and that half of the adult females were wed in polygamy. This statement was not challenged by the committee. Hemingray said the ballot was not safe in "the hands of a squalid peasantry who have never known and never will know the value of political and religious liberty." He said the ballots were marked with characters of the Deseret alphabet, so that each voter's ballot could be identified.

2. James G. Bleak ("Manuscript History of St. George," Book A, p. 401) mentioned the 1868 plan to migrate five or six thousand Saints from Great Britain at the rate of $100 each. This was the average.

3. The "Manuscript History of St. George," Book A, p. 172, contains a letter dated

February 15, 1863, from Apostle George A. Smith to Apostle Erastus Snow, regarding the missionaries who would gather the Lamanites "under the wings of Israel's Eagles." Hamblin would select one hundred energetic men who "do not worship the almighty dollar." Then followed instructions about the ferry, the road, and the forts to be built. That was the beginning of a work in Arizona which Jacob Hamblin continued the next fifteen years and which cleared the way for later unopposed Mormon settlement in that territory. George A. Smith, Jr., son of the apostle, was killed by Indians on one of these missions.

4. George W. Brimhall's *The Workers of Utah* is a little volume of recollections which, for some reason, did not please the church authorities. The report is that Brimhall destroyed all but a few copies, one of which is in the rare-book collection of the Library of Congress. Brimhall was told to go with his family (wife and five children—the oldest, George H., became president of the Brigham Young University) and traverse all the branch canyons of the Colorado River to which he could get access. It was his wish to go alone, but George A. Smith told him that "without a family along I would not know the methods of traveling, so that others might get along more safely from my experiences." He spent a hazardous summer on this mission and faced dangers which nearly cost the lives of his children and which "diminished my bravery and I became weak from the effects." He went through box canyons where the sand was so hot that he had to stop and move "alternately under the shade of the rocks, so to allow the hoofs of the oxen to cool off." At times the children cried from thirst. After several weeks Brimhall came out of the canyons, his horses and oxen "as poor as sandhill cranes." He said: "My children had made tracks where the squaw never took her papoose. . . . . My mission was complete and I was ready to report to those who sent me." Brimhall reported that he found along the Colorado no broad valleys that might be colonized, that the country was so barren that "not even the caw of the crow or the bark of the wolf was there to break the awful monotony."

5. In 1868 some of the Muddy Valley settlers became discouraged and proposed leaving. Erastus Snow telegraphed to Brigham Young, who sent by wire this order on February 17: "The brethren who are on the Upper Muddy must return to the place where they were sent, or else return home."

6. Some of the former "Muddyites" moved to Arizona. The rest remained in Kane County along the border of Utah. A few located on "the strip," that section of Arizona which is north of the Grand Canyon and is inaccessible to the rest of the state except by passing through Utah or Nevada. These most isolated of Mormon pioneers were the least influenced by change. Descendants of these families were involved in the church polygamy trials of 1935. They persisted in remaining loyal to the polygamy doctrines of Brigham Young, claiming the church had broken faith.

7. The principal settlement in the Salt River Valley was Mesa, near Phoenix. Several other communities were established along the Little Colorado River. The Sunset co-operative did not fare well. The men became unhappy under the rigid rule of Lot Smith. It was charged that he placed his personal brand on cattle that belonged to the co-operative.

Price W. Nelson wrote that Lot Smith would take orders only from Brigham Young. "When Brigham Young died, Lot Smith died in the Gospel. . . . . The only thing that will save him in the Kingdom of our Father is that he spill his blood to atone for his sins." Here in Nelson's life-sketch, on file in the St. George Library, is a remnant suggestion of the old blood-atonement doctrine. In June, 1892, Smith was shot by a Navajo Indian in the course of dispute about the use of some land and a watering place.

8. The writer reviewed the records of the United States Census Bureau for three southern Utah counties for 1870, when there were few Gentiles in the area. The three counties—Washington, Iron, and Kane—contained 6,872 persons—5,407 native born

and 1,465 foreign born. Of the foreign born, 689 were males and 776 females. Of the 6,872 inhabitants, 4,238, or 61.6 per cent, were under 20 years of age.

9. Corinne, founded March, 1869, once contained about two thousand inhabitants. The *Deseret News* remarked sarcastically on April 7, 1869, that the tent town was becoming civilized, "several men having been killed there already." The anti-Mormon *Corinne Daily Journal* began to issue from there May 2, 1871. The *Utah Reporter* began issue at Corinne on April 9, 1869, but did not survive very long.

Alexander Toponce (*Reminiscences*, pp. 231–33) reports that Brigham Young predicted the failure of Corinne. It was claimed that he brought to pass his own prophecy by having the railroad miss the place by several miles. Most of the businessmen from Corinne moved to Ogden. Phil Robinson (*Sinners and Saints*, pp. 269–70) reported Corinne in 1880 "a Gentile failure on the very skirts of Mormon success."

10. For information on this convention see "The State of Deseret," *Utah Historical Quarterly*, April, July, October, 1940, a single monograph volume on the subject; also B. H. Roberts, *Comprehensive History of the Church*, V, 457–64. Roberts ventured the opinion that the way was open in 1872 for a solution of the polygamy question, had Congress taken advantage of it.

11. Edward W. Tullidge's *History of Salt Lake City*, p. 589, contains a report of McKean using the *Tribune* to promote his "mission."

12. After being reversed in the Englebrecht case, McKean carried on without the use of either petit or grand jury. A report about his removal sent from Washington to the *Deseret News*, March 16, 1875, indicated that Grant came to the conclusion he was extreme and fanatical. See Roberts, *op. cit.*, V, 418–54. McKean resided in Utah until his death in 1879.

13. This gentile regime was fondly called by Gentiles, "The Republic of Tooele." See "Inventory of the Archives of Tooele County," pp. 26–30, a publication of the Historical Records Survey Project of the Utah W.P.A. This report indicates that the "Republic" collected $36,000 in taxes but spent $42,000.

14. See *Messages and Papers of the Presidents of the United States*, VII, 204, 208, 210. The Rev. John P. Newman, chaplain of the Senate, who went to Utah in August, 1870, to debate polygamy with Orson Pratt, was one of the leading lobbyists for antipolygamy legislation.

15. The following quotations are from testimonies of the sisters of the St. George Relief Society, as reported in the minutes for February 6, 1879:

"Hannah H. Romney referred to the stir that is being made in the courts regarding polygamy, said all who ever had the spirit of God would know that it is a command from God, and where practiced in righteousness would bring comfort and happiness to those who embraced it. . . . .

"Sister Dodge said that she had not tried polygamy and could not testify to the happiness it brings, but if the Lord ever gave a revelation, that was one. She believed the Lord to be on our side.

"Sister Ivins said she thought of the fuss the outsiders are making about polygamy. She felt like saying, 'Whose business are we meddling with? If three or four women wish to live with one man, where's the harm if they are satisfied?'

"Sister Margaret Snow said she must bear testimony to the truth of it. Said all the trouble she had was with herself. If we see a man whom we think is not doing right in polygamy, that is his business, not ours."

16. On the *Young* v. *Young* case see Roberts, *op. cit.*, V, 442–54; Ann Eliza Young, *Wife No. 19*, might have been a revealing report, but this divorced wife of Brother Brigham was too biased to distinguish between fact and fiction.

17. The records of the Commission for Indian Affairs from March, 1858, to April,

1860, contain a number of letters about the children orphaned by the massacre. These relate mainly to collecting them together and sending them back to Arkansas. For this purpose Congress appropriated $10,000—more than $500 per child. The *American Weekly*, a Sunday newspaper supplement, of August 25, 1840, contains a story by Mrs. Sallie Baker Mitchell, last of the seventeen orphans, who in her eighty-fifth year reported her recollections about the affair.

18. Joseph Fish, of Parowan, wrote in his journal, November 16, 1874: "There is considerable excitement here over the arrest of John D. Lee by Deputy Marshal Wm. Stokes. Lee was arrested for the Mountain Meadows massacre. They are watching him very close. . . . ." On November 18 Fish wrote that William H. Dame had been arrested and taken to Beaver. Fish commented on the character of the arresting officers: "There is a common saying that if you start proceedings against one of the cattle thieves that he will go through the courts and come out a deputy marshal. Nearly all who are assisting the marshal are generally reputed to be thieves and drunkards. This is the class of men that are employed to harass the Saints. David Page of this place is much pleased with Bro. Dame's arrest. . . . ."

19. Joseph Fish's journal, July 17, 1875: "There is quite an excitement in these southern settlements about John D. Lee, who it is claimed has turned state's evidence in the Mountain Meadows affair, and it is thought he will try to implicate W. H. Dame and others, if thereby he can save his own neck from the gallows. Very few put any dependence upon what he says, as the guards keep him drunk about all the time for the purpose of getting him to confess."

20. Joseph Fish's journal, October 2, 1876: "Spent the evening until a late hour with John M. McFarlane and U.S. Marshal William Nelson. The marshal was quite free to talk. He gave us a history of his labors in getting witnesses, etc., in the Lee case. He stated to us that the authorities of the Church were entirely innocent of the Mountain Meadows massacre. He said, 'I know more about that affair than Brigham Young. I have hunted up the evidence.' "

21. William H. Dame was able to prove that he was not near the Mountain Meadows at the time of the massacre; nor was Isaac C. Haight, president of the Parowan Stake. Bishop Philip Kingon Smith, of Cedar City, and his counselor, John M. Higbee, had probably been involved, but they had long since disappeared. As indicated by Lee, other Mormons were involved, including some 52 names, of which 32 were from Cedar City. These names were apparently listed not by Lee but by his attorney, W. W. Bishop, who edited the "confessions" (*Mormonism Unveiled*, pp. 379–80).

22. The *Journals of John D. Lee*, edited by Charles Kelly, contain a letter, of September 21, 1876, from Lee to Wife No. 17, Emma B. Lee (p. 242): "Six witnesses testified against me, four them purgured themselves by swearing falsehoods of the blackest character. Old Jacob Hamblin, the fiend from Hell, testified under oath that I told him that two young women were found in a thicket, where they had secreted themselves, by an Indian chief, who brought the girls to me, and wanted to know what was to be done with them. That I replied they was too old to live and would give evidence and must be killed; the Indian said they were too pretty to kill, that one of them fell on her knees and said, Spare my life and I will serve you all my days, and that I then cut her throat and the Indian killed the other."

23. On November 9, 1873, Brigham Young issued the following instructions for his burial: "I, Brigham Young, wish my funeral services to be conducted in the following manner: When I breathe my last, I wish my friends to put my body in as clean and wholesome state as can be conveniently done, and preserve the same for one, two, three or four days, or as long as my body can be preserved in good condition. I wish my coffin made of plump one and one-fourth inch redwood boards not skimped in length, but two inches longer than I would measure and from two to three inches wider than is com-

monly made for a person of my breadth and size, and deep enough to place me on a little comfortable cotton bed, with a good suitable pillow for size and quality, my body dressed in my temple clothing and laid nicely into my coffin, and the coffin to have the appearance that if I wanted to turn a little to the right or the left, I should have plenty of room to do so; the lid can be made crowning" (from a pamphlet, *Death of President Young*, issued by the *Deseret News*, 1877; quoted by M. R. Werner, *Brigham Young*, pp. 460–61).

24. The Mormon side of the case may be found in issues of the *Deseret News* of June 18, July 2, August 6 and 13, September 10, and October 8 and 10, 1879.

25. Alexander Toponce (*op. cit.*, pp. 196–98) gives a report of business deals with Young. Young bought from him 40 mules for use in pulling streetcars in Salt Lake City. Young could not then pay the full amount in cash. Sixty days was agreed on for payment of half the cost. This discussion took place in Young's office. "The Church office was a big room full of clerks and officials writing and working at their desks. Brigham's office was fenced off from the rest of the room by a low partition about as high as a man's shoulders. Brigham told one clerk to give me $1,500 cash and told Joseph A. Young, his secretary, to make up a note for $1,500 due in sixty days, with one percent interest per month after maturity, which Brigham signed.

"As he handed it to me he said, 'I guess, Alex, that will be all right without any other security, won't it?'

"I looked at the note and as I stepped out of his office I said, 'That will be all right, Mr. Young. I don't suppose you would go out and ask some Gentile to endorse it, not for the world, and as for the Mormon side of the house, all the names in Utah wouldn't make it any better. . . . .' The note was paid promptly. From first to last, I found Brigham Young the squarest man to do business with in Utah, barring none, Mormon, Jew or Gentile."

CHAPTER XII

ZION BOWS TO THE GENTILES

BRIGHAM YOUNG'S death came almost exactly thirty years after he settled the pioneer party in Salt Lake Valley; and in that period, against unrelenting opposition from Nature and the Gentiles, he lifted the church out of direst poverty into relative security. Under his guidance the Mormons went from dirt floors to carpets in a single generation. Except for the issues of self-government and polygamy, the frontier history of the Rocky Mountain Saints might have closed with the passing of their pioneer leader.

They had settled the land question and frustrated the land-jumpers. They had planted all the important settlements and kept the Gentiles off the land. The geographical pattern of Zion had been defined, and few changes were made after 1877. About all the water available for irrigation or for range purposes had been pre-empted. Mormon-owned flocks and herds had the run of the mountains and deserts. The area of settlement had been extended to Idaho, Wyoming, Arizona, and Nevada.

Brigham Young left the Saints with the thought out of mind that they would suddenly be called back to Jackson County. They were convinced that Zion was at home in the mountains. They were going ahead with the job of building temples. There were other problems in store, one of which was to become even more serious than the polygamy issue or the fight for control of local government. That was the problem of more land for Zion's increase. That question concerned the generation of 1877 much less than the generation of 1897.

The pressing problem at the demise of Brigham Young was polygamy, but it was one that could not be settled save on the basis of force and pursuit. Men of the law descended upon Zion, and there followed a long war between deputies and pluralists, a hide-and-seek contest in the "fastnesses of the mountains." The story is told of a tourist who engaged a Mormon in conversation about the impressive Bryce Canyon. This Mormon had lived within sight of the canyon all his life but without being impressed by its beauty. He said to the stranger: "I guess it's pretty all right, but it's a hell of a place to lose a cow."

In that region of crevices, rimrocks, and twisting watercourses, where the natives did lose their cows, it is small wonder that the deputies were frustrated in their man hunts. James J. Strang located with a faction of Mormons on Beaver Island in Lake Michigan. He instituted the system of plurality in his group. The Gentiles on the mainland rose up against him. It required but a single raid to break up and scatter his entire colony. Utah Mormons were much more secure. They found in their canyons many hiding places, and they were favored by the scattered character of their communities. It was this friendly environment which delayed the settlement of the polygamy issue and, therewith, that of the local government issue and Utah's attainment of statehood.

The story of the "tapering-off" years is one of a losing fight against a superior force. Collisions on the polygamy issue before 1877 were mere skirmishes by comparison. Each year thereafter saw the attack tighten until all the forces of assault and defense from Gunlock to Goshen, from the hut of the most isolated pluralist to the big house of the most prosperous apostle, were organized in a continuous line of battle.

Less than a year after Brother Brigham's death the opening gun of the polygamy war was fired in connection with the headline case of John H. Miles, the failure of which resulted in a demand for a more effective antipolygamy law.

Miles, of Salt Lake City, was arrested in October, 1878, on the complaint of his wife, Carrie Owen Miles, charging that he had previously "taken to wife" one Emily Spencer. Later she dropped the charge and consented to move with her husband to St. George.[1] This reconciliation did not last even until the summer of 1879, when she renewed the charges against Miles and received considerable support from gentile friends.

The trial dragged through May and June, the prosecution attempting to prove the marriage of Miles to the Spencer woman. An unsuccessful effort was made to force testimony from elders who presumably married the two at the Endowment House. Miles was found guilty of polygamy, fined $100, and sentenced to five years in prison. The decision was upheld by the supreme court of Utah but was later reversed by the United States Supreme Court. The upper tribunal ruled that the lower court failed to produce evidence of a marriage between Miles and Emily Spencer.

This Supreme Court reversal clearly showed that the Mormon brand of polygamy could not be prosecuted under the antipolygamy law of 1862. The court ruled in the Miles case that the wife is not a competent witness, and that was another reason for the Supreme Court reversal. It rested on the testimony of the wife.

A principal witness in the Miles trial was Daniel H. Wells, who admittedly married the Owen woman to Miles and allegedly married the Spencer woman to him previously. Wells could "not remember" in response to some questions, and other questions he refused to answer because they concerned the alleged "secrets" of the Endowment House. He denied that bloody oaths were administered or that terrifying threats were made to persons if they revealed anything they saw or heard in that holy place. He would not accept an offer to purge himself of contempt:

> I consider any person who reveals the sacred ceremonies of the Endowment House a falsifier and a perjurer; and it has been and is a principle of my life never to betray a friend, my religion, my country, or my God. It seems to me that this is sufficient reason why I should not be held in contempt.[2]

This did not satisfy the court. Wells was fined $100 and sent to prison for two days. Mormons were outraged. When he was released from confinement, they staged a demonstration in which thousands marched.[3]

In the Miles-Wells incident the prosecution was frustrated both by the refusal of Mormons to testify and by the Supreme Court ruling. The Gentiles, through the agency of the Liberal party, turned to Congress for a new antipolygamy law. They got support from President Rutherford B. Hayes, who in his message to Congress in December, 1879, urged "more comprehensive and searching methods" for preventing and punishing polygamy.

Again in his message of December, 1880, President Hayes called on Congress to act on the polygamy question. "It can only be suppressed by taking away the political power of the sect that encourages and sustains it." He proposed that Utah be placed under a body of commissioners, "a government analogous to the provisional government established in the territory northwest of the Ohio by the Ordinance of 1787." Or, he would give more power to the federal officials in Utah.[4]

Congress seemed in no hurry about the Utah question. However, while Congress was passive, events were moving on Utah's political front. In the election of 1880 Apostle George Q. Cannon of the People's party, was elected delegate to Congress over A. G. Campbell, of the Liberal party. Cannon received 18,568 votes; Campbell, 1,357. Governor Eli H. Murray, newly appointed Kentucky Republican, ignored the results of the election and certified Campbell.

This action caused the Cannon-Campbell election issue to be taken to the House of Representatives, where no action was taken for nearly a year. In the meanwhile, James A. Garfield had become president. In his inaugural address of March 4, 1881, Garfield said the Mormon church "not only offends the moral sense of mankind by sanctioning polygamy, but it prevents the administration of justice through ordinary instrumentalities of law."

Chester A. Arthur, elevated to the presidency after the assassination of Garfield, mentioned the polygamy question in his message to Congress of December, 1881. Thus, within the space of three years, three presidents had urged action against the Mormons. In the meanwhile public opinion was being inflamed. "Menace of Mormonism" sermons had become popular even in the exclusive churches. It was the Rev. T. De Witt Talmage who referred to the Mormon church as "that old hag of hell who sits making faces at heaven."

Possibly it was the contest between Cannon and Campbell for the seat as Utah's delegate that roused Congress to action. The Committee on Elections of the House reached a decision on January 25, 1882. It recommended that neither man qualified—Cannon because he was a polygamist and Campbell because he lacked a majority of the votes.

A week before the decision in this election case the Senate passed the Edmunds antipolygamy law. On March 22 the measure was signed by President Arthur.

So slowly moved the wheels of the federal government that ten years passed between the time when the Mormons publicly proclaimed polygamy (1852) and the time when the first law was passed against it (1862). Then another ten years went by before the first efforts to prosecute polygamy. That attempt was blasted in the decision of the supreme court in the Englebrecht case, which denied the federal courts the right to hear these cases. Two years later, in 1874, the Poland bill assigned jurisdiction over criminal and civil cases to the federal courts. Five years later it was found that the law of 1862 was unworkable, and it was not until 1882 that the first effective antipolygamy law reached the books.

The opposition was happy. After thirty years the "scarlet woman of the desert" would be brought to bar for her sins. The "plague spot of the continent" would be cleaned out. A stop would be put to the Mormons propagating the "doctrines of Christ with the instrumentalities of Momomet."

The Edmunds bill was mainly an amendment of the law of 1862, section 5352 of the *Revised Statutes of the United States*, "in Reference to Polygamy and for Other Purposes." It provided:

1. That the penalty for bigamy set forth in the law of 1862 continue in force. This penalty provided a fine up to $500, or imprisonment up to five years, or both.
2. That a male person cohabiting with more than one women should be guilty of a misdemeanor and should be fined up to $300, or imprisoned up to six months, or both.
3. That polygamists and persons believing in polygamy in Utah were to be denied the right to vote or hold public office. If the belief or practice was not a matter of record, it was to be determined by means of a test oath.

4. All registration and election offices in Utah were to be declared vacant, and a commission of five was to be created to supervise elections in Utah. Such commissioners would be appointed by the president and approved by the Senate. The commission supervised the test oath and qualified candidates for office.
5. Children born to plural wives prior to January 1, 1883, about nine months after the effective date of the law, were to be recognized as of legitimate birth, and those after that date would be illegitimate. The president had power to change this date.

The way was open for the Utah legislature to pass a law in conformity with the Edmunds bill. Had this been done, the federal government would probably have taken no action—at least not until local government had been given an opportunity to act. The Mormons took no such steps.

Three months after the passage of the Edmunds bill, on June 23, the Utah commission was appointed: Alexander Ramsey, of Minnesota; A. B. Carlton, of Indiana; A. S. Paddock, of Nebraska; G. L. Godfrey, of Iowa; and J. R. Pettigrew, of Arkansas. Apparently most of them were inconspicuous politicians, able to do well this job that imposed few duties. The commission reached Utah in August and received a jubilant welcome from Gentiles ready to besiege them with proposals, advice, confidential information, and requests for jobs.

The first official act of the commission was the rejection of a petition from the Liberal party to disfranchise women. The Liberal party would not have been much injured if suffrage had been taken from the women. It was a party of men, including most of the miners. While the commission rejected the petition on technical grounds, it said in its first report to the Secretary of the Interior, dated November 17, 1882: "We are satisfied that owing to the peculiar state of affairs in Utah, this law is an obstruction to the speedy solution of the 'vexed question.'"

While the Mormons defended female suffrage, they were probably no more converted to the principle than the Liberals. Whereas they piously advocated sex equality in politics, they never mentioned the possibility of women being elected to public office. Instead, they proceeded on the implied assumption that public office, like military rank, was a perquisite of the priesthood, according to rank. A bishop was not sent to the legislature if the stake president was a candidate, and a stake president would defer to an apostle. About the only importance of female suffrage was that it gave the Mormons, the People's party, so many more votes.[5]

The commission affected Utah elections in two ways: it cut down the number of votes, and it excluded polygamists from public office. Of a sudden there was a paucity of apostles, stake presidents, and bishops in the legislature. Instead of the polygamist George Q. Cannon being elected as Utah's delegate to Congress, the monogamist John T. Caine was elected, but he was no less faithful to the church. How the people of Utah voted in the election before, and in the election immediately after, the advent of the commission is shown in the contests of 1880 and 1882 to elect delegates to Congress:

1880

People's party: George Q. Cannon....	18,568 votes
Liberal party: A. G. Campbell........	1,357

1882

People's party: John T. Caine........	22,727 votes
Liberal party: P. T. Van Zile.........	4,884

The party vote was almost wholly Mormon against Gentile. After the commission began performing its office, Gentiles had the advantage at the polls, for they were the judges. Yet, with everything in their favor, Liberal votes only increased from 1,357 to 4,884; and, in spite of the unknown number of Mormons excluded, the People's vote jumped from 18,568 to 22,727.

Polygamy arrests did not begin until late in 1884. The delay was due to waiting for the Utah legislature to pass a conformity bill; but, when the bill was passed, it was vetoed by Governor Eli H. Murray on February 26, 1884. He claimed that not only did the conformity law not prohibit polygamy but that it placed such restrictions on civil procedure that it would have prevented the prosecution of a common seducer.

Rudger Clawson was arrested on October 15, 1884. The jury disagreed on October 21, and a new trial began on October 24. Lydia Spencer, alleged plural wife of Clawson, refused to testify, for which she was sent to jail. Clawson interceded, and she later admitted her marriage to him. Clawson was sentenced to four years' imprisonment and fined $800. His case was appealed to the United States Supreme Court asking the right of polygamists to be admitted to bail. On January 19, 1885, the high court ruled that bail was not a right, "but distinctly a matter for the discretion of the court to judge."

This decision cleared the way for the drive to begin and for speedy trials, because it placed polygamists in a position of standing trial or going to jail. Once caught, they were in custody until released or sentenced, unless the judge wished to be lenient and accept bail.

There were a few convictions in 1884: three in Utah, one in Idaho, and five in Arizona. The number was small but was sufficient to indicate that the courts were prepared to act, and this put the Mormons on notice. Within the church plans for defense were initiated.[6]

Early in 1885 the church sent out a circular to all stake presidents and bishops instructing them on the manner of raising funds for legal aid and of dealing with the deputies. "We do not think it advisable for brethren to go into court and plead guilty. . . . . Every case should be defended with all the zeal and energy possible. The families of those brethren who are imprisoned, and those who have been compelled to flee, should be looked after."[7]

This determination to avoid arrest and conviction involved resistance, by running and hiding, rather than active obstruction. It involved withholding information from strangers and telling nothing to federal officials that would help them in their hunting and convicting. It permitted giving false information and all but required wives to disown their husbands and children to deny knowing their fathers. This policy made a virtue of any tactics that would hinder the administration of the law.

To list the names of polygamists arrested or hunted in 1885 would amount to a roll call of all church leaders, from bishops up to apostles. On this roll would appear the names of many women who refused to testify. The list can be gleaned from the

POLYGAMISTS WITHOUT THEIR BEARDS

In this picture the Mormon "cohabs" are lined up with the regular prisoners. Normally they did not associate with other prisoners, called "tuffs." Last request of most polygamists upon leaving prison was for some part of their striped uniform. Generally the polygamists supplied their own shirts, socks, and underwear, which they sent home to have washed.

day-to-day items in the *Church Chronology*, from which it is noted that on September 15 "Miss Elizabeth Starkey and Miss Eliza Shafer were sent to the penitentiary by Judge Zane of the Third District Court for refusing to answer questions before the grand jury."

On October 6 Charles L. White came forward and admitted

PROMINENT MORMONS AT THE UTAH PRISON IN 1885

Reading from left to right, these gentlemen in stripes are: F. A. Brown, Moroni Brown, Freddy Selt, A. M. Musser, Parley P. Pratt (son of the apostle), Rudger Clawson (apostle), and Job Pingree.

unlawful cohabitation in order to free his wife, Miss Starkey, from prison. He was sentenced to six months in prison and fined $300. As for Miss Shafer, she stubbornly remained behind bars until December 19, when the judge weakened and turned her loose. She was brought to court the following February 15 and admitted being the plural wife of John W. Snell.

During 1885 the case of John Nicholson, associate editor of the *Deseret News*, caused some stir among the Saints because he pleaded guilty to polygamy. He condemned the law that required him to forsake a principle of his religion and break up his family. Also in 1885, Bishop John Sharp of Salt Lake City shocked all polygamists because he confessed guilt and agreed to abide by the law. Sharp said:

> I expect to remain under the political disabilities placed upon me, but I have so arranged my family relations as to conform to the requirements of the law, and I am now living in harmony with the provisions in relation to cohabitation as construed by this court and the Supreme Court of the Territory, and it is my intention to do so in the future until an overruling Providence shall decree greater religious tolerance in the land.[8]

Bishop Sharp was not sent to prison. He was released with a fine of $300. The court blessed him for his example, saying that his course "will have greater effect on society than any imprisonment the court could impose." Although Sharp had been a close associate of Brigham Young in business and a man of influence in the church, his course was condemned by all good Saints.

Two days before the trial of Bishop Sharp, Judge Zane gave an interpretation of the antipolygamy law that was distressing to the church. He took the stand that a polygamist could be indicted on a separate count for each violation of the law. This "segregation" principle was applied and tested in the case of Apostle Lorenzo Snow, husband of seven wives. For the period between January 1, 1883, the effective date of the Edmunds law, and December 1, 1885—a total of thirty-five months—Snow was alleged to have broken the law three times. The Supreme Court of the United States on May 10, 1886, denied the segregation principle. The decision read:

> Thus, in each indictment, the offense is laid as a continuing one, and a single one, for all the time covered by the indictment; and taking the three indictments together, there is charged a continuous offense for the entire time covered by all three of the indictments. . . . . The division of the two years and eleven months is wholly arbitrary. On the same principle there might have been an indictment covering each of the thirty-five months, with imprisonment of eleven years and a half, and fines amounting to $10,500, or even an indictment covering each week with imprisonment for seventy-four years and fines up to $44,400; and so ad infinitum, for smaller periods of time.[9]

While the Snow case was moving through the channels, Mormon lawyers were preparing another legal test in the case of Angus M. Cannon. The argument was advanced that unlawful cohabitation ("UC") could not be established unless the prosecution could produce evidence of sexual relations between the alleged polygamist and the alleged wives. Fortunately for the polygamists, the Supreme Court on December 14, 1885, ruled that the requirements of the law were satisfied if the evidence showed that the defendant "by his language or conduct or both" held the women in question out to the world as his wives. It was not necessary to prove sexaul intercourse.[10] Any other decision would have forced the prosecution into a program of prying and spying.

As it was, there was complaint about the methods of the deputies and prosecutors. On February 1, 1885, President John Taylor issued a statement, part of which is descriptive of the methods protested:

> When little children are set in array against their fathers and mothers, and women and children are badgered before courts and made to submit, unprotected, to the jibes of libertines and corrupt men; when wives and husbands are pitted against each other and threatened with pains, penalties and imprisonment, if they do not disclose that which among all decent people is considered sacred, and which no man of delicacy, whose sensibilities have not been blunted by low associates, would ever ask; when such a condition of affairs exist, it is no longer a land of liberty, and no longer a land of equal rights, and we must take care of ourselves as best we may, and avoid being caught in any of their snares.

This veteran, who had stood with Joseph Smith when he was shot by the mob, who had walked with Brother Brigham for more than thirty years, ended his diatribe with advising the polygamists, not to fight, but to run.

Then came the exodus of pluralists to "the underground," and all Zion entered into an unwritten compact to protect them. The *Salt Lake Tribune* on June 3, 1886, noted that dozens of polygamists had fled to Europe or to Mexico and suggested that those in prison "should be pardoned if they will go abroad." Many could not get away, since they were poor men. Many of these were caught. In 1885 and 1886 there were 151 convictions of polygamists in Utah, while 36 were convicted in Idaho.[11]

Those who were enforcing the antipolygamy statute were still not satisfied. They began to ask for more sweeping legislation. Congress gave them the Edmunds-Tucker bill of March

31, 1887, an act which placed Utah in the position of a conquered province. It was an elaboration of the law of 1882, adding to it four amendments:

1. It abolished the Perpetual Emigrating Fund Company, the pioneer agency which had brought thousands of converts to Zion and had become a repository or holding company for church wealth.
2. It abolished the Nauvoo Legion, Utah's church-controlled militia. Several unsuccessful attempts had been made to abolish this organization since 1870, because it was thought to have great secret strength.
3. It abolished female suffrage, which probably deprived the Mormons of about 10,000 votes. It also deprived the wives of polygamists of their immunity when called upon in court to testify on charges involving their husbands. In most polygamy cases the courts had not respected this immunity previously.
4. It abolished the Church of Jesus Christ of Latter-Day Saints as a corporation and called upon the supreme court of Utah to escheat all church property except houses of worship, the escheated property to be used in the interest of the public school system. This provision was a clarification of the antipolygamy law of 1862 which forbade religious bodies in the territories to hold property in excess of $50,000. That provision had not been invoked against the Mormon church because it might have been a precedent for action against other churches.

Before the court and the marshal could act to take possession of church property, the Mormons had taken action on their own. It has been claimed that considerable property was transferred secretly to individuals to hold in trust. On July 30, 1887, the Supreme Court appointed United States Marshal Frank H. Dyer to be receiver of escheated property. Church authorities at once began legal proceedings to halt the liquidation of this property, but in the meanwhile the Gentiles held it.

Pending the review by the courts, the Mormon economy was subjected to serious inconvenience. The prospect of ultimate loss of church property resulted in resort to various legal ruses to save the wealth held by the tithing offices.

The records of the St. George Tithing Office contain an inventory (see accompanying list) dated March 21, 1887, just ten days before the passage of the Edmunds-Tucker law. This inventory was made for the transference of the goods therein listed from the trustee in trust for the church to a private agency, called the "Church Association of the St. George Stake of Zion," obviously a device to place these properties beyond the reach of the law.

Apparently, this inventory was not included in the holdings taken over by Marshal Dyer. It can be seen, however, from the list below how deeply involved the church was in the economic

Lumber, shingles, adobies, etc.	$ 371.42
Fence posts and wood for fuel	286.40
Salt (rock salt from local deposits)	246.94
Wheat 1,259 bushels	1,236.57
Barley 767 bushels	524.14
Oats 64 bushels	38.40
Corn 478 bushels	401.76
Flour 6,208 pounds	186.25
Molasses 2,969 gallons	1,633.36
Wine 6,610 gallons	3,305.00
Vinegar 775 gallons	232.50
Dried fruits	215.45
Potatoes	147.35
Butter	6.74
Merchandise, foreign goods	1,720.43
Merchandise, home made goods	1,500.70
Swine	93.21
Sheep	147.75
Horses and cattle	1,215.50
Bees (37 hives)	185.00
Cash on hand	614.45
Scrip, mostly county and city	174.13
Equipment and fixtures	1,478.25
Investment in St. George Garden Club	2,944.58
Investment in Panaca cooperative store	1,041.79
Due on various personal accounts	8,325.65
Total	$28,273.72

life of local communities. Since banks were nonexistent in most places, the tithing offices were banks and credit agencies as well as stores.

With the additional power granted by the Edmunds-Tucker law the courts were able to press the prosecution of polygamists with renewed vigor, and with each month of effort the drive became more systematized. With so many polygamists in hiding, in custody, or in jail, there were costs to pay and labor to do. Nonpolygamists had to do their own work and the work of their polygamist brethren.

Deputy marshals became bolder and more numerous. There also grew up a class of informers who made a profession of helping the deputies, and some were not above bribing polygamists. The business of lawyers increased. A great deal of money changed hands in the prosecution or defense of polygamists. Since Mormons were not eligible as jurors in polygamy cases, for certain Gentiles jury service became an occupation.

Although deputies, in twos and threes, roamed the entire country, raiding house after house, none were physically interfered with. No deputy was killed and none injured in line of duty, but there were instances of deputies shooting at polygamists. At Parowan on December 16, 1886, Edward M. Dalton, wanted for unlawful cohabitation, was shot and killed by Deputy Marshal William Thompson. Dalton had been arrested previously but had escaped. Thompson and another deputy waited for him at the home of an apostate Mormon. When he came riding along the street driving some stock, he was shot without warning. Had the Saints of Parowan not been so well disciplined by priesthood authority, there might have been a lynching.

Judge Jacob S. Boreman, at Beaver, issued a writ of habeas corpus for Thompson, which the Mormons claimed would not have been granted to one of their number had a deputy been shot. Thompson was later indicted for manslaughter. The Mormons called it murder. Three weeks later, in a two-day trial before a gentile jury, he was acquitted.[12]

For this, the only killing in the polygamy war, the Mormons had to be content with writing their sentiments on Dalton's tombstone: "He Was Shot and Killed, December 16, 1886, in Cold Blood by a United States Deputy Marshal while under Indictment for a Misdemeanor under the Edmunds-Anti-Polygamy Law." Next was written the Lord's Word from Rev. 6:10: "And They Cried with a Loud Voice Saying, O Lord, Holy and True, Dost Thou Not Judge and Avenge Our Blood on Them That Dwell in the Earth."

After the passage of the Edmunds-Tucker law there was reflection among the Mormons. Many felt that still more restrictions were in store. The valiantly faithful were prepared for greater disabilities. Others took a more moderate view, for which they were called "radical" by the faithful. There grew up an organization for moderation called the "Loyal League of Utah." The avowed purpose of the League was to find a middle ground.[13]

Basically the League was anti-Mormon, although not as rabidly so as was the Liberal party. Some of the Mormons who joined it had come to the conclusion that the fight for polygamy was futile and that the day of church-managed local government was past. It was becoming clear to many that the church, disincorporated, voteless, and propertyless, could not carry on. Most of the leaders, being fugitives from justice most of the time, could not continue with their duties. We note a suggestion of discouragement in the journal entries of Charles L. Walker, a polygamist of St. George, who so often reflected the thoughts of others:

February 25–26: Hiding in the bushes so that I may escape being arrested by the deputy marshals. Feel rather under the weather through loss of sleep.

March and April, 1888: This month and part of April I have been obliged to hide from the U.S. deputies who are seeking me night and day to arrest me and drag me to prison for obeying the commandments of God, my Eternal Father. They came to my house and threatened to break down the doors if the folks did not open them immediately. They then ransacked the entire house, kicking the carpets and rugs about, trying to discover, as they imagined, some secret passage to a cellar or hiding place. Twice they came and found me not. They summoned my wife and four daughters to Beaver, 120 miles distant, to testify against me, and this is a Christian country where everyone has a right to worship God according to the dictates of his own conscience! The remainder of the month has been spent in hiding from my enemies, away from home in the daytime, and at night on duty at the Temple.

June 16, 1888: Today the U.S. Deps made a sudden descent on my house while I was sleeping about 1 oclock. As one was stationed at the back of the lot to come in the back way, the other was at the front to catch me. I ran east, not knowing anyone was in wait for me, and, having about ten seconds start, I hid in the foliage and thus escaped once more. I fully believe the Lord diverted his eyes in another direction, or the officer would have caught me.

In a later entry of his journal Walker said: "I don't feel very good to be hunted like a beast or a criminal." Orson W. Huntsman, of Hebron, wrote various notes in his journal. One is selected in which he refers to his father-in-law, Bishop Thomas S. Terry, who had three wives:

March 24–25, 1888: I atended St. George conference. I being the only one from here, was called to report the Hebron ward. Reported it in good condition and that we had our Bp. hid up so he could not be found. The last day of the conference at afternoon service the U.S. Marshal came in town and every man in meeting that had more than one wife slipped out and no one could tell anything about which way they went.

In Bleak's "Manuscript History of St. George" for 1887 and 1888 may be found various references to the "unsettled state of affairs." Mention was made for March 20, 1888, of the deputies shooting at Adolphus R. Whitehead while he escaped on a horse.

In the days when so much money could not be imagined, Brigham Young was wont to say it would cost the government $300,000,000 to abolish polygamy. What it did cost the government nobody knows, nor does anyone know what it cost the Mormons to defend themselves—court costs, fines, months in prison, years in hiding or going abroad. In 1886 Charles Ora Card and some other pluralists took a colony to Alberta, Canada, where they established Cardston in the valley of the St. Mary's River. The community today is center of a population of about 10,000 Mormons.

Similarly, in 1885 and 1886 a number of polygamists with their families fled over the southern border into Mexico and founded a number of small communities. These Saints, unlike the migrants to Canada, did not identify themselves with the alien country, and the settlements never grew.

For 1887 the Utah commission reported to the Secretary of the Interior 289 convictions in Utah for unlawful cohabitation since 1882. For that five-year period 541 polygamists had been indicted and were at large or awaiting trial. Fourteen persons during that period had been convicted of polygamy, this being a felony.[14]

Each case brought to trial served to place more information in the hands of the prosecution, until the private life of practically every Mormon was a matter of record. The more information the law enforcers had, the more difficult it was for Mormons, once caught, to escape conviction if they really were polygamists. Defense became more difficult. There was, for a while, a ray of hope from the thought that the Supreme Court would nullify the escheat clause. This hope vanished when the court, on May 19, 1890, upheld the clause and the provision abolishing the "late Corporation of the Church of Jesus Christ of Latter-day Saints et al."[15]

As the hardships increased, the number who wanted to carry on the resistance until driven to the caves were not so many. The leaders, most of them getting old, began to lose their determination. The inconvenience of hiding and fleeing was more than they could bear. Perhaps they had been spoiled by comfort. Early in 1887 John Taylor died while in hiding, and Wilford Woodruff became president of the church. Apparently, Woodruff and the apostles concluded the cause was lost, with the result that on September 24, 1890, he issued a "Manifesto," indicating that the church would "refrain from contracting marriages forbidden by the laws of the land."

This was a cryptic surrender which many Gentiles called insincere. To many Mormons it was a welcome pronouncement. Others were unhappy about it and could not believe that God would change his mind so abruptly on a principle given by revelation. Woodruff did not say that the Saints had renounced their belief in the doctrine, nor did he promise that all polygamists would obey the law.[16] He merely said that the church had surrendered.

While Gentiles did not accept the sincerity of the Manifesto, it must be said that some among them were also disappointed, or would have been had conformity with the law been complete and immediate. Strict obedience to the law would have inconvenienced many Gentiles who had jobs as prosecutors or deputies. Others earned money as jurors in polygamy trials. After the Manifesto many of these people lost business, especially as polygamists would appear in court and accuse themselves. Most of these, upon pledging to obey the law, would be dismissed with a fine of "six cents."[17]

President Benjamin Harrison on January 4, 1893, in response to a Mormon petition sent in December, 1891, and on the recommendation of the Utah commission made in September, 1892, issued a proclamation of amnesty. By this proclamation pardon was extended to all polygamists who had not violated the anti-polygamy laws since November, 1890. President Grover Cleveland later issued a similar proclamation extending federal grace to 1894.

Opposition to the Mormons waned in proportion as evidences of good faith multiplied. There was even a decline in opposition to the church efforts to recover its property held by the federal court. In March, 1896, with the approval of Congress and the president, the property was returned. Church leaders claimed the property had greatly depreciated, that the government took from them a full purse and handed back an empty one.[18]

They were happy in the hope of statehood and the prospect of getting rid of federally appointed governors, judges, marshals, attorneys, and commissioners, most of whom were poor political heelers, described by one observer as a "venomous and witless lot." Had the church yielded sooner on the polygamy issue, the riddance would have come sooner, and statehood would not have been delayed so long.

To the public outside of Utah, polygamy was largely a moral issue, but to most Gentiles in Utah it was only incidentally a moral issue. Even to the Mormons, it was not wholly a moral issue. It was tied on all corners to the struggle between Gentiles and Mormons for political and economic control. This is nowhere better illustrated than in the so-called "office-grab" incident of 1882, when jobless Gentiles tried to seize by appointment all public offices vacated by Mormons in accordance with the requirements of the Edmunds bill.

The commission provided by this law to supervise Utah's elections was not appointed until June, 1882, and did not reach Utah until two months later, too late to supervise the August elections. Utah stood to be without elected officials. Governor Murray ruled that when the incumbents' terms of office expired, the governor was bound to name their successors. The Mormon political leaders argued that the incumbents would remain in office until their successors were elected in the next election. Some offices which were held by polygamists were vacated, and the governor filled these by appointment.

Recognizing the problem, Congress, in August, 1882, passed

an amendment to the Edmunds bill authorizing the governor of Utah "to appoint officers in said territory to fill vacancies which may be caused by the failure to elect on the first Monday of August, 1882." Southern members of Congress opposed this amendment as carpetbagging legislation. The issue was taken into the courts, which served to frustrate the "office-grab" effort. By this process of delay from court to court the Mormons managed to prevent these wholesale appointments. Before the case reached the Supreme Court the election of 1883 had passed and a new set of officers was selected.[19] Had the Gentiles won the "grab" issue, they would have gained little in salaries, but the moral victory would have buoyed them up more than it would have depressed the Mormons.

In 1884 a group of young Mormons proposed a plan to abolish the old local party alignments, to get rid of the People's party and the Liberal party. This group, the "Sagebrush Democrats," advocated that the Utah voters join either the Republican party or the Democratic party. This suggestion was resisted both by the church-managed People's party and by the Liberal party, managed by federal office-holders and chronic Mormon-baiters. They could not settle differences until after the Manifesto had removed the polygamy barrier.

The issues which kept the local parties apart were minor and petty. Much was made, for example, of the Mormons' half-masting of the flag on July 4, 1885. They mourned thereby the loss of religious liberty. The Gentiles called it a lack of patriotic respect for the Day of Independence. The *Salt Lake Tribune* on July 10 denounced the gesture and suggested that, if the Mormons repeated the incident the coming Pioneer Day, July 24, there would be on hand a lusty and patriotic crowd from the mining camps. "It would probably result in a speedy effectual settlement of the whole Mormon business."

The Mormons accepted the challenge. In spite of preparations to have the soldiers on hand in the event of trouble, Mormons said the flag would be half-masted. It all came to naught. Former President U. S. Grant died on July 23, and all flags had to be half-masted.

Also, there was the question of the test oath, in which the Liberal party was very much involved, being determined to make the oath more exclusive and restrictive. The fight over the phrasing of the oath to be imposed upon the voters helped keep the parties alive; but that issue, too, was closed when the Manifesto committed the Saints to abiding by the law and permitted them to say they had abandoned polygamy.

After the Manifesto the Utah voters did give up their old local party affiliations; but, before the church leaders released the hold they had over the People's party, they had faced the necessity of setting the stage, and so the young leaders of the Democratic party did not displace them. Had the Mormon vote not received their coaching, it would have gone overwhelmingly for the Democratic party. The Mormons had always been partial to the Democrats from the day when Joseph Smith aspired for the presidency as a Jeffersonian Democrat.

But the leaders of the church, after the passing of Brigham Young, had become very active in Utah's business life. Their views were more in keeping with those of the Republican party. Their problem was to get the people to see eye to eye with them. With the power of the priesthood on their side, some of them went about among the people advising that it was not good for them to be in a single political party. It would be better if they were about evenly divided, Democrats and Republicans.

Aside from the personal motives involved, it was good advice for the Saints to be divided evenly between the parties, so that they would have friends whichever party was in power. Usually the Saints voted as a unit. They had done so in Missouri, in Illinois, and in Iowa; but each time they got into trouble. Later, in Idaho and Arizona, because the Mormons voted in a solid block, they had in their hands the balance of power. It was nothing new for the Mormon vote to support one party in one election and to switch over in the next.[20]

In connection with making Republicans by priesthood mandate, a meeting was held at Beaver on June 22, 1891. Church leaders from Beaver, Panguitch, Kanab, Parowan, and Millard stakes were present. The speakers were Apostles F. M. Lyman and A. H. Cannon, who presented the problem, gave the "advise of counsel," and then asked to see the hands of those who would volunteer to become Republicans.[21] Judge Orlando W. Powers, a Gentile active then in Utah's politics, reported later: "I know this of my own knowledge, that there were men in Utah, when we came to break upon party lines, who for years I know, claimed to be Democrats, who suddenly were Republicans." Powers cited the case of John Graham, an editor in Provo, who dutifully switched the influence of his paper from Democratic to Republican support.[22]

As a result of this campaign of conversion, an excess of Republicans was created, as indicated by the first test vote—that in the election of November, 1894, to select a delegate for Congress. Frank J. Cannon, Republican, received 21,326 votes, while only 19,505 votes were cast for the Democrat, Joseph L. Rawlins.

The next election was in November, 1895, when the first officers for the nascent state of Utah were named. Republican Heber M. Wells, son of the veteran Daniel H. Wells, received 20,563 votes for governor; while John T. Caine, Democrat, received 19,666 votes. Caine was normally popular in Utah, having been elected several times as delegate to Congress, but in that election priesthood guidance prevailed.

In November, 1896, Utah voted for the first time as a state. The franchise had been restored to the women, and the disabilities had been removed from the polygamists. Apparently, the priesthood mandate had been set aside. Mormons slid back to their old-time preferences. The Democrats carried the election with 64,607 votes for William J. Bryan; and for William McKinley, Republican, there were 13,491 votes.

Once it was clear that the church would abide by the Manifesto, the way opened naturally for Utah's statehood, after six failures between 1849 and 1887.[23] It is possible that the rejection of the 1887 appeal, taken to Washington in 1888, had some influence in hastening the decision of the apostles to foreswear celestial marriage.[24] Governor Caleb B. West in his report for 1888 to the Secretary of the Interior observed that in some parts of Utah a more tolerant attitude prevailed between Mormons and Gentiles. For example, they united "in celebrating the national anniversary upon the last two occasions." Yet, he concluded, the church still "stubbornly controls the people." Here was another influence which church leaders must have recognized: that Mormon-gentile antagonisms were beginning to abate.

Undoubtedly, whatever may have been the objectives of church leaders, the alignment of the people into the two major political parties which came after the Manifesto, served to dissolve the differences between them. It placed Gentiles and Mormons side by side in the ranks of each party, and both groups became interested in the common national issues of the parties.[25]

The seventh, and final, effort for statehood began with a constitutional convention on March 4, 1895. For the first time a convention to frame a constitution had the approval of Congress. This time the delegates agreed that polgyamy should be banned, and they also agreed to restore suffrage to women. When the people went to the polls on November 5, 1895, to vote on the constitution, they also elected officers for their pending state government. The vote on the constitution was 31,305 favoring it and 7,697 opposing it. As mentioned above, Republicans won the election.

Utah finally gained statehood through a proclamation by President Grover Cleveland on January 4, 1896. The day, even the hour and minute, got notice from the *Deseret News* issue of January 11: "The President's signature," it announced, "was affixed to the proclamation at three minutes past ten A.M., eastern standard time, or three minutes past eight A.M. standard time in Salt Lake City." Two days after the proclamation, with unprecedented ceremony, Utah's first state officers were inaugurated.

Although Mormons and Gentiles had learned to work together politically, the issue of church control of politics was still open. Church leaders did not—possibly could not—surrender the political power they had wielded so long. This situation gave rise to a controversy between Mormon factions. Gentiles were not greatly involved.

Church leaders took the stand that, if Mormons wished to became candidates for public office, they should first secure the approval of their respective priesthood quorums. In other words, the church would keep its hands off the elections but would insist on priesthood approval of candidates. The people were still willing to be guided at the polls by the priesthood mandate, and no Mormon candidate without priesthood approval could have been elected back in the nineties. The same is no longer true, but this change came about slowly.

Resistance to the mandate that the priesthood approve political candidates resulted in a number of brethren being disciplined. In St. George, when the order was submitted to the local priesthood organization, there was one vote against it. This devout pioneer, for his independent judgment, was all but disfellowshiped. Apostle Moses Thatcher, a Democrat, in 1898 aspired to be nominated to the United States Senate by the Utah legislature. He refused to ask the approval of the Apostles' Quorum. Sufficient pressure was brought by the church to nominate Joseph L. Rawlins, Republican and gentile. Thatcher was deprived of his apostleship.

After Utah's statehood the church was involved in a number of issues, each of which has a lively history but does not belong to the Mormon frontier as such. That frontier, for all practical considerations, had closed a decade before statehood. The frontier period was closing about the time that the federal deputy marshals began their hunt for polygamists.

Twice after statehood, Utah and the Mormons got conspicuous public notice. The first case was in 1898, when Brigham H. Roberts, Democrat and polygamist, was elected to Congress. He was denied his seat in the House of Representatives. The issue is pertinent only because, even at that late date, the Mormons believed that they could, if they wished, send a polygamist to Congress. In 1903 Apostle Reed Smoot, a Republican, was nominated by the Utah legislature to be United States senator. He was not a polygamist, but there was a nation-wide drive to deprive him of his seat because it was claimed that the church still secretly approved polygamy. After three years Smoot won his seat, and so ended the last drive of the Mormon-baiters.[26]

NOTES

1. For reports on the Miles case (*Miles* v. *U.S.*, 103 U.S. 304) see *Salt Lake Herald*, November 5, 1878; *Deseret News*, November 13, 1878, May 7, 1879; B. H. Roberts, *Comprehensive History of the Church*, V, 540–47. Carrie Owen Miles went to Washington, where she obtained a government clerical position. Later she became an active lobbyist for the Edmunds bill.

2. These heroic words by Wells were Mormon household slogans for many years. The *Deseret News* of May 7, 1879, contains Wells's statement. For an early account of the marriage ceremonies see John Hyde, Jr., *Mormonism: Its Leaders and Designs*, pp. 90–100. According to this report, oaths were pledged and hatred of Gentiles was encouraged.

3. Gentiles reported that the Mormons in this demonstration allowed the flag to drag in the dust. Although Mormons denied the charge, the story got wide circulation (*Deseret News*, May 14, 1879).

4. In 1879 Secretary of State William M. Evarts asked foreign governments to aid in discouraging Mormon evangelism and migration of Mormons to the United States. The request led to political fun-poking by the American press. The *New York Graphic*, October 15, 1879, wrote:

> I want you to see
> That every—e—e
> Man who migrates
> To the United States,
> Has no more than one wife
> To trouble his life.
> For it is not a good plan
> For a single man
> To marry and carry
> A harem with him.
> I've promised some ladies
> O'er a cup of Bohea
> To stop import of Mormons
> From over the sea.

5. The *Contributor*, October, 1882, p. 75, reports the platform of the People's party. The plank of suffrage read: "While the elective franchise is a privilege conferred by law, the qualifications for its exercise grow out of the condition of citizenship, and is not dependent upon sex or regulated thereby; whatever right of voting originates in the citizenship of men inheres also in the citizenship of women. . . . . The denial of suffrage to women is inconsistent with the principles which underlie our national institutions." Then followed a moral argument in favor of the women taking part in politics, the better to raise their children. "For twelve years the women citizens of Utah have enjoyed the right to vote at all elections in this territory and have exercised it with credit to themselves and to the benefit of the community."

6. Bleak's "Manuscript History of St. George," Book C, p. 493, contains a letter dated December 1, 1884, sent to all branches of the Female Relief Society in the region by Erastus Snow, J. D. T. McAllister, Henry Eyring, and D. D. McArthur, asking all

women to be alert because "the enemy is combining and making strong efforts to overthrow the faith of the Saints in the Holy Order of Celestial Marriage. . . ."

7. This document, issued in May, 1885, is found in *ibid.*, pp. 533–37. The minutes of the Lesser Priesthood Quorum of St. George, February 5 and March 5, 1885, also contain instructions: "Polygamists should cast about and not wait for a warrant or subpoena to be served on them, but take time by the forelock and keep out of the way. We must be wise and not stop around home until an officer comes around. When there are two wives living in the same house, it is better to separate them. Our enemies do not want to put the laws into force, but to grind down the people."

8. *Ibid.*, Book B, September, 1885. Sharp was bishop of the Twentieth Ward, Salt Lake City. He was removed.

9. *Snow* v. *U.S.*, 120 U.S. 274. The segregation principle came up again in the case of Hans Nielson in 1888. At the close of one sentence for cohabitation with one wife, he was arrested for cohabitation with another plural wife. The Supreme Court, May 13, 1889, ruled that the decision in the Snow case applied (*Nielson* v. *U.S.*, 131 U.S. 176).

10. *Cannon* v. *U.S.*, 116 U.S. 55.

11. Roberts, *op. cit.*, VI, 210–11. During 1887 and 1888 there were 314 convictions in Utah and 11 in Idaho.

12. The *Deseret News*, various issues beginning December 22, 1886. The *News* was so outspoken in its condemnation that gentile lawyers persuaded Thompson to sue the paper for $25,000. The case was settled out of court, the *News* paying $1,000.

13. O. W. Powers, of Utah, testified before the Committee on Privileges and Elections of the United States Senate, April 22, 1904, in protest against Reed Smoot being seated by that body. He cited the case of Joseph D. Jones, of Provo, excommunicated for membership of the Loyal League. Bishop J. E. Booth wrote Jones on January 12, 1887, that the principles of the League were opposed to those of the church. He told Jones to choose between his membership in the League and the church. Jones replied on January 15, saying Booth was "mistaken as to the principles of the League, some of which are, as I understand them to be, opposed to the political control and law-defining practices of this or any other church." Jones was excommunicated January 3, 1890 (proceedings of the hearing in *Senate Document No. 486* [59th Cong., 1st sess.], I [1906], 802–4).

14. Bleak, *op. cit.*, Book D, p. 27, contains figures released by the attorney-general in his report to Congress, September 10, 1888, indicating that, since 1875, convictions for polygamy in Utah totaled 16; convictions for unlawful cohabitation, 498; and convictions for adultery or fornication, 16; and that 293 persons were under arrest or awaiting indictment.

15. *Mormon Church* v. *U.S.*, 136 U.S. 2. The court ruled that the government faced the problem of disciplining "a contumacious organization, wielding by its resources an immense power in the Territory of Utah, and employing these resources and that power in constantly attempting to oppose, thwart and subvert the legislation of Congress and the will of the government of the United States."

16. Orson W. Huntsman, of Hebron, who was not a polygamist, wrote in his journal in March, 1892: "I will say that when polygamy was done away with it was a great blow to me. Not that I ever expected to take more wives, yet I might have done so if I ever thought I was good enuf, as I thought that law was only for good men and women. But the thing that bothered me was that the Lord had said to the Prophet Joseph that should be a standing law, and now it was done away. Could it be that the Lord had made a mistake? This question bothered me for a long time, but it came to me all at once that it is still a standing law, and will be forever, but we are not aloud to practice it for a while. I can now rest easy about it."

17. Bleak (*op. cit.*, Book D, p. 176) reported that on September 19, 1892, he went to Beaver and found two indictments against him. He paid a fine of six cents and promised obedience.

18. Joseph Fielding Smith (*Essentials in Church History*, pp. 601–13) offers a summary of the escheat experience but makes no estimates of the amount of property involved. The church has made available no listings of property taken or estimates of the losses. Bleak (*op. cit.*, Book D, p. 201, September 10, 1893) reported a speech made by Apostle Francis M. Lyman in St. George. Lyman said the government had taken a million dollars worth of church property, 40 per cent of which belonged to private individuals. This so-called "private property" had probably been transferred to individuals by the church for keeping.

19. Regarding the "office grab" see Roberts, *op. cit.*, VI, 61–67; *Congressional Record*, August 5, 1882. Note that southern members of Congress opposed giving so much authority to Governor Murray, calling it "carpetbag power."

20. Idaho met the power of mass Mormon voting by a test-oath law. See *Senate Document No. 486* (59th Cong., 1st sess.), II, 265–83. The test oath was upheld by the United States Supreme Court, February 3, 1890. This law, which denied the franchise to persons who believed in polygamy or gave financial aid to the Mormon church, was upheld by the courts (*Davis* v. *Beason*, 133 U.S. 333).

21. Affidavit by J. F. Tolton, of Beaver, dated October 29, 1895 (*Senate Document No. 486* [59th Cong., 1st sess.], I, 854, testimony of O. W. Powers, of Utah). Levi Savage, of Toquerville, wrote in his journal, June 11, 1892, that President Woodruff and Apostle George Q. Cannon had given political advice at a church conference in St. George. "They themselves seemed to favor Republicanism." Bleak (*op. cit.*, Book D, p. 157) mentions this meeting. The children of some of the Saints who "volunteered" on that occasion to become Republicans have for that reason remained Republicans.

22. *Senate Document No. 486* (59th Cong., 1st sess.), I, 802–4. Informed Mormons today readily admit that the church did wield such political influence during the pioneer period.

23. The *Deseret News*, March 8 and June 14, 1882. During this period before the polygamy raids, as during the Civil War, church leaders predicted a dire end to the government if it persecuted the Saints. Joseph Fish, then residing at Snowflake, Arizona, reported a speech made in that place by Wilford Woodruff, who "prophesied that there would be no United States in ten years from this time, that the government would be broken up."

24. Roberts, *op. cit.*, VI, 281–83. Utah in 1887 hoped to be on the bandwagon with several states admitted to the Union in 1888.

25. Democrats, not Republicans, were sent to Washington in 1894 to pave the way for statehood. The committee was headed by Governor West and the former congressional delegate John T. Caine. The latter, who had served the church so well, was apparently being shelved as a result of the trend toward Republicanism. Brigham H. Roberts was one of the young Democrats who had to be disciplined (*ibid.*, pp. 323–46).

26. Brigham H. Roberts, a polygamist, was elected to Congress in 1898. Congress denied Roberts his seat (*ibid.*, pp. 362–69).

Apostle Reed Smoot, a Republican, was nominated by the Utah legislature in 1903 to the United States Senate. Although not a polygamist, there arose a public clamor that Smoot be denied a seat in the Senate because he was one of the top leaders in a church that still believed in polygamy. It was also charged that the church had winked at the provisions of the Manifesto of 1890. The Smoot case was tried in the press and pulpit of the United States for three years. The Senate on February 20, 1907, voted to seat him (*Senate Document No. 486* [59th Cong., 1st sess.]).

CHAPTER XIII

PRIESTHOOD GOVERNMENT IN ZION

IN THE conflict between church and civil authority the issues did not concern so much the objectives of the government as its control. Gentiles and Mormons vied for control to gain economic advantage. However, Mormon reasoning was not altogether economic in motivation. It must not be forgotten that the Mormons believed they were, by divine designation, especially fitted to rule and that the Gentiles were not. They believed—

a) That there can be no just government that does not come from God;
b) That authority to govern rests with the priesthood bestowed by God upon his Chosen People; and
c) That the keys of knowledge and power inherent in the priesthood have been entrusted to them, making them the Chosen People.

Believing so, Mormons were not inconsistent with themselves in opposing gentile civil authority. They supported the Constitution and believed that the federal government had been designed by God, but they damned the people in control of the federal government. They expected all gentile government to fall during the Civil War, and they would be the government.

Mormon priesthood authority began when Joseph Smith asked questions of the Lord on May 15, 1839. He and Oliver Cowdery wondered "by what right can men speak for the Lord?" While they prayed for light, John the Baptist appeared before them. He gave instruction to Joseph and Oliver, ordained them to the priesthood of Aaron, and they baptized each other.[1]

Thus was restored to earth the Aaronic or lesser priesthood, named for the brother of Moses. It was limited to minor functions: the "ministering of angels" and the right to preach, to baptize, and to give blessings.

Soon thereafter Joseph and Oliver were visited by Peter, James, and John—apostles who walked with Jesus in ancient times. These holy men ordained Smith and his scribe to the Melchizedek priesthood.[2] This is the priesthood of miracles—of healing the sick, casting out devils, speaking in tongues, and prophesying. The greater priesthood contains all the powers which inhere in the lesser, plus the right to organize God's church.

Within the two levels of priesthood are several degrees of authority. A boy of 12 years enters the Aaronic priesthood when he is ordained a *deacon.* The pioneer deacon did chores and errands in the community. If a man were away serving the church as missionary, these boys were expected to offer their services to his wife: chop wood, carry water, hoe the garden. They helped the widows, too. They swept and started fires in the meeting house. Each boy was expected to keep the bishop informed about sickness, births, and other matters of record in his neighborhood. If the stock broke into a garden or field, it was for the deacons to drive them out and fix the fence.

Next step in the Aaronic priesthood is the *teacher*, after which the youth in his teens may be ordained a *priest.* With these higher degrees of priesthood comes more authority, much as the soldier gains if he is advanced to be a corporal and later a sergeant.

In the Melchizedek priesthood are two grades, the lesser of which is the *elder*, and the next is the *high priest.* Both are "elders," but the high priest is one of senior status. Stake presidents, bishops, and other men in authority and their counselors are generally high priests.

Priesthood is a blessing from heaven for the men. Women do not belong. But priesthood is not the church. That is an agency created by priesthood authority through which priesthood operates. Brigham Young once said the priesthood was a trust of the Quorum of the Apostles. They held the "keys." Others might organize a church, but it would not survive. One faction, however, did pull away and did survive, but it claims the same priesthood.

The church is both a geographical and organization concept. Geographically, it is spread over the earth in areas called *stakes* and *wards*. As an organization it is managed by men of the priesthood. One is *ordained* to the priesthood, but he is *set apart* or *called* to office in the church.

In 1941 there were one hundred and thirty-five stakes of the church in the United States. They have been organized wherever the Saints have gathered in sufficient number. For example, in the city of Washington the church once had a missionary unit. Later a permanent organization was set up, and local officers selected. This was a ward. As the number of Saints increased in Washington, the number of wards increased to three—sufficient to warrant a stake organization.

Functionally, the church operates through the quorums of the priesthood: the lesser priesthood, the Seventies (elders concerned with missionary work), and the high priests. Also, there are the Sunday schools, the primary schools (weekday play schools for children), the Mutual Improvement Associations for young people, and the Female Relief Societies for the mothers. There may be other auxilliaries as the needs demand. Each of these functions is organized from headquarters, down to the most remote place. For example, there is a general Sunday-school board in Salt Lake City, and in every stake there is a Sunday-school board from whence the line of authority extends through the bishop to the ward Sunday school. The programs for each function are made and distributed, with all instructions, from headquarters. This uniformity was less strict in pioneer times, but the line of authority was the same then.

It was this all-embracing unity and organization of the priesthood that agitated federal officials sent to hold public office in Utah. They were often puzzled or frustrated that the Mormons seemed able to govern themselves without civil agencies. Gentile public officials found themselves blocked by organizations from which they were excluded. They complained: "No matter what authority we hold from Congress, Brigham Young is governor and law-giver." They referred to the priesthood government to which local civil government was generally subservient.

THE ST. GEORGE TEMPLE

First Mormon temple to be completed fully and put into use. The Kirtland, Ohio, temple was finished for partial use when it was abandoned. The Nauvoo Temple had to be abandoned under similar circumstances at the point of being completed. The St. George Temple was started in 1870 and completed in 1877. It was built with labor donated from the settlements around and from contributions of cattle, wheat, wood, and dairy products. The upper picture shows the temple near completion, the black lava masonry walls about to be plastered. The lower picture shows the temple in 1933. It stands apart from the town and is the first structure seen by travelers approaching from the north or the south.

The operation of priesthood government is the subject of this chapter.

The materials offered here to illustrate the operation of priesthood, were taken, in the main, from the church records of the St. George Stake of Zion. Similar material and similar cases could be found in other stakes of Zion.

For the period under review—1862 until about 1890—Washington County was the civil division corresponding to the St. George Stake, although from time to time the stake exercised authority over communities beyond, some of them in Nevada or Arizona. The structure of the High Council presiding over the St. George Stake was the same as that which formed the first government in Salt Lake Valley, which was patterned after the model designed by Joseph Smith at Kirtland. The Council is presided over by a president and his two counselors, who sit at the head of the table. Along the table, six on each side, sit the twelve councilmen, all high priests and some of them also bishops of the wards comprised in the stake.[3]

As the records show, the High Council received cases or problems either directly or on appeal from the wards. In the bishop's court, procedure was informal. At meetings the bishop or one of his councelors presided, and the elders of the ward shared in the deliberations. If the problem was a complaint, the two sides were heard. The aggrieved party might appeal from the bishop to the High Council.

High Council procedure was usually more formal. In the case of a trial the accused person would have assigned to him one or two councilmen to aid in presenting his case. Councilmen do not act as lawyers to supress evidence and browbeat witnesses. This is reminiscent of early church dislike for court methods. There was in the pioneer council no swearing on earth, since all were expected to be truthful; else, God help them!

There used to be disagreement in the St. George Stake about the lines of jurisdiction between the priesthood and civil authority. The High Council on May 11, 1869, sought to state the bounds of its authority. Elder Wooley remarked that the councils in Salt Lake City restricted their authority, but "we have a wider field of usefulness." He thought the High Council had jurisdiction over "all matters pertaining to the welfare of the Stake of Zion, either spiritual or temporal: to see that bishops, presiding elders, civil authorities, and others do their duties in their official capacity."[4] The High Council agreed with Elder Wooley.

In April, 1872, Levi Savage, Jr., lodged charges against John Nebeker, probate judge of Kane County, which then included Toquerville, alleging "unfair decisions and awardings." Savage asked the High Council to review an action of the judge. Also a member of the body, Nebeker argued that his official acts as judge could not be so reviewed, but he was told that the Council had "jurisdiction over the acts of every member of the Church, whether officials or otherwise." However, the Council upheld Nebeker's court decision.

The court of the bishop also took precedence over the justice of the peace, and this is seen in the story of a Gentile from Silver Reef who paid court to a young lady in Washington. This happened about 1875, when Dixie was disturbed by the influx of so many miners. The young Gentile received notice to appear before the bishop's court, which he did, only to scoff at the elders. "You can't try me without a charge; just asking me if I'm guilty of something. I am a free citizen and can go or come as I please. If you have a real charge, I demand a trial by a real court."

One of the elders was also justice of the peace. He said: "Bishop, we have a right to know who this man is and whether his intentions are honorable. It is our duty to protect our women against strangers who would pick the grape and trample the vine. As justice of the peace, I can try this man for vagrancy, but I shan't. I say the bishop's court is good enough for any man who will not lie."

Another elder spoke up: "Bishop, I favor giving this man one hour to think it over. If he does not then want to submit to this court, then he better high tail away. If he stays and you don't shoot him, Bishop, I will."

They sent the man outdoors to make his decision. Ten minutes later he was riding toward Silver Reef, never to return. The much amused elders concluded that he really did not love the girl.

The High Council on May 29, 1876, issued from St. George instructions to probate judges for handling domestic cases in which there was some legal property settlement. The courts were advised that children in divorce cases might be assigned to the mother only if she was "able to support the children herself; but if the mother could not support the children without aid, then let the father have the care of them."

Orson W. Huntsman wrote in his journal for July 14, 1899, about an altercation between Jefferson Hunt and William Pulsipher. Hunt (not the Mormon Battalion veteran) injured Pulsipher with a stone, bruising his head so that several stitches had to be taken. Justice of the Peace Daniel M. Tyler was to hear the case when Bishop Terry interceded and "placed it in the hands of the ward teachers, but they could not settle the trouble as it was of too long standing." There had been a sort of feud between the five Pulsipher and six Hunt families. The bishop had to settle the case.

A bishop's court in St. George in 1865 heard the case of *Wilson* v. *Grange.* The latter borrowed a wagon from Wilson; and, when pressed for payment two years later, he made shoes for the Wilson family. Wilson claimed the shoes were poorly made. Grange countered that the wagon was old and rickety, not worth the $142.50 demanded. The bishop valued the wagon at $90.00, the sum due Wilson; the shoes at $71.45, the amount due Grange. This left a balance due Wilson of $18.55, to be paid in shoes of good quality or in greenbacks, at Wilson's option.

A year later there came before the same bishop's court the case of *Keats* v. *Contcher.* Keats sold some land to Contcher, for which he was to receive twenty sheep and goats, two 3-year-old heifers, one 2-year-old heifer, and $55 in other stock, in firewood, or in fence posts. The agreement was oral. Contcher paid two 3-year-old heifers, some posts, and some wood. He also made some shoes for Keats and considered the bill paid.

Keats appealed to the bishop, who ordered Contcher to deliver a 2-year-old heifer and "20 head of sheep and goats as per contract without expense to Brother Keats, and with their growth and increase," and within reasonable time to pay Keats $36.60, after which he would have "peaceable possession of the lot."

In a priesthood meeting in St. George on January 4, 1871, the brethren settled the rules for managing the cowherd against Indian raids:

> The herdsmen of the cowherd shall receive 25¢ per head per week. Produce to be rated at the following prices: flour 10¢ per pound, molasses $2 per gallon, corn $2 per bushel, and other produce proportionate, 20 pounds of flour per head per annum to be paid quarterly in advance. . . . .
>
> Herd to be shut up in the fartherst corral from the point of driving, the horn to be blown while passing to and fro through the city. Herdsman to be responsible for any damage stock may do while under his charge, also for any damage or loss that may occur by stock being left out of the city at night. Herdsman to collect his bills quarterly, and should there be any delinquents, report them to their respective bishops. Bishops will collect the same at the expense of the delinquents.

In December, 1878, a petition was presented to the priesthood of St. George protesting the Canaan co-operative's monopoly of the meat market. The people wanted a competing market. But it was their duty as Saints to support the Canaan butchers and to have "strong confidence" in the co-operative. However, some of the leading brethren were in an uncomfortable position with their monopoly, and another market was permitted. Where was the city council when this issue came up? These gentlemen were members of the priesthood quorum that made the decision.

The items below were copied, without correction, from the ward records of Santa Clara, the Swiss community settled in 1862. These pious and literal pioneers built from deep poverty one of Dixie's edens.

> *February 25, 1879:* Gotfried and Edward Stucki have been appointed for fieldmasters in the lower field, and Conrad Naegeli for the upper field; for each head have to pay 50 cent for teiting out, and when the owner could not be found, the should bring them to the strepound. Jacob Graf, Richard Wilson and John S. Stucki have to take charge of the diferent gates to shut, if ene man or boy left the gates open must pay 25 cent to the gate kipper.
>
> We all have unamously voted for to pave the watterditch with rock and

make headgates and boxes; a committee where appointed to pave the upper-side of the ditch. John Hafen, John Stucki, Sen. and Casper Gubler and Richard Wilson with them as watermaster. All the owner on the main street have to help together. . . . .

March 30, 1879: The subject wars to build a haus for the poor in our ward of Santa Clara and it wars taken a vote and excepted that we will build a haus 12 by 15 feet between John S. Stucki and Friedrich Riber. Sam Stucki, Casper Gubler and John Stucki, Sen. have been appointed as a building committee to gather the lumber, neals and glas from the bretherin in the ward.

July 27, 1879: Bp. Ensign lead bevor the bretherin the mader if we all would be willing to tacke the cowherd to the creekbead for a season to safe feet for the winter. We all agree with annammous vote to do so. Two men wars appointed as assistance to herd. Captain John Stucki, Sen. with names be Marthin Bauman and Sam Stucki we as a people give unto these three men the power to say where the herdsmen has to go with the herd, and how menne have to help together on the diferent plases, and evere time has to be a good man with the herd. . . . .

Another important subjeckt wars lead bevor the bretherin was selling wein and liquor to the Indians. Bp. Ensign ask the people if they are willing to be on the watsh for such ackt and make their report to the proper pleace. We all prommis we would by saing I. The next subjekt wars to find a home for Bro. Waites family, witch wars given in the hand of John Hafen as teacher to see to.

Santa Clara had no civil government, being a village; but with the elders around the bishop, none was needed. The priesthood handled problems simply and directly, as indicated above, and the people were satisfied.

A man named "S." in St. George was accused of stealing from the Wooley, Lund, and Judd store. The bishop referred the case to the High Council. S. argued that he did not steal the boy's hat and the ax handles, as charged. He admitted looking at these articles in the store, but he made no purchase. On the way home he met a man with boys' hats and ax handles for sale. The man owed him money; so he took these articles in payment. He would not name the man. The High Council was offended that one of its members should offer such an alibi. S. was suspended until he could bring proof of his innocence. Some time in 1888, several months later, he was cut off the church.

In 1869 the High Council heard the case of two men who disputed over priority rights to cut timber on Pine Valley Mountain. Erastus Snow said for the Council that the right to cut timber had to be regulated by the probate court. Brown said that the court had ruled that the timber was free to all. Snow took issue, claiming that the court had no right to give such free access to the timber supply. The court had a responsibility to see that the natural resources were used without resort to waste.

Some days later the Council considered the matter again, because there had been some criticism of the priesthood for presuming to advise the probate court about its duty. The *Brown v. Burgess* case was then passed back to the court, with this reservation: "If we find that after proper investigation we shall be obliged to differ with the county court, we shall represent this to them."

The High Council of the St. George Stake handled some cases which might have been tried by the bishops, but there was a special reason in each case. For example, Brother W. of Washington and Brother H. of St. George agreed to purchase a threshing machine in 1869. W. freighted the machine from Salt Lake City, but he paid nothing on the original cost. He used the machine a year and took half the profit. H. demanded the machine at the end of the season. W. refused to comply. The Council ordered H. to pay W. for freighting the machine and then H. could take possession. This case was probably handled by the Council because it involved disputants who lived in different wards.

Normally, fisticuff cases were handled by the bishops, but here is one that went to the High Council and involved one of its members, Brother Moody. The year, 1871. Moody bought a lot from Brother Paddock. The question arose whether Moody was pledged to pay cash. Each man called the other a liar, with the result that Moody got knocked down. The Council rebuked both men—Paddock for striking Moody, and Moody for "giving more or less provocation and for having it in his heart to strike Brother Paddock." Each had to apologize.

In November, 1867, Bishop A. P. Winsor, of Grafton ward, was brought before the High Council by his neighbors. The fiery bishop later became riding boss for the co-operative herds because Brigham Young trusted him. On this occasion the issue involved possession of some lumber that had been salvaged from a flume recently torn down. The bishop attempted to haul the lumber away. The neighbors objected, claiming that the lumber had been jointly paid for and should be divided. Winsor ignored them, and they took the case before the magistrate, a Mormon. Winsor was offended and would not accept the decision of "the court of the land."

The neighbors appealed to the High Council, claiming that they could not take the case to the bishop himself. They charged "unchristianlike conduct in insulting, abusing and threatening a number of men that were peacably met to transact business"; also the use of profane language "and otherwise conducting himself in a most disgusting manner." They deposed that Winsor said in the presence of the magistrate that "he did not give a damn, and turned his buttocks to the brethren, clapped it with his hand . . . . ," and told them what they could do, swearing all the while.

For this shocking deportment the Council ordered Winsor to resign from the bishopric and to "make acknowledgment of the wrong done the brethren, and far as known, to the ward; also that he may be forgiven of the brethren; and that the brethren make acknowledgment to the bishop for being in too much haste in dividing the lumber without the bishop being consulted . . . . and for their action in taking him before the magistrate."

Winsor was the kind of man of force and decision who could get things done, which was the reason Brigham Young first placed him in charge of the Canaan co-operative herd and later of the Winsor Castle Stock Growing Company. In 1874 he was brought again before the High Council, this time by John R. Young for "unchristianlike conduct in using abusive language and for publicly and at different times stating that he knows that I have stolen 20 head or more of tithing sheep." The men had an argument, and Winsor was knocked down. The Council ordered Winsor and Young to apologize to each other.

There lived in St. George a good Saint named Romney, who sometimes drank too much wine. In January, 1872, he answered to the Council, of which he was a member, for "acting up" on New Year's night and for challenging Brother Samuel Adams and others to fistic combat. He admitted the charge and promised to deport himself more correctly. Two years later this brother asked to be taken again into the fellowship of the Council. The request was granted because he "had taken the chastisement in a proper spirit and had suffered a great deal." The priesthood was that tolerant.

To the priesthood a demonstration of humility meant more than it can mean in the courts of law, and many a sin was wiped out by the sinner standing up in the congregation and confessing. However, there was an occasional Saint who found repentance and apology quite easy. For such the priesthood used harsher methods—for example, excommunication and rebaptism.

Two families in Toquerville got into a feud because of a collision between their teen-age boys. Willie A. called Jimmie B. a hard name. Jimmie's father went to see Willie's parents: "What are you going to do about your Willie swearing that way?" "Going to do nothing," Brother A. replied. "Your Jimmie is one of the worst profaners in this place." Brother B. went to the bishop, who said: "It is an affair of the boys and they will settle it naturally. We should be patient."

Some days later Jimmie was returning with his young lady from choir practice. Willie passed remarks. An hour later the boys met, and Willie was worsted in a fight. This time it was Willie's parents who demanded action by the bishop. Other families got interested. Willie and his friends were blamed for many pranks. Jimmie and his friends were blamed for other pranks, including the rape of a squaw.

The hearing lasted an afternoon, with all the elders of the town present. The bishop said he could not determine the worse offender. Much of the hearing was devoted to learning whether one of the boys had called the other a "God damned" so-and-so, or merely a "damned" so-and-so. The elders concluded it was high time an example was made of boys who profaned; so both boys, to the agony of their parents, had to publicly apologize.

Public apology was a potent discipline for the forgiving as well as for the forgiven. In the case of the boys at Toquerville, the public apology put an end to the issue. In cases that stirred gossip before being handled by the priesthood, gossip generally ceased after public apology had been made. It was priesthood policy to limit apology to the area of knowledge. If only members of the priesthood knew of the offense, then forgiveness was required only of the priesthood.

In 1866 a St. George bishop heard the case of Brother J. B., of Pine Valley. Apparently this man was rough at times, because later he was brought up for carelessly and in fun frightening a man with a gun. On this occasion Brother J. B. had a family quarrel. In the course of the argument he tipped over the table and broke some dishes. Dishes were precious. His wife was angry, and his daughter took sides against him. He "pushed and kicked her out of the house." A neighbor came "and clinched him and threw him down." J. B. got an ax and threatened the neighbor. The bishop ordered J. B. disfellowshiped. His wife interceded; so the bishop concluded that perhaps J. B. had suffered enough. He reversed his decision, saying to the repentant man: "If your family will forgive you, we can."

Although Mormon young people did a fair share of yielding to temptation, the priesthood was generally patient. In reviewing the records in the St. George Stake it appears that tolerance served the community as well as discipline, but it generally came after repentance. In these records are found many morals cases, some of which, although taken seriously in Zion, might have been overlooked elsewhere. For example, a St. George man in 1879 confessed to his bishop that he had had "unlawful cohabitation with his wife before marriage." The case was referred to the High Council, but the high priests could not agree, although praising the brother for accusing himself.

Erastus Snow said: "Who is hurt by this act, the sin being with them?" He answered: "It is a sin against the community by taking the fruit before it is ripe." No punishment was meted out to the woman in this case, but the man had to be rebaptized.

Some years previous to the above case a man confessed to the High Council that fifteen years earlier and five years before marriage he was working in the California gold diggings. While there, he yielded to temptation and patronized a prostitute. He waited several years before confessing to his wife. She forgave him but feared his soul would burn if he did not tell the bishop. The bishop appealed to the Council. The man was excommunicated with the understanding that he would be reconfirmed after baptism.

Another conscience case was that of a man who confessed sin with his deceased wife before their marriage. He wanted to clear her record by taking the blame, so that she would not have to answer in the next life. He was sent out to be rebaptized. Then there was the case of a brother from Toquerville who confessed adultery with a servant girl. The girl was about to be honorably married in the temple; and, according to the record, since "he knew that not only himself, but several others, had shared the lady's favor, he felt he should stop her being married in the temple." The record did not indicate what action was taken against the woman, but the self-confessed sinner was cut off the church and told that after a period of penance he would be restored, but first he would have to make public apology in his community.

In 1883 a Brother G. was summoned before the High Council on a charge of drunkenness and adultery. Bishop Charles Terry referred the case because he failed to get the truth about Brother G.'s illicit relations with his divorced wife, Jerusha. When Stake President J. D. T. McAllister asked G., "Have you had sexual intercourse with Jerusha G. since being divorced?" he answered: "I never have nor never will do or say one act that will reflect censure on that lady, Jerusha G."

Here was "stiff neckedness" where humility was expected. The Council ruled that Brother G. "be allowed one month to set himself right before the brethren in the ward where he belongs, and in the event of such a thing not taking place . . . . he will be cut off the Church."

Brother G. made public apology in his ward. The bishop ordered that he be rebaptized. Brother G. replied: "I need not be re-baptized for I was not cut off the Church." Bishop Terry was not moved by this technical argument. Then Brother G. pleaded: "I ask further time for baptism, until warmer weather." To this request the bishop's counselor, Brother Empy replied: "Cold water will not hurt a repentant man."

The case of an unfaithful plural wife was brought before the High Council in 1883. She pleaded that Brother A. H., her husband, had beaten her, that he was often drunk, and that he failed to provide. She wanted to be free to marry Brother F. B., but her husband would not divorce her.

Councilman Cannon, who was advising the woman, offered the explanation that "she probably did not realize the nature of the charge. . . . . She had applied to the probate court for a bill of divorce but was told that the law did not recognize plural marriages. She may have gone away and done this deed thinking she was free from all restraint." Decision was deferred. Within a few days the woman eloped and married her young man. Both were cut off the church.

The records of the High Council of the St. George Stake indicate that between 1882 and 1885 a moral purge was under way. Perhaps this drive for virtue had been prompted by the pending prosecutions for polygamy under the Edmunds bill of 1882. Morals cases were numerous until after 1890, when the Manifesto relaxed the drive against the polygamists. In that period of strict moral surveillance many young couples were brought to task only because they were betrayed by the birth of a baby too soon after marriage.

After the Manifesto there began a division of opinion among the High Council members. The overstrict brethren "did not see why all who commit sin should not confess." They thought that too much was being condoned. Apostle Francis M. Lyman was visiting with the Council during one of these discussions. He said: "Young people who sin against each other and afterwards fix the matter up and marry each other, they by doing this have made full satisfaction." Concerning secret sinners, Lyman said: "If a person makes satisfaction to another and it is known to them only, it is nobody's business but theirs, and should not go further."

The priesthood had its share of domestic problems. For example, in 1869 a man named Reese in St. George was brought before the High Council because he failed to support one of his wives. He answered: "I am patriarch in my family, and I am responsible directly to God for my acts." The Council ruled that "no patriarchal rights take precedence" over the authority of the priesthood. Reese accepted the verdict and agreed to provide.

A Brother Hall was hailed before the High Council in St. George in 1864. He had divorced one of his wives in 1861, when he was living in Ogden. He moved with the rest of his family. It was too expensive supporting his divorced wife and her children in Ogden; so he set out to move them to Beaver. In the course of transporting the woman and her children, he and his former wife became reconciled and resumed marital relations. This caused gossip when Hall arrived in Beaver. His loyal wife became offended and went to Ogden. Later Hall and his divorced wife separated again. With both wives away, Hall found himself in more trouble when called to answer a charge of adultery. By that time he had moved to Washington County.

Hall was offended by both women. The estranged wife in Ogden was demanding support, and the divorced one had already transferred her affections to a Gentile at Beaver. She had married the Gentile, but he soon deserted her, and she was asking Hall to support her children.

The High Council referred this case to Brigham Young for untangling; but, pending the decision, Hall was disfellowshiped. During the next several years the Hall family problems came up two or three times. The wife who went to Ogden came back but soon left him again. The priesthood was appealed to. Hall charged her with "violent, boisterous and unbecoming" conduct toward him and alleged that she had turned her children against him. "I have suffered ten deaths. I dare not take a second wife."

Sister Hall replied: "He says I am down on plurality. I deny it. The wives that left him say they could live with me but not with him." The Council ordered a separation and named a committee to divide the property. The wife was warned to accept the division of property without resort to litigation. The committee made the division, designating each cow, pig, article of furniture, and kitchen utensil to be given Sister Hall. Hall then, according to order, provided a house for her; but later Sister Hall would not accept the house. She repulsed Hall's "peace overtures," and the Council granted a divorce.

Polygamy cases before the Council were not so numerous as the writer expected to find. This does not prove that plurality did not cause friction; but it does seem that, once entering polygamy, the plural wives did not try to make an issue of it. Most polygamists were responsible men and financially able to support their families. A number of cases were found of widows of polygamists disagreeing about the division of property. In once instance, Widow No. 1, the first wife, claimed a larger share of the estate because she was older than the other widow and less able to care for herself. The second woman wanted most of the estate because she had young children, whereas the children of the other woman were grown and could care for her. Unable to satisfy both widows, the Council ruled that both were good women and had been faithful wives. The estate was divided equally.[5]

In 1876 Brother M., of Washington, brought charges against Brother C. for retaining portions of his property and for assault. The bishop sent the case to the High Council. It developed that the real trouble was because Brother C. had been courting M.'s daughter. There was disagreement between the parents about the courtship, but there had been other disagreements which the son-in-law had tried to adjust.

The Council found Brother M. at fault: "When a man cannot live at peace with his family, it is better that he stay away from them." He was ordered: "Let her have your property in Washington, except your tools, and give her a divorce, and you get another wife. . . . ." He was not told to support the children; merely ridded of his wife, who complained about his conduct.

By virtue of his priesthood the huband is patriarchal head of his family, although accountable to the priesthood. His wife and children are subject to him, for there must be order in Zion. A good wife did not nag. A nagging wife was brought before a St. George bishop by her husband, Brother B. He alleged she created scenes, disturbed the neighbors, and used shocking language against him. She countered that B. was giving attention to other women and neglecting her. For this she followed and nagged him.

Elder William Carter said he considered Brother B. a good man, "although he lacks in not being master of his own house at times." Bishop Robert Gardner ruled that the charge against Sister B. had been sustained, that she was not worthy of a standing in the church because she tried to blacken her husband's character. She was cut off the church until she repented, and Brother B. was told to appeal to the president of the church for permission to take another wife.

Occasionally the High Council was called on to settle some matter involving the next life, on the theory that what the church binds or frees on earth is bound or free in heaven. Two widows from Washington came with the request that one of them be divorced from their mutual deceased spouse. Widow No. 2 said that the divorce had been promised before the husband died, but he took no steps to fill the promise. The first wife, Widow No. 1, confirmed this testimony. The other woman had an opportunity to marry again, but she wished to be divorced so as to be free from her deceased husband in the next life. Without such a divorce any children she might have by the second husband would be claimed by the first in the hereafter, and she, too, would be claimed by him. No good Saint wanted to marry a woman if she and her children were to be claimed by another man in the hereafter.

Normally the Council would not divorce the living from the dead, but in this case it was decided that the dead would not be offended, because before his demise he had agreed to the divorce. Then came the problem of the children, who could not be claimed by a mother without a husband. They were given to her father until she should marry again, when, if to a good man, she and her husband might adopt them in his name.

In 1886 a woman in Pine Valley appealed to the High Council with this problem:

> My first husband . . . . became insane and went back east. My second husband apostatized. I was sealed to him as a second wife. I had two children by him. My third husband . . . . was disfellowshipped for not conforming to requirements made of him by the United Order, and afterwards was shot and killed by A. B., the seducer of his daughter. He also shot and killed A. B. This is my true condition, in short. I now have the opportunity of being sealed to a good man, which has been my desire for many years. If you will consider this a proper course for me to pursue, please answer the accompanying recommend.

Technically, as far as church records were concerned, this woman had no husband. Being a faithful Saint, she was freed from each of them when they lost their church standing. She was as unattached "as though she had never known them." The "recommend" mentioned is a form statement signed by a bishop declaring that the bearer is worthy to enter the temple. The Council saw fit to honor the recommend of the Pine Valley woman.

In 1876 Wife No. 2 of Brother V. complained that he failed to support her. He stated that "in their marriage contract she promised not to be an expense to him, as she had means of her own that she wished to use and control in the maintenance of herself and three sons." The hearing revealed a misunderstanding between the two wives of Brother V. The second wife said the first had suggested marriage to her husband. Wife No. 1 denied the statement, saying that the second wife, then a widow, came to her with this plea:

> Sister V., I guess you think I am very bold to want to come into your family. Brother Young counseled me to get a good husband. . . . . It is just to carry out the principle of our religion that I wish to be sealed to Brother V. I would never think of having pleasure with a man at my age. That is not the design of this proposition.

The Council decided that Brother V. had assumed a responsibility and could not shirk it, even though Wife No. 2 had wanted only to be sealed to a good man so that she would not be alone in the next world. Her purposes were in keeping with her religion, but it was difficult for her not to impose earthly claims on the husband she initially wanted only for heavenly status.

The priesthood assumed to bind in heaven economic agreements that were made on earth. This is illustrated by the following letter from Dan C. Sill, a literal Saint of Dixie, sent on March 27, 1899, to President Lorenzo Snow, then head of the church. The devout man's letter was referred by Snow to the stake president in St. George, where it reposes. After relating some of the facts leading up to the loan made more than forty years before, the 69-year-old Sill wrote:

> At the time Elder Orson Hyde was presiding over the Carson Valley Mission, I was living in California and had saved some money. I went to Carson Valley and stayed at Brother Hyde's. He had been having a mill built, and explained to me that he was in debt, and asked if I would pay one of his creditors $500. I agreed to do so, and paid the man, a Gentile, that amount in gold coin. I gathered in Salt Lake in 1857 with other members of the Carson Valley Mission. I accompanyed Brother Hyde to President Brigham Young's office and it was arranged that I receive credit in tithing for $150 cash, out of the loan to Brother Hyde. Afterward Brother Hyde gave me an order for $200 on Eli B. Kelsey, which was paid in sheep and a cow and calf.
>
> In due course the balance of $150 was called to the attention of Brother Hyde, and at the time of the dedication of the St. George Temple, April, 1877, and it was agreed between Brother Hyde and myself, here in St. George, to defer the payment of $150 for this life, on condition that the transaction and balance due be entered on the Church records. I have neglected to see that this was done, and now respectfully ask that it be recorded in such a way as you may designate. I have no desire to draw this amount, and have not had since the agreement with Brother Hyde, that payment be deferred, but would like to have it recorded in our Church records somewhere.

For such evidence of faith the angels in heaven rejoice. Apostle Hyde died a few months later. It should be noted that the humble Brother Sill had collected no interest on the debt and that no mention was made of collecting interest hereafter. Did Elder Sill, after waiting so many years, suddenly have doubts about the apostolic debtor? The answer is: Whatever his opinion in 1899 about Apostle Hyde, he had no doubts about the power of the priesthood to bind the debt in heaven.

One of the ideals of the United Order was to create a new society in which there would be no lawyers, for in the true society of the Saints lawyers were useless. This may have been the basis for pioneer priesthood discipline of Saints who took their issues to court. Mention has already been made of this aversion. Another example was the case of Brother D., who was brought by a neighbor before the High Council in 1872 but would not consent to a priesthood review. The neighbor objected to the "gentile court" and complained to the Council. The term "gentile court" was a misnomer in this instance, for the judge would have been a Mormon; but it was objected to because that was the gentile way. Brother D. was censured by the Council.

In 1885 a Brother E. brought charges against a Brother W. "for taking him before the law of the land and endeavoring to defraud him of his property." Brother W. forced the case into the civil court, and when he was called before the High Council he insisted that it was his right under the law. The Council ruled: "It is not for any member to say he will not be amenable to the High Council when a charge is preferred." For his stubbornness Brother W. was disfellowshiped. He appeared later before that body and apologized for his conduct.

After 1890 the Council began to relent in its prejudice against courts of the land, and men were not rebuked for taking their problems to a justice of the peace or the probate court, where they used to go only in cases in which Gentiles were involved. In 1893 the High Council of the St. George Stake indicated with reference to a dispute over water rights: "We are told to not handle legal questions or questions liable to be taken to the courts."

Most precious of the powers claimed by the priesthood is the power to heal the sick and to cast out devils. The Saints have good biblical support for their belief in evil spirits. Pioneer records are replete with cases of healing the sick and of casting out spirits.

While the Devil may enter a person's body and cause him to writhe in pain, he may also torment persons ill from other causes. For example, this story is told by Thomas S. Terry and is found under his name in the *Latter-Day Saints' Biographical Encyclopaedia*. This took place about 1874, after Terry had been several days in bed.

> While lying in my room I was visited by the Devil. Standing before me with his hand upon the bedpost, he said, "You are sick and you had better give up and die, and not go through the sickness in store for you. You will never have another passage through your bowels." I did not answer and the evil one left the room. I immediately called my wife and said, "I am going to be very sick. I want you to see that I have a passage of the bowels every day." For six weeks I was at death's door, but through the administration of the elders I recovered.

The priesthood was not baffled by illness known to be caused by evil spirits in the body. Illness not caused by evil forces was treated by prayer and anointing, but there was no objection among the pioneers against the various home remedies in vogue at the time. When the elders were called in to deal with illness, perhaps they formed a prayer circle about the bed of illness, men and women kneeling and holding hands. Perhaps the elders would anoint the head of the sick and pray for him with their hands touching his head. There is in Mormon lore no end of testimony of healing by "the laying on of hands."[6]

A legendary case of healing relates to the construction of the St. George Temple. John Burt, a plasterer, fell from the scaffold, dropping about seventy feet. To quote the official record:

> When picked up he was apparently lifeless, but Elders John O. Angus, Wm. H. Thompson and Jos. H. Randall at once laid hands upon his head and administered to him; Bro. Angus being speaker. While doing so, the man began to gasp for breath and showed signs of life. He was put upon a stretcher and taken to his boarding house. Upon medical examination, it was found not a bone was broken. By the blessing of the Lord, he was back upon his work on the temple in a couple of weeks.[7]

Often the priesthood resorted to the device of baptizing the sick for their recovery, a practice still followed in the temples. In 1856 came the "Reformation" and a wave of repentance. Everyone had to be rebaptized, just as a considerable number were rebaptized in 1847, when the first pioneer community was formed. Again in 1874, when the attempt was made to establish the United Order, whole communities were rebaptized.[8]

While any Saint may pray for good in his soul and health in his body, the prayers of the priesthood have behind them the

BAPTISM OF THE SHIVWITS INDIANS AT ST. GEORGE ABOUT 1875

These would submit to the rite only if they were baptized in clear spring water. The Mormons obligingly dug this pool for the occasion. The bearded gentleman in the pool is Daniel D. McArthur, veteran Indian-fighter and president of the St. George Stake. The tall man with the long beard is Augustus P. Hardy, who, with Jacob Hamblin and three other white men, established among these Indians in 1854 the Santa Clara Mission. Hardy was for many years county sheriff.

force of authority. Here is the story of a clash between a pioneer doctor and an apostle, as reported by Joseph Fish, of Parowan, in his journal for March 11, 1860:

My wife, Mary, gave birth to a daughter about 10 PM (Sunday). The infant was rather small, but well, weighed $6\frac{1}{2}$ pounds. Everything did not work right with my wife. The nurse gave her an emetic which threw her into spasms. These spells lasted about 36 hours, having one every hour. She was insensible all the time. They put hot rocks on her to steam her and burnt her feet and legs so bad that quite large pieces came out. The whole ball of one of her big toes came off from the burn. Dr. Meeks was called in; afterwards Dr.

Pendleton. They did not agree in their methods of treatment. Pendleton finally had her bled in the ankle to bring the blood from the head. Meeks got mad at this and left. He was quite stubborn about the case. Brother Lyman called the case up in Council and reprimanded Meeks for his cours. Lyman spoke about it in public meeting.

So the doctor was criticized by the priesthood because he did not believe bleeding at the ankle to draw blood from the head would aid a woman recovering from childbirth.

Elder Charles L. Walker, devout St. George pioneer, wrote in his journal on March 28, 1871:

One night my wife was very bad with severe pains in her hip and groin. She seemed to lose all hope of ever getting well, and thought she surely would be a cripple all her life. The tears flowed down her pale and haggard cheeks as she looked at her thin and puny babe without a mother's attention, she not being able to attend it, owing to her sickness. I felt bad for I had done the best I could. I made a fire, put my wife in an easy chair and placed the babe in bed. Then I went out in the lot and knelt down and prayed to God to help me and bless me in the house of trial and affliction, and asked him in mighty prayer to heal my wife of her infirmities.

When Walker returned to the house, he found his wife resting easier. She fell asleep and thereafter improved rapidly.

This pioneer prejudice against resort to doctors in case of illness has been gradually replaced by another viewpoint, which favors the use of doctors but does not dispense with the priesthood. The ideal doctor is one who, after prescribing as a physician, will join with his brethren in administering to his patient.[9]

The priesthood is a fraternity of ordained men who employ in faith the powers which they believe came down through the organization from God. Priesthood claims the authority to guide, counsel, and order and expects unquestioning obedience. That was the test of pioneer faith. The Saint obeyed his file leaders, as a soldier in the service.

Lyman L. Woods knew he had been sent to Clover Valley to keep the Indians quiet. But he was expected to hold the place. Thousands of Mormons were sent to places to establish homes and to places where they would not have gone of their own volition. Obedience to these calls distinguished the Mormon frontier from all others. It was desertion to leave a settlement post.

The year 1879 was a dry one in southern Utah. The supply

of water in the Santa Clara Creek was so low that there was not enough to meet the needs of the two settlements, Gunlock and Santa Clara. The Gunlockers, higher up on the creek, were accused of using more than a fair share of irrigation water. The case was taken to the High Council.

At the hearing the Santa Clara brethren proved that they had been unfairly dealt with in this arrangement, which required each community to use less water than it needed. Bishop Joseph L. Huntsman, of Gunlock, said to the decision of the Council: "If we have no right to water in Gunlock; we cannot make homes. We had better move. . . . ." President J. D. T. McAllister answered that times were hard, that each community would have to sacrifice, and that the Santa Clara brethren had been patient; and he warned Huntsman to dismiss from his mind the feeling about moving. He ordered the bishop to go with his brethren on the following Sunday to Santa Clara and apologize to the people for taking more than a fair share of the water. Huntsman obeyed. The minutes of the Santa Clara meeting contain the note that he spoke at the meeting and "made satisfaction."

On November 18, 1888, Bishop Marcus Funk, of Washington, wrote the High Council that he would like to move with his family to the San Luis Valley in Colorado. He had served in the Dixie Mission fourteen years. "I have worked hard trying to make a living by farming; have suffered much loss by floods washing away our dams and ditches, and losing my crops several years." He was given permission to move. Funk had, only a few weeks before, been released from prison, where he had served a term for unlawful cohabitation. Colorado was safer.

About the same time, the Council received a similar request from Bishop F. W. Jones, of Pine Valley, also a polygamist. He wanted to move to Mexico, but he wished to be honorably released and leave with "the approval and blessing of the priesthood." He was given permission to go with the good will of his file leaders.

The insistence of church authorities that Saints go where they were called and remain until released was an essential regulation without which the Mormon frontier would have failed. This theme is impressively developed by Maurine Whipple in her recent novel of Dixie, *The Giant Joshua*. Some of the women, the young wives, were unhappy. It was a hazardous place to bring up babies. Yet one of Miss Whipple's characters insisted to his wife: "A man whom Brother Brigham has trusted doesn't leave a mission unless he's carried out feet first."

Such a man was Levi M. Savage, one of the Mormons to pioneer Arizona. Year by year, he did all that duty required. He entered polygamy and reared a large family. In his old age he wanted a little rest. He would not ask to be relieved. The following item is from a letter, dated March 29, 1918, sent by the president of the church to the president of the Snowflake Stake:

> We have just received a letter dated 27 inst. from Parley Savage, son of Levi M. Savage of Woodruff, Arizona, stating in effect that his father who is now near 70 years old, is obliged to work for his living, that he is doing day's work on the Woodruff Dam, walking six miles to and from the place of his work; that he has been eager for years to leave Woodruff, that he thought that after 40 years on the Little Colorado, shoveling sand a great part of that time into the river only to see it washed away, was sufficient to bring him release, but he is willing to stay provided we think it is best for him to do so.

The president of all the Mormons sent the assurance that Bishop Savage should "consider himself free to make his home elsewhere." However, according to his own journal, Savage changed his mind and remained some time longer, until a new dam was built "to get the water into the valley again," after which he felt relieved of a duty imposed by priesthood authority in 1871.

NOTES

1. Apostle Joseph Fielding Smith (*Essentials in Church History*, pp. 67–68) reports that this was the same John the Baptist who baptized Jesus and who later lost his head. He laid his hands on the head of Joseph Smith and then of Oliver Cowdery and, in ordaining them, said he had been instructed to do so by Peter, James, and John. Smith then baptized Cowdery, and Cowdery baptized Smith, but they kept the matter secret for some time.

2. Concerning this event, Apostle Joseph Fielding Smith (*ibid.*, pp. 69–70) reports that the date of the visit of Peter, James, and John is not known. In Doctrine and Covenants, Sec. 128, it is indicated that the meeting took place on the Susquehanna River between Harmony, Pennsylvania, and Colesville, New York.

3. Andrew L. Neff (*History of Utah*, pp. 521–29) discusses the Mormon version of the "Kingdom of God," the priesthood government out of which would grow the leadership for temporal government. A brief summary of Mormon religion is given in *Utah: A Guide to the State*, pp. 91–97.

4. As far as seems proper, the real names of persons figuring in the illustrative cases will be given. In cases involving charges which might be embarrassing to descendants of the persons involved, other names or disguised initials will be used.

5. Normally, the probate courts did not handle cases for adjusting the estates of polygamists because the plural wives had no standing before the law. The following case was recorded in Book C of the Washington County Probate Court, January 23, 1872, and concerned Patty and Mary Jane Perkins, widows of the late William J. Perkins, and the three children of Mary Jane Perkins

To Patty Perkins was given half-interest in a house and lot valued at $700; 2 acres of land valued at $80; stock in the Canaan Stock Company, in the textile mill, and in a co-operative store valued at $610; cash in gold, $200; and household furniture valued at $300. Total $1,340.

To Mary Jane Perkins was given a house and lot in Canaan valued at $250; stock in a co-operative store valued at $240; livestock and equipment valued at $270; furniture valued at $145; cash in gold, $80; and for her three children livestock valued at $580 and cash in gold, $120. Total $1,685.

A homestead of unspecified value was to be owned equally by the widows. "And all the residue left of the estate of said William J. Perkins, deceased, after payment of debts, if any, and expenses of administration, to be set apart for the three minor children."

6. B. H. Roberts (*Comprehensive History of the Church*, VI, 167) contains the report of the shooting of Joseph W. McMurrin, night watchman at the tithing office in Salt Lake City by Deputy Marshal Henry F. Collin in December, 1885. The polygamy issue was involved. Attending physicians thought McMurrin's wounds were fatal. "But he was visited by two of the twelve apostles of the Church, John Henry Smith and Heber J. Grant. They anointed him with oil and blessed him with the laying on of hands . . . . and promised him recovery and life and health. He speedily recovered." In 1930, when Roberts wrote the above, McMurrin was still alive.

7. The *Church Chronology*, January 18, 1890, reports a similar accident to a worker on the Salt Lake Temple. This man, Robert H. Ford, fell from a window. Ford apparently was not helped by administrations. He died.

8. Ordinances in the temples concern many matters, in addition to baptism for the living, the sick, and the dead. The first year's work in the St. George Temple, reported by Bleak ("Manuscript History of St. George," December 31, 1878), showed: baptisms: for the dead, 23,197; for health and healing, 356; and for renewals of covenants, 86. The same report showed proportionate numbers of endowments, sealings, and adoptions for the living and the dead.

9. The writer obtained information regarding the age, sex, and cause of death of 1,660 persons interred in the municipal cemetery of St. George from 1862 through 1931. The data for the early decades seem to indicate that neither the two doctors nor all the elders were able to halt the high death rate of little children. During the first 20 years, ending 1881, burials included 324 children under 5 years of age, 57 children 5–14 years of age, and 125 persons who were 15 years of age or older at the time of death, making a total of 506 deaths. Over 3 deaths out of every 5 in the first two decades were of children under 5 years of age. Each decade during the next forty years witnessed a lowering of the total death rate, but the lowering of the infant death rate remained high until after St. George discontinued drinking water from open ditches.

CHAPTER XIV

ECONOMY OF FAITH AND PLENTY

IT WAS not a distinctive venture for the Mormons about 1831 at Kirtland, Ohio, and at Independence, Missouri, to initiate economic communism. Many small sects and fraternal groups were then committed to some form of communal living. Besides the Shakers, Harmonists, Perfectionists, and Separatists, there were many more—some well known, others obscure.[1] Smith knew some of them.

Whereas these plans differed in detail, all had certain elements in common. The religious communal groups held that the earth and its resources belong to the Lord, that the Lord suffers man to use the resources of the earth, that the Lord expects man to be grateful and use these things for social good, and that man is only a steward of whatever he holds.

Such philosophies of property apparently were natural responses to the hazards and poverty of the frontier. They were common-sense adaptations under the dictates of expediency. People had to unite their labor to meet their needs. Communal economy was often the imperative to individual survival. The newly formed Mormon community was one that had to co-operate or perish. Before Joseph Smith could build Zion to fill the world, he had to build a strong organization in some locality. The resources of all members had to be united.

To converts who had property, Smith said in effect: "You must share your surplus with our poor brethren." To others he said in effect: "You must consecrate your surplus to the Church, so the Church will be able to aid those who have little." On April 26, 1832, Smith received a revelation which enlarged the plan of voluntary consecration into a systematic program called the "United Order of Enoch." The United Order did not succeed, but it was in substance a scheme of communal living.[2]

It failed because of opposition from without and confusion within. The prophet could not effectively administer a plan, one part of which operated at Kirtland and the other at Independence, a thousand miles away. The Saints were not secure against their gentile opponents, and many were not really converted to the plan. Smith blamed the failure on the weakness of the people.

However, he assured the faithful that some day the Saints would be strong and ready to live according to the "greater law." Until then they would be governed in their community economics by a less complicated system, the "lesser law." This was the law of tithing, based on Smith's revelation of July 8, 1838.[3] Under the law of tithing, each would assess himself one-tenth of his increase, hence every tenth cow, horse, pig, ton of hay, pound of butter, or bushel of produce added to his wealth. The mechanic would pay a tenth of his earnings or contribute labor to the church.

Since the Saints believed that the earth and the fulness thereof belonged to the Lord, tithing was a form of rent. According to the logic of this reasoning, the church retained a proprietary interest in all holdings of its members. It was for them, if called upon, to consecrate their all. Consecration was a transference of stewardship to the church. An effort was made to effect such a transfer in the consecration movement in Utah from 1855 to 1857.

William Chandless, visiting Utah in 1855, reported a sermon on consecration by Apostle Orson Pratt. The apostle assured the people that church ownership of the property would give the Saints greater security, especially Saints who remained faithful. Chandless quoted Pratt as follows:

> If the Church owned the whole of Salt Lake City, and any one, Gentile or Mormon, become an abomination to us, the Church would say to the man, "Leave this house. It is our house"; and to others, "If you let this man live with you, you also shall leave your house and the city." And if the Church owned all the settlements, it could say to the offender, "You shall not stay in this land at all." And all this could be done without violating a single law of the United States.[4]

Many of the faithful responded to this call, as is shown by the county records. Below is copied in substance the deed of consecration[5] of a Swiss convert in Box Elder County:

Frederick Roulett to Brigham Young, trustee in trust for the Church of Jesus Christ of Latter-Day Saints:

One 5-acre lot of farming land bought of William Davis in the Big Field, Box Elder Survey, not numbered	$ 50.00
One city lot in Brigham City, and improvements, not numbered	120.00
Household and kitchen furniture, including bedding, clothing, "and all kinds of cooking and farming aparatus & utinsils"	200.00
"Also my daughter, Fanny Charlott Roulett, born Genia, Switzerland, Oct. 26, A.D. 1844"	....
	$370.00

Here is the case of John Brown, of Lehi City,[6] who in "good will" consecrated to the church, in the name of Brigham Young:

Several pieces of land, each of which is identified in the instrument, and the total stated value of which was	$ 775.00
"3 Yoke of Oxen and one Wagon	300.00
"6 Cows at $30 & five Calves at $8 each	196.00
"1 Yearling 15$ & Two pigs at 5$ each	25.00
"Farming Tools 75$ & one Rifle 30$	105.00
"Household Furniture Beds Bedding etc.	150.00
"12 Sheep at 5$ per head & Two Horse 'Pistoles' 12$	72.00
"1 Silver Watch $25 & 1 Cooking Stove $30	55.00
"60 Bushel of Wheat @ 2$ per Bu.	120.00
"5 Bushel of Corn @ 1.50 per Bu.	7.50
"60 Bushel of Potatoes @ 1 per Bu.	60.00
"Garden Vegetables 30$, & 6 Tons of Hay $48	78.00
"Cloth in Progress $25, & outstanding Ac/s 50$	75.00
"1 African Servant Girl	$1000.00
"Total Value of John Browns Property	$3038.50

"Three thousand and Thirty Eight Dollars & 50¢, together with all the 'rights,' 'privileges' and appurtenances thereunto belonging or appeartaining. I also covenant and agree, that I am the lawful claim-ant and owner of said property, and will Warrant and forever defend the same, unto the said Trustee in Trust, his successors in office, and assigns against the claims of my heirs, assigns or any other person whomsoever."

While the total does not add correctly, this document is the evidence of John Brown's faith. He gave everything to the church, even his watch and the "African Servant Girl"; and he would defend the right of the church to this property against the claims of his own children.

These consecrations were possibly not widespread, but they must have been numerous. They turned out to be gestures, because the church did not take possession of this property. Had all the Saints given their all, the church might have become mighty in its power, and under self-seeking leaders the people might have entered a helpless subjection.

While the church did not take advantage of the consecration program, the tithing principle did continue in force, and the pioneers were full and dependable tithe-payers. There has never been a record of the church income from this source. It was, however, not the full income, because the people, in addition to tithing, made other contributions to Zion.

Had the Mormon leaders been rich men, their industrial and commercial co-operatives might not have been undertaken. The best evidence is the speed with which they turned to capitalistic enterprise when they were financially able. If, in 1851 or 1852, they wished to start some enterprise, such as the Deseret Iron Company, they had to pass the hat and collect from all Saints. Apostles Erastus Snow and Franklin D. Richards, who later headed the Iron Mission, also collected some money in England and received an appropriation of $3,000 from the Utah legislature. The Iron Mission failed, but it did evidence the willingness of the people to support such undertakings.

Thus, the church in 1850 started a paper, the *Deseret News*, which for many years was the voice of Mormondom, read in every Latter-Day Saint home. Also, the church passed the hat to get money and means to build its own telegraph system, beginning in 1865. In all settlements money, poles, and labor were donated, and sixty-five wagons went east to bring back wire, fixtures, and instruments. Within two years the Deseret Telegraph Company had five hundred miles of line connecting settlements from St. George to Logan.[7]

By 1871 the Deseret Telegraph Company had extended its lines to the mining communities of eastern Nevada and to the outposts of northern Arizona, where the co-operative cattle and sheep herds were grazing.[8] All the telegraphers were Mormons; many were young women, which served a good purpose in later years, when polygamy raids began. By their code messages these alert telegraphers were able to keep all communities informed of the goings and comings of the deputy marshals.

The rates of the Deseret company were much lower than those of other lines. When Western Union was charging 10 cents a word for sending messages about five hundred miles, the Deseret Telegraph Company was charging community rates. According to the record of the Lesser Priesthood Council of St. George, March 6, 1879, a community could then receive 800 words of news daily at a rate ranging from $8.00 to $10.00 per month;[9] the telegraph office was a popular gathering place when news came over the wires. The Deseret company was sold to the Western Union about 1900.

Although co-operative herding companies existed from the start of Utah settlement, there was a movement about 1868 to formally incorporate these herds. The church collected as tithing each year great numbers of cattle and sheep, which were then leased. When the herds were incorporated, the church took shares in the new companies, and the co-operative herds became the repositories of tithing-office wealth.

Possibly the largest of these co-operative herds was the Canaan Co-operative Stock Company, organized April 10, 1870, in St. George on instructions from Brigham Young. He directed Erastus Snow to buy the land and water rights at Pipe Springs in northwestern Arizona for a stated price of $1,000. He also directed that A. P. Winsor, former bishop of Grafton, be the riding boss of the herd at a salary of $1,200.[10] Thus, on Young's order, a co-operative began. Snow passed the orders to the bishops, and the bishops to the brethren. Shares in the co-operative were sold until a capital stock of $100,000 was secured. The herd was incorporated on January 31, 1871, empowered to own dairies, to own meat markets, and to employ "all needed agents and work hands and discharge them at pleasure."

Those who turned cattle into the herd received stock certificates to the appraised value of the animals. Canaan stock were branded with the company brand, a cross in a circle. Cash being scarce, the Canaan company issued scrip, which circulated like money and was redeemed by the Canaan company in livestock, beef, or dairy products. The meat market in St. George was operated by the company as a monopoly for a number of years.[11]

A co-operative sheep herd was formed at Cedar City in 1869, the church contributing, for shares, a considerable number of the twelve thousand sheep owned by the company. There were several such sheep herds, and church sheep were included in them all, including the co-operatives at Kanarra, Pinto, and in the mountain country back of Parowan.

Two years after the Canaan cattle herd got under way, Brigham Young joined with A. P. Winsor and other brethren in what seems to have been a business proposition, the Winsor Castle Stock Growing Company. Of the $50,000 capital stock, $10,000 was owned by the church, $2,350 by Brigham Young, and $3,500 by Winsor, who became riding boss. Apparently all the stock was not subscribed then but accumulated with the natural increase. For the first eighteen months the company paid a dividend of 33 per cent.[12]

In 1879 the Winsor Castle herd was sold to the Canaan company, which continued for a number of years, although gradually losing its co-operative character. Sheep herds also changed from community to individual enterprises.[13] Although co-operative herds were discontinued, co-operative herding and range-riding took its place, and still continues.

Mention was made in an earlier chapter of the effect of the railroad on Mormon insularism. The church turned to industrial and commercial co-operatives as defense measures. Zion's Co-operative Mercantile Institution was such a protective agency, the guardian of other co-operatives, because it gave prior consideration in selling homemade products.[14] Z.C.M.I. made a specialty of goods produced in Mormon textile mills, shoe factories, and canning factories; and Z.C.M.I. also made clothing.

It was because the church had this extensive mercantile system that small industries dared to begin. Except for a few woolen mills, which later turned to special products, most of these small industries were later abandoned.

The prospect of failure was then no deterrent. For example, in 1871 for the region around St. George a plan was launched for co-operative marketing. Farmers hauled quantities of fruit and vegetables to the mining camps. Because of losses often sustained, a plan was launched for the farmers to bring their products to a central place for grading and packing. Express wagons would haul this produce to Pioche, Hiko, and other Nevada camps. There would be a uniform flow. Prices would be standard and fair. The plan was a good one.[15]

But this co-operative failed. Some farmers acted in good faith. Others would slip away with their own products, hoping to better the "co-op" prices. Even Mormon human nature could not resist the temptation of taking a chance. Some farmers, lucky enough to get to market when others were not there, got good prices. Others would arrive to find several loads in town ahead of them and the limited market overstocked. They were happy to get any sale. The co-operative would have better served both farmers and customers.

Dixie's primary crop was to have been cotton. Every man called to that mission was expected to give prior consideration to cotton and to produce other crops only to meet extreme needs. It was also his duty to produce fruits which would not grow elsewhere in Zion, to be traded with other regions. Initially, most of the farmers obeyed the cotton call. The 1863 cotton crop approximated 56,000 pounds. Most of it was hauled north and traded for wheat, flour, or store goods. But some cotton was hauled on the sly to California and sold for cash, with which the farmers could buy much-needed harness, saddles, shoes and, for the women, stoves, dishes, and cooking utensils, so lacking in the homes.[16] Thus, 11,000 pounds of precious Dixie cotton went to benefit the Gentiles.

This offended Brigham Young, who, when he heard of it, sent riders to tell Dixieites that he would buy the cotton for cash. He said that he was planning a textile mill for Dixie and that steps were being taken to bring in the machinery—to haul it fifteen hundred miles by ox team. On Pioneer Day, July 24, 1866, people from the settlements gathered at Washington to celebrate the start of work on the new mill, "Brigham's factory." The church invested $44,000 to buy the machinery, which was installed in 1869.

COTTON TEXTILE MILL NEAR ST. GEORGE, UTAH

This was the factory of the Rio Virgin Co-operative Manufacturing Company, completed in 1869 for the purpose of processing the cotton produced in the region. The machinery was hauled by ox team from the East. This picture was taken about 1890. The mill operated intermittently until about 1900, when it had to be closed because cotton could not be economically produced in Utah's "Dixie."

In 1870 church leaders of Dixie incorporated the venture as Zion's Co-operative Rio Virgin Manufacturing Company, with a capital of $100,000. Erastus Snow was named president. It was always that way with church-sponsored enterprises. the highest man in the priesthood among the organizers would be named president. If it were a ward enterprise, the bishop would be president.

Assisting Snow as members of the board of directors were

other ranking brethren, including bishops of wards. The bishop of each ward had the task of persuading every family of his flock to buy stock in the factory. Orson W. Huntsman wrote in his journal on May 10, 1871, that he had subscribed for factory shares to the amount of $64.[17] When cash was to be had, it was used; but most of the stock was paid for in the produce of the country or in labor.

Zion's Co-operative Rio Virgin Manufacturing Company was fairly efficiently equipped, but it started under difficulties. All the cotton and wool produced in the region was not sufficient to keep the mill going half-time. They hoped to increase the supply. Moreover, the cost of production, especially of cotton, was prohibitive—generally about a dollar a pound. It was an imposition on the faith of the brethren to ask them to grow cotton when it was more economical to grow other crops. Yet, many farmers kept at it and counted not the loss, believing they laid up treasures in heaven for the losses on earth. The mill never had enough work to pay its debts.

Information is lacking about operating costs and production for the "factory." The records of the priesthood quorums contain occasional exhortations that the brethren grow more cotton and use more "home made." In 1890 the stock was selling for 68½ per cent of the face value, but it probably had no value outside the area of responsibility and faith. We quote some figures given by Stake Historian Blake for 1892, which was near the end of the experiment: "Wages paid, about $1,000 per month. Dividends about $4,000 from July 1, 1891 to December 31, 1892. Cotton used about 50,000 pounds. Goods produced during this period of 18 months valued at about $40,000."[18] A few years later the factory closed.

Some of the cotton missionaries were alive as late as 1912. They still cultivated small patches of cotton in their gardens because they said they had "not been released from the work." Some of them ginned the product by hand, rolled it in bats, and peddled it to housewives in the Mormon communities for lining quilts.[19]

Brigham Young, often offended because the women of Zion

were tempted by fashion, would deliver tirades against the follies of the world. There is reason to suspect that much of this anger, exploded over the heads of the sisters in the congregations, was really intended for some of his own wives and daughters or for other women of the first families who were "approximating after the things of the world." Thus he charged that the Devil was tempting Zion's sisters from the simple life.

Young was especially irritated because the following of fashion was costing good Mormon cash for the baubles of the Gentiles. Charles L. Walker wrote in his journal on May 13, 1876, of a speech made by Brother Brigham in St. George. He "spoke of the folly and indecency of present fashions. Said some of the sisters of Zion acted like damn fools, and the whores of London and Paris would be ashamed to act like they did, and said it would serve them right for someone to take a knife and slit their dresses from their navel to their knees." He urged the mothers to teach their daughters to cook, wash, iron, and sew.

Silkworms and mulberry trees were brought into Utah about 1850. Before 1860, attempts had been made to produce silk in several localities in Salt Lake City and Ogden. The *Deseret News* of June 4, 1864, contained this self-explanatory advertisement, inserted by T. Whitaker of Centerville:

> I wish to say to all those who have mulberry trees (muro multicaulis) that I have succeeded in raising some 1,400 healthy silkworms of a large kind. Whoever may wish to avail themselves of this opportunity of securing some of these useful insects can leave their orders with Henry E. Phelps; opposite the Telegraph Office, or at H. A. Squires, opposite Jennings' store, East Temple Street, Salt Lake City.

The climate of northern Utah was not congenial to the silkworms. Mulberry trees did not thrive there, and the worms did not do well on the leaves of other trees. Young then thought the silk industry might be tried in Dixie. He was in St. George in November, 1872. He spoke of the blessings of the textile mill and suggested that, while the men raised cotton, the sisters could serve Zion by raising silkworms. The day would come when Babylon would fall and the merchants would cry: "There is no one to buy our merchandise." Zion would then be secure and dressed in fine raiment. "If we profess to know how to use silk dresses, we must first learn how to produce them."[20]

St. George women accepted the mission to produce silk. They were more committed to the mission two years later, when the United Order was established. There was much to learn; and few of these women, with large families to care for, had the time for this mission. But they did have the spirit, as may be gathered from the following sentiments reported in the minutes of the St. George Female Relief Society:

February 7, 1878: An unnamed sister said, concerning mulberry trees: "Her experience had not been good in raising them from the seed, that the plants looked very good for a season, and then looked yellow, as though it was too hot for them or the soil was not right. She encouraged us to persevere and carry out the counsel that had been given us, that perhaps some could do better than she had done."

May 2, 1878: Sister Ivins of the Third Ward said: "They were making a start in the silk business. Said as she looked upon the worms and realized that all the silk came from them, they seemed quite near to her. She hoped to see the day when we would be able to make our own fine apparel, and that which we would not be ashamed of."

"Sister Snow said that she had a number of worms. They were not much trouble to her, as they did not require their food cooked. Said they were not hard to take care of. Said it was not for what she could gain that she undertook the business, but because it was obeying the counsel of the authorities and was building up Zion."

June 6, 1878: Sister Elizabeth Morse said: "Her mulberry seed had not come up. She thought silkworms were not fit to have in the house where we have to eat and sleep; felt encouraged to persevere and do all we can." Sister A. Church was also interested in silkworms. "She hoped yet to have a silk dress."

May 1, 1880: In this meeting Sister Church showed a necktie that she made from home-produced silk. Sister Eyring said: "She did not think we should make a great deal of money out of silkworms, but if we learn to handle them and plant the mulberry we are making that much progress in the Kingdom and doing our duty. We will get our reward, whether we make much or little."

On May 6, 1880, Stake President J. D. T. McAllister spoke to the St. George Relief Society sisters. He wanted to encourage them in the silk business. "As the brethren in the north are laying out money to buy machinery to work up silk, we ought to do all we can to make it profitable."

Then Bishop David H. Cannon stood up. He "felt interested in the business, but would not labor as he has seen the sisters do to take care of them [worms] and get nothing for it. He would feed them to the chickens. Does not like to see the sisters go out into the fields and around and carry bundles of mulberry boughs on their backs." Some brethren were complaining that the women were turning the parlors over to the worms; that the smell of the worms drove them from the house to eat in the woodshed.

The women went piously and stubbornly on, learning each year something new about mulberry trees, the ways of the worms, and the making of silk. Each month at the testimony meetings of the Relief Society they would tell of their progress or failure. Here are some expressions from the minutes of June 3, 1884:

> Sister Ann Woodbury said: "I would like to say with regard to silk, that the coccoons are worth looking after. I feel it a mission placed upon us, and I know that silk can be raised without much trouble. . . ."
>
> Sister Emmaline Winsor said: "This has been a singular year for me without worms. I have raised a great many coccoons and I do not wish to give it up, for I know it will be a useful business."
>
> Sister M. B. Eyring said: "Raising silkworms is like any other machinery, so much easier when you get used to it. . . ."

The experiment continued many years, until the sisters were weaving the silk and making small articles with the product. A shawl had been presented to Mrs. Hayes, wife of President B. Hayes, when the president and his wife visited Salt Lake City in September, 1880. The Utah Silk Association in May, 1895, presented a silk gown to Susan B. Anthony when she presided at the Intermountain Woman Suffrage Convention in Salt Lake City. Governor Caleb W. West, in his report to the Secretary of the Interior for 1887, indicated that $1,000 was invested in the Utah silk industry, that ten workers were employed, that ten looms were in operation, and that that year $5,000 worth of goods had been produced. He did not include the work in the homes.

Wine-making was another Mormon enterprise that came to the same end as the cotton, iron, and silk missions. The St. George Tithing Office reported on March, 1887, a supply of 6,610 gallons of wine, valued at 50 cents per gallon.

There were practical reasons for producing wine. Here was a product for the Gentiles. It could be stored in small bulk, kept indefinitely, and hauled with little waste. It was thought that the cultivation of grapes would not greatly interfere with raising cotton and that a man could make wine at odd times. Bishop Henry Eyring said to the High Priest Quorum of St. George on June 30, 1866, that the settlers would not "make a fat living here," but he said of grapes: "We can lay a foundation, get barrels, etc., or dry grapes. They will pay best."

The making of wine and some whiskey and brandy went ahead without organized direction for more than a decade. On March 26, 1874, when Brigham Young spoke to the women about making silk, he mentioned ways of keeping Mormon money at home by making articles normally bought from outsiders. He favored making wine for sale to outsiders. The presses could be located at central places. "First, by lightly pressing, make a white wine. Then give a heavier pressing and make colored wine. Then barrel up this wine, and if my counsel is taken, this wine will not be drunk here, but will be exported, and thus increase the fund."[21]

Since the church encouraged wine-making, it was not possible for the tithing offices to refuse wine as tithing. Some paid their tithes in poor wine and kept the good. Others brought in the grapes, only to have them spoil. The tithing office at St. George received wine of many grades. It met the problem by setting up standards. The tithing clerk issued these instructions on September 20, 1879:

> In order to obtain a more uniform grade of wine than we are able to obtain by mixing together the tithes of small pressings in the hands of sundry individuals; it is suggested that those having but small quantities of grapes to make up into wine, deliver their tithes in grapes at this office. This may be arranged under the direction of the bishop so that economy may be preserved in the hauling, for which, of course, credit will be given on the tithing account.

Thus the church found itself the chief single producer of wine in the Dixie area and the agency for establishing uniform standards for quality. Because the tithing offices held the largest amount of wine for the market at any time, it was in a position to name the price. Church interest is evidenced in a letter sent by the St. George Tithing Office August 12, 1880. This letter was a bill sent to the managers in charge of building the Manti Temple, to whom had been sent a quantity of wine—4 barrels, or 158 gallons. It was not sold, but tithing credit was asked as follows: $187.50 for the wine; $20.00 for the barrels; for hauling the wine to Manti, $16.00; total $233.50. This was given in pay to the builders of the temple.

In 1889 Edward H. Snow, clerk of the St. George Tithing Office, wrote the presiding bishop at Salt Lake City regarding wine: "Our sales during the year do not amount to half of what we are obliged to make up from the grapes that are brought in. . . . . We have made at this office alone over 600 gallons this year. We cannot refuse the grapes or the wine, and I see no way to get rid of it." Snow wanted the presiding bishop to take the surplus. Later the tithing office sent men with loads of wine to the northern settlements, where they traded Dixie's liquid wealth for wheat and flour or took it to the mining camps, where it brought cash.

Dixie brethren did not follow Brother Brigham's counsel. They drank so much of the wine that by 1890 drunkenness was a worry to the church leaders. The tithing office discontinued accepting wine for tithes and abandoned its own presses. An effort was made to discourage individual wine-makers, but this made slow headway, since money was invested in vineyards and presses. Before 1900, however, the preaching had taken effect. Wine-making had all but ceased, and wine-drinking had become taboo.[22]

These co-operative and home-industry efforts mentioned were part of a general scheme of Brigham Young for Mormon economic security and isolation. The objective was the United Order of Enoch, which Joseph Smith said would eventually have to be established before the Saints would be ready to meet Christ on his second coming. He predicted that there would yet be a full participation in the United Order.

Brigham Young was in St. George in February, 1874. Work on the temple was progressing. He was pleased with the attitude of the people, which encouraged his belief that this area would in time be Zion's center. Should not St. George be the first to enter the United Order? The time seemed ripe. He had a personal reason for wanting the Order started, for his own life was closing and he wanted to supervise the beginning of the great experiment.

He told the local elders of his plans. They rejoiced. He called a meeting and found the Saints pleased with the thought. He mentioned the great panic then hampering the economy of the gentile world. He stressed the need of building home industries, lest the Gentiles in Zion get too much power. He called for a show of hands and found all ready to go along with him. A committee was named to draw up a plan.

This committee reported on March 29, offering a document entitled: "The Preamble and Articles of Agreement of the United Order of the City of St. George." Some of the "whereas" clauses in the "Preamble" indicate the thinking by which church leaders were then motivated and the relation of this united effort to the panic of 1873:

> Realizing the signs and spirit of the times, and from the results of our past experience, the necessity of a closer union and combination of our labor for the promotion of our common welfare:
>
> *Whereas:* We have learned of the struggle between capital and labor; resulting in strikes of the workmen, with their consequent distress; and also the oppression of monied monopolies; and
>
> *Whereas:* There is a growing distrust and faithlessness among men in the political and business relations of life, as well as a spirit of extravagant speculation and over-reaching the legitimate bounds of the credit system; resulting in financial panics and bankruptcy, paralyzing industry, thereby making many of the necessities and conveniences of life precarious and uncertain; and. . . . .

One reason for concern about "strikes of workmen" was a growing wage class in Utah. Only a few years earlier, church leaders had warned the Saints against joining any movement to raise wages, for the church way was better. The church program called for sacrifice and co-operation, as in the United Order. That problem may have stimulated the "whereas" clause which ended: "To be friends of God we must become friends and helpers of each other." The Order would join their labor in the business of farming, manufacturing, merchandising, fruit-growing, stock-raising, dairying, and such other pursuits "as will tend to the material prosperity of the Order."

There were eighteen articles of agreement, which concerned organization and management; accumulation, handling, and distribution of property; classification, assignment, and payment of labor; keeping books; the adjustment of claims; and the sharing of losses. Articles pledged the members to temperate habits; to wearing simple garb and abhorring "foolish and extravagant fashions"; and to "energetic, industrious and faithful" dealings.[23]

To speed the Order program, Brigham Young and other organizers during March toured the southern Utah and eastern Nevada outposts.[24] When the organizers reached a community, they called together the leading elders and laid out the plan. The bishop was placed in charge, and the brethren were counseled to line up behind him. A work superintendent was appointed; perhaps there were subforemen, depending on the activities. It was expected that the supervisors would hold regular meetings with one another and with the workers, to plan the labor for the day and week. There would be a clerk to keep account of the contributions of each Order member and the amount of work done by each member.

In addition to the Order in St. George, there was a church-owned farm at Heberville, a place later named "Price." This was really the only unit of the vicinity that approached the ideal of the Order. The venture had been initiated by a group of men sent from Brigham City, where Apostle Lorenzo Snow had been operating a community co-operative program since 1864. Church leaders in St. George assumed direction of the Price farm, and some of the local men and families worked there.[25]

After the formation of units of the Order in the southern area, Brigham Young and his party started north, holding meetings and organizing all communities en route. This was a sort of revival not unlike the "Reformation" of 1856. Each day was

No. 3635 5 Cts.

Good for Five Cents,

IN

HOME PRODUCTS.

Brigham City Co-operative.

Secretary.

G. S. L. City. Jan. 20. 1849.

No 1.00d

GOOD to N. K. Whitney or bearer.

one DOLLAR on demand. B. Young

1.00d

T. Bullock Clerk. H. C. Kimball

No 17452

This is not intended to be used as Money.

5c

THIS WRITING WITNESSETH THAT THE

BISHOP'S GENERAL STORE HOUSE

AGREES TO FURNISH THE BEARER

PRODUCE AND MERCHANDISE

TO THE AMOUNT OF

FIVE CENTS

AT SALT LAKE CITY, UTAH

Date Oct 1st 1898. Wm B. Preston

Above, a piece of scrip issued about 1865 by the Brigham City co-operative, forerunner of the United Order. The Brigham City scrip was later rated as money by federal authorities and subjected to a tax, no doubt on a legal technicality.

Center, an emergency dollar issued by Salt Lake City on January 20, 1849. It is signed by Brigham Young, Heber C. Kimball, and Thomas Bullock. The note is made to Newell K. Whitney.

Below, an example of tithing-office scrip. It reads: "This is not intended to be used as money," to avoid federal tax. Most tithing offices and stores issued some form of scrip which served when cash was scarce.

a spiritual feast, and each day began new units of the Order from Kanarra to Salt Lake City.[26] Brother Brigham promised the people: "Do as I say and Zion will prosper." Before the end of June the organization drive had reached down into Sanpete, up to Cache Valley, and over the border into Wyoming and Idaho.

Good work was done in that drive, making 1874 a high point in church history. There was no end of inspirational resolve; but, when the inspiring speakers moved on, the people were left with their usual everyday worries and the greater problem of tearing themselves free from their practiced and established routine. The bishop was boss and was generally accepted as such. Nonetheless, here was a practical problem with which even the most saintly of bishops could not cope. How to get together horses, wagons, implements, seed, and buildings; how to credit people; how to put them to work—every step was a baffling one. Some of the faithful gave all they had. The less faithful, or more skeptical, gave little. Some who had nothing came expecting to be cared for or to be put to work, expecting the Order to regulate their lives. The Gentiles and apostates looked on cynically, if they did not actively lend opposition, as they could have, believing that the Order was another form of Mormon plotting against them.[27]

Questions were asked that local officials could not answer, and so many inquiries were sent to Brigham Young. The questioning letters followed him wherever he went. Many are on file in Bleak's "Manuscript History of St. George" for 1875 and 1876. The writer copied a number of these questions, which indicate the obstacles that stood in the way of ideal Order management, but they also reveal the faith of the people in their leader.

If a man in one settlement has property in another, will he join the Order in both places? And where would he pay his tithing? In paying his tithing would the man pay as an individual, or should he pay with his brethren through the Order?

If a man went on a mission, would his wife have a claim on the Order for support, or would people individually help her out? And how would the numerous Church contributions be made?

Could a property with a small mortgage on it be accepted by the Order? Could a man mortgage part of his property and get cash for joining the Order? How can the Order take possession of unclaimed land?

If a man gave his best team to the Order, and one of the horses died, could he hold the Order for the value of a new horse, and would he lose dividends to the value of the dead horse?

If a man is elected to be director of one branch of the Order, could he also be a director of another branch?

How about voting; will voting be done by shares, or will each person have one vote regardless of his investment?

Is it fair to give wages to workers in the trades, when farmers work for little or nothing, and may lose if they have a poor crop?

Why incorporate the Order after the laws of the land? Is it not organized by the higher law of the priesthood? When we incorporate it are we not making it like a Gentile organization?

If some work is hard and some work is easy, should the young men be given the hard work, or should each member take turn at the work he can do? What should be done with workers who are lazy or careless?

Such were some of the questions that stood in the way of the perfect society, and they reveal the elemental human nature which even the Saints could not surrender to the demands of their ideal. No wonder Brigham Young, then harassed with the polygamy issue and personal litigation, was often discouraged. While trying to defend himself and safeguard the church against gentile opposition, here he was bombarded with detailed questions about managing an order that all were committed to.

Possibly the apostles near Brigham Young, and other leaders cold to the Order, took their cue from him. When he asked a prominent Mormon near Salt Lake City why he had failed to join the Order, the brother answered: "Brother Brigham, when I see you join the Order, then I'll go in."

"Whenever," answered Young, "I can find a man or set of men who can manage my business better than I can, then I'll join the Order."

Yet Brother Brigham found fault with others who thought the same. Some did not like his idea that the Order units should be incorporated. It was sound advice and of a class with his insistence that written records be kept. Much of the trouble that did follow was due to the lack of proper records.

Bleak wrote in the "Manuscript History of St. George" on

October 7, 1877, of growing opposition to the Order. Two leading local elders were quoted. One called the scheme "priestcraft instead of priesthood." The other said: "I have no idea that the thing which we have attempted here called the United Order, is the plan designed by the Almighty."

Some of the staunch believers were men who lost most in trying to make the Order succeed. Orson W. Huntsman was one of the believers. He wrote of the experiment in his home community, Hebron, that his share was "15 bushels of grain, 10 bushels of potatoes, cloth to make a pair of pants, 58 pounds of beef, 20 pounds of salt, one gallon of molasses, and perhaps about perhaps one dollar's worth of other articles." Huntsman concluded that the Order was good but that men were weak.

Price W. Nelson, in his unpublished recollections, wrote about the Glendale United Order, which failed after a few months:

> The young men and boys destroyed things shamefully. "They belong to the Order," they would say, and they would break their tools, or throw them away, or bury them in the sand, so when the boss came around and asked why they were not working they would tell him they didn't have anything to work with. I believe some of those picks are buried in those sandbanks yet. In the fall they went to harvest the crops. Every person tried to see if he couldn't get it all, and there was no system about anything, so that some got a great deal and some nothing. . . . .

Another believer was Zadok K. Judd, who then lived in St. George. He said of the Order: "There was only five cents difference between the man that worked and the man that idled, and the man that idled generally got the five cents; for he was always on hand to know if anything was brought into the treasury, and would call for the first and best."

A number of families at Santa Clara were disappointed because the Order failed there. Under the leadership of Edward Bunker, these families moved to the Muddy Valley (abandoned by the Mormons in 1871) and founded the village of Bunkerville. They lived as one household during 1877 and 1878—the women cooking, washing, and sewing as one family; the men working as one gang in the fields.

The Bunkerville arrangement, all eating at a common table like the Spartans, became irritating to the women; and, beginning the third year, each wife took her husband and children to her own home. The men carried on for another year, raising cotton and cane. In terms of efficiency the plan was successful, but the men were not satisfied. At the beginning of the fourth year each man took his own farm, but the individual farms were, all together, less productive than the co-operative had been.

When Lot Smith established Sunset, Arizona, in 1876, it was organized as a communal United Order family. Levi M. Savage, one of the Sunset founders, wrote in his journal shortly after arriving:

> All who join us turn all of their possessions into the compact, and labor and share equally in the profits, if any. Each man is expected to do as much as he can reasonably perform of the work; and all eat at the same table, each fares as well as the other. We consider it the way of the Lord to live in this manner. Otherwise we would prefer living in the old style, for there are a great many trials connected with this style of living not known to the other. . . . . It is truly a work of love and kindness, but our weaknesses are so many, and our natures still so strong and selfish that it often requires a great deal of patience and forbearance.

Savage never confided to his journal what the trials were. Nor did he write down why it was the Lord's will that the old-style family ménage should be replaced by the community family. Several months later Savage wrote that the women had rebelled and turned from the heaven-blessed community way of living. The men were not happy either. They worked as if in bondage or in the service of Lot Smith. One by one the families departed until the co-operative had to be abandoned.

Best known of the co-operative experiments was the Orderville community in Long Valley, founded in 1875 by a number of families from Mount Carmel and Glendale who were offended when the Order units in those places closed at the end of the first season. The *Deseret News* of July 15, 1875, printed a letter from D. B. Fackrall, secretary of the unit at "Order City." This new community, located three miles from Mount Carmel, had already completed its first organizing steps:

> Our dining hall is far enough complete to hold our meetings in. . . . . All those who have moved from the old place eat together all their meals. Our

hall is 25×40 feet. As each family move up, they fall into line and help swell the family circle. We have all lived from the general fund for some time, and all fare alike. We have no individual property. Our bishop, Howard O. Spencer, is indeed a father to his people, and much loved by all. The spirit of the Lord is with us. Our aged brethren, some that were in Zion's Camp, say these are the best days they ever saw.

The *Deseret News* of October 5, 1875, reported that Orderville had 285 acres of land in crops, not counting 15 acres of garden and 10 acres orchard. Livestock included 500 sheep, 125 cattle, 400 chickens, and 30 hogs. Mention was made of various shops, and there were two items not to be neglected: first "There is no doctor or lawyer in town," and second, the statement that 5 acres of grain had been planted for the Indians.[28]

The faithful elsewhere who had been disappointed by the failure of the Order were heartened by the early reports from Orderville. Zion's Camp veterans living there called it the fulfilment of their dreams. Martin Harris, one of the witnesses to the Book of Mormon and one of the first members of the church, died in northern Utah in 1875, in his ninety-second year. He had lived to see come to pass Joseph Smith's prophecy about the Order.

In April, 1877, Brigham Young was at St. George on what turned out to be his final visit. He opened there the conference of the church dedicating the temple. Then he set out for Manti where he dedicated the site for another temple. Later he arrived in Salt Lake City, where he was due to settle the long-battled suit against him by his estranged wife, Ann Eliza Young. The test case of George Reynolds was moving through the courts with the prospect that the United States Supreme Court would decide the polygamy issue against the Mormons. That was a busy and troublous period for Brigham Young, the last half-year of his life.

Yet he came from southern Utah much encouraged. One temple was complete, and another begun. Moreover, the Order was well reported in three places: Bunkerville, Sunset, and Orderville. He had seen the Order fall apart elsewhere, but here were three places that offered a small ray of hope.

In 1878 the Order at Bunkerville and Sunset began to disintegrate. At the same time the seeds of discontent were beginning to take root in Orderville. In 1880 there was trouble between the idlers and workers. In 1882 Erastus Snow was sent to Orderville to investigate the unrest. He found fault with the practice of "giving equal credit for unequal labor." It was not until 1887 that Orderville was able to come to a private division of the property of the compact.

Earlier in this chapter the principle of tithing was referred to as the "lesser law," given after the failure of the first United Order, then called the "greater law." Comparing tithing and the United Order as "lesser" and "greater" carries the implication that one was substitute or preliminary to the other and that the "greater" could obviate the "lesser." This was not the case. The United Order in Utah did not replace tithing, but itself paid tithing to keep the supply system of the church going. By the use of the tithes the church was able to aid the new or poor communities from the contributions of the older communities to the Lord's Storehouse.

Basically, the United Order was designed to integrate and implement the co-operative security program of Zion. The effort found its most consistent response in the co-operative irrigation undertakings, which continue to operate. The settlers had to work together on their ditches and dams. They had to use their irrigation water co-operatively to get from it the maximum benefit. Thus developed the unique village type of agriculture in Zion.

In the story of Enterprise, mentioned in the first chapter, is illustrated the place of co-operation in community building. This town was parented by and succeeded the pioneer Hebron on Shoal Creek, founded about 1865 by several families sent there to raise cattle and to operate dairies. The site chosen was able to support about twenty families, but the population had outgrown the land by 1885. There was plenty of land six miles down the stream, where the water ran out on the flat country and sank into the desert, as do all the streams flowing into the Lake Bonneville basin.

There was insufficient water in Shoal Creek to serve Hebron farmers and to permit another community farther downstream. Some young men of Hebron came forward with a plan, suggesting that a dam be built up the stream, where the canyon narrowed and where, above the narrows, there was a natural basin

THE ENTERPRISE RESERVOIR IN PROCESS OF CONSTRUCTION

This project was completed almost entirely by labor contributed by the farmers. Building the eighty-foot dam and digging the ditches to conduct the water about twelve miles to the desert was an undertaking that occupied them for more than ten years. Approximately one hundred families in the Enterprise community are sustained from water stored in this dam.

for a reservoir site. Foremost promoter of the plan was Orson W. Huntsman. He saw the possibility of an ideal project, but it would take ten years to build the dam and the necessary ditches. To accept the plan would require that, when completed, Hebron would have to be abandoned and all would have to move.

The older people were not favorable. They were not ready to abandon their stone and brick houses, their gardens and shade trees; to give up twenty years of work to start a new community on the sagebrush flats.

Huntsman measured, surveyed, and estimated. Although not an engineer, he was able to report with fair accuracy the amount of stone needed for the dam, the cubic yards of earth needed to fill behind the dam, and the number of man-months of labor required to finish the job. The cash outlay would be small because all the material was on the site, even the stone to make lime. The result would be a dam 80 feet high, sufficient to impound 5,000 acre-feet of water. It looked good on paper, but the brethren were skeptical.

The more Huntsman talked of his plan, the more opposed some of the Hebronites became. Some called him eccentric and avoided him. He wrote of these things in his journal, saying that he knew the Devil was working to defeat the project and so he set out to thwart the Evil One.

On a Sunday after meeting, Huntsman mounted his horse and rode up the canyon toward Little Pine Valley, the site of the proposed reservoir. He dismounted at the narrows where he had envisoned the dam, and he called on God to bring to pass his dream. He dedicated the site for a dam that would hold back the waters and be a blessing to the people. He rode out into the valley, where today the dam backs up two or three square miles of water. He dedicated the place for a reservoir and for no other use.

Huntsman then appealed to the stake officials at St. George. Those high priests came and held a meeting with the elders of Hebron. They thought the plan had merit. Someone remembered that a high church official once stood on the desert at the site of the proposed community and said: "I see here in vision a beautiful city." In was decided to build the dam, decided that Hebron would move.

While some Hebronites were still not convinced, they were good Saints and followed their file leaders. All went to work; and after a few years, about 1900, Hebron families were migrating to the new location, called "Enterprise." It began like a frontier community, the people living in tents or small board shanties. But there was room in Enterprise, and the land was good. There were no trees, but the years have solved that problem. There was space for yards and gardens and for a hundred families instead of twenty.

Still there were some who entertained homesick memories for the old location where they grew up and where the pioneer dead were buried. It was hard to believe God wanted them to give up all that to live on the desert.

This story ends with a moral, which concerns the earthquake that leveled San Francisco in 1905. A tremor of that quake reached through the mountains to the abandoned village. No other place in the area was touched but Hebron. Every vacant house was shaken down or badly cracked and caved. Six miles above the village the stone barn and brick houses of the Terry ranch were not molested. Even the doubters, who opposed in their hearts the move to Enterprise, realized that lives might have been lost had they remained in Hebron. That was a testimony. God was pleased with their efforts to make a new home so their children would have land.

NOTES

1. William A. Hinds (*American Communities* [1902]) describes some thirty types of co-operative societies, most of them before 1850, most of them religious. Practically all ended with disagreement.

2. J. A. Geddes (*The United Order among the Mormons*) deals with the early effort. See Doctrine and Covenants, Sec. 82, and later revelations.

3. Doctrine and Covenants, Sec. 119. This revelation was given in Missouri, when funds were badly needed to bring the Saints from Kirtland.

4. Chandless (*A Visit to Salt Lake*, pp. 270–73) reported that he asked top leaders of the church if they would consecrate their property, but he received no positive affirmative answers.

5. *Box Elder County Records*, Book A, No. 34, p. 415, April 17, 1857.

6. *Utah County Records*, Book F, pp. 81–83, January 8, 1857.

7. Bleak "Manuscript History of St. George," Book A, p. 256, April, 1865. St. George contributed $683.33 cash and pledged in service $890. Snow apologized because more cash was not available. The St. George telegraph office opened with elaborate ceremonies on January 15, 1867.

8. Journal of Orson W. Huntsman, July 10, 1871: "This summer the Deseret Telegraph line is being put up from St. George to Pioche. This will bring us in connection with the hole world. In the year 1866 or '67 this same company connected all the settlements from Salt Lake City to St. George, also from Salt Lake City to Logan with the

Deseret Telegraph Lines. The people here and other places put up the poles from this place [Hebron] to Pioche and got tithing pay for it, in fact the hole line of Utah were built out of tithing and are operated by the Church. I put up seven miles of poles west of Nephi Canyon, or I might say, west of Terry's ranch for which I received tithing scrip $275.00. This amount I turned to the carpenters toward building my house."

9. Andrew L. Neff (*History of Utah*, pp. 729–31) reports on telegraph in Utah. The transcontinental line reached Utah in 1861. It cost then $7.50 to send ten words to New York City. In 1880 the cost was $1.50.

10. This ranch, now a national monument, was owned by the widow of Dr. James Whitmore, who had been killed by Indians at Pipe Springs in 1866.

11. Bleak (*op. cit.*, Book B, p. 581, September 26, 1875) indicated that the Canaan herd for the year ending June 30 paid a dividend of 25 per cent. *Ibid.*, p. 688, January 2, 1877, shows the capital stock increased to $125,000.

12. *Ibid.*, July 1, 1874.

13. Letter of St. George Tithing Office to Presiding Bishop William B. Preston, November 25, 1885, regarding renting church sheep: "Brother Archibald Sullivan and sons of this place are desirous of establishing a sheep herd in this vicinity and south of St. George. They have had a considerable experience with sheep, and wish to get the Church sheep now in the Kanarra herd. I have their proposition before me in which they say they will take the tithing sheep and give half the lambs and half the wool, and keep the old stock good. Or they will guarantee 13 lambs for each 100 sheep and one and three-fourths pounds of wool to the head, and keep the old stock good. They would also like the tithing sheep in the Pinto and Hebron herd, amounting to about 1,000 head. I will here state that in talking with the secretary of the Pinto and Hebron herd the other day he notified me that he contemplates breakup the herd next fall, in September, and wishes us to make provision for receiving the tithing sheep at that time."

14. Edward W. Tullidge's *History of Salt Lake City*, pp. 728–32, contains the report of Z.C.M.I. progress to July, 1875, showing total sales of $15,000,000 for a period less than five years.

15. Bleak, *op. cit.*, Book B, p. 145, May 29, 1871, reports details. A charge of 12½ per cent was to be made for receiving, packing, forwarding, and collecting. The market was 100 miles away. The cost for individuals making the same trip would have been more. The co-operative express teams made the trip in forty hours. It required three days for individual farmers, and their produce was not delivered in as good condition.

16. *Ibid.*, Book A, pp. 194–95, letter from Brigham Young to Bishop J. W. Crosby, November 6, 1863. Young was astonished that they should sell to strangers what was badly needed at home, as if the brethren had "a determination, ignorantly or wilfully, to put beyond my reach, as far as they can every facility by which I might be enabled to benefit the community." Bleak reported the 1863 cotton yield thus: St. George, 8,500 pounds; Santa Clara, 6,810 pounds; Grafton, 4,784 pounds; Toquerville, 14,500 pounds; and Washington, 21,500 pounds. All of it was needed in Utah.

17. *Ibid.*, Book B, p. 317, indicates that Erastus Snow was anxious to raise contributions to pay $40,000 due Brigham Young. This debt probably really involved church money. Young said in 1874 that the debt would be forgiven if the people willingly joined the United Order.

18. *The Union*, a short-lived St. George paper on May 7, 1896, pleaded with the people to produce cotton, saying: "Our farmers need to turn a new leaf."

19. Bleak, *op. cit.*, Book B, p. 102, contains a letter of December 1, 1870, indicating

that the farmers of Muddy Valley had 25,000 pounds of cotton but were destitute of food. They needed to find means of trading their cotton.

20. *Ibid.*, p. 230, March 29, 1874, quotes from the "Preamble" of the United Order: "We believe that the beauty of our garments should be the workmanship of our own hands, and that we should practice more diligently economy, temperence, frugality, and the simple grandeur of manners that belong to the pure in heart."

21. *Ibid.*, Book A, p. 356, indicates that the probate court of Washington County issued licenses in 1866 permitting the making of brandy at Toquerville but that the enterprise might be closed if later it proved to be "subversive to the public good."

22. *Ibid.*, Book B, p. 276, February 15, 1873, quoted Brigham Young: "Keep your eggs at home . . . . and use them in building the temple." If the Gentiles would buy Mormon products "let them come after them. . . . . Make and sell them wine freely, but take it to them."

23. *Ibid.*, pp. 310–29.

24. Orson W. Huntsman wrote in his journal, March 25, 1874, the day after the Order was formed in Hebron with Thomas S. Terry as superintendent: "The meeting bell rang at eight oclock and all hands gathered there to get their orders for the day. From there each man went to where he was sent, and the United Order of things began in earnest." Instead of each farmer having his own separate potato, wheat, etc., patches, there was a single field for each crop. Huntsman indicated in later entries that he thought the Order went to extremes in some things. He opposed the "Order shoes," made of wooden soles with canvas or leather uppers. Huntsman traded potatoes to an Indian to have him make a pair of moccasins, which, he wrote, "took the shine off the old wooden shoes for comfort and hansom."

25. The Brigham City co-operative was reported by Eliza R. Snow in her *Biography of Lorenzo Snow*. She was his sister. Snow followed Wilford Woodruff as president of the church. The Brigham City Mercantile and Manufacturing Association included a tannery, woolen mill, and other shops. In 1879 the woolen mill burned, a loss of $30,000. The association had to pay a federal tax of $10,200 on its scrip, ruled by a court to be money. For a report on the Price farm, started by the Brigham City association, see *Deseret News*, April 12, 1875.

26. The United Order farm at Price became a farming corporation. During the co-operative period some of the Santa Clara Swiss were working on the farm. There arose differences between the Swiss and other women on what constituted good housekeeping. A Swiss mother became so angry at the others that, when the call came for all to be rebaptized into the United Order, she refused. Baptism required that one should forgive his enemies, which she was not willing to do because they said her cooking was not clean. When the Order died, Robert Gardner was placed in charge of the farming company. The stone building used as Order headquarters, and the dining hall became his home. Professor Angus Woodbury of the University has written an unpublished report on Price, Orderville, and other United Order efforts.

27. Before the United Order started, Brigham Young made occasional mention of the ideal. On October 9, 1872 (*Journal of Discourses*, Vol. XV), he answered queries regarding how one would live in the new society: "I will tell you how I would arrange for a little family, say, about a thousand persons. I would build houses expressly for their convenience in cooking, washing, and every department of their domestic arrangements. Instead of each woman getting up to cook breakfast for a few, she would go direct to her work. Have a hall large enough for 500 people to eat in, and sufficient cooking apparatus in rooms attached to the hall; a person at the farther end telegraphs that he wants a beefsteak, coffee, toast, etc.; it would be conveyed by a little railway under the table. When through, dishes would be placed on the railway and carried back

to the kitchen. For washing, use Chinamen if you prefer. Women would make clothing, hats, bonnets, etc. Adjoining the dining room would be the prayer room, large enough for 500 at a time for morning and evening prayers. Then to business, each man to his own job. Houses would be built in a variety of styles. There would be no loafing. Dairies in one place, pigs and horses in other places, all out of the city. City streets would be gravelled and the paths paved. Sleeping rooms up high with plenty of air." Followed a description of schools for the children and subjects to be taught. "No lawyers would be needed in this society, and doctors only for the purpose of setting bones or amputating diseased and damaged members."

28. For a brief report on the United Order in Utah see Edward J. Allen, *The Second United Order among the Mormons;* Hamilton Gardner, "Communism among the Mormons," *Quarterly Journal of Economics*, March, 1922, pp. 134–74.

CHAPTER XV

SOCIAL IMPLICATIONS OF POLYGAMY

WHEN Tom Thumb, the diminutive Englishman, toured the United States under the auspices of the mighty P. T. Barnum, father of the circus, he stopped in Utah to visit Brigham Young. Perched on the edge of a chair in the parlor of the Beehive House, he conversed with several church leaders. Said the minute Tom to the massive Brigham: "There is one thing I cannot understand about you Mormons, and that is, to put it bluntly, this here polygamy." President Young stood casually by the fireplace, leaning his elbow on the mantle. After a moment's pause he turned solemnly to Mr. Thumb. "Don't worry," he replied, "when I was your size I didn't understand it either."

In 1932 another distinguished Englishman visited the United States. He stopped in Hollywood and later came ashore in New York City long enough to make a speech. This gentleman, George Bernard Shaw, spoke of many things, including the political mindedness of Americans. "Make any issue political," said the sage of the drama, "and the American people will understand it." He mentioned the Mormons and polygamy. "With them polygamy was not a sex issue. If it had been, the Latter-Day Saints would not have tolerated the practice for a moment. It was for them a great political issue."

Many politically minded Gentiles tried to make of polygamy a moral issue. The Mormons hedged the institution of celestial marriage about with various moral tests and safeguards. In the heat of the battle they would not have called polygamy a matter of politics. But it was essentially a political expedient for speeding the rapid growth of Zion. This is a fact about polygamy that the Saints did not admit or recognize, and one that Gentiles did not or would not understand.

Now that the sound and the fury of the battle is over, even the Mormons are much more objective about the plurality issue. Many Mormons will admit now much that they once denied. The revelation sanctioning polygamy was allegedly dictated by Joseph Smith to William Clayton on July 12, 1843. It is now known that Prophet Joseph had taken plural wives to his bosom even in 1841, and church history concedes that he probably taught the principle ten years earlier. It was not deemed wise then to make the principle known.[1]

The objective of celestial marriage in the mind of Joseph Smith is not clear. Except in terms of beauty or some other intangible value, polygamy is not explained. But there was no mistaking the reason for polygamy under Brigham Young. It was for the purpose of producing children. It would be a snug harbor for any woman—widow or spinster—of child-bearing age and in need of a husband. Here was clearly a social purpose.

There is no need to discuss here the validity of the Mormon claim that Joseph Smith espoused a number of wives. It is generally known that his first wife, Emma Hale Smith, who later joined the Josephite branch of the church, denied that the prophet entered polygamy. The Josephites say: "If he married so many women and lived as a husband with them, why were there no children? Smith had children by his wife, Emma." To this the Brighamites have no answer, but they do name the women who were wed to Brother Joseph, and the testimonies of these women are made available.

One of the alleged wives was the poetess, Eliza R. Snow, sister of Apostle Lorenzo Snow and later one of the wives of Brigham Young. Another was Louisa Beeman, said to be the first woman to become a plural wife. She later married Brigham Young. Lucy Walker, the tenth of fifteen alleged wives of the prophet, later became one of the wives of Heber C. Kimball. She was one of the several women who in later years acknowledged her marriage to Smith.

When Lucy Walker's mother died in 1842, leaving ten children, Prophet Joseph took a number of the children, including the 16-year-old Lucy, to his home. Sometime during that year, according to her own report, he called her to him. "I have a message for you. I have been commanded of God to take another wife, and you are the woman." The girl was shocked and responded in some negative manner. Smith then demanded: "Do you not believe me to be a prophet of God?" The girl responded in the affirmative, but she did not accept the proposal. Smith assured her: "If you pray sincerely for light and understanding . . . . you will receive a testimony of the correctness of this principle."

The girl did pray for faith and light. However: "Gross darkness instead of light took possession of my mind. I was tempted and tortured beyond endurance until my life was not desirable." Some days later the prophet approached her again saying: "I have no flattering words to offer. It is a command of God to you. I will give you until tomorrow to decide this matter. If you reject this message, the gate will be closed forever against you."

Of her reaction, Lucy Walker wrote: "This aroused every drop of Scotch in my veins. . . . . I felt at this moment that I was called to place myself upon the altar, a living sacrifice. . . . . This was too much. . . . . I had been speechless, but at last found utterance and said, 'Although you are a prophet of God, you could not induce me to take a step of so great importance, unless I knew that God approved my course. I would rather die.' "

The prophet mellowed and assured her that she would yet receive a testimony which would convince her. Her account then indicates that in response to prayer the dark cloud left her and a sweet calm entered her soul. Next time she saw the prophet he noted the change in her attitude. He said: "Thank God, you have the testimony. I, too, have prayed." Then he led her to a chair and blessed her with every blessing. They were married by William Clayton on May 1, 1843.[2]

In the course of his abrupt courtship of Lucy Walker, Joseph Smith said that the time was near when "we will go beyond the Rocky Mountains, and then you will be acknowledged and honored as my wife." Perhaps this was one of the basic reasons for his urgent interest in migration. The tanglements of the net which he had woven in all these secret espousals must have been discomfiting. He was not sure that the doctrine of plurality would be accepted by all the leaders of the church, although it had been revealed by him to a few.

There were already enough tensions in the Mormon community at Nauvoo without permitting the polygamy issue to come out in the open. Smith did well to keep his own wife from publicly exploding. William Clayton, private secretary to the prophet, who kept the revelation secret for so many years, related in 1874 the following episode.

On July 12, 1843, Joseph Smith and his brother Hyrum came into the office. They were discussing the plurality doctrine. Hyrum said: "If you write down the revelation, I'll take it to Emma and convince her." "You don't know Emma like I do," Joseph responded sadly. Nonetheless, Joseph dictated the revelation to Clayton. Hyrum left with the document, to reason with Emma. Very soon he came back, reporting that he never met so much fury before. Later on, to appease his wife, Joseph tore up the revelation in her presence. But a copy had been made and preserved.[3]

This revelation, which the prophet did not put down on paper until two years after instituting the doctrine, turns out, upon examination, to be largely an argument for the principle and a warning to the one woman who would have none of it. The fifty-fourth verse of this document reads: "And I command mine handmaiden, Emma Smith, to abide and cleave to my servant, Joseph, and to no one else. But if she will not abide this commandment, she shall be destroyed, saith the Lord."

How did other women accept the teaching of plurality? Probably the case of Mary Ann Price Hyde, Wife No. 3 of Apostle Orson Hyde, is typical. She was a convert to Mormonism who migrated to Nauvoo about 1842. Some time after her arrival in that place she received a call from Hyde, bearing letters from her friends in England. In response to his invitation she visited his home, where she met the prophet. In the course of the evening Smith launched forth on the principle of plurality. As Hyde later took her home in his carriage, he asked what she thought of the principle. She answered that it was "repugnant" to her feelings, and she rejected Hyde's offer of marriage.

> Thus it rested for a while, and Mr. Hyde married another young lady. In the meantime I was trying to learn the character of the leading men, for I sincerely hoped they were men of God. . . . . I soon learned to my satisfaction that Mr. Orson Hyde was a conscientious, upright, noble man, and became his third wife. Mrs. Hyde had two sweet little girls, and I soon learned to love them and their dear mother, who in the spring of 1843 received me into her home as her husband's wife, sealed to him by Joseph Smith, the Prophet, in her presence.[4]

In Nauvoo during the period of clandestine plurality the brethren were very cautious. It was not so ten years later in Utah. Those who accepted the Gospel on the first tenets of the faith, little by little found themselves enveloped with all the schematic mesh of related principles. The Saint who elsewhere might have rebelled against polygamy, in the utopian Mormon community found it not at all repulsive. It was one of the important guide signs on the road to eternity and was evil only to those who thought evil. Whatever some wife may have thought of the principle privately, the social pressures did not encourage outspoken opposition even to her husband. The women could approve and defend polygamy much easier than contemplate the end to which the church would come if Mormonism succumbed to gentile opposition.

It would be helpful if some statistical information were available on Mormon polygamy, but the time seems not yet ripe for the church to delve into its records for that purpose. The author attempted to obtain some information for southern Utah from the books of the United States Bureau of the Census. The census-taker did not hesitate to write down the facts about plural families. It is not possible to identify all such families, because the wives sometimes lived in different towns or even in different counties. It was possible to identify by name in Washington County for 1880 a total of 71 plural families. This would constitute one polygamist to each ten or twelve monogamists. In other parts of the church the proportion of polygamists was doubtless smaller.

Of the 71 polygamists identified, 61 had only two wives and 10 had three or more. If there were others with more than two wives, they were not identified. The fact that the typical plural family included but two wives may be significant. To illustrate: the husband would humbly inform his wife that he had been commanded to enter polygamy, that it had not been at his own suggestion, that he still loved his wife, but that a good Saint must follow his file leaders. When one southern Utah woman was approached by her husband in this identical manner, she answered: "I will give my consent if you select a woman I can approve. But don't come to me next year and say you have been commanded to take a third wife." Had this brother brought up the subject of a third wife, he might have been suspected of other motivations than obedience to the Gospel.

The writer examined the record books of the United States Census Bureau for 1860, 1870, and 1880. The task of reviewing the records for the whole of Utah was too much of an undertaking; so the examination was confined to southern Utah communities. The findings for twelve communities in Iron and Washington counties were reviewed for 1860.

In these twelve communities in 1860 were 1,664 persons, or 293 households. In the 293 households were 897 children under 15 years of age. This is mentioned because it indicates the extent to which children shared in the hazards of that frontier.

It was possibly to identify among the 293 households a total of 25 polygamous families in which two or more women were listed as "wife." There were doubtless other plural families that could not be so identified. This would apply especially to some of those families that had recently moved to the south from elsewhere but where the husbands had not taken more than one wife along.

Nineteen of the 25 polygamists had two-wife families. Three others had three wives. Two men, Isaac Haight and Dudley Leavitt, each had four wives. Leavitt, who lived in Pine Valley, was then 30 years of age; and his wives were 22, 19, 17, and 14 years old. Leavitt was a Canadian. Two of his wives were born in Iowa, one in Illinois, and the fourth in England.

THE FAMILY OF THOMAS D. LEAVITT OF BUNKERVILLE, NEVADA

Beside Leavitt are his two wives. Behind each wife are her eleven children, twenty-two in all—four daughters and seven sons by one wife, and seven daughters and four sons by the other—all healthy, normal people.

The most-married man of the 25 polygamists was John D. Lee, of Harmony, then in his forty-seventh year. His ten wives ranged from 17 to 46 years of age. It is known that Lee had married other women; but, if they were living and still loyal to him, they were not in southern Utah.

The two youngest of the polygamists were G. W. Adair and H. Dalton. Adair, age 23, had two wives—one 16 and the other 14 years of age. Dalton was 25. One of his wives, age 27, was born in Illinois; the other was an English woman of 28 years. The median age of the 25 polygamists in 1860 was 42 years; that of their oldest or older wives, 41 years; and that of other wives, 26 years. It was not possible to determine from the census records which women were first and which were "other wives." It was assumed that most of the "oldest" were the first wives. There were 39 additional wives to whom the designation "other" was conveniently applied.

Regarding the place of birth of polygamists and their wives, it was found that 15 of the 25 men were born in the United States, 7 were born in England, and 1 each came from Canada, Denmark, and Scotland. Of the 25 oldest wives, 12 were born in the United States, 9 in England, 2 in Denmark, and 2 in Scotland. Of the other wives, 21 were born in the United States, 14 in England, 3 in Denmark, and 1 in Australia. These figures indicate that, of the 64 wives in the 25 families, 31 were foreign born, 26 being of English or Scottish extraction and 5 of Danish.

From the same source the writer obtained data on polygamists reported in the census enumerations for 1870 and 1880. Unfortunately, the data for 1890 were not available, these records having been destroyed by fire. Also, because the review of the records for a wider area would have involved an excessive amount of labor, the writer limited the examination of the 1870 records to three southern Utah counties—Iron, Kane, and Washington. This examination yielded 82 polygamist families which could be identified. For 1880 the examination was limited to Washington County and yielded 71 polygamist families. The 82 families for 1870 and the 71 families for 1880 were deemed to be samples sufficient for comparative purposes.

The following table shows the comparative distribution of husbands and wives in polygamous families according to three age groupings.

Age Groups	Husbands		Wives	
	1870	1880	1870	1880
Under 20 years	0	0	7	0
20–44 years	35	15	130	86
45 years or over	47	56	52	64
Total	82	71	189	150

Polygamists who were under 45 years of age diminished relatively between 1870 and 1880. Of the 25 polygamists reported above for 1860, only 7, less than one-third, were over 45 years of age. Ten of the 64 wives of the 25 polygamists reported for 1860 were under 20 years of age, and only 11 were 45 years of age or older. The above table shows 7 of the young wives in 1870 and none in 1880, but there was a relative increase of wives 45 years or older.

Aging of polygamists and their wives is shown in the table below, which sets forth the median ages for 1860, 1870, and 1880.

	Median Age		
	1860	1870	1880
Polygamous husbands	42	48	56
Oldest wives	41	45	46
Other wives	26	31	36

This table scarcely needs any comment, except the caution that it represents but a small number of polygamists in a remote area of Zion.

On the matter of age of polygamous spouses, additional information is obtained by comparing the ages of polygamous husbands and wives with monogamous husbands and wives. This is done in the next table for Washington County in 1880. At

Silver Reef, a gentile mining camp located in the county, there were no polygamous families. The monogamous families at Silver Reef were not included, and it is safe to say that practically all the cases reported in the table below were Mormon families.

Age Groups	Polygamous Families		Monogamous Families	
	Husbands	Wives	Husbands	Wives
Under 20 years	0	0	0	13
20–44 years	15	86	124	153
45 years or over	56	64	128	86
Total	71	150	252	252

Daughters of Zion in Dixie in 1880 were not entering polygamy, although they were getting married at an early age. Speaking in terms of percentages, the comparison of the husbands and wives 45 years of age or older is most pertinent. Of the polygamous wives who were above the normal child-bearing age there were 64, or 43 per cent of the total number, whereas but 35 per cent of the monogamous wives were in this age group.

One measure of social sanction of polygamy would be the proportion of Utah-born men and women who entered plural marriage. In 1880 the church had been in Utah more than 30 years. The age of marrying for women on the frontier was at about the age of 20, and for young men the marriage age was about 22. The next table shows the nativity in general of polygamous and monogamous husbands and wives in Washington County in 1880.

Nativity	Polygamous Families		Monogamous Families	
	Husbands	Wives	Husbands	Wives
Born in Utah	2	15	45	77
Born in other states	31	46	99	69
Born in other countries	38	89	108	106
Total	71	150	252	252

Only 2 of the 71 polygamous husbands and 15 of the 150 polygamous wives were born in Utah. Put another way, 10 per cent of the polygamous wives, compared with 30 per cent of the monogamous wives, were natives of Utah. Utah had in 1880 a large percentage of Mormons of foreign birth. Presenting the percentages in whole numbers, 54 per cent of the polygamous husbands, compared with 43 per cent of the monogamist husbands, were foreign born. Of the wives, 59 per cent of those married polygamously were foreign born, compared with 42 per cent for the monogamous wives.

Why were so many foreign-born wives found among the polygamous families? Two answers have been given: (*a*) Foreign-born single women who came to Zion were sometimes older women, many of them ranging from 25 to 35 years of age. They were anxious to obtain husbands but could not compete with the younger Mormon women for the younger men. Polygamy was a boon for them. (*b*) These female converts from abroad were usually sent to families of their own nationality—Danish women to Danish families, English to English families, Swiss to Swiss families. The element of proximity, coupled with social necessity, encouraged plural matches.

A look at the population of Utah as reported by the census for 1870 and 1880 would show that the number of males and females were about equal. The outsider, viewing this array of information, might argue that polygamy was not fair or democratic. In Utah there were men enough to furnish husbands for the available women. Mormon women who migrated to Utah to get husbands were determined to marry in the church, if possible. A good share of the Gentiles in Utah were eligible men but were nonexistent as far as the Mormon women were concerned. It was frowned upon for Mormon women to have friendly social intercourse with Gentiles.

One of the bishops of St. George in 1867 brought to trial one of the plural wives of Brother Bleak on the charge of

> unchristianlike conduct in permitting men to visit her at untimely hours and for indulging in immoral and indecent conversation with them upon such occasions and for making false statements in reference to the extent of the in-

timacy between herself and these men: Charles Dowthett, George Miller and Charles Hawes, they being Gentiles of disreputable character, stopping in our midst.

Actually what Sister Bleak had done was to take in three strangers as roomers and boarders. Not only had she been cordial with them, it was also charged that she had been indiscreet. The neighbors, who listened and peeked, reported that she had complained against her polygamist husband, saying that he did not love her, that he did not provide for her; and she showed the hem of her underskirt as evidence of the ragged clothing she was obliged to wear.

It was also testified by neighbors that Sister Bleak made merry with the strangers in a jumping game and that Gentiles called her by her first name. It was alleged, too, that one of the men brought whiskey into the house and that another of the strangers boasted that he had killed a man.

The husband said he did not believe the evidence revealed that his wife had enjoyed "any criminal connection with any of these men," but he was offended that she should speak ill of him to strangers.

This problem might never have arisen had the three Gentiles first presented themselves to the bishop, asking for help in finding a place for room and board. He would have selected a lodging in a home where there were no young children or young women. The bishop said that Sister Bleak had ignored the duty of the priesthood "to protect the people here from these Gentiles while she made them comfortable at her fireside."

It was ruled that Sister Bleak "rendered herself subject to censure and must stand rebuked and disfellowshiped until she gives satisfactory evidence of repentance." A year later, in company with her husband, she came before the bishop's court, showed her humility, and was forgiven.

The census of Washington County for 1880 showed that 77 per cent of the women 15 years of age and older were living in wedlock, compared with about 60 per cent in 1930. In 1880, by the same census report, 14 per cent of the women were single, compared with 25 per cent in 1930; and 9 per cent were widowed or divorced in 1880, compared with 15 per cent in 1930.

Out of each 100 women in Washington County in 1880, when polygamy was in flower, 77 had husbands; but in 1930 monogamous Washington County showed but 60 women of each 100 married and living with their husbands.

It was a policy of the church that all bishops, stake presidents, and other persons in ecclesiastical authority were expected to be plurally wedded. In some cases men were advised to enter polygamy as a preparation for being promoted to some position of authority. But no man entered polygamy without first getting the consent of those in authority over him: his bishop, his stake president, and, sometimes, the president of the church. He could not take a plural wife without being married in the church by officers with authority to perform such marriages.

Charles Walker wrote in his journal on September 16, 1865. that he had asked Brother Brigham if could take another wife, President Young answered: "I have no objection if it is all right with your bishop and president." Walker remained a two-wife polygamist.

There was a man in Cedar City who already had two wives. He reported that he had had a dream in which he saw the faces of two women, and they belonged to him. Sometime later he went to Salt Lake City. While visiting a friend, he met two women. He recognized their faces as the faces of his dream, and on the first opportunity he told them of the dream. They were converts who had recently come from England. They had come to Zion to marry and rear families. They had prayed that the Lord would provide them with acceptable husbands.

The good brother went to see Brigham Young, reporting his dream and the prayers of the women. Brother Brigham said: "Bring them on and I will seal them to you, for you are the kind of a man I like to see get ahead."

There was a young man in the town of Virgin who became a counselor to the bishop. President McAllister of the St. George Stake reminded him that he was duty-bound to take another wife. He hesitated. Then he asked his wife, a good and reasonable woman who had borne him seven children. She gave her consent, provided he married a "sensible helpmate and not a silly little girl."

His duty from that point on was clear, but still he hesitated. He went to the Lord in prayer. Each time that he saw a woman who might qualify as Wife No. 2, he would ask of the Lord for light. Would the Lord give him some sign whether he should propose to the girl in question, or wait. He kept on waiting. It should be added that the period of his hesitancy was from 1887 to 1890, when the polygamy raids were on. Then came the Manifesto, and the issue passed. Of this experience he later wrote: "I felt greatly relieved, for in my heart I never really wanted two wives."

Polygamy was not romantic. It was marriage primitive and practical, as it would have to be to serve the celestial objectives of the New and Everlasting Covenant. The wife who would prevent her husband from entering plurality would thereby detract from her glory and lose her husband in the hereafter.

The reader can fill in the blank places between items found in the journal of Joseph Fish. He wrote on July 17, 1869: "I started for Salt Lake today. Went as far as Beaver. Took my wife with me, also a young lady by the name of Eliza Jane Lewis." On Monday, July 26, at Salt Lake City, Fish wrote: "Eliza Ann Lewis was sealed to me today. My wife, Mary was willing for this step to be taken, but still she took the matter a little hard, but she tried to be reasonable, but she did not quite come up to the mark at all times. We went to the theatre in the evening." Of his courtship with Mary Steele, Fish confided much to his journal. There were no entries of his courtship of the second wife. He later married two additional wives.

It must be remembered that frontier life itself was not romantic. Pioneer people were motivated by elementary survival interests, and none were more practical than some of those pioneer women, many of whom favored men who were most secure economically and able to provide the substance for living.

John D. Lee, however much of a villian he turned out to be, was such a good provider. He had nineteen wives.

Lee wrote in his journal for February 23, 1847, regarding the event leading to the accession of his twelfth wife:

> Had some conversation with Sister Nancy Gibbons, who had come to me for that purpose. She told me that she was without a friend that she could in reality claim as a counselor or lodge the secrets of her breasts with, and that she had thought rather hard of me, for I was one of the first elders that brought the Gospel to her and a man in whom she always reposed the most exquisite trust and confidence in, and that I had never been to see her and advise her since her exodus to the mountains, and why I should treat her so cooly and be a stranger, she could not account. She had often thought of speaking to me and asking me the reason why I was so distant to her.
>
> I told her that I always had the warmest feelings of friendship for her, and the reason for my not being more familiar with her was that her sister, Sarah, was sealed to Brother A. O. Smoot, and that inasmuch as he had brought her [Nancy] from Tennessee that he likely had claims on her, and always wishing to attend to my own business, I said nothing to her for fear that I might cause feelings with Bro. Smoot.
>
> She assured me that it was not, nor never had been her mind to be connected with him, that she traveled with his family through necessity because she was not acquainted with any other family, and that she wanted I should take charge of her and her effects, that is if I considered her worth taking off.
>
> I asked her if she wished to be connected with me in marriage according to the seal of the covenant. She replied, I do, and am willing to fare as you do in all things in adversity. Your request shall be granted.[5]

At the time of making the above entry in his journal, Lee was about 35 years of age and Nancy Gibbons was 48. She needed a home and a man to take charge of her and her affairs. Lee's decision in her case was a generous one.

The story which follows was told to the writer by the granddaughter of one of the St. George pioneers. It is an example of latter-day romanticizing by the children about the polygamy of their pioneer progenitors. The man in the case was a leader in the southern frontier. He had charge of several companies of Saints crossing the plains and had brought to Utah at least one of the handcart companies. He was one of the first elders publicly to preach polygamy to the world, but the story reports that he did not himself take a plural wife. Several times he had been reminded of his duty; and finally, in the presence of the man's wife, Brigham Young ordered the good brother to enter polygamy or he would have to surrender his position of authority in the church.

According to the story told by the granddaughter, this great pioneer leader, who could fight Indians without a twitch of fear, trembled at the prospect of taking another wife. When he appealed to his wife, she gave her consent but refused to help him with his courting.

He called on a neighbor and spoke to the woman of the house, asking permission to court her daughter. The mother appreciated the offer but suggested that the daughter was too young. She did not want her daughter to marry until she had passed her sixteenth year.

Then the brother went to another neighbor and in the same manner appealed to the mother. Again he received the answer. The mother did not think her daughter should consider marriage before she was sixteen.

Discouraged with these efforts, the brother was about to give up when the first mother came to him, saying that she had talked the matter over with her husband. She and her husband had prayed about the proposal. They had talked with their daughter and had reached the conclusion that the marriage would be desirable.

Next day the second mother came; and she, too, related that she and her husband had prayed. They had spoken to their daughter. They had come to the same conclusion, and the proposed marriage was approved.

This left the brother in a serious quandary; both proposals had been accepted, but neither mother knew that he had proposed to the other for her daughter's hand. The brother went to his wife. She answered that she had done her part by giving consent; it was for him to do the rest.

It was then that the baffled brother called the two mothers together. He explained how he had been told to enter polygamy, how he had gone to one and then the other, and how both had accepted. It was an honest explanation. He hoped they would forgive him if he had caused hard feelings.

Neither of the mothers cared to withdraw from the proposal;

so the good brother, according to the story, took both young ladies to the temple the same day. On the same day he brought both young brides to his home. His wife took them in as she would daughters. She retired from the kitchen to the front room and thereafter took life easy and deported herself toward the new wives as if they were children; and their children she treated as if they were grandchildren. All lived happily in the same red-stone house.

Such is the story the grandchildren tell. However, several years later the writer found that the facts as written in the census records for 1880 were quite at variance. The pioneer did have three wives. The names were as reported. But the plural wives were not wedded to him on the same day and were not the same age. In 1880 the census showed that the husband and his oldest wife were each 59 years of age. The ages of the other two wives were 39 years and 24 years.[6]

Whether the above story is true or false, parents did not rise up and protest if their daughters married in polygamy. True, the issue did not often arise, because there were young men on hand to supply husbands for the daughters of Zion. There were stories of older men pushing the young men aside in order to obtain the young women as plural wives. The statistics given above would not confirm that report. Only a single case of an older man taking over younger women came to the attention of the writer. One of the pioneers of Toquerville in 1856 married a widow. Her husband died crossing the plains with a handcart company. It is now a legend that this brother offered to marry her and care for her two little girls, who were twins, provided she would consent to his marrying the daughters when they reached the proper age. He kept the young men away, and when the girls were 16 years of age he married them both. He had two children by the mother, but none by the two daughters. Like most polygamists, he was persecuted and was one of those sent to prison. The two wives survived their mother (co-wife) and their mutual husband by many years. There were numerous cases of pluralists marrying sisters, but few of the same man marrying mother and daughter.[7]

Frontier Mormons who were economically secure were most likely to be called to positions of authority, which was the road to polygamy. Some of the brothers who were economically well situated were instructed to take additional wives. There were, also, men who assumed the obligations of polygamy but who were not good providers. Here is the case of a polygamist who was lazy and parasitic:

Sister Cragin, second wife of James Cragin, brought a complaint before one of the bishops of St. George in December, 1867. She had been married two years, but her husband had not provided, although he had eaten often at her table. She was tired of having him appear every alternate day, doing nothing and bringing nothing. He had not worked on her house. He did not haul wood. He took her wagon and a span of horses and killed a beef which belonged to her. He sold twelve gallons of molasses of hers and gave in return only a hundred pounds of flour. He replied that she kept asking him to come to see her, but he was getting tired of her cooking. He said that now she takes her bedding and sleeps separate from him.

The bishop told Cragin to give the woman a divorce and pay the expenses of the same, but he was not required to pay back what he had taken or consumed.

The "beauty and order in plurality" of which the elders spoke, and the security that women enjoyed in such marriage, if they conformed, did not gainsay the fact that it was an institution for exalting the male side of the house. Polygamy imposed responsibility on the husband, but the penalties for neglect of duty were not generally so severe for men as for women. Plural wives fared well only if they were fortunate enough to have husbands who were fair and generous.

This arrangement was not without its compensations. The plural wife found comfort in her children, probably more so than other wives; and she was more the head of her own household than other wives. For example, in Bunkerville, Nevada, lived the fourth wife of a polygamist. Although this brother lived in fairly comfortable circumstances, he did not provide well for his fourth wife. Possibly this was due to the fact that she had been previously wedded and was a widow. She became mother to seven children by her second husband.

In the next life, according to Mormon doctrine, all of her children would belong, not to their earthly father, the husband of four wives, but to her first husband. Naturally, a man who enters polygamy to rear children for his own glory in the next life feels reluctant about expending his substance for the benefit of his children who will belong in the hereafter to another man. So Wife No. 4 was greviously neglected, but she never complained. She provided for her children and sent all of them through college. The father practically faded from a place in the family; and, while his name was held in proper respect, she was the honored head of a clan.

In the town of Washington dwelt a pioneer brother, a pluralist who once was bishop of Virgin. About 1887, when he was quite an aged man, he married a young woman. When polygamy prosecutions began, to avoid arrest, he left the country. She was unhappy about the marriage and appealed for a church divorce, that she might marry again and rear a family. She sent her appeal to the presidency of the St. George Stake. Those brethren on October 24, 1888, wrote to Wilford Woodruff, then president of the church:

> Sister Sina M. stated she wanted a bill of divorce from Brother P., as he had never fulfilled his marriage vows with her; that she was as much of a virgin as she ever had been; that although he had slept with her every Sunday night for a considerable time, he had never had intercourse with her, alleging the cause that he was ruptured; that he had been the means of her going to Salt Lake City and had made no provision for her, although, in her opinion, he might have done so. She feels that if he was ruptured so as to make him incompetent he should have told her so before marriage. She further stated that her love for the Gospel and desire to be fulfilling her duty as a wife makes her desire a divorce by the Church authorities.
>
> The brethren, on hearing her statement, felt that she should be released. Brother P. is now in England, an indictment for polygamy has been found against him since his departure for that country. We submit the foregoing for your consideration. We feel that when a woman wants a bill of divorce, it is hard to satisfy her without one.

The files of the High Council contain a letter of later date in which President Woodruff sanctioned the divorce. It must be said of the plural wives in southern Utah that the records of the High Council reveal no cases of women wanting to shake off the responsibilities of polygamy because of hardship. On the contrary, when the antipolygamy laws went into effect and polygamists were forced to go into hiding, there was a great rallying to their defense. The wives of the plurally married, to the extent that they shared the persecution, enjoyed a preferred status, even a little social distinction in the united Mormon community.

Charles L. Walker, of St. George, wrote several poems dealing with the "vexed question." Space limitations permit the inclusion of but one offering of this poet-polygamist. He wrote in his journal on May 17, 1885, that the lines were read before a "Sunday School jubilee at the tabernacle" and were "received with much enthusiasm."

The sun is still shining,
The miners are mining,
And the Liberals are whining . . . . In Utah.

The bees are yet humming,
The summer is coming,
The jurors are bumming . . . . In Utah.

The judges are packers
Of juries, their backers,
The attorneys tell whackers . . . . In Utah.

The 'taters are growing,
The waters are flowing,
There's a bad legal showing . . . . In Utah.

The stars still keep shining,
Bootlickers are pining,
For trade is declining . . . . In Utah.

There's an underground railroad
Evading the bail road,
Which ne'er was a jail road . . . . In Utah.

The girls still keep singing,
While washing and wringing,
There's none of them cringing . . . . In Utah.

The cows are yet eating,
The sheep are still bleating,
While the lawyers are cheating . . . . In Utah.

While the marshals are slumming,
There's no thought of succumbing,
For the babies keep coming . . . . In Utah.

As stated at the outset of this chapter, the political objective of polygamy was to increase the population in order to spread the might of Zion. As a consequence, men and women had honor by the patriarchal standard. As late as 1904 an apostle, speaking in St. George, extolled large families. He mentioned a Kanab polygamist who, at the age of 49, was father of fifty-three children. It must also be recorded here that many of his children had been added to his family after the Manifesto.[8]

During 1917 the writer visited the home of a Jones family in St. Johns, Arizona. The head of the family introduced his two wives and two or three grown children by each wife. He sat at the head of the table with the first wife on his right and the second on his left. It was a regular family meal, with about ten persons sitting down to eat; and it was a genial gathering, with considerable banter between the young folks about affairs of the heart. The fact that there were two wives present did not in any way enter the conversation, nor did it seem to be a matter of thought.[9]

During the several years from 1908 on, the writer became acquainted intimately with the three-wife family of Thomas S. Terry. The first occasion, in his presence when all three wives and their husband gathered about the fireplace and made conversation, was for the writer one of uneasiness. Later it became a matter of routine to be at dinner, with all three wives present and the old patriarch presiding over the meal.

In 1849 Terry married Mary Ann, daughter of Zera Pulsipher, a pioneer who had been with the church from Kirtland through the persecutions in Missouri and later in Nauvoo. To this union was born three sons and nine daughters, all of whom lived to rear families.

In 1854, while still residing near Salt Lake City, Terry married Eliza Ann, another daughter of Zera Pulsipher. To this union, also, was born twelve children—three sons and nine daughters—and these also lived to rear families of their own.

THE HOUSE OF TERRY

The gentleman with the snow-white beard at the center is Thomas S. Terry, Sr. At his right and left and at front are his three wives. Also present are most of his thirty children and a considerable number of his grandchildren. This picture was taken at Terry's Ranch in 1905. Most of the grandchildren in the front and others who came later have since reared families of their own, and some are now grandparents. The living descendants now number more than nine hundred.

Incidently, both Pulsipher sisters were married to Terry at the age of 16 years.

Terry did not take his third wife until 1885, which was years after he had settled on Shoal Creek. He was then bishop of Hebron. He married as his third wife, Louisa Hannah Leavitt, a daughter of Dudley Leavitt,[10] a polygamist who later settled in Bunkerville, Nevada. To this union was born six children—two sons and four daughters.

In July, 1933, the writer made an effort to obtain some statistical information about the House of Terry. It was not easy to get full reports, because the parts of families had scattered to several states and the information about new marriages and births had not been so faithfully gathered as when the patriarch and all his wives were alive. Only the third wife was alive in 1933. Terry died at the age of 95, his first wife at the age of 82, and his second wife at the age of 78 years. The table below shows the living and dead in the Terry family at the time of the count to be 919. Of the 92 dead, 76 were infants or small children.

Children of T. S. Terry	As of July, 1933—		
	Living	Dead	Total
Children of the three wives	24	6	30
Grandchildren	165	29	194
Great-grandchildren	506	47	553
Great-great-grandchildren	132	10	142
Total	827	92	919

The next table shows the number of descendants of Terry's Wife No. 1 in 1933, which was eighty-three years after the birth of her first child in 1850.

What manner of people were these descendants of polygamist Terry? There was no record of feeble-mindedness or of social maladjustments.[11] Physically, they were strong, well-sized, and healthy. In about one hundred and fifty marriages up to 1933, there had been but three divorces. The first and second generations were mainly farmers and ranchers. There was not land enough in that region to provide farms for the third generation, and a considerable number of the young men and women migrated, some to become farmers elsewhere, some to enter industry, and still others to enter the professions.[12]

The real test of Mormon loyalty came when the government assumed the task of abolishing polygamy by law. The behavior of the Mormons was disappointing to the gentile advocates of

Descendants of Wife No. 1	As of July, 1933—		
	Living	Dead	Total
Children	11	1	12
Grandchildren	79	16	95
Great-grandchildren	347	25	372
Great-great-grandchildren	104	10	114
Total	541	52	593

antipolygamy laws. They expected the plural wives and others to come to the deputy marshals, the judges, and prosecutors bearing complaints. They found the Mormons united. Even Mormons who may have been privately against polygamy were among the ardent opponents of the "deps," those catchers of "cohabs," as the polygamists were called.

The two most-mentioned "deps" in southern Utah were James McGeary and John Armstrong. A Dixieite who was a youth in the polygamy days said of them: "Some were afraid to sell wine to the deps, or even give it to them, but they would say they did not care about wine sellers. Their job was to catch cohabs." Armstrong and McGeary, however unpopular their job, were not unpopular in the communities. They had a habit of calling at the homes of polygamists, where they were often invited to stop for something to eat; and, while eating, they would jokingly say: "We know your husband is out hiding somewhere. Maybe we'll catch him next time we come to town."

Delaun Cox was a polygamist who lived in Orderville. Normally he was hiding when the deputies came to town, but on this occasion he was surprised. While at work in his blacksmith shop, Armstrong burst in on him and began reading a warrant for his arrest. A neighbor came rushing in just in time to hear the officer pronouncing the words "for the arrest of Alonzo Cox."

"Brother Cox," said the neighbor, "this warrant is for some other man."

"That's right," replied the polygamist, "I am not Alonzo Cox. My name is Delaun, commonly called "Laun."

Tricked by a technicality, Armstrong joined in the laugh on himself and promised to be back soon. Cox sportingly wished him "better luck next time."

John S. Stucki, of Santa Clara, related in his autobiography an experience he had had with Armstrong and McGeary. He had just learned that his name was on the list of wanted men and was on the alert. One day he came home and found both deputies waiting for him. He had in his hands some fruit from his orchard, which he graciously handed to them. He asked them to remain for dinner. When they offered to pay for the dinner, he refused their money. To his surprise, they made no move to arrest him. Stucki wrote that all the while he prayed silently for deliverance. He concluded: "We can see how wonderfully God can protect His humble children."

In the records of the St. George Stake is a letter, dated September 3, 1887, sent by one polygamist to another who was in hiding. The letter reported two surprise raids on the town. On both occasions the "deps" came after midnight, and each time the alarm went from house to house, *after* the raids started. No arrests were made.

They raided President McArthur's, A. R. Whitehead's two houses and Edmund A. Hendrix's lot first, then his two houses; after which they concluded to leave town, for it was by that time daylight. In going out they stopped at Booth's second wife's, and there being no curtain in the way, McGeary looked in and saw the woman in bed. She being awake, asked him what he wanted. He said that he was a U.S. officer and wanted Mr. Booth.

She said he was not here but she would get up and let him search, but he said she need not mind, at present he was satisfied Booth was not there.

I feel gratified in stating that, so far as I have heard, those three officers: McGeary, Armstrong, and another whose name I have not learned, acted in all their questionings and searches, which were very close, in a gentlemanly, officerlike manner, giving no unnecessary annoyance.

That could not be said of all the deputies. Their behavior was far less cordial in other places. At Parowan, as mentioned in a previous chapter, one of the "deps" shot and killed a polygamist. In St. George there is a record of at least one polygamist, A. R. Whitehead, mentioned above, having been shot at twice while escaping on horseback.

When the Manifesto was issued in 1890, the church was confronted with new problems. Thereafter no good Mormon would enter polygamy, but some did. Some went to Mexico and there espoused plural wives. Some were charged with having wedded plural wives on the high seas, where the "law of the land" does not prevail. This was to be expected. The sudden reversal of church policy could not have gone into force with full and faithful observance. Many people had doubts about the Manifesto. President Woodruff had to plead with the Saints. This is shown in an item written by Charles L. Walker in his journal on November 7, 1891:

> Wilford Woodruff said, no man that has a plurality of wives is required to break his covenants. He should feed, clothe and educate them and children. He also said the Lord told him to ask the Saints the question, whether it was better to have our temples and places of worship destroyed and our brethren imprisoned and their families suffer, and that to forego the practice of plural marriage? Said he had it word by word from the Lord as to the course to pursue, and that the Manifesto was given to him by inspiration; that the first presidency and the twelve knew what they were doing, and were led by God. President Cannon endorsed his sayings. This, I think, will have a good effect upon the people, and will have a tendency to calm their feelings of disquiet. . . . . Polygamy is at an end.

After the Manifesto there were some cases before the High Council of the St. George Stake of plural wives charging neglect or nonsupport. One wife asked for a divorce so that she could marry again and because her husband "took his bed to himself." At Pinto was a polygamist who lived at peace with his wives until after the Manifesto. The plural wife testified: "When Brother G. came at night to my bed, in a few minutes Sister G. came and smashed the bedroom window with her hand and pulled him out of bed by the whiskers and thrashed him, so of course he went back to her." The High Council reminded Wife No. 1 of her duty. She replied: "I am willing to share my cows and my flour, but not my house and my husband."

Such talking back to the brethren would not have been tolerated by the High Council twenty years, or even ten years, earlier. Here is another case that was heard by the High Council in 1891 and again in 1892: There was in St. George an aged polygamist who had three wives. After the death of his first wife in 1881, he supported the other two as well as he could; but he was practically unemployable in 1891. He began then to expect support from his wives, both of them women under middle age. They charged that he was cantankerous and dominating. They would no longer tolerate him and joined together to expel him. On his final appeal to have the power of the priesthood invoked against his plural wives the Council refused to act.

Not until 1899 was any attempt made by church authorities to obtain information about the status of polygamy. At that time a request was received by the St. George Stake for the number of polygamists in the area about 1890. The report of the clerk showed that there had been 101 polygamists in the stake at the time of the Manifesto, but only 44 were reported for 1899. In 47 families the polygamous union had been broken by the death of the husband or one or more of his wives. Five families had been broken by divorce, and five had moved to other places.[13]

According to this census taken in 1899, it was reported that there had been in all the church a total of 2,451 polygamous families. The same report contained the following information:

Polygamous families broken by death, 1890–99..........	750
Polygamous families broken by divorce, 1890–99........	95
Polygamous families removed from the United States....	63
Polygamous families still existing in 1899...............	1,543

In May, 1902, the church conducted another survey and found that the number of polygamous families had declined to 897, "the great majority of whom were of advanced age."[14]

More than a generation of Mormons have passed to their reward since the heat of the battle on the polygamy issue. All the valiant defenders of that lost principle are gone except a few, including the man, now past 80 years, who heads the Church of Jesus Christ of Latter-Day Saints. Like all the presidents of the church before him, he is, or has been, a polygamist. On April 6, 1885, at the annual conference of the church, the then Apostle Heber J. Grant made a speech in which he defended polygamy. This was reported in the *Deseret News:*

> No matter what restrictions we are placed under by men, our only consistent course is to keep the commandments of God. We should in this regard, place ourselves in the same position as that of the three Hebrews who were cast into the fiery furnace. . . . . It is sometimes held that the Saints are in error because so many are opposed to them. But when people know they are right, it is wrong for them to forego their honest convictions by yielding their judgment to a majority, no matter how large.

What he called a "virtue for sacrifice" in 1885 was less than a virtue in 1935, when, as president of the church, Grant raised his voice with the Gentiles in condemning the clandestine polygamy of a few isolated Saints in the Dixie region.

Out in that area of northwestern Arizona called "the strip" were a few Mormons who were living in polygamy in 1935. Church authorities said they were moved by lustful urges. They were condemned by bishops, stake presidents, and apostles in the same language that Gentiles used against bishops, stake presidents, and apostles in 1885, when Bishop Sharp was removed from ecclesiastical office because he had decided to obey the antipolygamy law.

NOTES

1. In the *Elder's Journal,* issue of May, 1836, Joseph Smith listed some of the questions commonly asked him about the new religion, including: "Do the Mormons believe in having more wives than one?" Smith's answer was: "No, not at the same time." Roberts in his Introduction to Volume V of *History of the Church, Period I* (pp. xxxii–xxxiii) ventures the opinion that Smith was thinking about polygamy as early as 1831.

2. From the statement of Mrs. Lucy Walker Kimball, written by herself and in the possession of her niece, Mrs. Lydia Rogerson, of Ogden, Utah. This document was copied by the Federal Writers' Project, January, 1940. In this statement Mrs. Kimball gave an account of the Haun's Mill massacre, which she as a child witnessed. "They ordered my poor delicate mother out into the deep snow, searched our wagons, took from us our arms and ammunition, pointed their guns at us children to intimidate us, and cursed and swore in a most frightful manner. . . . . I did not tremble. I did not fear them."

3. A copy of this document was made by Joseph C. Kingsbury and was preserved by Newel K. Whitney, whose eldest daughter, Sarah Ann, was one of Smith's plural wives. See *History of the Church, Period I*, Intro., pp. xxxiii–xxxiv.

4. The original letter, dated August 20, 1880, is filed with the notes of H. H. Bancroft in the Bancroft Library, University of California. Many such personal documents were collected by Bancroft for his *History of Utah*.

5. This part of Lee's journal was published at Salt Lake City in 1938 by Charles Kelly. Lee joined the church in 1838, and Kelly claims he was one of the original Missouri Danites. He entered polygamy in 1844.

6. The Daughters of the Utah Pioneers have been active in this urge to sweeten the memory of polygamy. That organization in 1937 issued a lesson booklet entitled *The Other Mother*. It contains a number of biographies of plural families that lived happily. These were written by daughters or granddaughters of those families.

7. Cases of polygamists marrying sisters were frequent. There were cases of polygamists marrying mother and daughter. In his book, *Across the Continent* (p. 123), Samuel Bowles wrote: "Polygamy introduces many cross-relationships and inter-twines the branches of the genealogical tree in a manner greatly to puzzle a mathematician, as well as to disgust the decent-minded. The marrying of two or more sisters is very common. One young Mormon in Salt Lake City has three sisters for his three wives. There are several cases of men marrying both mother (widow) and her daughter or daughters; taking the 'old woman' for the sake of getting the young ones; but having children by all. Please to cipher out for yourselves how this mixes things."

8. An example is found in a story taken from the *Washington County News* for November 7, 1899, reporting that Mother Huntsman, 84 years of age, had a family reunion at which were present 11 children, 88 grandchildren, 142 great-grandchildren, and 7 great-great-grandchildren.

9. In his book, *The Mormon Country: A Summer with the Latter-Day Saints* (p. 65), John Codman reported a visit with the Robbins family on the Bear River in northern Utah: "Mr. Robbins is a family man, and a very good hospitable man we found him. He and his boys, of whom there was quite a number, took care of our horses, and when we entered the house, his wives and daughters, of whom there was another number, amply provided for us. Two of the Mrs. Robbins were nursing babies of about the same age. Each Mrs. R. was dressed exactly like the other. A third Mrs. R. who did not appear to be troubled with a baby just then, cooked the dinner. Several young Robbins of ages intermediate between babyhood and youth, were chirping about, roosting on beds inside, and on fences without, and Mr. R. himself strutted about among them all, with the air of a happy husband and father."

10. Dudley Leavitt had five wives and 53 children. Mrs. Juanita Brooks, of St. George, a granddaughter of two polygamist families, Dudley Leavitt on one side and John Hafen (four wives) on the other, wrote an article about her two grandfathers, "A Close-up of Polygamy," *Harper's Magazine*, February, 1934, pp. 14–18.

11. The following opinion is found in *Californians and Mormons* by A. E. D. De Rupert (p. 161): "Mormon children by the first wife are well-formed, strong and

healthy, but the offspring of wives number two, three and four are generally feeble in body as well as in mind."

12. Arthur K. Hafen, of St. George, wrote a booklet, published locally in 1929, reporting on the family of John G. Hafen, one of the Swiss pioneers of Santa Clara. Hafen had four wives and 27 children. In 1927 his family numbered 211 children, grandchildren, and great-grandchildren. Hafen was then in his eighty-ninth year. The Swiss families expended great effort to send their children to college.

13. Whereas in 1890 there were 101 polygamists in the St. George Stake, the number in 1907, according to records of the High Council, was but 22. Probably none of the 22 polygamists reported for 1907 is alive in 1942.

14. The church figures on these statistics about polygamy were presented on March 5, 1904, to the Senate Committee on Privileges and Elections by Joseph F. Smith, then president of the church, in the hearings to determine the eligibility of Senator Reed Smoot (*Senate Document No. 486* [59th Cong., 1st sess.]).

CHAPTER XVI

THE MORMON WAY OF LIVING

"WE ARE a peculiar people," the Saints often say of themselves, and that self-description has always been developed in terms of contrasts. Gentiles who describe this attitude on the basis of acquaintance with the Mormons are sometimes reminded of a story about a man who entered heaven. As he went about getting acquainted, he noticed a great number of people in an isolated valley. All were facing the center of the valley, their backs to all other people in heaven. The stranger was interested, and he asked why those people kept to themselves when all other inhabitants associated freely. A celestial guide answered: "Those people are Mormons. They call all the rest of us Gentiles and refuse to associate with us, but as long as they are happy that way nobody bothers them."

It must be conceded that the Mormons would never have achieved the status of a "peculiar people" had they not isolated themselves from the Gentiles. Free association with outsiders would have minimized the differences between them and other people. They might have remained in Missouri, but they would not have developed the cultural pattern which still distinguishes them from other frontier people.

It must also be conceded that the Mormon policy of strict nonintercourse with Gentiles could not have been maintained within a zone of tolerance. The Gentiles became "people of the world." The very existence of such an insular attitude stimulated like responses among the Gentiles, and to these responses the Mormons reacted in kind.

Pioneers in Zion could hardly have been good Saints without holding Gentiles in contempt. It was their duty to glorify their uninviting habitat, and that was not easy; but it was easier if they could sincerely dislike the Gentiles, who had made their migration necessary. For the Saints, their hate for the Gentiles made easier the obligations of co-operation in economic matters and stimulated appreciation for their social exclusiveness.

Invidious comparisons fostered this satisfaction with their insular objectives. When Brother Brigham said to the Saints in conference: "We are the best people in the world," he meant what Heber C. Kimball said: "The Gentiles are our enemies; they are damned forever." The people shouted "Amen" and were in accord when Kimball said of the Gentiles: "They come here in large numbers and decoy our women. I have introduced some Gentiles to my wives, but I will not do it again."[1]

Some of the outsiders who looked with favor upon the daughters of Zion were probably men with honorable intentions, but that made no difference. The elders of Israel stood firm on their principles. "Let these men join the Church and prove by their works that they are willing to be one with us. Let them bring forth fruit meet for our confidence."

But the elders and high priests were no less adamant about the men of Zion fraternizing with the Gentiles. Such friendships served to develop intolerable laxness; and many a young Mormon, because of his friendly relations with Gentiles, was excluded from community socials, as if he were himself a Gentile.

Sometimes conflicts resulted from the Mormon policy of social exclusion. At Beaver, for example, lived a number of Gentiles. Under their influence some men in surrounding communities had grown cold toward the authority of the church. These apostates, like the Gentiles, were excluded from social functions. Joseph Fish of Parowan wrote in his journal for July 4, 1872:

> Our celebration of the day did not get off very well. The party in the evening was broken up by a crowd of rough boys who had not been invited. The rowdy and lawless element in this place has increased very much of late. This spirit is encouraged and fostered by apostates, of which we have a number in this place who will aid any measure which goes to break down good order. Mormonism being the thing they are all striking at, and they would readily sustain thieves etc., in opposition to the people. This has made it quite difficult to punish thieves and they have become very bold. Several have been

arrested and taken before the courts. They were immediately bailed out and appointed U.S. deputy marshals. This showed a determination of the courts to sustain anyone who would encroach upon the rights and property of the Saints.

Beaver, gentile city of safety, was the seat of the United States district court. More than a year later, on December 25, 1873, Fish wrote in his journal of another demonstration by the same "rough and lawless" young men. "Our dance committee have not invited them to our dances, nor will they sell them tickets." The excluded young men were determined to force themselves into the party. "They got their Henry rifles and marched around town with their guns in their hands. . . . . They went up to the meeting house but did not attempt to go in. One of the party, L. D. Watson, got a pretext and knocked a man down." When an attempt was made to arrest the young men, they retreated to an old saloon and offered armed resistance. They were arrested the next day and fined by Fish, who was justice of the peace.[2]

Social exclusiveness might have been much less of a problem for the Mormons in the frontier period had they not been a fun-making people. Dancing was blessed to the point of being a type of sacrament. When a group of families was sent out to start a settlement, provisions were made to have at least one fiddler in the company. The Cotton Mission had two bands and enough instruments for an orchestra besides.

Ward and stake records in St. George are silent on recreational problems during the first few years of the settlement. The journals of individuals report a great amount of social activity. Like every other community in the church, St. George had glee clubs, dramatic clubs, and literary societies—of course, for Mormons only and for the entertainment of Mormons.[3] During the first few years, when there was no cash in any pockets, dance admissions were paid in kind. Lyman L. Woods told the writer: "Many a time I went to a dance or theatre with my lady on one arm and a bag of potatoes under the other." Here is a report of the earnings of the St. George Relief Society from a Leap Year ball on December 31, 1868:

15 yards of calico and bleached muslin..........	$ 4.25
56 pounds of flour..............................	5.60
5 gallons and 1 quart of molasses...............	10.25

There was no gentile problem in St. George on that occasion. But the gentile and apostate problem was present that year in

THE SALT LAKE THEATER COMPLETED BY BRIGHAM YOUNG IN 1862

It was for years the "number one" theater west of the Mississippi. While the states were at war over slavery, Brigham Young was erecting such buildings to give work to the unemployed. Much to the regret of the American theater world, this structure was torn down in 1928.

some of the communities farther north. For example, the young men of Parowan staged a wolf hunt, a sport common to most frontier communities. Leaders were chosen, and the leaders selected for opposing teams all the men of the place who could bring guns and use them. The rival teams would then scour the country, hunting wolves, bear, cougar, and other predatory animals. The losing side was required to give a party and dance for the whole community. The Parowan hunt resulted in complications, because some of the socially unacceptable young men took part in it. An effort was made to bar them from the dance. Joseph Fish wrote on March 9, 1868:

> The dance came off last night. Some who belonged did not attend and gave their tickets to others who were objectionable to many who were there, so they were not allowed to dance. This was about to cause trouble and break up the party. William Roberts was the main one who was trying to crowd in, and E. C. Clark was backing him up in it. About this time President W. H. Dame took the floor and made quite a speech. He got terribly excited and acted like a crazy man. He yelled and hollered until he could be heard all over town. His enemies used this against him, and his friends were ashamed of it.

President Dame stood out loudly for the purity of the town's social life—an issue serious enough then to divide the town into factions. This problem of excluding some and admitting others to social functions did not appear on church records in St. George until about 1875, when there was an influx of gentile miners. There had been only the problem of protecting the dances against the wine-drinkers.[4]

Any sign of "approximating toward the things of the world" was reprehensible conduct. Playing the popular gentile tunes at dances, adopting new dance steps, or even employing itinerant gentile musicians were all taboo. High Councilman Smith of St. George complained in 1883 that "a Gentile fiddler recently came here and was permitted by one of our private citizens to play for some young people and form associations with them." Before a meeting of the lesser preisthood in 1879, Stake President McAllister, who may well have been the Giant Joshua in Miss Whipple's novel of that title, scolded the youth. He said: "We should not encourage transient persons to make fun for us, and for which give them our hard-earned dollars."[5]

Many of the outsiders were men of worldly interests—prospectors, promoters, bribe-takers, political job-seekers. They were symbols of evil, of the pride that goes before the fall, and of all the false values, including vanity, which were so repugnant to the Mormons. "The Gentiles are crawling up and will go where the money goes," said a member of the Quorum of High Priests of St. George in 1871. He said woe to the brethren if they follow the example of the Gentiles. He had "no objections to a paper collar," but he did object to the attitudes made manifest by the collar.

In so far as the Gentiles were able to gain a foothold in Zion, it was in relation to those forms of commerce that operated on a cash basis. They were entertainers, lawyers, public officials, miners, and traders. Utah's wealth may have been owned largely by the Mormons, but Utah's cash after about 1870 was largely in gentile pockets. When the mines began to operate, many young Mormons were tempted to go to the camps for jobs. Here they exchanged work for cash—a matter of great concern to the elders, because many of these men were weaned away from the simple ways of living.

Many who went to the mines brought little of their earnings home. There were, of course, exceptions. Erastus Snow said, in a southern Utah conference at St. George in 1873, that he had given permission to some of the brethren to work in the mines because they needed cash to buy "new wagons and stoves and a great many other family necessaries, but they were forgetting that they were neglecting the interests of Zion and were building up strangers." Brigham Young spoke to the young men of St. George in February, 1873, saying: "I have noticed that those who work all the time for others are more or less slaves, and do not build themselves up, rather go down."

Some of the Gentiles who went among the Mormons tried to be friendly. For example, in 1882 a Gentile approached Bishop David H. Cannon, of St. George, and requested to be baptized. The bishop would not baptize him. Had the bishop been out in the world on missionary service, he would not have hesitated.

On March 17, 1882, President McAllister spoke to the Relief Society of St. George. He was concerned about the flood of gentile preachers then going from place to place in Utah. In some communities these "agents from Babylon" were courteously received. The bishops "furnished audiences," but rarely did the missionaries get any converts. McAllister was not that tolerant. "These sectarians come into our midst proposing great sympathy with us and kindness for our children, offering to teach them free of charge, but really they are our worst enemies and are continually writing and publishing the most palpable falsehoods concerning us, thereby bringing persecution upon us as a people."

McAllister's advice was based on an experience many Utah communities had had the previous year. Dr. H. D. Fisher, of the American Bible Society, came to St. George. With him were a number of other ministers, including T. B. Hilton, of Salt Lake City, and Erastus Smith, of Beaver. They were given the use of the St. George Tabernacle, and the people were encouraged to attend. The gentile preachers spoke sympathetically. The brethren were pleased at this demonstration of tolerance. Some weeks later Dr. Fisher joined with a number of gentile ministers in Utah in writing a "Report on Affairs in Utah." Among other statements offensive to the Saints, they wrote: "Mormonism nullifies the laws of the Lord; controls elections, and protects its followers in the commission of the most heinous crimes. Mormonism creates Saints and Prophets out of thieves and murderers, and clothes with a halo of sanctity perjury and deeds of villainy."

The Mormon way of life would scarcely have been achieved had not such an attitude toward outsiders maintained. We may well ask what was this way of life that the Saints were seeking to establish or conserve? Was it the Mormon family? Except for the doctrine of celestial marriage, the Mormon family was little different from the family of New England. The family was expected to keep the First Commandment and to multiply. If there was any difference, it was that the Mormon church had embarked on a systematic program for building Zion by imposing upon the family a greater devotion to the First Commandment. It was this greater emphasis that justified polygamy.

Celestial marriage was a distinctive doctrine, for it linked man's earthly existence to the eternities and gave to his family a continuity from the beginning to the end of time. Babies born to this life are migrants from the spirit world, but those born to good Mormon families are choice spirits. They are born to mortality so that they might be tested and gain bodies which will rise with them purified in the resurrection. They enter the next life on a merit basis, according to their deeds in this one. Heaven is not a place of total glory for all—all are excluded who have sins marked against them. There are degrees of glory—many degrees—in the Mormon heaven, and there is progress in heaven. These beliefs are very important to the Mormon family, for the family continues in the next life.

Celestial marriage in the church was not exclusively marriage in polygamy. Any marriage for this life and the next assumed celestial character. It provided for eternal family union of husband and wife and of parents and children. Marriage of a Mormon woman to a gentile man was not celestial, even though a church official married the pair. It was marriage for this life only. The same would hold for the marriage of a Mormon man with a gentile woman. Here is the basic reason for church opposition to fraternization with Gentiles, for such associations, if allowed to continue, would lead to mixed marriage. Mormons married to Gentiles and the children of such unions might go to heaven, but they could not enter the celestial glory.

The Saints were a peculiar people in their community life also. Families were required to live together—a distinctive pattern for agricultural communities. Their insistence on following this order of community life led to some difficulty in securing title for their lands; but they resisted the forces that might have scattered them, got title to their land, and carried on with their village society.

In 1882 a problem arose in Cache Valley in northern Utah. Some families in the vicinity of Logan wished to move from their village and build homes on their farming land, located two miles or more outside. Stake President William B. Preston asked for advice of the church presidency. He received an interpretation of community policy from President John Taylor, written on December 26, 1882. The answer, in brief, placed the responsibility on the bishop to hold his people within sight and hearing as much as possible.

In all cases in making new settlements the Saints should be advised to gather together in villages, as has been our custom from the time of our earliest settlement in these mountain valleys. The advantages of this plan, instead of carelessly scattering out over a wide extent of country, are many and obvious to all those who have a desire to serve the Lord.

By this means the people can retain their ecclesiastical organizations, have regular meetings of the quorums of the priesthood, and establish and maintain day and Sunday schools, Improvement Associations, and Relief Societies. They can also cooperate for the good of all in financial and secular matters, in making ditches, fencing fields, building bridges, and other necessary improvements.

Further than this they are a mutual protection and a source of strength against horse and cattle thieves, land jumpers, etc., and against hostile Indians, should there be any; while their compact organization gives them many advantages of a social and civic character which might be lost, misapplied or frittered away by spreading out so thinly that inter-communication is difficult, dangerous, inconvenient and expensive.[6]

The problem of retaining the village agriculture came up in 1882 because at that time there was an expansion into Wyoming and Idaho. Some farmers who were homesteading land found it less expensive to live on their homesteads. Taylor, in this letter to Preston, opposed such scattering. "We know of no reason why the methods that have been pursued in the past on these matters are any less applicable to the Saints in Idaho and Wyoming than they have proved to those in Utah and Arizona." The village agriculture was established by the Mormons in Idaho, Wyoming, and later in Colorado, Mexico, and Canada.

A frontier Mormon agricultural community was compact, much like a gentile mining community; but there was a world of difference between the two. This difference can be shown in the contrasts between two places in southern Utah; St. George, a Mormon agricultural town, and Silver Reef, a gentile mining camp. The two were about twenty miles apart. The year of comparison was 1880, when the "Reef" was at the height of its prosperity and gentile assertiveness.

Silver Reef was a mushroom, boom town of 1,112 persons, less than 5 per cent of whom were Mormons in good standing. Possibly not more than 3 per cent of the 1,364 persons in St. George in 1880 were Gentiles. The "Reefers" were of the bonanza-minded, carefree, reckless types portrayed by Bret Harte in *The Outcasts of Poker Flat* and *The Luck of Roaring Camp*. Silver Reef was *worldly*—a treeless, grassless, red-sand location.

St. George was *otherworldly*—a community of fields, gardens, and flowers.

Silver Reef was a shack town, its main street lined with saloons, gambling places, and other conveniences for sinners. St. George was a moral family town, where the humble domestic virtues were glorified.

From the records of the United States Census Bureau the writer was able to extract certain items of information about the people in Silver Reef and St. George as reported by the census of 1880. The first table below shows the place of birth of males and females in both places. A considerable number of "Reefers" reported as born in Utah were children of gentile miners.

Place of Birth	St. George		Silver Reef	
	Male	Female	Male	Female
Utah	438	444	113	120
Elsewhere in the United States	99	106	347	109
Foreign countries	118	159	344	83
Total	655	709	804	312

Silver Reef was a man's town. Of its population, 28 per cent were females, while 52 per cent of the population of St. George were females. Silver Reef reported 37 per cent foreign-born persons, compared with 20 per cent for St. George. The next table shows a considerable difference regarding countries of origin for the foreign born in the two places. Not many Danes are shown for St. George, but there were many in other Mormon communities, especially in Sanpete Valley.

In Silver Reef foreign-born females were outnumbered four to one by the foreign-born males. In St. George there were no Chinese; in Silver Reef, 51. St. George reported only 1 Irishman, but in Silver Reef there were 111 Irish males and females. There were relatively more Swiss in St. George, that place being but five miles from the Santa Clara Swiss community. The Swiss at Silver Reef may have come from the same place.

Principal Countries of Origin	St. George		Silver Reef	
	Male	Female	Male	Female
Canada	5	10	28	2
China	0	0	41	10
Denmark	1	4	9	8
England	73	98	98	18
Germany	3	2	28	5
Ireland	1	0	86	25
Scotland	14	18	20	4
Sweden	0	2	8	1
Switzerland	14	22	4	3
Wales	2	0	9	4
Other foreign countries	5	3	13	3
Total	118	159	344	83

The next table shows the age distribution of St. George and Silver Reef residents. The same information is graphically presented in the accompanying chart for the age and sex data.

Years of Age	St. George		Silver Reef	
	Male	Female	Male	Female
Under 10	227	207	102	97
10–19	145	170	45	55
20–29	107	114	186	88
30–39	42	63	251	44
40–49	34	62	149	22
50–59	41	43	55	5
60 and over	59	50	16	1
Total	655	709	804	312

Silver Reef was an adult's community in which 73 per cent of the inhabitants were 20 years of age or older, compared with 45 per cent for St. George. On the other hand, 32 per cent of the inhabitants in St. George were children under 10 years of age, compared with 18 per cent for Silver Reef. Women of family-

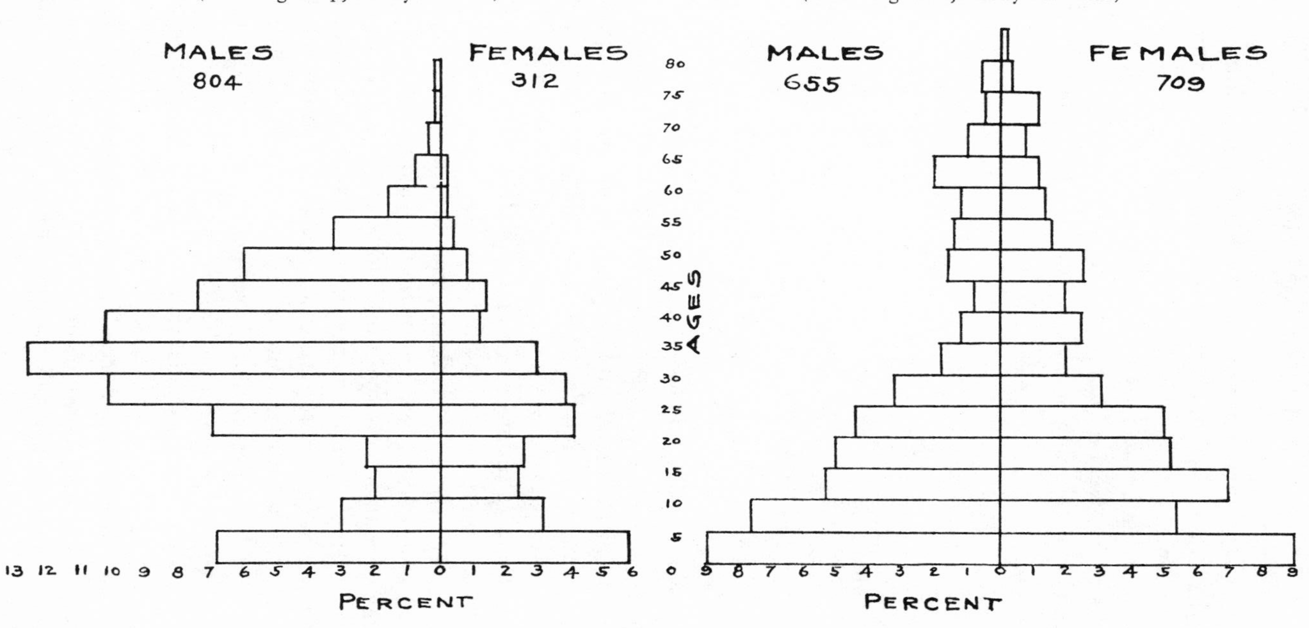

AGE AND SEX DISTRIBUTION IN TWO "DIXIE" TOWNS, 1880

rearing years outnumbered men in St. George, but in Silver Reef the women within those age groups were far outnumbered by the men.

As the table below shows, there was a shortage of unmarried females in St. George, but in Silver Reef the shortage was far greater. This table includes all persons 16 years of age and older.

Marital Status	St. George		Silver Reef	
	Male	Female	Male	Female
Unmarried	72	35	458	27
Married*	208	266	196	133
Widowed	14	29	18	9
Divorced	3	4	1	4
No marital status reported	1	13	7	0
Total	298	347	680	173

* Plural wives account for the excess of married women over married men in St. George. In Silver Reef there was an excess of married men over married women, explained by the fact that some men at Silver Reef kept their families elsewhere.

Figures in the above table explain eloquently the opposition of Mormons to having Gentiles share their social life. In exclusive St. George there was a shortage of unmarried women, even though the total number of women in that place exceeded the men by about 16 per cent. In Silver Reef there were about 12 unmarried, divorced, or widowed men for each woman not married. A considerable portion of the 29 widows reported for St. George were women above the child-bearing age. It was probably not an error on the part of the Mormon census-taker that 13 women in St. George were not reported for marital status. It is a safe assumption that some, if not most of these, were wives of polygamists residing elsewhere.

The year 1880 was one of great prosperity at Silver Reef. Four mills had been installed there to extract silver from the red sandstone. A union had been formed with a membership of more than three hundred men. The going rate of pay was $4.00 per day. Owing to market conditions, the companies decided to reduce wages to $3.50 per day. A strike was called about the first of February. The strikers took Colonel W. Allen, one of the mine superintendents, and escorted him out of town. He appealed to the federal court at Beaver for protection against the miners.[7]

The Mormons were greatly inconvenienced by the strike. Church leaders opposed their people working at the mines for wages but favored trade relations. They profited by selling wood and timber or in freighting for the mines. Also, they were able to sell to the "Reefers" considerable quantities of fruit, vegetables, and wine. When the strike came to the attention of the United States marshal at Beaver, he went to Washington County and called on the Mormon sheriff, Augustus P. Hardy, for a posse.

St. George Mormons gladly responded. To them, the strike was only another form of gentile badness. The posse assisted in the arrest of thirty-six of the union leaders. The Saints helped load these men in wagons and transport them to Beaver for trial. This event was the beginning of the decline of Silver Reef, which had yielded in a few years about 6,000,000 ounces of silver. Later, when the price of silver declined, it was no longer a profitable venture. Silver Reef by 1890 had become a ghost town, which was an economic loss to southern Utah communities; but, because it marked the exodus of the Gentiles, it was for the Mormons a social gain.

Silver Reef stood for most values which were repugnant to the Mormons. The "Reefers" also held the Mormons in low esteem. They lent active support to the anti-Mormon political group, the Liberal party. While the mines operated and the place was thriving, it was the haven for all opposition to the Mormon way of life. Even the Presbyterian minister who located in St. George in 1880 went to Silver Reef for encouragement and support in his crusade against polygamy.

After a rough-and-ready manner of their own, the "Reefers" believed in law and order much as did the Mormons surrounding them, but they were individualists. Any man among them was free to drink, gamble, carouse, backbite, and even idle away his time. If he wished to engage in brawls, those were affairs between him and his opponents. He might be arrested if he assaulted others without provocation, as he might be for stealing or for any untoward use of deadly weapons. Law and order in the Mormon communities allowed the individual much less freedom.

Some months after the strike, which was lost by the miners partly because of the part played by the Mormon sheriff and his posse, there was a murder at Silver Reef. In his proper line of duty the sheriff arrested the murderer and locked him in the county jail at St. George. The miners did not want the case tried before the Mormon judge of the county, their dislike of the Mormons being so much the more because of their experience with them in the recent strike. They raided the jail at night, took the prisoner from the sheriff, and lynched him. That was irregular procedure. The Mormon County officials, since the victim was a Gentile, took no action against the lynchers. No effort was made even to identify them. This also was irregular, but it evidences the great gulf of feeling between the opposing societies at Silver Reef and St. George. The Mormons at St. George, in a body, protested against the gentile murderer being buried in the local public cemetery.[8]

It was not shocking to the Mormons that a mob from the "Reef" should break into the county jail and lynch a man. Gentiles were like that. Over in Pioche, another frontier mining town, it was commonly said that "the Gentiles there kill a man a day." Pioche did have a huge graveyard for a place so small. Pioche and Silver Reef were cash customers for large amounts of the red wine made by the Dixie Mormons, some of it by the church authorities there. Mark A. Pendleton, a former resident of the "Reef," wrote in 1930 of the drinking propensities of the miners:

> The Reef was noted for its stocks of wines and liquors, and Peter Welte knew how to make good beer. One saloon keeper had the reputation of making a barrel of whiskey last a long time by adding tobacco, strychnine and water, but it was Dixie's red wine that had a kick worse than a government mule, as many newcomers learned to their sorrow. Leeds, with its wine cellars was a convenient distance away. Wine was placed on the table in goblets. The natives were immune, but woe to the "stranger within the gates."[9]

The Mormon wine business proved the entering wedge for a kind of fraternalism between Mormons and Gentiles which was very disturbing to local church leaders. Mormons who drank wine with the Gentiles became friendly with them. Besides breaking down the social barriers, wine-drinking became a vice to some of the brethren. Women complained that young men who had been associated with the Gentiles were acquiring the habit of drinking wine at the dances.

The High Council complained that some wine-drinkers did not pay their tithing, that others neglected their families, and that still other wine-drinkers were degenerating into loafers. Conduct which did not matter at Silver Reef became an issue of great moment in the Mormon communities. The bishops were required to take offenders to task; but this was not easy, since in some wards most of the brethren made wine for sale and most of the brethren had become wine-drinkers to some degree.

To make the problem more difficult, there began to emerge the attitude that wine-drinking was a private matter. Such an attitude could not have been found before the miners established themselves in Silver Reef. But ten years after their arrival, faithful Saints were arguing about personal liberty. Brother Gray told the High Council in 1885: "I drink my own wine. I do not buy it and never pay for it, consequently no one is the sufferer in this respect. No person is injured or wronged but myself."[10]

In St. George there was a certain lady who occasionally sold wine to the Gentiles. It was charged that she took Gentiles into her home as boarders and that she also drank wine with them. Neighbors reported that she had been intoxicated. Also, she rode in a wagon to Silver Reef with a Gentile.

The ward teachers were sent to visit the offending sister. She conceded that perhaps she drank too much wine "once in a while and sometimes twice in a while" but that other charges against her were "as false as hell," including the charge that she had fallen from a wagon when intoxicated. The Council did not believe that any Mormon lady should harbor Gentiles; and it was that count against her, more than her drinking, which moved the brethren to cut her off the church. She took her discipline lightly, an attitude which came from gentile influence.

Since the St. George Tithing Office, as a practical measure, had originally joined with the farmers in making wine, the church authorities were much embarrassed in pushing their drive against wine-drinkers. About 1887 the tithing office discontinued making wine. The passing of Silver Reef as a market left the producers with quantities of wine on hand.[11] The tithing office managed, as well as it could, to get rid of the more than six thousand gallons on hand.

From the moral angle, church leaders were forced to recognize that their people could not be makers of liquor without being drinkers of it, too. There were too many drinkers of wine and too few moderate drinkers among them. There were too many relaxing outbursts. Possibly wine afforded an escape occasionally from rigid and paternalistic priesthood supervision. Levi Savage wrote in his journal on July 24, 1888:

> The good people of Toquerville enjoyed themselves in celebrating this the 41st anniversary of the Pioneers of the Saints entering Salt Lake Valley; President Brigham Young at their head. After noon, a few of the boys having drunk too much wine, ran their horses and wagons thro the streets at a fearful rate. Eventually two of the wagons collided and ruined the forward wheel of one.

The ranking members of the priesthood decided to take firm measures against wine and whiskey. Here is an example of the way this resolve was carried into action. A prominent elder at Gunlock had been in the habit of making whiskey, for which he found a market in other settlements. A complaint was lodged against him by some of the elders of Pine Valley, where he sold whiskey to some young men; and these young men had created scenes at social gatherings. The stake president wrote to the bootlegger, reminding him that whiskey-making could no longer be countenanced. The man answered, saying that he was sorry there had been a complaint. This letter was sent to him September 28, 1887:

> Your letter of 19th inst. is before us. We appreciate the candor with which you write relative to your wrong-doing in disposing of intoxicants. You ask for our fellowship and standing in the Church; these we should be very sorry

to have withheld from you. But all these matters are as you well know, subject to conditions.

You may have intended to have stated that it was your intention to stop the practice of what you have been charged with—but it is not so stated. Presuming that it is your intention to quit the practice, we suggest that you visit Pine Valley, see the Bishop and meet with the people, and just as frankly as you write us, speak to them, expressing it as your intention to quit such practice as unworthy the calling of a servant of God. When this is done, get a few lines as report of the meeting from Bp. F. W. Jones and forward to us, and write your own feelings relative to stopping the practice, addressing your letter to us from Pine Valley, as your letter will more readily reach us from there than if you try to get it to us from Gunlock.

Yesterday we had here in St. George a United States officer of the Internal Revenue who avers that there are illicit stills in this County—at least one is reported to be in your Ward. Now, it is our intention to use our influence to stop this unlawful practice, and we expect *all* who are members of the Church in this Stake to unite with us, or they, whether officers or members, must not expect to retain our fellowship.

Now, we would like you to have this letter read to your ward so that our brethren and sisters there may clearly understand our views on the subject and govern themselves accordingly.

This letter was signed "Your Brethren in the Gospel, John D. T. McAllister, Daniel D. McArthur, David H. Cannon." So the high priests sent a prominent Gunlock brother out to get a switch by which he would submit to a whipping in his own town and in Pine Valley. He obeyed.

Thus priesthood supervision saved the day, and the dances were soon free of rowdiness born of strong drink. This was the price of attempting to introduce the industry—wine-making in the low hot communities and whiskey-making in the canyon communities. It did not square with a social life guided by prayer.

As noted above, the pioneer Saints were a fun-making people, but their amusements had to be sanctified. One of the pioneer cotton missionaries of St. George was a man named Hicks, who, with his wife, was called to Dixie from a little farm in Cottonwood, near Salt Lake City. He stopped for a while in Washington and then moved to St. George. In 1864 he wrote a song: "Once I Lived in Cottonwood." This was a parody on a popular song, "Sweet Betsy from Pike," which had vogue in the West. It was intended to be a humorous song; but, when Erastus Snow heard it, he ordered that it be sung no more. After several narrative verses about troubles in getting to Dixie, the song then tells of the plight of the Dixieite.

> I feel so sad and lonely now, there's nothing here to cheer,
> Except prophetic sermons, which we very often hear.
> They will hand them out by dozens, and prove them by the Book.
> I'd rather have some roasting ears to stay at home and cook.
>
> I feel so weak and hungry now. I think I'm almost dead.
> 'Tis seven weeks next Sunday since I have tasted bread.
> Of carrot tops and lucern leaves we have enough to eat,
> But I'd rather like to change my diet for buckwheat cakes and meat.
>
> I brought this old coat with me, about two years ago,
> And how I'll get another one, I'm sure I do not know.
> May Providence protect me against the wind and wet,
> I think myself and Betsy, these times will ne'er forget.
>
> My shirt is dyed with wilddock root, with greasewood for a set,
> I fear the colors all will run when once it does get wet.
> They say we could raise madder here and indigo so blue;
> But that turned out a humbug; the story was not true.
>
> The hot winds whirl around me, and take away my breath.
> I've had the chills and fever, till I'm nearly shook to death.
> "All earthly tribulations are but a moment here,"
> And, Oh if I prove faithful, a righteous crown I'll wear.[12]

This song did not die when banned by Snow. It was sung on the sly by many a Saint who would not have given up his Dixie mission whatever the cost. So serious was the mission that the Saints did not learn to laugh at themselves until a generation later. That was one phase of the Mormon way of life: to take life seriously, because all this is preparation for a more important existence to come. All living was part of a scheme of things extending out of the limitless past into the endless future.

One was drilled to duty from the cradle to the end of his days; taught to work and pray for wisdom, strength, and virtue to be a good father or mother, to rear many children in wisdom, strength, and virtue. This was, for the pioneer, the great imperative of eternal progress, for, "as man now is, God was once. As God now is, man may become."

To this end the "Word of Wisdom" is given as a guide to building a strong body, and education is glorified as the means of gaining intelligence. The "Word of Wisdom" was given to Joseph Smith by revelation on February 27, 1833. It was Brigham Young who attempted to make this doctrine of clean living mandatory.[13] With Brother Brigham, however, keeping the "Word of Wisdom" was not the supreme test of faith. Some of his apostles and some of his most trusted aides were users of tobacco and drinkers of whiskey. For him the test of a man's faith was his integrity to an assignment given by the church. Could a man take a company of Saints to a desert and hold them to the task of building a community; then it didn't matter much to Brother Brigham if he was a user of whiskey and tobacco. Those "Word of Wisdom" virtues were precious to him but secondary.

Much of the strength of the Mormon way of life is contained in its taboo system, for which the "Word of Wisdom" has become the general repository. This is the negative phase of their culture. Here is the catalogue of all that is forbidden. And this system has increased in importance as other phases or tests of faith have faded with the frontier. The way of life in Zion is still as serious as in pioneer times, but it has been reduced to simple rules and regulations. The children sing "In Our Lovely Deseret," to the tune, of "The Little Busy Bee":

That the children may live long,
And be beautiful and strong,
Tea and coffee and tobacco they despise.
They drink no liquor, and they eat
But a very little meat;
They are trying to be great and good and wise.

Orson W. Huntsman wrote in his journal on December 25, 1871, of the death of Bishop Crosby. The old gentleman gathered a group of young folks about his deathbed and told them "to be temperate in all their habits, eating, drinking, working, playing, sleeping and dancing, and not rest too much." Had he added that ill would result from any excesses, he would have spoken the essence of the "Word of Wisdom."

On the positive side the Mormon way of life quite logically leans on what is almost a pious adoration of education. This is logical, because life is a probation and preparation for progress.

One must gain knowledge, and by knowledge one gains power. This conceptual area of the Mormon way of life is summed up in the household expression: "The Glory of God is intelligence." Here is a possessing and dominating interest, an ideal which has gained in importance each year since the pioneer period.

While modern Mormons point with pride to the various phases of their way of life which merit them the designation of "peculiar people," no phase today receives greater emphasis than this pursuit of knowledge.

In the history of every pioneer community may be found a chapter on education, telling of the first schools, generally taught by volunteer pedagogues in tents or covered wagons. Usually the bishop called someone, or "set apart" someone, to be teacher. The superintendent of schools in Washington County made his first report in 1864. He wrote:

> The recent settlement of a great portion of the county and the great labors required of the brethren opening their farms, have prevented them giving much attention to school matters. . . . . In most settlements the school houses are temporary buildings, or the schools are taught in private houses. . . . . The school teachers generally through the county charge by the scholar, and collect their bills themselves. This prevents a systematic report on amounts paid to teachers being given.

The Washington County school report for 1865 indicated that, of 1,044 children of school age in the county, 673 had attended school for a brief period. The report for 1875 indicated that 93 per cent of the children of school age (4–16 years) in the county had registered and that 74 per cent of the school-age children had attended school an average of seven months. This was a good record for a pioneer people and was typical of most Utah counties.

Utah's school system was not a bona fide public agency. It would be more correct to say that Utah had a policy in favor of education, as much as the people could afford. It was not compulsory, merely a duty that every parent should provide education for his children.

Joseph Fish wrote in his journal on October 28, 1867, that he had been called to teach in Parowan. "I commenced teaching school today, had a good attendance. I teach in my own house

PIONEER DAY IN ST. GEORGE ABOUT 1890

At the left of the picture are several bearded survivors of the 1847 pioneers. At the front is the band, some of the players in uniform. At the center of the picture are the handcart pioneers who took part in the parade of the day. The flags ceremoniously spread on the ground are given the honored place in the picture. No disrespect was intended.

as there is no school house in the place, and no good teachers. Our schools are in a bad condition, and it is the necessity of one that has induced me to teach, for I do not feel competent for such a task."

If the Mormons failed to institute a system of public schools until many years had elapsed, it was probably due to their unwillingness to encourage any organization that might benefit the Gentiles. In so far as public schools were established in the larger cities, they were an offense to the Gentiles, who objected to Mormon teachers and charged that their children were exposed to the teaching of Mormonism. This Mormon control of the schools was made a political issue by the Liberal party in 1880.[14]

It was doubtless in response to gentile opposition that the provision was injected into the Edmunds-Tucker bill of 1887 to escheat all church property in excess of $50,000 for the benefit of the public schools.

Pending the legal review of the escheat order, the church set about to establish a parochial school system. This order was the subject of a letter sent to all stakes on June 8, 1888, by President Wilford Woodruff. He indicated that religious education had been "practically excluded from our district schools" and that the reading of divine books had been forbidden. He concluded:

> To permit this condition to exist among us would be criminal. The desire is universally expressed by all thinking people in the Church that we should have schools where the *Bible*, the *Book of Mormon* and the *Book of Doctrine and Covenants* can be used as text books, and where the principles of our religion may be a part of the teachings of the schools.

The public schools were not discontinued; but, as indicated by Governor Arthur L. Thomas in his report for 1889 to the Secretary of the Interior, they were not adequately supported. He said: "The tax collected for the support of the schools does not pay one half of the expenses of maintaining the schools; consequently the pupils must pay tuition fees or the schools be closed." In wholly Mormon communities the schools were able to carry on; but in communities where there were gentile children the schools could not be maintained if the Mormons sent their own children to church schools.

It was not until after statehood that Utah settled down to the serious business of building up a public school system, which in time gained a high rating. After statehood, Utah put forth effort to the point of sacrifice to perfect the public school system.

On the one hand, this striving for knowledge, this drive for education to promote the Kingdom of God, was an effort to conserve in the Mormon group the cultural values developed on the frontier. On the other hand, the education fetish has resulted in reversing intellectually all the old processes of pioneer insularism. It has forced the Mormons to turn around. It used to be a sin to "approximate after the things of the world." That was the justification for the Deseret alphabet—to shut out the intellectual influences of the Gentiles. There was no concern about approval of outsiders; in fact, disapproval was a compliment.

This is no longer true. Zion has turned from insularism to identification—a process which has been speeded by the modern striving for the knowledge that comes in books, an interest that never greatly concerned the pioneers. There is a practical reason for this reversal. The urge for identification is more a matter of expediency than is generally realized even by the Mormons and is as much a matter of expediency as was the pioneer urge for isolation.

The isolation ideal in terms of community-building had to be surrendered when the Mormons came to the end of their land supply. By the time Utah attained statehood practically all the acres that could be brought under irrigation had been occupied. Already the overflow youth of the Utah settlements had begun to migrate to other places, looking for land. Before 1900 the agricultural opportunities in the entire Mormon area had become exhausted; and the overflow population had to seek employment in the mines, on the railroads, and in such industries as the area afforded.

Since 1900 many thousands of young men, patiently trained

in the Mormon way of life and expensively educated in the knowledge of the world, have been forced to migrate from towns and farm villages in Utah, Arizona, Idaho, and other places. They have gone to the cities of Babylon, from whence their fathers escaped to build an isolated civilization in the valleys of the mountains.

All this boils down to a conflict between the Mormon ideal and the realities of the Mormon habitat. The Mormon community remains the same, except as it is harassed with the cost of educating its youth. The Mormon family follows the pioneer ideal, but it faces a future of little promise, for now it produces offspring for the Gentiles. The Mormons are being forced to recognize that Zion can no longer produce two blades of grass where one was before, but the Mormon family goes piously on producing two or three children where one was before.

It is a conservative estimate to say that Mormon communities have "exported" since 1900 as many as 100,000 of their sons and daughters. That figure would probably equal the number of emigrant converts brought to Utah from the east and abroad during the pioneer period. Pioneer Zion was an "importer" of people, and most of these additions to the population were able-bodied under-middle-age adults. The cost of their rearing and training had been met elsewhere. They arrived in Zion ready to go to work.

This influx of converts was already on the wane in 1890, when the Manifesto was issued. By 1896, when the land frontier was closing in that region, Mormon emigration had about ceased. That was the closing of the period when Zion could add able-bodied Saints to her population, at a cost of $200 per head, to have them add thousands of dollars to her wealth.

Before 1890, Utah mothers in the hinterland communities averaged seven to eight children per mother. In these same communities the average may have dropped to five per mother today, but even a family of five children is called on to export at least three. Three children out of five—in some families two out of five—must be brought up and trained for export. Here is the reason Zion has turned from her pioneer insularism, and the reason for the rising interest of Mormons in education.

From 1859 to about 1870 the Mormons put forth their maximum effort to bring in thousands of converts anxious to migrate to Zion. Every sacrifice was the sacrifice of investment. The emigrants were adding to Zion's wealth. Today the tables have turned. Sacrifices are now being made to rear and educate thousands of youth who will go away to the great cities to enrich the Gentiles, and most of these have been expensively educated.

Perhaps this is the long-predicted expansion of Zion to the world, another kind of missionary movement. Certainly it is not a militant, old-fashioned evangelical approach to the outside. On the contrary, the Mormons are now themselves on the other side. They are straining to adapt themselves. They have succeeded so well that their name is no longer anathema. Preachers no longer sermonize about the menace of Mormonism. Is this dilution process thinning out the old distinctiveness? Will Mormonism spread and adapt until it loses its identity? That has not happened yet. It is still a distinct way of life.

NOTES

1. Samuel Bowles in *Across the Continent*, pp. 397–98, includes at the close of the volume a number of excerpts from speeches of Mormon leaders given to illustrate Mormon antagonism to the government.

2. Joseph Fish wrote in his journal, June 14, 1874: "Beaver is full of apostates and the feeling against the Mormons is quite bitter. Nothing but the Mormon question is talked about upon the streets. Oaths are uttered against them on every corner and it is a common saying to say they ought to be hung. The apostates are most bitter and are cursing around the streets every day predicting that the Church will be broken up. . . ."

3. Every community had its dramatic associations. Sometimes there were several groups, and they took turns giving plays. The first production in St. George was given on July 24, 1862, before a meeting house had been erected. In 1868 Brigham Young sent a Professor Thomas to St. George to give dramatic instruction. Mormon interest in drama is described by George D. Pyper in his *Romance of an Old Playhouse*.

4. In 1876 Bishop Ensign of Santa Clara brought before the High Council of the St. George Stake a number of boys who had behaved in a rowdy manner at a dance. He thought an example should be made of them for the purpose "of upholding the proper usages and customs of our social gatherings. Stated that the accused have used improper language and acted in an unbecoming manner. Henry Hug had danced twice in succession contrary to the rules of the party. John Hug had made a bleating noise when the people were called upon to rise and be dismissed." The young people being disciplined objected because the dance started at seven o'clock, instead of six, and closed at ten o'clock.

5. On December 10, 1887, the High Council of St. George issued some rules for dancing which had been sent out by the church. Dances would be under control of the bishop; opened and closed with prayer; no dancing after midnight; "loud or boisterous talking, stamping and other unseemly noises should be avoided; and all double or exces-

sive swinging in cotillions, quadrilles or contra dances are hereby disapproved"; two-round dances permitted each evening but close holding forbidden; bishops and other authorities expected to be invited to all dances.

6. This letter was included in a Ph.D. thesis by F. Y. Fox, "The Mormon Land System," pp. 142–43.

7. President J. D. T. McAllister wrote to Sheriff Hardy: "We understand that you have summoned twenty men from this city to form part of a posse to assist you in the service of writs on certain parties at Silver Reef; and take the liberty of offering the following suggestions: Be careful of yourself and those thus summoned. In making service of your writ or writs, do not have all your men go in at once; have enough around to watch that no person being served, or their friends have opportunity to draw arms and use them. Have total abstinance from any intoxicating liquors strictly observed in your party. Should the brethren be fatigued, a cup of coffee is recommended. Do not stroll away from each other, or visit saloons or gambling holes. Keep together and be on the watch. All attend to your prayers in the morning and at night before retiring. Do not forget God, and He will not forget you" (Bleak, "Manuscript History of St. George," Book C, October, 1880).

8. For a report of the lynching see *ibid.*, October 6, 1880. Three days later 270 citizens protested the burial of Forrest's body in the municipal cemetery. Three years later a stranger named Quinn died in St. George. The people decided that he was a "friendly stranger" and should not be buried in the potters' field started for Forrest.

9. Mark A. Pendleton, "Memories of Silver Reef," *Utah Historical Quarterly*, October, 1930.

10. Men who made wine resorted to every device to sell. Wine became such a temptation that church headquarters in Salt Lake City became concerned. Levi Savage wrote in his journal for September 13, 1891, that Apostle Francis M. Lyman spoke to the Saints in St. George. "He said there was a large percentage of the young men of St. George who used tobacco and wine, also some old men indulged, too. One or two brethren in the audience told him he was wrongly informed. He said he had the figures in writing and when figures were brought to rebut it, he would yield, but not before." He also said that if wine-drinking did not stop, there would be a shortage of fit young men in Dixie to marry Dixie's young women.

11. On November 21, 1885, Frank Snow, clerk of the St. George Tithing Office, wrote the presiding bishop of the church that he had on hand about 6,000 gallons of wine, and suggested sending men with loads of this wine to the northern settlements to exchange it with Mormons there for cash, grain, and flour. The tithing office later ceased to accept wine, and the High Council on July 9, 1892, issued a ruling that wine would no longer be used for the sacrament. Water has been used instead, from then to now.

12. "Once I Lived in Cottonwood," was included by the Daughters of Utah Pioneers in a book entitled *Pioneer Songs*, published 1932.

13. There is a legend that the "Word of Wisdom" was given to Joseph Smith after a session at his home with a number of his apostles. Wife Emma Smith was offended because some of the apostles chewed tobacco and spit tobacco juice on her stove and floor. They tried to spit in the ash pan but did not aim properly. She asked Joseph: "Is that a good way for men of the Lord to do?" Joseph pondered the question. Soon thereafter he received the revelation.

14. One consequence of the failure, or refusal, of the Mormons to provide public schools free from church domination was the gentile missionary movement. Practically all the sectarian organizations that did missionary work in Utah collected money on the plea that Utah did not have free uncontrolled schools. Almost all the missions began their work by starting schools.

BIBLIOGRAPHY

I. UNPUBLISHED MATERIALS

BLEAK, JAMES G. "Manuscript History of St. George," from 1862 up to about 1900. Four scrapbook volumes of journal entries, letters, and other documents, kept and compiled by Bleak in his capacity as stake historian. A synopsis entitled "Annals of the Southern Utah Mission" (1932) of 342 pages, is on file at the Brigham Young University, Provo, Utah.

Private journals, letters, and other documents by the pioneers or about them, collected and copied by the Historical Records Survey of the Utah Work Projects Administration. These relate mainly to southern Utah and adjoining states. This material is typewritten, and copies are on file at the St. George Public Library, the Utah Historical Society, and the office of the Historical Records Survey Project in Salt Lake City. In this collection is a volume of material sufficient to occupy the researcher or general reader for months.

Minutes of the High Council of the St. George Stake of Zion from 1862 up to the present. These minutes are large hand-written ledger books, a whole shelf full on file in St. George. Various problems of family, church, and community were handled. There were trials and complaints. The reports are full and informing but may not be readily available.

Other records of the St. George Stake, including minute books of the ward organizations, priesthood quorums, Relief Society, letters between local and stake officials, tithing records, and other documents. Some of these materials are filed in letter boxes, and all are the property of the stake organization.

"History of Brigham Young," 1844–77, a collection of books of documents chronologically arranged and on file at the Church Historian's Office, Salt Lake City. The materials include entries dictated or written by Brigham Young, letters written by him or to him, and other documents pertinent to his administration. These materials are not indexed.

"Latter-Day Saints [L.D.S.] Journal History," 1830 to the present. Many loose-leaf books of documents chronologically arranged, on file at the Church Historian's Office, Salt Lake City. The contents are not indexed, and the books are kept open, so that as new materials are discovered they may be inserted for the date and year.

Other original documents include materials on file in the offices of the city of St. George, or Washington County, Utah, or in the files of the federal government. Federal records include those of the War Department, Office of Indian Affairs, Department of State, Department of the Interior, and the

Attorney-General. Most of these documents are on file or are being filed in the National Archives. The census data were viewed at the Bureau of the Census.

II. PUBLISHED MATERIALS

This is not a complete bibliography on the subject of Mormons and Mormonism, but it should serve the interests of the general reader. There are many references in the notes following the chapters which have not been included. For those wishing more references attention is invited to a special bibliography published in 1940 by the Utah Historical Records Survey: *Inventory of Church Archives of Utah*, Vol. I. There is a classified bibliography in *Utah: A Guide to the State*.

ALLEN, EDWARD J. *The Second United Order among the Mormons.* New York, 1936. Pp. 149.

ALTER, J. CECIL. *James Bridger.* Salt Lake City, 1925. Pp. 546.

BANCROFT, HUBERT H. *History of California.* 7 vols. San Francisco, 1888. Volumes V and VI have information about the Mormon Battalion, the voyage of the "Brooklyn," and the San Bernardino settlement.

———. *History of Utah.* San Francisco, 1889. Pp. 808. In writing this book Bancroft had the blessing of the church while collecting material.

BASKIN, ROBERT N. *Reminiscences of Early Utah.* Salt Lake City, 1914. Pp. 252. Baskin was active in politics opposing the church.

BEADLE, JOHN H. *Life in Utah; or the Mysteries and Crimes of Mormonism.* Philadelphia, 1870. Pp. 540.

———. *Western Wilds and the Mean Who Redeem Them.* Cincinnati, 1880. Pp. 624. These and other books strongly attacked the church. Beadle was a news reporter.

BEAL, SAMUEL M. "The Salmon River Mission." Berkeley, 1914. (University of California, Ph.D. thesis, typewritten.)

BEARDSLEY, HARRY M. *Joseph Smith and His Mormon Empire.* Boston, 1931. Pp. 421. Contains good bibliography on the Joseph Smith period.

BENNETT, JOHN C. *The History of the Saints; or an Exposé of Joe Smith and His Mormons.* Boston, 1842. Pp. 344.

BIRNEY, HOFFMAN. *Zealots of Zion.* Philadelphia, 1931. Pp. 217.

BOWLES, SAMUEL. *Across the Continent: A Summer's Journey to the Rocky Mountains, the Mormons and the Pacific States, with Speaker* [Scuyler] *Colfax* (1865). New York, 1868. Pp. 454.

BRIMHALL, GEORGE W. *The Workers of Utah.* Provo, Utah, 1889. Pp. 95. Author destroyed all but a few copies because book did not have church approval.

BROWN, JAMES S. *Life of a Pioneer.* Salt Lake City, 1900. Pp. 520.

BROWNE, ALBERT G. "The Utah Expedition," *Atlantic Monthly*, March, April, and May, 1859. Browne was a correspondent with Johnston's Army.

BRYANT, EDWIN. *What I Saw in California*. New York, 1849. Pp. 455. Revised as *Rocky Mountain Adventures* (New York, 1888).

BURTON, SIR RICHARD. *The City of the Saints*. New York, 1862. Pp. 574. Friendly report by the translator of the *Arabian Nights*.

CHANDLESS, WILLIAM. *A Visit to Salt Lake*. London, 1857. Pp. 346.

Clayton, William: The Life of (from his journal). Salt Lake City, 1921. Pp. 376.

CODMAN, JOHN. *The Mormon Country: A Summer with the Latter-Day Saints*. New York, 1873. Pp. 225.

COOKE, PHILIP ST. GEORGE. *Conquest of New Mexico and California*. New York, 1873. Pp. 307.

CREER, LELAND H. *Utah and the Nation* (1846–61). Seattle, 1929. Pp. 275.

DALE, HARRISON C. *The Ashley-Smith Explorations and the Discovery of a Central Route to the Pacific, 1822–1829*. Cleveland, 1918. Pp. 352.

DE RUPERT, A. E. D. *California and Mormons*. New York, 1881. Pp. 166.

DE VOTO, BERNARD. *Forays and Rebuttals*. Boston, 1936. Pp. 403. A collection of essays. See "The Centennial of Mormonism," pp. 71–137, a philosophical view of "utopia and dictatorship" in church history.

EGAN, HOWARD. *Pioneering the West*. Richmond, Utah, 1917. Pp. 302.

EVANS, JOHN H. *Charles Coulson Rich: Pioneer Builder of the West*. New York, 1936. Pp. 400.

FISHER, VARDIS. *Children of God*. New York, 1939. Pp. 769. Historic novel of merit dealing mainly with period of Brigham Young.

FLINT, DR. THOMAS. "Diary of Thomas Flint from California to Maine and Return, 1851–1855," *Annual Publications of the Historical Society of Southern California*. Los Angeles, 1923.

FORD, THOMAS. *History of Illinois, 1818–1847*. Chicago, 1854. Pp. 447.

FOX, FERAMORZ Y. "The Mormon Land System." Chicago, 1932. (Northwestern University, Ph.D. thesis, typewritten.) Pp. 332.

FREMONT, JOHN C. *Memoirs of My Life*. Chicago, 1887. Pp. 655.

GARDNER, HAMILTON. "Co-operation among the Mormons," *Quarterly Journal of Economics*, May, 1917. Also, "Communism among the Mormons," *ibid.*, March, 1922.

GEDDES, JOSEPH A. *The United Order among the Mormons*. New York, 1922. Pp. 172.

GOLDER, FRANK A. *The March of the Mormon Battalion*. New York, 1928. Pp. 210.

GOVE, CAPTAIN JESSE A. *The Utah Expedition: Letters of Captain Gove to Mrs. Gove and the New York Herald*. Concord: New Hampshire Historical Society, 1928. Pp. 442.

GREELEY, HORACE. *An Overland Journey: From New York to San Francisco in the Summer of 1859*. New York, 1860. Pp. 786.

GUNNISON, CAPTAIN JOHN W. *The Mormons or Latter-Day Saints.* Philadelphia, 1852. Pp. 168.

HICKMAN, WILLIAM A. *Brigham's Destroying Angel.* New York, 1872. Pp. 202.

HOWE, E. D. *Mormonism Unveiled.* Painesville, Ohio, 1834. First attack on the church. Republished as *History of the Mormons* (1840), pp. 290.

HYDE, JOHN, JR. *Mormonism: Its Leaders and Designs.* New York, 1857. Pp. 335.

JENSEN, ANDREW. *Church Chronology.* Salt Lake City, 1899. Pp. 259.

JONES, DANIEL W. *Forty Years among the Indians.* Salt Lake City, 1890. Pp. 400.

Journal of Discourses (London), annual volumes, 1854–66. Reported and later edited speeches of Brigham Young and other Mormons.

KANE, THOMAS L. *Private Papers and Diary: A Friend of the Mormons.* Limited 500 copies. San Francisco, 1937. Pp. 78. Introduction by OSCAR O. WINTHER.

KELLY, CHARLES (ed.). *Journals of John D. Lee* (mainly 1846–47). Salt Lake City, 1938. Pp. 251.

———. *Salt Desert Trails.* Salt Lake City, 1930. Pp. 178.

KELLY, CHARLES, and HOWE, MAURICE L. *Miles Goodyear: Utah's First Citizen.* Salt Lake City, 1937. Pp. 152.

LEE, JOHN D. *Mormonism Unveiled: The Life and Confessions of John Doyle Lee*, ed. W. W. BISHOP. St. Louis, 1879. Pp. 406. Abridged version, *The Mormon Menace*, by ALFRED H. LEWIS (New York, 1905).

LINN, WILLIAM A. *The Story of the Mormons.* New York, 1902. Pp. 637.

McCLINTOCK, JAMES H. *Mormon Settlement in Arizona.* Phoenix, 1921. Pp. 307.

Messages and Papers of the Presidents of the United States, 1789–1897, ed. JAMES D. RICHARDSON. 10 vols. Washington, D.C.: Government Printing Office, 1899.

Millennial Star. Church periodical published in Liverpool since 1840. Has been at times a weekly, bi-weekly, and monthly.

MORGAN, DALE L. "The State of Deseret," *Utah Historical Quarterly*, combined three issues, April, 1940. Pp. 192.

NEFF, ANDREW L. *History of Utah, 1847–1869*, ed. LELAND H. CREER. Salt Lake City, 1940. Pp. 955.

PETERS, DEWITT C. *Kit Carson's Life and Adventures.* Hartford, 1874. Pp. 604.

POWELL, JOHN W. *Explorations of the Colorado River of the West.* Washington, D.C.: Government Printing Office, 1875. Pp. 291.

POWELL, JOHN W., and INGALLS, G. W. *Report to the Commissioner of the Study of Indian Affairs in Utah, Nevada, etc.* A pamphlet published by the

Office of Indian Affairs. Washington, D.C.: Government Printing Office, 1874.

PRATT, PARLEY P., JR. *The Autobiography of Parley Parker Pratt.* New York, 1874. Pp. 441.

PYPER, GEORGE D. *Romance of an Old Playhouse.* Salt Lake City, 1937. Pp. 405.

QUAIFE, MILO M. *The Kingdom of St. James.* New Haven, 1930. Pp. 281.

REMY, JULES, and BRENCHLEY, JULIUS. *A Journey to Great Salt Lake City* (1855). 2 vols. London, 1861. Pp. 1113.

RILEY, I. WOODRBIDGE. *The Founder of Mormonism.* New York, 1902. Pp. 446.

ROBERTS, BRIGHAM H. *A Comprehensive History of the Church of Jesus Christ of Latter-Day Saints.* 6 vols. Salt Lake City, 1930. Pp. 3100. Published by the church.

ROBINSON, PHIL (Philip Stewart). *Sinners and Saints.* London, 1883. Pp. 370.

SMITH, JOSEPH. *History of the Church of Jesus Christ of Latter-Day Saints, Period I.* Salt Lake City, 1932. Seven volumes published by the church; the first six volumes cover period 1830–44, and the seventh volume covers 1844–47. Materials are chronologically arranged.

SMITH, JOSEPH FIELDING. *Essentials in Church History.* Salt Lake City, 1928, Pp. 694. A church publication.

SMITH, LUCY MACK. *Biographical Sketches of Joseph Smith, the Prophet, and His Progenitors for Many Years.* Liverpool, 1853. Pp. 279.

SMOOT, REED. *Proceedings before the Committee on Privileges and Elections of the United States Senate in the Matter of the Protests against the Right of Honorable Reed Smoot, a Senator from the State of Utah, To Hold His Seat.* Senate Doc. No. 486 (69th Cong., 1st Sess.). 4 vols. Washington, D.C.: Government Printing Office, 1906.

SNOW, ELIZA R. *Biography of Lorenzo Snow.* Salt Lake City, 1884. Pp. 581.

STANSBURY, CAPTAIN HOWARD. *Exploration and Survey of the Valley of the Great Salt Lake of Utah.* Philadelphia, 1852. Pp. 487. Also as Senate Doc. No. 3 (spec. sess., March, 1851). Washington, D.C.: Government Printing Office, 1853.

STENHOUSE, FANNY (Mrs. T. H. B. Stenhouse). *Tell It All.* New York, 1874. Pp. 623. Introduction by HARRIET BEECHER STOWE.

STENHOUSE, THOMAS H. B. *The Rocky Mountain Saints.* New York, 1873. Pp. 760.

STUCKI, JOHN S. *Family History Journal.* Salt Lake City. Pp. 164.

TOPONCE, ALEXANDER. *Reminiscences of Alexander Toponce.* Ogden, 1932. Pp. 248.

TULLIDGE, EDWARD W. *History of Salt Lake City.* Salt Lake City, 1886. Pp. 1063. Contains documents not found elsewere.

Tullidge's Quarterly Magazine. 4 vols. Salt Lake City, 1880–85.

TYLER, DANIEL. *Concise History of the Mormon Battalion in the Mexican War, 1846–1847*. Salt Lake City, 1881. Pp. 376.

Utah: A Guide to the State. New York, 1941. Pp. 595. Materials were compiled by the Writers' Project of the Utah Work Projects Administration.

WAITE, CATHERINE V. *The Mormon Prophet and His Harem*. New York, 1886. Pp. 280.

WATERS, WILLIAM E. *Life among the Mormons*. New York, 1868. Pp. 219.

WERNER, MORRIS R. *Brigham Young*. New York, 1925. Pp. 478.

WHIPPLE, MAURINE. *The Giant Joshua*. Boston, 1941. Pp. 633. A novel about Mormon life and polygamy, competently and sympathetically told.

WORK PROJECTS ADMINISTRATION FOR UTAH. Various publications, including histories of cities and counties. These documents are compiled from the public documents by the Historical Records Survey Project. Each contains valuable information and a pertinent bibliography.

YOUNG, ANN ELIZA. *Wife No. 19*. Hartford, Connecticut, 1876. Pp. 605.

YOUNG, LEVI EDGAR. *The Founding of Utah*. New York, 1923. Pp. 445.

INDEX